Negotiating the Curriculum:
Educating for the 21st Century

Edited by

Garth Boomer
Nancy Lester
Cynthia Onore
Jon Cook

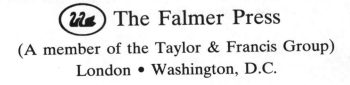

The Falmer Press

(A member of the Taylor & Francis Group)
London • Washington, D.C.

UK   The Falmer Press, 4 John Street, London WC1N 2ET
USA   The Falmer Press, Taylor & Francis Inc., 1900 Frost Road, Suite 101,
      Bristol, PA 19007

First published in 1992

**A catalogue record for this book is available from the British
Library**

**Library of Congress Cataloging-in-Publication Data are available on
request**

ISBN 1 85000 931 7 cased
ISBN 1 85000 937 6 paperback

Jacket design by Caroline Archer

Typeset in 9.5/11pt Times by
Graphicraft Typesetters Ltd., Hong Kong.

*Printed in Great Britain by Burgess Science Press, Basingstoke on
paper which has a specified pH value on final paper manufacture of
not less than 7.5 and is therefore 'acid free'.*

Contents

Contents

Acknowledgments

The editors wish to thank The Teachers Assistance Trust for permission to reprint Chapters 1, 2, 3, 4, and 9 of this book and the many teachers in networks in Australia and the USA who have contributed to growing knowledge about negotiating the curriculum. Those teachers whose work appears in this book represent many others who are part of a committed community of reflective practitioners.

Preface: About This Book

Origins and Intent

Negotiating the Curriculum: Educating for the 21st Century is an invitation to educators at all levels and in all sectors to reflect upon your present teaching or administrative practice; to assess critically the practice of others; to consider changed action and then to act in the spirit of the educational investigators who have contributed to this book; not in order to test a *new method* but in order to extend and enrich your *present theories* of teaching and learning. The investigations and speculations represented here all move in the direction of student emancipation, increased self-reliance, improved critical-reflective capacity, and a growing awareness and subtlety in exerting influence and control both individually and collectively. This is the democratic spirit of the enquiry that readers are invited to embrace.

The book is also a continuing, amplified conversation about the ideas presented originally in the book, *Negotiating the Curriculum: A Teacher-Student Partnership* (1982). In this foundation text, over twenty Australian teachers reported on their practical enquiries into negotiation of the curriculum, keeping a strong focus on the questions: 'How do human beings learn?' and 'and, therefore, how might we teach?' In conducting their enquiries, the teachers demonstrated a powerful form of teachers' liberation, if by 'liberation' we mean coming to think and act according to one's own principles rather than conforming out of habit or according to someone else's fiat.

Since 1982, a range of educators and teachers in North America have joined the Australians in taking the ideas further through new forms of action and reflection-on-action. In particular, Nancy Lester and Cynthia Onore in New York have developed an international dialogue with Garth Boomer and Jon Cook, Australians who were key contributors to the original book. As a result, we have this new book which, a decade on, provides windows and new thinking about enduring notions and principles, this time including American teachers and educators alongside the Australians and so introducing us to new contexts and different educational cultures.

Readers will notice that we have retained the title *Negotiating the Curriculum* from the original text, but have given this volume a new sub-title. While the 1982 *Negotiating the Curriculum* was widely known and used in Australia, it never made it across the oceans, except through copies of individual chapters. When it went out of print in 1988, and we decided to create this new volume for a wider UK/US/Australian readership, we felt it was both appropriate, given our intention to promote curriculum negotiation as a theory of teaching and learning, and sensitive to readers coming to the ideas for the first time, to keep the original title. Because we are moving into a new century that challenges us to transform teaching and learning in order to educate all our citizens, we hoped to underline the place that negotiating the curriculum will have in supporting and guiding that transformation; thus the new sub-title, *Learning for the 21st Century*.

Negotiating the Curriculum is, therefore, a 're-vision'. It aims to reconsider and reconstrue a way of thinking about teaching and learning which proved to be generative and productive during the 1980s. The reconsideration and reconstrual is necessary because the theory of negotiation has built into it the necessity of continually striving to modify and disconfirm its own present understandings. It is also necessary because a key component of the theory is that acts are always embedded in a rich sociopolitical context which must be acknowledged, interpreted and dealt with since it strongly influences and constrains classroom and institutional possibilities.

Clearly, the sociopolitical contexts, including the frontiers of educational debate, have changed since the early 1980s. This book takes account of those changes and seeks to reposition 'negotiating the curriculum' to show its continuing, indeed heightened, relevance as nations face burgeoning economic, cultural, and ecological dilemmas, all of which point to a need for society to develop enhanced capacity to think and act wisely.

It is also an aim of this book to confound and complicate those who may have responded more to the surfaces than to the essences of the original presentation of negotiating the curriculum. There is a deliberate critical/speculative intent in the writing as an antidote to sloganism and formula. In this way *Negotiating the Curriculum* hopes to distance itself from the various forms of educational virus which periodically sweep across states and nations, invariably leaving behind an educational scene essentially untransformed and not a little jaundiced.

The Book's Structure

The book is divided into three parts, the first being a re-presentation of three key theoretical chapters of the original book. Here, the reader may explore and come to understand the rationale and some significant foundational ideas which were developed into an operational framework for those who might want some guidelines on how to begin negotiating the curriculum. These chapters remain largely unchanged and so in tone and emphasis they remind the reader of some of the concerns, hopes and possibilities of the early 1980s. There is a technical orientation to these chapters although they go well beyond the confines of a how-to-do-it manual.

Part B presents a range of cases. It is the belief of the editors of this book that, by and large, teaching acts are shockingly private and undocumented. There is an urgent need across all facets of education to accumulate records of theorized practice where the infinitely complex business of teaching can be studied through cases. In some ways this means learning from the profession of law which affords very high status to case studies. Unfortunately, education has too often preferred to fragment itself by deferring to distinct and separate disciplinary or foundational studies in psychology, sociology, philosophy, management theory and so on.

The teachers in Part B are seen choreographing and reflecting upon teaching and learning in all its complexity, with all its layers, nuances and uncertainties. Contributors include teachers from the original book alongside new writers from both Australia and the US. Significantly, this section includes a chapter on investigating the efficacy of negotiation in higher education.

In the final part, contributors re-work many of the original ideas and bring new perspectives to negotiating the curriculum. There is a strong drive to complicate and problematize, so that the readers can be in no doubt that this book's project is to invite and provoke further ongoing theorizing and practice in ever-changing contexts rather than to popularize a method. The aim here is to demonstrate strongly-held principles at work while guarding against naive romanticism and evangelism.

An Invitation

This book is directed to all those who share an interest in the theory and practice of education. It is particularly concerned to reach those who are intending to teach and those who are out there teaching, educating for the twenty-first Century in the sense that those at school today will graduate into a new millennium and play a key role in shaping new societies.

In each part there is an invitation to interpret critically what is offered and to join in the quest to wonder, act and document in the service of wiser, more subtle, more alert, and more democratic teaching and learning.

As editors, we've had the privilege to see the chapters in this book grow from idea to finished product. In the process of reading and rereading them, we were guided by the questions we raised in our responses to the emerging texts. We would like to share our questions with you without intruding on your own interpretive meaning making processes. There are no right answers. And there are no right ways of using the questions. You may choose to read the questions now as a guide to your own reading, or you may decide to refer back to our questions when a question comes to your mind as you're reading along, or you might wait until you've finished reading and writing your own response before you take a look at the questions we've raised.

We see our questions contributing to the conversation between the multiple voices in these chapters and your own. Collaboratively and communally, we enrich each other's learning.

Part A

Theoretical and Technical Framework [Foundations]

INTRODUCTION

Context and Origins

The origins of the three chapters retrieved here from the original book *Negotiating the Curriculum* (1982) need a brief account. It is a story of the work of a close-knit national educational network in Australia. From 1974 to 1980, 'language and learning' teams within education systems in four states of Australia — South Australia, Victoria, Western Australia, and Tasmania — worked with teachers to document and reflect upon classroom problems in learning, using an action research process of hypothesis/action/reflection. The impetus of this work came originally from the 'language across the curriculum movement' (Barnes *et al.*, 1971) which began in London in the late 1960s. In the early stages of the Australian inquiries, the focus was on the role of language in education but, as Garth Boomer points out in chapter 1, the focus gradually changed to learning in the curriculum.

In 1978, the National Curriculum Development Center helped to formalize links between state language and learning teams by establishing the *National Working Party on the Role of Language in Learning*. All states of Australia, except Queensland, were represented on this working party, which had the tasks of gathering together and sharing the best of state inquiries and of collaborating to do further work.

During 1978, a paper by Garth Boomer (represented here as chapter 1) was taken up as a basis for inquiry in each state. Both in schools and at inservice conferences, teachers were invited to question, in practice, the principles that other inquiring teachers and working party members together had formulated.

At this time, Garth Boomer and Jon Cook were working in the shifting territory between educational bureaucracies and classroom teachers as consultants, change agents and curriculum developers. It was, therefore, essential that they should find ways of making accessible and useful to teachers what they had been discovering through their action research networks and, at the same time, find ways of rendering it accessible to their teaching colleagues.

These first three chapters, especially chapters 2 and 3, subsequently became widely used templates or guides for a range of teacher enquiries and system-wide work in curriculum development. Indeed, chapter 3 was adopted almost in its entirety in a major system-wide curriculum framework for drama in South Australia. Jon Cook's 'four questions', presented in chapter 2, have proved to be inviting, elegant, and richly generative entry points and shaping influences when teachers are building learning/teaching episodes in the classroom.

Orientation

These three chapters could each be seen as attempts to consider and deal with power inequities in teaching. Studies of early childhood learning are usually inspiring testaments to the power of human minds (Smith and Miller, 1970; Wilkinson, 1971). The infant learner is a powerhouse of private and public investigation. Infant apprentices use a continuing battery of 'Why?' and 'What's that?' experiments in play and imitations after demonstration, and display a tenacity to get their own way as they power into the world. Usually adults are excitedly generous in providing answers, offering models, revealing secrets, and acknowledging success. They are usually prepared to meet the young more than half-way.

Studies of classroom interactions are not always so inspiring (Barnes *et al.*, 1971; Novick and Waters, 1977). Perhaps because of the obligatory nature of schooling, or because adults now have a mandate to teach, or because society has designs on what is to be learnt, there is by and large, a dramatic shift in power when children enter school. There is a clear tendency for children to become more acted upon than acting. Teachers possess a formidable battery of teaching techniques — most of them instruments of motivation, attention getting, and judging — to be summoned and deployed with the full backing of the education industry.

Schools are much more responsible than parents for what society sees as learning and the transmission of knowledge, and so they tend to require children to put aside their intentions in order to engage with those things which adult society deems important and necessary. In the clash of intentions, responsible and powerful teachers must win over children at least at the overt level of what is said and done in classrooms. Quite often, through their own enthusiasm and 'interpersonal skills', they move off into new territory with a happy and compliant class. Yet, unwittingly, through the use of powerful motivators, teachers may be *sapping* or *turning off* the learning power of children. Each time they prevail in such a way, they may also strengthen their belief that children *like* and *need* to be stimulated in this way.

In these chapters, Garth Boomer and Jon Cook set about finding ways of redressing power imbalances and making space for the learning intentions of students. In doing this, they begin to develop templates and protocols which may help teachers to break away from old reproductive habits and rituals.

Invitations to Inquire

1   In chapter 1, Garth Boomer contrasts the so-called motivation and negotiation models of teaching. He does not deal with the reasons why the 'motivation' model has persisted for over a century in western societies. What reasons can you give for its persistence? How might the negotiation model help us to abandon the motivation model?

2   Garth (chapter 1) is also relatively silent about the nature of the 'constraints' which prevail in any teaching act, particularly about systems of public testing and assessment. Given the palpable reality of these testing and assessing structures, how can a negotiating teacher honor students' needs to do well on externally imposed tests?

3   Jon Cook (chapter 2) could be accused of Machiavellianism in his rationale for securing student ownership. Do you think his capital metaphor of making students shareholders in the company is just a more subtle way of coopting the workers?

4   Would it be possible for teachers to increase their power over students by using Jon's method? (In other words, is chapter 2 sufficiently clear about the values implicit in his exposition?)

5   What are the prospects of teachers taking up both chapters 2 and 3 as recipes?

6   What important aspects of the teaching act are lost in Garth Boomer's attempts to anatomize the curriculum in chapter 3?

7   Garth (chapter 3) lists an array of questions which teachers might ask themselves when evaluating the progress of the curriculum-in-action. These are all questions looking inward to the classroom. What questions might teachers need to ask about what is happening in relation to how the school community, the school principal, the wider educational system, and, indeed, politicians might be seeing it?

With these and other questions in mind, read on . . .

References

BRITTON, J.N., BARNES, D. and ROSEN, H. (Eds) (1st ed.), TORBE, M. (replaced Rosen in 2nd ed.) (1969/1986) *Language, the Learner and the School*, Portsmouth, NH: Boynton/Cook.

NOVICK, D. and WATERS, D. (1977) *Talking in School*, Adelaide, Australia: Education Department of South Australia.

SMITH, F. and MILLER, G. (Eds) (1970) *The genesis of Language*, Cambridge, MA: MIT Press.

WILKINSON, A. (1971) *The Foundations of Language*, Oxford: Oxford University Press.

Chapter 1

Negotiating the Curriculum

Garth Boomer[1]

Introduction

In the late 1970s in Australia, it had become fashionable for schools in Australia to produce language policies *across the curriculum*. Because I was at that time convinced that such policies would be ineffectual unless they were accompanied by changes to the school's administrative structure, its curriculum and its educational philosophy, I wanted to explore an issue that went behind language to the eternal triangle of education: the *teacher*, the *child* and the *curriculum*.

This exploration owes a considerable debt to Professor James Britton, who offered valuable encouragement and advice in the early years of the work of the various 'language and learning' teams in Australia. Britton supported our growing belief that the more profitable question to put to whole school staffs is not 'How can we develop the child's language?', but *'How do children (and for that matter, we) learn?*

The first question quite often threatens those teachers who consider themselves unqualified to teach language, and it can also lead to petty bickering about the perennial bogey surface-features of spelling, punctuation and 'proper' presentation. If language across the curriculum is associated with the English faculty, Sampson's 'Every teacher is a teacher of English' (1926) becomes a misleading focus.

But put the second question, and all teachers, lecturers and administrators are, or should be, equal. This is a question to which we all should have personal, articulate and perpetually speculative responses.

Allied to the question of 'How do children learn?' are further teasers, such as *'Under which conditions do children learn most effectively?', 'What is learning?', and 'Do we all learn in the same way?'*

On Learning Theory

Since 1975 the Language Across the Curriculum project team in South Australia, and more recently the Curriculum and Learning Unit that grew out of it, had been asking teachers questions like this, as well as looking into official, departmental curriculum statements to see if any of these address themselves directly to what may loosely be called learning theory. Few departmental statements addressed learning theory. Certainly *teaching* theory abounded, either implicitly or explicitly, and it was possible to argue that, however tenuously, teaching theory must be based on some notion of how people learn. However, our team in South Australia concluded, on the basis of widespread inquiry, that few teachers could articulate what they assumed about learning.

By having a learning theory I do not mean being able to precis Piaget, Skinner and Bruner. I mean being able to state one's own best-educated understanding as to how people come to internalise new information or to perform new operations. It can be argued that we come into the world *theorising*. Certainly Year 1 children can very easily be encouraged to talk about how they learnt to talk. Teachers likewise can examine the learning theory implicit in their classroom practice.

So I come closer to the topic of negotiating the curriculum through classroom practice. Imagine education-department curriculum guides, with no explicit learning theory, being taken by teachers with no explicit learning theory and turned into lessons for children who are not told the learning theory. Some of the best of these children then graduate to become teachers. And so on. Isn't it about time that we all tried to articulate what is surely there behind every curriculum unit, every assignment, every examination?

If we can tell ourselves our present theory, we can also tell it to our students in terms that they can understand, so that they can try it out to see if it works in helping them to learn. From our joint evaluation we can then modify the theory, and try again. So, collaboratively, teachers and students may build learning theories, if by 'theory' we mean a kind of working hypothesis.

But learning theory cannot be disconnected from the criteria used to select what is to be learnt and when (i.e. our theory about the *curriculum content*: the subject offerings and the subject sequencing). These, in turn, are framed by a theory about society or culture.

Professor Basil Bernstein talked about the framing and sequencing of curriculum (at the National Language Development conference in Canberra, January 1978). He spoke of the way in which we often attribute divine universality to what may be simply culture-specific subject offerings and lock-step teaching sequences. When I look back on many years of work in schools, I think that education is an almost self-perpetuating chain of subjections. The education system is subject to the ingrained educational myths of society (deified into theories in the universities); the teachers are subject to the myths of the system (reified into curriculum guides, textbooks, standardized tests and public examinations); and the children are subject to teachers who choreograph all the myths in subjects, each educational genre with its own ritual, language, sequences and decor and each with its own value (e.g. classical physics is worth more than popular art, which is worth more than punk-rock, sex education).

The aim of this chapter is to suggest tentatively how this chain may be broken by articulating the mythologies or theories at all levels and then taking a constructively irreverent stance towards them. I have already suggested that teachers and children may collaboratively build learning theories. I now extend this to include curriculum theories and theories about society — and I mean this quite seriously *from Year 1 to Year 12*.

Summarizing, I have so far questioned language as a *way in* to whole-school teacher development, and I have suggested learning as a more profitable topic. Learning is, or should be, inseparable from curriculum theory, but curriculum theory is shaped by the mythologies of a specific culture and based on teaching, handing down and initiating children into valued ways of looking at the world. Teachers who become their own learning theorists also need to become their own curriculum theorists.

Experiments by the Curriculum and Learning Unit in South Australia have shown interesting consequences when teachers, each having reflected on something recently learnt, together build up a learning theory, after which they are asked a simple question: '*How would you then fare as a learner in your own class?*' They are generally forced to conclude that schools are institutions of teaching, not of learning.

On Power

Before focusing specifically on the curriculum, it is necessary to reflect a little on power. It was not the brief of the Language Across the Curriculum project to inquire into the politics of education, but the project officers came to believe that no discussion of language and learning can afford to ignore the structure of systems and schools. We sat for hours reflecting upon teachers' problems, our own problems and data gathered in classrooms. Inevitably, we kept returning to the question of power relationships: inside the classroom, within schools, within the system and in society itself. Perhaps initially we inclined too hastily to apportion blame to teachers; we would now want to question the very bases of our society.

With our interest in learning, we set out to gain insights into how teachers perceive knowledge and how they think wisdom is achieved. With exceptions, of course, we found that a kind of pharmaceutical metaphor is widely applicable. Teachers define the knowledge to be dealt with, prepare the medication, and dispense the knowledge according to the prescribed dosage. Knowledge is perceived as transmittable, and the learner's mind as a passive receptacle. The assumption is that teachers *have* the knowledge and that children *have not*, the 'have nots' being dependent on the 'haves'.

Now, even when teachers profess humanism, democracy, respect for the learner and horror at the mere thought of manipulative behaviour, we have come to have doubts — not about the teachers' sincerity, but about their ability to perceive the power vested in them, simply because they are *adults* and control the dispensation of knowledge. Indeed, we are beginning to wonder whether the outright autocrat is not less dangerous than some self-deluding humanists. At least the former may make the rules of the power game explicit. We looked closely at so-called 'child-centred' progressive teaching techniques, where teachers purport to take a largely facilitative role. Here, teachers who still retain the significant, ultimate powers often pretend to divest themselves of power by giving limited decision-making opportunities to the children. For example, children may be free to choose one of several options without having the option to reject the options. Moreover, many attractive learning packages in schools demand little creative, individual, teacher and learner contributions.

A crucial question arises: '*Are schools dedicated to the promotion of the child's power to learn, and ultimately to learn independently of instruction and guidance?*'

I am sure that administrators and teachers throughout Australia would answer with an unequivocal 'Yes'. Why is it, then, that we find dependent learning rather than inquiry and experiment? Why is it that we find so few questions from children? Why is it that *fact* is so often revered above *principle*? What is the reality?

On Constraints

The teachers with whom we have worked in South Australia have impressed us greatly with their concern to help children to learn and with their self-critical approach to the craft of teaching. Many devote themselves to education with awesome energy, but we are left with the feeling that, in isolation, these teachers have little power to affect the many feudal structures long embedded in both schools and the system. Sadly, we have talked to many good teachers who are frustrated and often plagued with guilt because they are falling short of their ideals, when the real cause often lies not in themselves but in a subtle combination of various manifestations of external control. These may include a fragmented timetable, disguised streaming of children and teachers, external examinations, large classes, or a limited choice of commercially-produced resources all with an implicit, behavourist learning theory. The more we have speculated about the nature of schools, the more we have come to believe that a massive deep-seated inertia, not of the school's wishing, persists — despite cosmetic changes from closed to open space, from forty minute lessons to hour modules, from English to general studies. It is devilishly difficult to effect change, yet we feel that radical structural changes are needed to produce a school context in which language can flow powerfully between teachers and students in the pursuit of action knowledge.

For example, where individual teachers wish to change the emphasis from teacher as Examiner to teacher as Collaborative Evaluator with the students, they act in a broad context quite inimical to their intentions: students socialised for years into seeing the teacher as judge, a school system geared to external reward for effort, and a society based on competition. Depending on their own personal charisma, teachers may begin to succeed in winning the confidence of some students, who may then feel aggravated by their other teachers; but the more usual result is that such teachers are devalued as soft or even slightly crazy. It is therefore very difficult for teachers to share their power with students, because society and schools are not based on such a philosophy.

It is my belief that *there are some existing strategies that can be improved*. For instance, our reflections on power have led us to question our South Australian team's strategy of working with individual teachers in the hope that good things will ripple out. There may be some rippling, but the steady hands of custom and ritual soon calm the waters.

To summarize again, I accept that there is an inevitable inequality between teacher and child and that teachers have wide powers. In turn, I see individual teachers as relatively powerless themselves within the governing frames of society and the education system, so they are often reduced to the status of intermediaries, translating society's values and initiating children into these values. Where administrators of the system, with respect to teachers, or teachers, with respect to children, purport to hand over powers, I believe that the harmful effects of their power may be increased, because the subjects of this power are likely to be more mystified about the actual sources of control.

On Demystification

Now, our specific concern in the South Australian team was to promote more open communication, more talk to exchange and seek information, and more questioning to relieve mystification. This follows from one of our basic assumptions: that learning is vitally connected with the language resources that can be brought to serve it. A more equitable distribution of power (or at least a more healthy exercise of power), which we know can be used either benevolently to let in or maliciously to exclude, will not come while those in power monopolise the talking space (i.e. the language), thereby keeping other people in relative ignorance.

So what should be done? I believe that there are three important areas of action:

- Strategies should be applied at *all levels* of the system and society. That is, politicians, parents, administrators, teachers and children all need to be brought into *discussions about how we learn*, if we are to raise the quality of thinking and learning in schools and society.

- There will always be inequalities of power in both schools and society and the harmful effects of power will be offset only *if those in power make quite explicit* the values, assumptions and criteria on which they base their actions. In this way others will have a better chance to defend themselves, more opportunity to question and more chance of negotiation, at least where the power figure is not totally despotic.

- Significant change will come only *through collaboration at all levels*. Individual action is usually contained and rendered ineffectual when it begins to threaten the established order.

This does not mean that individual teachers should delay action until they can find support from their colleagues. At least, teachers can talk to their students openly about why they do what they do, about how they think people learn and about the societal consequences of various behaviours.

I have found perhaps the most exciting and challenging strategy offered in the book *Language, Truth and Politics* (1975) by Trevor Pateman. Pateman says that we should ourselves be able to do, and then in turn to be able to teach children how to do, the following:

- question an unreasonable assertion
- say that we don't understand if we don't understand
- pause to think
- say that we don't know if we don't know.

This should be accompanied by a good deal of thinking aloud in front of students, so that they can have open access to the teacher's thinking powers.

On Motivation versus Negotiation

Motivated learning

Now, Model A represents the traditional curriculum model in which, after reflecting on past experience and the content to be taught, teacher A, within the practical constraints of school and society, intends to teach a certain program.

Before teaching can proceed the students must be motivated in some way. If the topic is 'Weather and Climate', this may be achieved by a trip to the local weather station, or by a lesson in which the coolers are turned off to draw attention to the topic in hand. The powerful motivator thus *by indirection finds direction out*, and the children, to varying degrees, come to intend roughly in the same direction as the teacher. Throughout the planned curriculum unit there is tension between the teacher's goal and the children's intent, but most students eventually receive marks or grades for written work, which tell them how close they have come to the teacher's intentions. Sometimes the mark is externally decided.

As Model A shows, even at best the children's learnings only approximate to the teacher's goals, so the curriculum may touch only a little of each child's key and associated interests. This leaves a good deal of what has been learnt unexamined and unevaluated, because the teacher, or external examiner, tests only what is set on the curriculum. Of course, the overlapping shown in the model may not occur at all, and the child is failed or subjected to remediation, which requires more intense motivation. In either case the child appears to have learnt much less than is actually the case.

Irrespective of the teaching style of the teacher, there will be great wastage if this model is applied.

Negotiated learning

Armed with a Pateman-like outlook on open communication, a personal learning theory and an awareness of the harmful effects of inexplicit power, a teacher may develop strategies for negotiating the curriculum as represented in Model B.

Here, teacher B reflects in the same way as teacher A to find worthwhile curriculum content and strategies based on past experience, coming to fairly non-negotiable conclusions about the basic content of the unit. If the unit is 'Weather and Climate', the teacher finds some core input that should illustrate the key *principles* and *concepts* to be learnt. At this stage the teacher talks openly to children about the topic to be covered, why it is to be included, why it is important and what constraints prevail (e.g. it may be a set topic in the mandated geography curriculum; it may have been made obligatory by the faculty head; it may have to be finished in three weeks). The talk centres on what the children already know, how the teacher thinks the new information may be learnt, how the necessary tasks are to be shared and what constraints the children have (e.g. 'We've got an enormous amount of reading in English this week').

The next step is for teacher and children to plan the unit, the activities, the goals, the assignments and the negotiable options. (Compare with Model A, where this programming takes place *without children present, before* the sequence begins). Collaboratively, a fairly tightly structured unit of work is prepared, in which the class, the groups, each child and the teacher all contract to make contributions. The unit takes into account unforeseen learning related to the

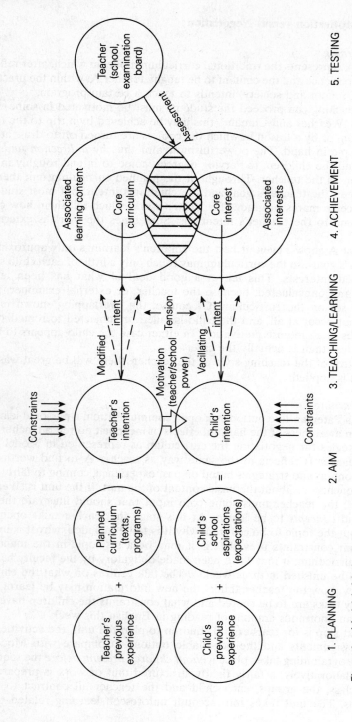

Figure 1: Model A: Motivation

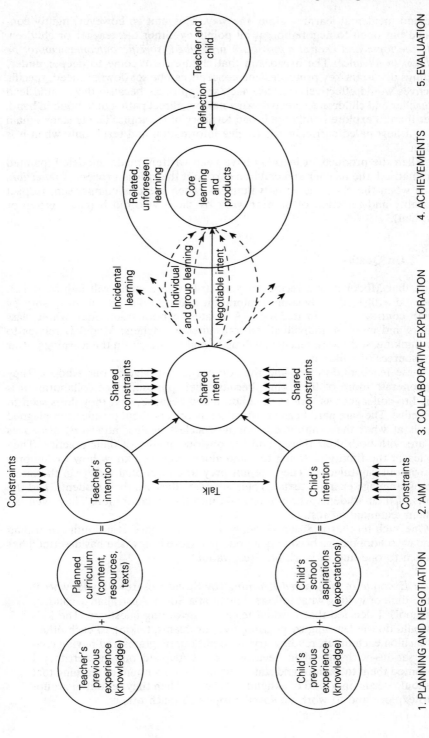

1. PLANNING AND NEGOTIATION   2. AIM   3. COLLABORATIVE EXPLORATION   4. ACHIEVEMENTS   5. EVALUATION

Figure 2: Model B: Negotiation

topic and incidental learning along the way. This unit is, however, tightly constrained but open to negotiation at all points by either the teacher or children. *While the topic and central content are prescribed, specific outcomes cannot be set down in advance.* The broad aim that children will come to deeper understandings of certain key principles and concepts can be set down. Indeed, specific objectives would effectively sterilise such an approach, because they would lead the teacher and children to creep down a narrow, direct path, guide book in hand, rather than to explore boldly the broad territory of the topic. The teacher's main role in a negotiated curriculum is to give information and teach only when it is needed.

When the products of learning have been written, made, modeled, painted or dramatised, the teacher and children carry out the crucial process of *reflection*. This is when the class shares its valuing — when there is comparison, respect for quality and rejection of inferior work by those who did it (class, group or individual).

On Quality

I think that Model A is a recipe for standards where many will fail; Model B, if adopted, will lead to dynamic exploration and rigorous pursuit of quality by all who contract to be in it. Model A relates to both traditional, whole-class teachers and modern, individualized-transmission teachers; Model B relates to clear-thinking, self-aware teachers willing to make a wager on the learning power and resources of children.

These teachers do exist, and they do not just survive in our schools. They even generate more of their kind, because their philosophy of collaboration is applied to colleagues as well as to children and because what they do is seen to be effective. They are hard-headed, articulate theorizers about practice, not plagued by guilt at what they cannot do, nor defenceless against attackers, armed as they are with both their theory and the obvious quality of their practice. They have learnt the futility of trying to stand alone, and they know how to compromise without capitulating. They are not prey to educational fads (e.g. the latest spate of language exercise texts). Their greatest allies are their students, and the parents of their students who are brought into the collaboration. They even get excellent examination results.

One such teacher is Susan Hyde, who taught science at a South Australian secondary school before becoming a principal. Here is how she has described her approach to one unit of work on 'Respiration'.

> *An Example of Negotiated Learning* (by Susan Cosgrove/Hyde, who at the time of writing what follows, taught at a South Australian secondary school): I decided that I would teach by answering questions. The kids would do the learning by puzzling over problems, talking to each other, teaching each other, reading, trying to nut out diagrams and having conversations with me when necessary. So, I mapped out the territory I wanted them to explore and stated the minimum amount of learning that should occur (in a kind of assignment sheet). Then they set out in groups to explore and to work up specific topics to teach others.

My challenge met with responses that convinced me that answering questions beats teaching any day, if you want the kids to learn and understand. But stick to teaching and asking the questions if you, the teacher, want to learn.

I should point out at this stage that these students had been using topic booklets, written by a teacher and produced at the school. They involve a series of activities, with information or references, experiments to do and questions to answer in each activity. The assignment sheet is a condensation of the information in one of these topic booklets.

So, when they got the assignment sheet, they had to decide their own strategy for learning the information. They had to choose their own questions and choose how to search for the answers; and to be able to choose where to start, they had to work out what they already knew about the subject. This is exactly what they did. They formed themselves into groups and began talking:

'Okay, what are we going to do?'

'I know, blood. Let's do blood. My mother, she works at the Blood Bank at the Plaza.'

'Blood Bank? What's that?'

'Hey, remember that lung cancer film we saw?'

'Yuck!'

'Yeah, we could do the lungs, and get some and cut it up and all that.'

So they began, drawing from their own experience and knowledge of the subject, beginning at an area that interested them.

They appreciated being able to do this. In a letter to me about this experience, Susan and Paul wrote:

'I learnt this topic reasonably well because we could choose the part we were most interested in and because we could do some research on it, but with the topic booklet, they tell you the answer by putting notes at the beginning of the activity.'

Susan and Paul

But what about the students who couldn't decide or who didn't catch on? Well, they came to me for advice. 'I don't get what to do, Ms. Hyde'. We sat down and talked about it. I asked them a question or two about what they might be interested in. If they still couldn't decide, I told them a few things about each area to give them more ideas about where to start. At this stage I asked them to keep a diary of what they did each day. In this way I could keep tabs of where each group was moving, and it also made them aware that they did have a strategy of learning.

At first our lesson time was spent in group activities. They were reading books, making notes, talking to each other and to me:

'Did you know that . . .'

'Where do you think I could find out about this?'

'Could you explain . . .'

I spent my time answering questions like these, directing them to sources or to another group that was studying the same area, and just talking about some fact that interested someone.

How did the students learn? By talking, writing, reading and listening to each other, and by being able to choose their own strategy for their learning. Oh, and after all of this, we did have a test. After seeing the test, my senior wrote: 'In general the results indicate a good grasp of the subject. Pleasing'. But the people most pleased with the test results were the students themselves. They then went full speed ahead into the next challenge ('Measurement', 'Pressure' and 'Density') and did even better.

Conclusion

If teachers set out to teach according to a planned curriculum, without engaging the interests of the students, the quality of learning will suffer. Student interest involves student investment and personal commitment. Negotiating the curriculum means deliberately planning to invite students to contribute to, and to modify, the educational program, so that they will have a real investment both in the learning journey and in the outcomes. Negotiation also means making explicit, and then confronting, the constraints of the learning context and the non-negotiable requirements that apply.

Once teachers act upon the belief that students should share with them a commitment to the curriculum, negotiation will follow naturally, whether the set curriculum is traditional or progressive, and whether the classroom is architecturally open or closed.

Note

1 This chapter is an adaption of the article, 'Negotiating the curriculum', first published in *English in Australia*, **44**, June, 1978.

References

SAMPSON, G. (1921) *English for the English*, London: Cambridge University Press.
PATEMAN, T. (1975) *Language, Truth and Politics*, Nottingham: Stroud & Pateman.

Chapter 2

Negotiating the Curriculum: Programming for Learning

Jon Cook[1]

Why Negotiate?

Negotiation means about the same in education as it does in politics or industry. All the parties in an operation come together, bringing with them their own points of view, needs and wants, and together they work for the outcomes most satisfactory to all concerned. In educational terms, the result of negotiation may come to a meshing of minds, an interlocking of intentions, an agreement about means and ends between teacher and learners. The focus is on bringing about the best possible learning for the learners.

The key to negotiation, both in theory and in practice, lies in the ownership principle: people tend to strive hardest for things they wish to own, or to keep and enhance things they already own. The inverse is just as true and observable all around us: people find it difficult to give commitment to the property and ideas of others. Most teachers would acknowledge the difference between the gardens of the houses they've rented during country service, and those of their own homes; most enthusiasts would admit, wistfully, that the greatest proponents of their enthusiasms are themselves.

For the present discussion there is an important corollary. Children also are people and are capable of being successful negotiators. Like adults, children have needs, wants and points of view; they will work hard to get what they want; and they can understand the trade-off, involving the recognition of inevitable constraints and the impossible. More than most adults, children are willing to strive to please, often for little better reason than that it is expected of them. This willingness both to please others and to accept the inevitable has, I believe, been unwittingly played upon by educators, who often seem too prepared to interpret that willingness as a lack of decision-making ability and a lack of individual intention. I would argue the contrary to be the truth: that when the opportunity to exhibit abilities is unavailable, those abilities will remain hidden and under-developed.

I think that a partial explanation for Australia's educational history of classroom autocracy, chalk-and-talk, teachers as purveyors of knowledge to passive child recipients, is our (i.e. educators from primary to matriculation and beyond) refusal to recognize children as being capable of the ownership principle in practice (i.e. children as decision makers, intenders, owners of their own ideas, willing partners with their teachers in the active pursuit of their own learning).

Yet it is demonstrable that classroom autocracy has been less than ideal. Students who are passive or acquiescent, unwilling, resentful or coerced, even externally 'motivated' (as described in chapter 1), do not make the best learners. Equally, *laissez faire* has proved generally inoperable and indefensible in the classroom. Freedom without discipline is aimlessness at best, and chaos at worst. Of course, owners recognise the constraints of ownership, just as they do its freedoms.

The analogy of capital and labour is not inappropriate here. For high productivity there must be a willing partnership between the two. When labour's rights of, or urge for, ownership — whether of an adequate return for effort rendered, or an equable say in things — are denied, capital flounders. Strikes play havoc with productivity. But children can't overtly go on strike, which may help to explain why teachers generally may appear to get away with owning all the classroom capital (i.e. the means, content and outcomes of education). So, children develop more subtle ways of giving teachers the message that all is not well. They withhold their learning power. Classroom productivity (i.e. learning) suffers.

So I reiterate my answer to the question 'Why negotiate?' Negotiation of the curriculum offers our best chance of maximising the learning productivity of the classroom. The rule is simple. Learners will work harder and learn better, and what they learn will mean more to them, if they are discovering their own ideas, asking their own questions and fighting hard to answer them for themselves. They must be educational decision makers. Out of negotiation comes a sense of ownership in learners for the work they are to do, and therefore a commitment to it. Learning is an active process. Teachers can't do it for learners. Information may be imposed, but understanding cannot be, for it must come from within. Students learn best when they want to. They want to when they are doing it for themselves, as a result of their own needs. Active (i.e. intentional, participatory) involvement in classroom decision making and in the enactment of the decisions, results in more effective learning than does the passivity that attends the performance of a teacher's imposed pedagogical pattern.

This is not personal fiction. Learners will tell the truth of it for themselves if we ask them. In the past several years many hundreds of teachers and students have been asked the question 'How do you learn best?' by the language and learning/team in Western Australia (and elsewhere). Learning has been defined loosely as 'coming to new understandings'. The emphasis has been on how learners learn *best*. We've asked them to focus on what needs to happen for them to learn at full power, on the conditions that need to apply and on the processes they go through. The answers have kept forming, with remarkable consistency, the pattern that follows now, expressed from the point of view of learners, and organised in the way that has evolved from what they say.

Learners' Description of How They Learn Best

1 Engagement

• We learn best when we intend to learn, when we become personally engaged and interested in the learning we are to do. Our learning should be purposeful, and *our* purposes are more important to us than those of the teacher. So we need to know *what* we are to do, and *why* we are to do it. We need to sort out the what and the why, so that a clear sense of direction emerges for us. But we would like our intentions to mesh with our teacher's purposes, so that as much as possible we are all thinking along the same lines.

• Given that we respond better to internal motivation (i.e. intention) than to external motivation (e.g. examinations, fear, or our teacher's enthusiasm — though these also may be powerful), our intention to learn becomes engaged when we become curious or puzzled by the things we are to learn. We need to recognize the problematic, and it must matter to us (not just to our teacher) that we resolve our puzzlements and find satisfactory solutions to our problems.

• We want relevance. Our new learning should relate to what we already know, so that we can grow from where we are now and draw on our experience to relate to the new understandings we are struggling with.

2 Exploration

• But we need it acknowledged that we are not all equal in experience or in what we know and can do. So we need the learning experiences to be as individualized as possible, to cater for our differences in starting points, needs and interests, abilities, preferred ways of doing things and purposes for doing them.

• While we may need to work together, and while it helps if we have purposes in common, we also need the teacher to open up the range of options and modes for our learning. The style, amount, kind, timing and order of things may need to be as variable as we are individual.

• But either way, we all need to bring our learning means to bear, especially our language, and most especially our talk. We need to inquire, speculate and hypothesise; to test our ideas and engage in trial and error; to learn by doing and by finding out, rather than by being told or having ideas inflicted on us. This means that we need to be active participants in real learning experiences, not passive recipients of our teacher's knowledge and experience. We understand best when we can do things for ourselves and arrive at new knowledge by discovery, by trial, application, and often reshaping and reapplication.

• In our learning we often need to work with, and relate to, both other learners and our teacher. We need individual, paired, small-group and whole-class structures and learning situations, depending on such factors as the work's purpose and context, its stage of development, its audience and individual needs or preferences. But the small group is our preferred base, because it gives us the greatest involvement and flexibility. It allows us to learn together and from each other as we go. We can use each other as sounding boards and generators, and as audiences; we feel most secure when working with our peers.

• We need help from our teachers, but not dominance by them. We want a supporter and facilitator, not a dictator. We need to take risks in struggling for new understandings and skills, and we will only take those risks in a supportive and conducive environment — one in which we are challenged, but encouraged; can feel the tension of the struggle, but not fear, can strive to get things right, but not feel shame if we get them wrong; and can make mistakes, but know that the teacher will help, not punish us.

Besides this supportive role we want the teacher to be available to work with us when and as we need help. This need usually arises individually or in small groups, rather than in all of us at once. We don't want to be bored, insulted or confused by the teacher's telling things to all of us in the class together, if in fact some of us already know what is being explained, or are hopelessly lost because we don't know enough to understand, or if the timing simply is not right for some of us to be given that input. Anyway, in the whole-class situation too often we can't ask real questions, or respond thoroughly or talk it all through; and we need to do these things when the need arises, not simply when we are told to do them.

3 Reflection

• At the 'end' of our learning experience, we want to feel that we have achieved something worthwhile to us. We need to come up with products that mean something important to us and that will please the audience we are preparing for. We like to share what we have found, and in fact the sharing can often be a way of testing for ourselves how well we have learnt. We need to reflect, both individually and collectively, on our learning and its consequences and implications for us, and to ask where we have arrived. Out of this reflection, sharing and presentation we often find that useful new questions, challenges and directions emerge. Thus we can continue to grow and learn.

Meeting Learners' Requirements by Negotiation

If this picture formed from what learners say is true, other reasons for negotiation begin to emerge to keep company with the ownership principle. The teacher's job of programming for his/her students' learning (as differentiated from the norm of programming for teaching) suddenly seems to become impossibly complex if he/she is to keep all the learners' requirements in mind. Teachers cannot be in all the minds of all learners at once; cannot know all their experiences, needs, wants, interests or intentions; cannot prejudge all the modes of learning experience, let alone the order and timing of them, that learners will need once they get going. Also, teachers can't be working with perhaps thirty people individually at the same time. All the learners' questions cannot be foretold, nor can all the required resources be predicted. Yet learners demand that all these factors, and more, be considered by the teacher if their learning power is to be optimised.

So, if teachers alone *cannot* do the kind of programming demanded by learners, help must be provided. Only learners can provide that help, since only they know their own minds, intentions and experience — or can work them out, given encouragement and talking and thinking time. So teachers must genuinely ask learners to tell what they know, think and hope, so that teacher and learner may together plan for profitable work. That is, they must negotiate the curriculum. Teachers and learners must negotiate together because neither can go it alone, if optimum learning is the aim.

But it is still not as simple as that. Neither teacher nor student is free always to decide everything to suit the self. The optimum program is now further compounded in difficulty by some realities facing teachers and therefore, indirectly, students. Super-ordained constraints do exist. Usually there is such a thing as an imposed syllabus or course, which usually constitutes a non-negotiable element. Daily timetables and room allocations cannot simply be dispensed with or changed around. Senior staff and education department officers have their requirements. There is only one teacher, but there are perhaps thirty students, and this averages out at about one minute only per period per student. And so on. We all know the constraints.

None of these constraints meshes with the requirements of learners. Yet they are real enough. Small wonder then that so many teachers ignore the requirements for optimum learning, and opt for teaching at the collective norm, often whether effective learning is happening or not.

But I believe that the negotiation approach does embrace these constraints, by meeting them head on — not by pretending that they don't exist, but by admitting them and working around them once they're out in the open for all to see. Too often teachers know them, but students, like sprouting mushrooms, are kept in the dark. Yet, just as scientists will accept realistic constraints in their research, so will students (who are, after all, a kind of scientist by definition) if these constraints are recognised and understood. The first thing that good negotiators do is face up to the impossible, accept what can't be changed and then go to work on the possible, on what can be changed and won.

In Summary So Far

Still it is not that simple. I have proposed some reasons for negotiation and some suggestions about why negotiation may solve some oft-experienced classroom conundrums. Yet the practicalities of how negotiation is to operate remain unraveled. Given a set of guiding principles, a methodological approach is required. The remainder of this chapter is given to such 'nitty-gritties'. Illustrations of the approach in practice are to be found in Part B.

But first, by way of summary, I propose two models (emerging from the guiding principles outlined above), which may help to crystallize where I have to go: Model 1, of learners' requirements for optimum learning; and Model 2, of negotiation as an aid towards meeting these requirements.

One Practical Approach to Classroom Negotiation

First the learning area (i.e. the content of a unit of work) must be chosen and declared. If there is no imposed syllabus or course, there is an obviously strong argument (e.g. the ownership principle!) for even this decision to be negotiated, whether from a range of possibilities suggested by the teacher or from the interests of students.

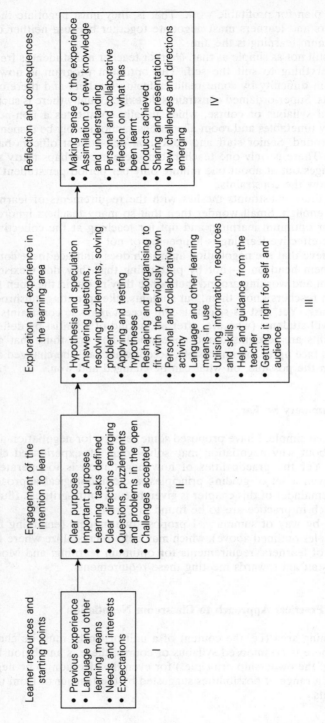

Learner resources and starting points

I

- Previous experience
- Language and other learning means
- Needs and interests
- Expectations

Engagement of the intention to learn

II

- Clear purposes
- Important purposes
- Learning tasks defined
- Clear directions emerging
- Questions, puzzlements and problems in the open
- Challenges accepted

Exploration and experience in the learning area

III

- Hypothesis and speculation
- Answering questions, resolving puzzlements, solving problems
- Applying and testing hypotheses
- Reshaping and reorganising to fit with the previously known
- Personal and collaborative activity
- Language and other learning means in use
- Utilising information, resources and skills
- Help and guidance from the teacher
- Getting it right for self and audience

Reflection and consequences

IV

- Making sense of the experience
- Assimilation of new knowledge and understanding
- Personal and collaborative reflection on what has been learnt
- Products achieved
- Sharing and presentation
- New challenges and directions emerging

Figure 3: Model 1: Learners' requirements

If there is the constraint of an imposed syllabus, the teacher must declare the fact, explain why and clarify the constraints. An alignment with the students, if necessary, against the external constraint, may be useful for the teacher: 'I have no more choice in this than you do. The fact is we *have* to do it. That examination is at the end of it all. Let's unite to defeat the thing . . .' But with or without this negotiation ploy, the challenge for the teacher must be to engage the intention of the learners to meet the challenge of an imposed task. *They must come to own something that, to begin with, is not theirs.* (This is by no means impossible. For example, few of the ideas in this chapter are peculiarly my own invention; but they are nonetheless mine, since I have come to own them as much as their originators do. They are mine now because I have made them so.)

The chosen topic may be 'Making and Telling Stories' with a year 3 class, 'Electricity' with a year 6 class, 'The Industrial Revolution' with a year 8 social studies class, or 'Metaphor as a Way of Viewing the World' with a matriculation English class. But whatever content is chosen, by whatever means, the learners should know *why* they are tackling it.

Given that the content is selected, and at this stage perhaps not yet willingly accepted, teacher and learners together should then ask four questions, and together negotiate the answers (the wording may need to change, but the focus should not):

Concerning the topic:
1 *What do we know already?*
(Or where are we now, and what don't we need to learn or be taught about?)
2 *What do we want, and need, to find out?*
(Or what are our questions, what don't we know, and what are our problems, curiosities and challenges?)
3 *How will we go about finding out?*
(Where will we look, what experiments and inquiries will we make, what will we need, what information and resources are available, who will do what, and what should be the order of things?)
4 *How will we know, and show, that we've found out when we've finished?*
(What are our findings, what have we learnt, whom will we show and for whom are we doing the work, and where next?)

There is much common sense in the progression of these questions. They represent a very logical approach to tackling a problem — in fact, most kinds of problems — and so they may have wide application in the classroom, across the whole curriculum. The scientific method — problem, clarification, hypothesis, test, conclusion — is embraced within them; and an approach that has so satisfactorily met the needs of the scientist may surely be useful also for learners in other fields, because in a sense all learners at best are scientists — seekers of understanding, problem solvers, people who need to satisfy their curiosity about the things they don't know but want to know.

Jon Cook

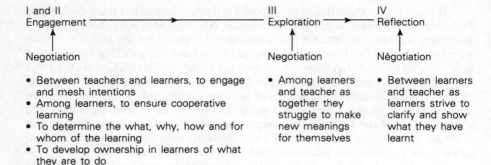

Figure 4:   Model 2: Negotiation as process helper

Questions 1 and 2: What we know now, and what we'll find out about
The two questions go together, since question 2 emerges essentially out of question 1. The very act of asking what we know tends to expose what we don't, and so raises the consciousness of questions to be answered about the gaps in our knowledge. So often, too, one question will lead to another. However, it is crucial that it be the learner who is the questioner, and who leads on from one question to the next. The process going on here is the engagement of the learner's intention to learn. Asking and answering questions will help, but not if the teacher is doing it all for the learner.

So the point and focus of these two questions may be to achieve for the learner, through his/her own efforts:

- the arousal of the intention to learn
- a mobilisation of thinking power
- a kind of clearing of the decks, as the sorting out of the known and unknown takes place
- a marshaling of experience relevant to the topic, and a clarification of the problems and issues at hand
- a developing curiosity, interest and puzzlement, as the exploration process begins
- the start of hypothesis and speculation about answers to the questions arising
- a sense of ownership for the topic
- a sense of direction for the learning inquiries.

Four stages may be involved in putting questions 1 and 2 into practice:

1   The topic is agreed upon between teacher and learners. The individual learner now makes notes for him/herself, preferably in two columns headed 'known' and 'questions' or ('unknown').

2   In small groups, the learners pool their ideas. They sound each other out; inevitably, they generate additions to their two columns as one statement or

question sparks another; they in fact negotiate together their sharing under-standings, experience and prospective inquiries. Probably, they will also begin to answer some questions, quite naturally, and so clarifications begin to emerge.

3   The groups come together as a class, and, with the teacher as their scribe, the collected notes of the groups are placed on the blackboard.

By this stage the students will have done their best to work out, both individually and collectively, what they know and wish to find out. Four factors now probably emerge for the teacher to consider:

- It is probable that the students will have raised much of the content required anyway in a prescribed course.

So much the better if so, since any content that is non-negotiable (i.e. *must* be done) is much more powerful if raised or decided upon by the students out of their own intentions, than if preimposed by the teacher. Still, it is also probable that not all of the prescribed content will have been considered by the students on their own. So it is at this point that the teacher may reasonably have his/her say. Negotiation is, after all, a shared procedure, not a unilateral one on the part of students. I believe that students will readily accept that there may be some things that they have not considered but that it is both necessary and interesting to consider. So much the better if the teacher can now introduce these things, to round off the students' picture. The students are likely to see the value of the teacher's suggestions if they are raised in the context of their own ideas. In this way student ownership of the teacher's share in the action comes naturally and logically.

But, it is my confident prediction that (unless a prescribed content area is badly selected or inappropriate) most often students raise for themselves the very issues and questions that the teacher knows must be covered anyway. Any additions or qualifications the teacher must make are likely to be quite minor.

- The second factor to emerge at this stage is that the blackboard notes in the two columns will represent the *collective* understandings and questions of the students, not the individual ones.

By no means all the students will know what has been noted under 'known', nor will all be ignorant of the answers to all the 'questions'. This is to be expected. What is important is that, with the addition of any teacher suggestions, the ground will now have been fully exposed, and individual students' horizons of inquiry broadened.

- Thirdly, both the relative importance of the various content questions, and the question of for whom they are important, may now emerge.

My suggestion is that the teacher now leads the class in deciding these things. That is, if there are things under 'questions' that every student must consider, now is the time for the teacher to say so — and, of course, to say why. Similarly, if there are things that profitably may be considered by groups, this should be discussed with the class.

- Finally, there may be many questions that are of individual rather than collective concern.

(Bearing in mind my responsibilities as a teacher, I may well expect that students will also *prove* — in various negotiated ways, as raised in the discussion of question 3 below — that they know and understand what they have detailed in the 'known' column. But much of this proof will have been demonstrated anyway through the discussion that ensues as the columns are placed on the blackboard and considered.) We can now lead into stage 4.

4   The students now reshape, on the basis of their collective considerations and their teacher's suggestions or requirements, their lists of 'knowns' and 'questions'. This is a kind of second draft operation. What each student considers that he/she can prove knowledge of is written up in the 'known' column, and the questions to be answered may be written up in three sections:

- things that all students must answer
- things to be considered in groups
- things of individual interest or concern

In taking this step the students draw on their own first draft columns and on the notes from the blackboard.

Question 3: How we find out and make our discoveries
The students should now know what is to be done in the unit of work, and why. The question to consider now is how best to do it all. The process may well follow the lines of questions 1 and 2. Thus, a useful starting point may be for the students in their small groups (so continuing to induce them to help and use each other, and to bring their language, especially talk, to bear on the problems) to focus on determining the means for discovering their answers to the agreed, whole-class, essential questions. Groups generate possibilities for approaches to be taken, and then again the class comes together to have their ideas documented on the blackboard. The teacher adds suggestions, and discusses a plan of attack: the resources required, work to be done, who does what, and so on. These whole-class questions are considered first, because it keeps the class together in a united effort.

It may be that the class, after considering question 4 (the evaluative component of the process), gets to work now on the actual answering business. Alternatively, it may be preferable for the process to be repeated for the small group questions, and then for the individual questions. But it is worth bearing in mind that some regrouping of students may be necessary here, so it may be better for the teacher to move around and make such arrangements with the students once they are into the business of working on the consensus questions.

If this latter approach is not chosen, then clearly, after the whole-class questions have been treated, question 3 will have to be considered for the small group and individual questions. The problem with this approach is that by this time the students may be at different stages, since some are quicker in their work than others, and so some inevitable disruptions occur. For this reason I prefer the former approach. Either way, the class will be busy redrafting its plans of attack in the light of the collective, blackboard notes, and will soon be ready to get down to work. But first, question 4.

Question 4: Showing and Sharing Our New Learning
The question of evaluation (i.e. of how students and teacher can know and show that the work has been done, and done well, and that all the right work has been done) should be raised before the students get going on the work itself, for a major reason. Since all work should have a purpose and an audience, it is clearly necessary for students to know what these are before the work is commenced. The audience (i.e. those for whom the work is to be done) will influence the way in which it will be done and shaped up for presentation. This situation will be similar for the purpose or function of the work.

The most effective and efficient method of presentation will be one determining factor in helping students to decide on drama, scientific experiment and write-up, discussion and debate, reading and writing, or whatever, as the approach. But surely the audience for the work, and its purpose, must also be major influences. It must help to know what the goal is before beginning to travel towards it.

Again, the processes used in questions 1, 2 and 3 may be useful for question 4. Individually and/or in small groups, and then as a whole class, the students ask themselves how their answers to questions 2 and 3 can be shaped to prove their new knowledge gained — to themselves, to each other, to the teacher, and to any other audience that may be identified — and always, how this may be managed in a manner useful to the students as learners.

Particularly once students become accustomed to the whole negotiation approach, they will come up with some remarkably imaginative and profitable answers to question 4. But in early days the teacher may need to step in with some suggestions and requirements (e.g. students teaching each other, groups sharing their findings with other groups, drama in science, experiments in English, short stories in social studies, or presentations to other classes in the same or other schools). One group I worked with came up with the examination it considered would be fair for me to set them as a test of their new knowledge — a clever and cunning device indeed! One way or another, by the time questions 1–4 have been negotiated, the students should be clear about what they are to do, why, how and for whom, and how the work is to be shared, assessed and evaluated. Hopefully, the intentions of the students will have been so raised that motivation by the teacher will no longer be an issue; they will be bursting to get at it, which is precisely what they now should do. Whether a contract basis, tight or loose, individual, group or class structure is decided on, or a step-by-step approach, is up to the teacher and the class. The choices hardly require spelling out here. But the principles of enactment should be much the same as those of conception and plan, and are worth a brief reiteration now.

A Restatement of Principles

- The learners make the running. The teacher guides and helps, but as a negotiator, not as a dictator.

- Timing, order and depth of treatment are negotiable factors, determined by *learner* need, purpose and intention, not teacher prejudice or predisposition.

- Language must be allowed to work for the students, who must talk, write and read themselves into clarifications, understandings and decisions. The teacher-like temptation to do it all for them is to be avoided. (The latter way, teachers learn, but students don't.)

- Learners need to work *together* as well as individually. Their needs and best learning means should determine when and why the effort is to be individual or collective.

- Students should be helped *when* help is needed, not before or in case. Owners will call for help to preserve what they own, much before employees will call for help in serving their masters.

- I believe that an overriding goal of the classroom is process oriented. Thus, what is to be learnt is only part of the classroom context. Students need to acquire the ways and processes of finding things out, of working alone and together to solve their problems. The whole negotiation approach is focused on inculcating this principle. It is a principle that enhances the acquisition of information, not one that encumbers it.

Some Conclusions

The work the students do consequent to completing negotiations for its conception and planning (i.e. negotiations of answers to the four questions) does not follow on as a separate business or by a different process. It is a part integral to the whole learning process derived from the principles of negotiation and learner-centered curriculum enactment proposed in this chapter and in this book. Almost inevitably, by the time the questions have been fully considered, some of the work itself has been done. At least it has been begun, and the students' explorations follow logically on from the engagement of their intentions and the sorting out of their directions and decisions.

If negotiation is a useful means of bringing about a meeting of minds and a meshing of disparate intentions and directions, it will work as much in the operation of learning as it does in the design or programming for learning. Learners still need to negotiate meanings, information, understandings and conclusions together as, and in order that, they learn — through talking, listening, reading and writing; through acting and experimenting and reflecting; through negotiating truth out of a maze of possibilities and paths.

It is not until the unit is finished that the negotiation is concluded. A final element is the reflection or evaluation process itself, when teacher and students together ask themselves at the unit's conclusion: 'What have we learnt?', 'What is it worth?', 'Where have we got to?' and 'Where do we go next?' Even the process of individual reflection leading to small-group and whole-class probings may usefully be repeated at this stage. The growth and consolidation this process causes is one of the things negotiation is all about.

The central factor in all of this is that the students own the work they do. It is that they know the why, what, how and for whom of their work, and believe that the best means of achieving valuable learning for themselves are always in operation, so that they will intend to do the work as best they can for the best reasons. They, and the people they must live and work with, will profit from it as fully as possible within an understood and accepted context of needs, interests, expectations and constraints.

Seven Corollaries

1 The time factor

In discussions on the negotiation approach to programming, the bugbear of time is usually raised: 'Will this approach take longer? Because if it does, I can't afford it. There's too much work to get through as it is . . .' A lot of classroom investigation remains to be done on this one by teachers. But on the basis of my experience with the approach in practice to date, I make the prediction that it's not so much a case of requiring *more* time, as a case of *reorganizing* available time. Certainly the initial planning takes longer than the traditional approach whereby the teacher makes the programming decisions (in his/her own time) and then announces them to the class, perhaps accompanied by a motivational session. Still, much useful learning occurs during class planning sessions; and once the planning has been done, I believe, the work proceeds more quickly and more efficiently and effectively than it would otherwise, since the students both intend to do the work well, and are clear about the methodology of doing it.

So I think that extra time should be required only for the best of reasons, such as that extra work is being done, and done well. To put it in rather more extreme terms: since I believe it does no harm for us to question the validity of some content areas in school courses, and ask whether too much is included at present, and whether it's all the right stuff anyway, I'd rather spend four weeks on a truly valuable unit of work (learning-wise), if it came to it, than three weeks on a relatively valueless one (learning-wise).

2 K-12 and across the curriculum

Another group of questions frequently asked relates to subject areas, ages of students, and the ability levels appropriate for the approach. My response is that, since the vast majority of all the humans I've come across, from zero to ninety years, respond well to appropriate good sense, like to be involved and learn in much the way delineated earlier in this chapter, I'd try the approach with all ages, at all levels, and in all subject areas. For all, I have confidence that it works — or that, at least, it *can* work.

The process of freeing-up from traditions, and from artificially institutionalized patterns of expectation and behaviour, may take some time of course. I believe that passive acquiescence genuinely may be replaced by active decision making, and that power sharing through negotiation within declared boundaries of constraints and intentions is profitable and responsible. It certainly does not mean teachers' abdicating from their proper roles and responsibilities. So it's a case of allowing time for students and teachers to grow with the approach, perhaps by easing into it gently at first; then, as setbacks and hesitancies occur, acknowledging that, while it takes time to negotiate constant open reflection on what is happening, among students and teacher, will remove the doubts and make the process fluent.

3   *The role of the teacher*

The teacher's role in the classroom and as programmer of classroom life changes significantly in the shift from dictator to negotiator. Much of this shift has been stated or implied in the text of this chapter, but some further points may now be made. The teacher is still in charge. His/her goals and responsibilities have not changed, but the methodology for achieving them has. In educational jargon, the new role is one of process helper, facilitator, resource linker, and public documenter. These concepts of role provide the context within which the teacher is still a source of ideas, an expert, a provider of information, a guide and leader. Briefly, I wish to detail five teacher tasks that seem essential.

• The teacher must coordinate operations. The teacher must start things and oversee the whole process. The teacher may not be the one to answer the four questions, but is the one to ask them. Someone must link up people, gather resources and make the arrangements necessary as the learning is planned and implemented; the person best equipped is the teacher. The students do the learning; the teacher facilitates its efficient progress.

• During the process of individual and small group work, both in the course of answering questions 1–3 and when the planned work is going on, the teacher has the opportunity (which is lacking in whole-class, teacher-centred activity) to take a roving facilitative commission. It's possible now to help students on a needs basis, as and where required. Wrangles and confusions within groups can be sorted out. Groups can be linked up, or individual students linked across group borders, since the teacher is in the ideal position to be aware of what all the students are doing, and the students aren't. It's during these parts of the process that the teacher can really teach and consult with students, and this is one of the most rewarding aspects of the whole approach.

• In the whole-class stages of the process, the teacher may be the scribe on behalf of the students, noting their ideas on the blackboard, on butchers paper or an overhead transparency. At first the role is simply one of recorder. The concern is first to get the *students'* ideas out into the open; then the teacher chips in, to help clarify, decide, develop, penetrate murky issues, and unravel tangled ones. The questions are of the process order (e.g. 'What do you mean?' 'Tell me more . . .' 'What's the point of that idea?' 'Where does this lead us?') rather than content laden. But the teacher also must be ready now to step in and add his/her own ideas or requirements. If there are non-negotiable things, such as the demands of prescribed courses, that the students have not raised thus far, it's now that the teacher introduces them. This applies to content, to audiences for the work, and to methods of presentation. It also applies to establishing key focuses or directions, and to deciding on what must be done by all, by some or by individuals. I find that, given that the students have had first go, they will accept constraints and teacher suggestions very readily. After all, they are being helped in *their* endeavours, not dominated by another's prescription as base.

• Probably, the teacher has the role of writing up the program once it has been worked out. It should be done in a public mode (e.g. duplicated and distributed to all students, inscribed on a wall chart). Students could do this, but they're better off getting on with their work while the teacher does legwork of this kind.

• Finally, when reflection and evaluation time arrives the teacher must lead the class in its response to questions like: 'What do we know now that we didn't before?' 'Where have we got to?' 'Where next?' and so on. Students need help in this, and the teacher's greater experience and ability to stand back from immediate contexts are invaluable

4 *Wall charts*

Because the process of the negotiation approach is learner-centred, the sources and products of the learning experiences must always be available for the learners. There's little point in asking the learners to do the programming publicly, if the teacher keeps private and secret the kinds of questions to be asked, the source of resources, or the program the students devise. Thus, the processes, possibilities and conclusions of the negotiation approach must be made public, shared and made available for free use in the service of the students' learning. The answers to the four questions must, at both planning and conclusion stages, be 'up front'. They must be documented as publicly as possible in the sphere of the classroom. My suggestion is wall charts.

In the classroom I envisage, standard wall chart or pin-up board requirements will be:

• the program itself: the four questions, the answers to them raised by the students, and the ensuing plans for action

• the range of available resources and sources of information

• the ways open for students to use in finding out answers to their questions: the testing, searching and experimenting methods; the kinds of writing and talking and reading etc.

• possible audiences, and possible forms of presenting and sharing students' findings

• the kinds of questions students may ask in making plans and decisions.

How are these wall charts devized? The answer is commonsensical: as the life of the negotiating classroom develops. The first time the approach is tried, up go the large pieces of paper onto the walls. As the relevant bits of information, or questions, or resources or decisions are suggested, they are added to the appropriate charts. The next time a unit of work is tackled in this way, the charts are there to be drawn on, and more will be added to them. The point is to make the tools of learning available for the learners, not to keep them guessing or reliant upon the teacher. So, wall charts of these tools should be public, ongoing and growing. They are built by the students and their teacher, they belong to all and are freely available for use by all.

5 *Small groups*

The basic unit of classroom organization and student structure must be the small group, which typically may comprise four students. That is to say, rather than the norm of a single-class structure numbering perhaps thirty students, which occasionally breaks into small groups for specific tasks, I advocate the norm of small groups, which will occasionally, according to specific needs, combine together to form a single class.

Two factors demand this organization. The first is found in the learners' requirements for optimized learning, detailed in the first part of this chapter: they learn best when they can naturally and extensively interact with each other as peers, according to need and the task at hand. The whole, teacher-centred class cannot allow this; the small group can. The second factor is found in the structure suggested for the approach. Frequent consultation, pooling of ideas etc. between students are essential. The small group of four students, with its inherent opportunities for individual, paired, small group and combined-group activity, enables this as the whole class cannot. At the same time, the discipline of the negotiation approach acts as a safeguard against the usual excesses that teachers often find accompany small-group activity. Small groups are essential. The approach will founder without them as its basic student organizational structure. I would add only that no other structure can provide such flexibility, opportunity for negotiation, possibility of cooperation, audience access, challenge and debate, and language resources. Talk is the language mode closest to thinking, and the small group of peers is the structure that most facilitates talk.

6 *When to use the negotiation approach*

I have thus far suggested using the approach for the planning and implementation of a curriculum unit or topic. But I suggest that it may be equally useful, because of its basis in sound educational and learning theory, and because of its fundamental good sense, for a single period or activity. In short, the process of asking and answering the four questions seems as appropriate to tackling a single issue within a geography topic, making a chair, understanding a poem, or unraveling a conundrum in science, as it is to doing a complete unit embracing many such activities. If it works, why not use it?

7 *Constraints*

Finally, a note on constraints — the things that tend to define, limit and frustrate the life of our classrooms. Constraints are, realistically, an inevitability. But while they may be part of the context for learning, they need not be — in fact, must not be permitted to be — the underpinning inhibitor of good learning. As I've remarked earlier, we all know the 'Oh buts', the problems and the limitations. So often, however, we teachers know them, but the students don't. The first rule in dealing with constraints is to bring them out into the open and, by acknowledging their existence, to meet and beat them. The constraints of such things as timetables, prescribed courses and limited resources are reasonably explained by the teacher, and understood by students, once they have been given an honest explanation.

I have remarked earlier that learners are all scientists, explorers of knowledge and seekers of understanding. My contention is that negotiating the curriculum with them will prove their struggles as good scientists, and good scientists will usually accept the inevitability of realistic constraints.

Note

1 At the time he wrote this chapter, Jon Cook was Senior Master in English at Scarborough Senior High School, Western Australia.

Chapter 3

Curriculum Composing and Evaluating: An Invitation to Action Research

Garth Boomer

Introduction

This chapter attempts to map some parts of the exceedingly complex course of a curriculum in action, and to offer some strategies for evaluating the quality of the learning taking place.

Teachers gain great satisfaction from successfully steering a passage through a difficult section of the course. Every day, and at almost every moment of their teaching lives, they have to make delicate choices in order to avoid the classroom equivalents of reefs, shallows, squalls and looming cliffs. In this sense teaching has always been a matter of 'negotiating the curriculum'. The physical environment, the set syllabus, the nature of the local community, the available resources, the school policies and the children themselves all present challenges that must be accommodated. Teachers need artistry, experience, knowledge and their own reliable maps to find a way.

Each child in the class who strives to meet curriculum requirements must also be engaged in a similar kind of negotiation and accommodation, involving a similar use of artistry, experience, knowledge and maps.

Traditionally there has been an 'apartness' in classrooms. Teachers teach and children learn. Teachers guide and children are guided. Teachers decide what is to be done and children usually try to comply. Teachers accommodate children and children accommodate teachers, but they have different roles.

In those classes where there is 'rapport', or where there is an outside enemy in the form of an external examiner, this apartness may give way to collaboration and a blurring of roles. Together, 'we' may begin to negotiate our way through the curriculum. This book shows teachers, at all levels, in a variety of subject areas, *deliberately* striving to collaborate and negotiate with children. What may formerly have been occurring intuitively and occasionally is raised to the level of conscious, principled activity in the cases presented in Part B.

The curriculum is no longer a prepackaged course to be taken; it is a jointly enacted composition that grows and changes as it proceeds. A new definition of curriculum is needed, and new ways of evaluating it must be found.

It would be aesthetically offensive to coin the word 'curriculuming', but that is what I mean when I think of 'curriculum'. The noun can too easily seduce educators into a notion of curriculum as simply a plan of content, activities, methods and outcomes. Curriculum is a process beginning with the teacher's or the curriculum writer's conception, proceeding through planning, and eventually reaching enactment and evaluation. Ideally, the enterprise is directed towards promoting valued knowledge, abilities and attitudes in the learner, where 'valued' encompasses the world view of both teacher and learner. Curriculum, in the sense in which I use it, can therefore be described and fully comprehended only in retrospect. The quality and scope of what children learn, both foreseen and unforeseen, are the proper focus of evaluation.

'Learning', which any curriculum aims to promote, is defined as becoming able to make new meaning and to understand and apply underlying principles. It is also mastery of new abilities that enable the learner to use 'tools' deliberately to act upon the world. Very broadly, to learn is to expand one's ability to say and to do.

This book is concerned with curriculum and learning so defined. There is evident danger in trying to put a map or grid over such a subtle word as 'curriculum'. Nevertheless it is irresponsible not to attempt to share with others what one has come to believe to be useful and good. The cases that follow try to take account of, and describe in general terms, what teachers in this book do in negotiating the curriculum, so that other teachers wishing to enter this world can find a way in.

Considering Learning

In planning a year's curriculum or a short term program of work, it is important always to keep the learning process in mind. Jon Cook, in chapter 2, presents his interpretation of what learners say about their own learning. A picture emerges of what seems naturally to occur when groups of children or individuals deliberately take up an intention to learn.

I have developed a simplified chart that divides this process into five stages (see Model A). This can be used as the basis for planning and evaluating any program of work that we carry out with children. Any program following the principles espoused in this book will take account of every stage. It must be stressed that learning does not always proceed smoothly, logically and sequentially through the stages. But on looking back on the behaviour of children during a completed piece of learning, it should be possible to see examples of the five sets of activities, despite the movement backwards and forwards between 'stages'. Model A shows a learning sequence that begins with a challenge of some kind. The learners then gather together and clarify what is already known, before seeking out further information.[1] Eventually, after interim trials, one possible solution or strategy is put to the test. The sequence ends with the learner reflecting on, and evaluating, the success of the venture.

A formula for curriculum composing or planning follows logically from this learning model

Considering Curriculum

A curriculum process consistent with the learning model would have the five stages shown in Model B. At all stages teachers informally evaluate their progress.

1	2	3	4	5
The Origins of Learning (The Challenge)	A Gathering to the Task (The Preparation)	Going Out Into the World (The Search)	Trying It Out (The Test)	Valuing the Learning/ Doing/Performing (The Reflection)
Having become aware of demands, constraints, pressures, needs, we reach a state of:	This is where we define our problem, gather our own resources and work out what we need to know.	We now need to extend our previous knowledge having decided to 'have a go'.	Eventually we settle on a possible solution and try it out.	Now it's time to see how well we know it or did it.
• puzzlement • tension • dissonance • expectation.	And so we: • consider the problem • cast around • imagine • try to predict • work out what we already know • assess our ability to succeed.	And so we: • question • select • rehearse • talk it over • narrow the field • sort • discard • shape an hypothesis.	This is where we: • make errors • have success • modify • consolidate • assess.	And so alone or with others we: • reflect • confirm • see where to polish it • plan new things • celebrate.

All the time we need to be powered by our own *intention, tenacity, ability to struggle.*
At any time we may incidentally learn many things.
All the time we are at risk if there is no one to support us, to talk to, to help, to give information.

Figure 5: Model A: The Learning Process (Simplified) from the Point of View of the Learner

1	2	3	4	5
Planning	*Negotiating*	*Teaching and Learning*	*Performing*	*Evaluating*
Teacher planning ('Mapping the territory')	Teacher-class negotiation and organising ('Preparing for the journey')	Student exploration, research, trying out, improvising etc. Specific teaching	Consolidating learning to show understanding through various 'outcomes'	Teachers and students reflecting on the quality of the process and the outcome

Figure 6:   Model B: A Curriculum Process Consistent with the Learning Process

They may also wish to apply more deliberate checks to assess the quality of what is happening. The following sections deal with each stage and offer evaluation checklists as well as some strategies for informal and formal evaluation.

Stage 1: Planning a Unit of Work

Elements of the curriculum
Whether planning the year's program or a specific unit of work over, say, two weeks, teachers may find it useful to consider the following seven elements of a curriculum plan:

- content
- justification of content
- products
- skills and media
- learning activities
- aids and resources
- methods of evaluation.

Information to be used in programming
A group of teachers within a school, or an outside examining body, may draw up a detailed list of topics for a particular subject. Ideally, these should be accompanied by brief justifications, possibly in the form of focus questions that children will be exploring. It is important to note that the quality of the programme in terms of depth and long term value will be greatly enhanced by the quality of the key questions that the teacher will be exploring with the children.

The year's curriculum plan ideally should also offer a list of possible outcomes in terms of attitudes, knowledge and abilities. Similarly, skills and media that children will be practising, as well as useful resources, may be listed in broad terms. Then, according to the style of the teacher and the level and abilities of various classes, the possibilities for learning activities are endless. It is our contention, however, that learning activities should be consistent with the learning process outlined above. While teachers will vary in the style and sequence that they follow in planning a programme, it may be useful to outline one possible 'recipe' for turning general curriculum ingredients into 'scripts' to be performed.

35

A grid indicating the various elements to be considered in planning is shown in Model C. The grid has been a useful tool for teachers who have experimented with the 'negotiation' model in South Australia.

Starting

Program ideas can start anywhere. They may start with a desire to teach a specific skill from the list of skill objectives for the year. They may start with the finding of a good story, article or chapter from a textbook that promises to provide challenging content. They may start with the aim of working towards a performance outcome etc. The starting point may be followed by a short or long 'incubation' or 'fermentation' period.

Deciding on the content

While the original inspiration for the programme may be a skill, or a resource, a medium (e.g. puppetry), a product, a text or an experience, teachers following the principles offered in this curriculum guide would move from the starting point into a close consideration of *content*. This means deciding on something (a text, some poems, some content material from another subject, an excursion etc.) that will challenge the children and provide opportunity for the whole class, small groups and individuals to explore. The teacher considers such questions as 'What shall we study that is worthwhile and justifiable and will lead them to practise the skill (or use the medium etc.) upon which I wish them to concentrate in this unit of work?' and 'What questions about self and the world will we be exploring?' A unit of work without solid *content* will be 'at risk'.

Deciding on products

Once the broad 'territory' has been mapped, the teacher can imagine a set of worthwhile outcomes, products or goals. Considering goals decided upon within the school, the teacher can specify the end points in terms of what children should be able to say and do as a result of the learning.

Further outcomes can be negotiated with the children, according to the circumstances.

Imagining the possible learning activities

At this point, without tying themselves down to day-by-day planning, teachers need to be able to imagine this journey taking place. It has to be possible within the constraints that prevail (learners, time, buildings, equipment, resources etc.). So, in broad terms, teachers may map out a set of possible learning activities consistent with their own view of the learning process. The degree to which this sequence now becomes fixed will depend on the confidence of the teacher and students in the process of negotiation about learning activities.

Listing the media and skills to be used

It is now possible to list the 'media' that children will most likely be using during the programme of work. A 'medium' is any vehicle that students use in order to learn and do things (e.g. talking, reading, writing, listening, acting, miming, painting, making models, moving, using music).

It is also possible to list both the specific subject skills and the general skills

Content ('Worlds to be Explored')	Justification of Content	Products	Skills to Be Built Up and 'Media' to Be Practised	Learning Activities (Process)	Aids and Resources	Methods of Evaluation
Problem or intention This is the content or territory that we want children to explore. We decide upon this on the basis of our knowledge of the children and our own intuitions about what would be worthwhile and suitable. The content may be: • poem or story • the students' own stories or anecdotes • a theme • a social studies topic etc.	This is where we justify the content chosen and make *hypotheses* about what things may be learnt etc. *Aim* To decide what they already know and then to introduce new perspectives. *Key question* This is where we outline the key questions that we think will be addressed. They may not be specifically treated by the children, but they will lie beneath all that is done. *Note* The quality of the question will affect the quality of learning. The key question offers the teacher a philosophical framework which will give purpose, direction and shape to the learning activities. It will almost certainly imply a value stance.	These are what we hope the children will be able to *say* and *do* as a result of the work. *Can say* Through sharing language and new experiences in the process, students will accumulate a wider set of meanings in the 'world' they are exploring and be able to articulate some of their new thoughts about the 'world' in a finished product. *Can do* Students can make some representation in a performance etc. *Unforeseen outcomes* Add to the above planned goals, things eventually achieved but not initially planned for.	To achieve the planned goals children will have to develop various skills and use various 'media', e.g.: • enactment • mime • puppetry etc. • talking • painting • mask making. *Unforeseen skills and media practised* Children may take divergent paths, and in the process practise applying other skills and media.	This column can only be completed after negotiation with the children. It may not be fully completed until *after* the work has been completed. However, whatever specific learning sequences and activities are decided on, *all the stages of the learning process* (see Model A) *should be covered.* Teachers will come to the students with suggested approaches, but these will be modified and polished in discussion. The constraints on what can and cannot be done should be made quite clear to the children.	Here we list the resources that will help. These will vary according to the topic. Some things that may be used are the: • students' experience • teacher's experience • experience of other people around the school • stories • poetry • films • pictures • music etc. *Unforeseen resources* In retrospect it will be possible to add resources not envisaged but proved to be useful.	Here teachers and children list the kinds of evaluation they will use to see how well they have done. They will evaluate both the *process* and the products. Methods may include: • keeping a journal • performing to an audience • sharing criticisms • formal testing • making tapes • comparing with others.

Figure 7: Model C: Curriculum Planning and Programming

(e.g. discussing, cooperating) that students will be using and learning in the process of achieving the outcomes. Certain skills may be specially emphasised in any one unit of work.

Establishing some criteria and strategies for evaluating the process and the outcomes

In the process of planning the unit, teachers will also (intuitively or deliberately) have in mind the criteria by which they will judge success both during the learning process and in the outcomes.

Some deliberate evaluation plans will probably be developed at this point. These may be shaped and extended as the work proceeds.

Evaluating Stage 1: A checklist of questions and strategies

Questions:
- Is the proposed topic or content justifiable in terms of its potential for challenging, engaging, extending and offering points of connection with the children's experience and previous knowledge?
- Is it justifiable with respect to overall aims, goals and values?
- Is it appropriate in terms of what has gone before?
- Does it provide opportunities for children to contribute to the detailed planning and to the enrichment of the experience?
- Has the plan taken account of all the constraints and practical difficulties that may arise, and do the goals seem achievable in the time allotted?
- Is the plan flexible enough to allow for alternative treatments if necessary?
- Does the plan allow room for individual children to pursue a special interest outside the common course?
- Are there sufficient resources to enable children to achieve the goals?
- Does the proposed culmination of the program seem likely to lead children to be pleased with their achievement and eager to pursue further learning?
- Does it allow for exploration of the concepts through a variety of learning media (e.g. art, talk, music, dance, enactment)?
- Is the proposed process consistent with my learning principles?

Note: These questions, in the past tense, will also provide the basis for an evaluation of the program after the work has been carried out.

Some strategies for finding answers:
- Ask yourself and reflect.
- Show a trusted colleague.
- Invite rigorous criticism from an acknowledged 'expert'.
- Ask another class.
- Ask your own class these questions (in terms they understand), and seek out their critique and suggestions.

Stage 2: Negotiating with the Children

Degrees of negotiation
Many factors (e.g. age, experience, accommodation, school policy) will influence the degree to which the teacher allows the class to make or suggest changes to the plans. If the class is new to the process of negotiation, the plans may simply be discussed but not altered, so that at least the children will know what is going to happen and what is expected of them. At the other extreme, where the class and teacher are quite accustomed to collaborating, the teacher's plan may be presented as only a tentative proposal, to be shaped into a tight program only after concerted consultation with the children.

Why negotiate?
This curriculum is based firmly on the assumption that children will learn best when they *intend* to take up a challenge and reach a goal. It therefore follows that children are more likely to learn if they understand and accept the program plan. If they are invited to contribute to the planning, and if the teacher demonstrably takes account of their contributions, the likelihood of their 'owning' the tasks to come will be increased. Therefore, some form of negotiation and consultation is seen as essential if the spirit set out in this book is to prevail, and if the program is to be consistent with the underlying principles of learning.

The process of negotiation is a preparation for the journey to be taken and will involve justification of the proposal to the children. It will also involve asking the questions:

- What do we already know?
- What do we need to know?

Preparing for the journey
First there is the question of resources:

- What resources do we already have?
- What resources will we need?

Questions of organization and evaluation can also be asked, depending on the teacher's assessment of the class's ability to handle them:

- How are we going to reach our goals?
- How are we going to divide the labour?
- What additional outcomes may we work towards?
- How are we going to assess the quality of what we have done?
- By what criteria shall we assess this quality?

Whether the teacher alone answers these questions, or whether they are answered after consultation, they need to be answered if the learners are to have a sense of purpose that will discipline their activities and allow them to make judgments about their progress. This will also enable children to inform their parents and others about the curriculum.

Garth Boomer

The teacher's responsibility

It is not suggested that the children decide the curriculum. Constraints and non-negotiable demands must be spelled out by the teacher. The teacher must exercise professional judgment in the selection of content and goals and in the organization of appropriate learning activities. After consultation and explanation, the teacher has the responsibility of drawing up a structured programme of work that will be binding on all the children. The plan should, however, be subject to adjustment if it is not proving successful.

Some negotiation activities

At this stage of negotiation and preparation, children may contribute in any of the following ways:

- suggesting some resources (e.g. books, photographs) that they can bring or acquire
- deciding individually or in groups some product or goals in addition to those which the teacher may have made obligatory
- making suggestions about learning activities and sequencing
- working with the teacher to arrange deadlines and contracts
- 'brainstorming' with the teacher on possible methods of final evaluation
- suggesting modifications or extensions to the content
- contracting individually to follow an alternative programme in special circumstances.

Evaluating Stage 2: A checklist of questions and answers

Questions:
- Did I arrange for the children to marshal their existing knowledge in such a way that they all felt that the journey was worth taking and possible for them to make?
- Did I succeed in getting the children to understand and accept the rationale for the proposal, and the details of constraints, non-negotiable requirements and ultimate goals?
- Within the constraints that operated, did the children have the opportunity to contribute to the shaping of the course in terms of proposed learning strategies, sequencing, resources, additional outcomes and the proposed evaluation?
- Did I value and use the children's contributions or properly explain why a contribution was not used?
- Did I make a 'quality' decision with regard to my requirements of those children who tended to reject or to be indifferent to the proposals?
- Are the children now committed to the contract and aware of areas where modification may be necessary if the plan is not working?

Some strategies for finding answers:

- Informally observe the children outside the classroom to see whether they are continuing to talk about what is intended.
- Informally observe behaviour in class (e.g. obvious 'tension' to get on with it, evidence of anticipation, tendencies to divide into interest groups, unsolicited organizing behaviour).
- Invite another teacher in to evaluate you on your own criteria.
- Tape-record class interaction and small-group discussions, and reflect on them later (alone or with someone else).
- Reflect 'diary'-style in writing about what has happened.
- Write up in detail the negotiated proposal, and seek evaluation of it by some other teacher.

Stage 3: Teaching and Learning

This is the stage at which the program moves from being a script, to being a 'performance'.

The teacher's role is to present new information, to demonstrate new skills, to organise group activity, to arrange for resources, to answer questions, to direct children to other potentially profitable sources of information and to offer critical, constructive advice as necessary.

If the children have become committed to achieving the contracted outcomes, the classroom should take on the appearance of a workshop as various groups and individuals work at their problems.

According to the learning processes already outlined, this is a stage at which children will be engaged in using a variety of media in order to find answers and to reach understandings. They will also be practising skills needed in order to complete the assignments.

Evaluating Stage 3: A checklist of questions and answers

Questions:
- Are the children seeking available resources and contributing resources of their own?
- Are the children initiating questions and discussions?
- Are the children exchanging anecdotes, understanding, information, resources and equipment?
- Are the children showing and teaching each other things?
- Are the children facing problems, making errors, and coping positively and constructively with these difficulties?
- Are the children taking up different media to help them in their explorations (e.g. improvizing, drawing, writing notes, talking, recording)?
- Are other people outside the classroom becoming involved in the course (e.g. the librarian, the history teacher, parents, a community worker, 'experts')?

- Am I giving the children access to my own experiences and skills in a way that is helping them with their tasks?
- Are they cooperating to make things and then using these outside the classroom?
- Am I getting confirming feedback (from parents, other teachers, other students, etc.) that the children are carrying out their ideas into other areas?
- Does the process continue when I leave the classroom?
- Am I teaching to the whole class, small groups or individuals according to clearly recognised problems or demands for information?

Some strategies for finding answers:
- Get the librarian to document, or to report on, the uses being made of resource material.
- Ask the children to tell you (either in informal discussion, by question-naire or by extended writing) which of the above criteria they feel are working for them (e.g. whether they continue to work when the teacher leaves the room).
- Ask the children to evaluate which things are working best and to say why.
- Ask the children to suggest modification to the process.
- Apply any of the previously suggested strategies.

Stage 4: Performing

'Performing' refers to that stage of the programme when children test, shape and show what they have achieved and know. The traditional teacher test is only one means of 'performing'. This is therefore the stage of consolidation and polishing, of producing quality products, of applying what has been learnt. If children are absorbed in their tasks, teachers should observe peer-to-peer disciplining, and a growing intensity of concentration, as the demands of working towards the product assert themselves with more immediacy.

The teacher's role is to act as critic, advisor and trouble shooter. This requires that the teacher become a kind of generalized 'audience', giving the children insights into the kind of acceptance their work might have in the world outside schools.

Evaluating Stage 4: A checklist of questions and answers

Questions:
- Are the children redrafting, revising and rehearsing out of a commit-ment to producing a product of quality?
- Are they showing signs of owning their product (e.g. defending it, talk-ing about it, improving it, seeking out interim evaluations from trusted colleagues)?

- Are they continuing to work on the product in their own time?
- Is there a growing tendency for quiet absorption and respect for the need that others have to work without disruption?
- Are the children electing appropriate people to take a leading role when this is required, and do the leaders change according to the demands of the situation?
- Is the self-imposed demand for quality intense to the point where temporary frustrations are emerging, and are they coping with these frustrations by tenaciously seeking alternative strategies?
- Are the unsuccessful students able to accept for themselves the failure of a product to meet their own requirements, and if necessary, are they willing to begin again?
- Is there evidence that the children are sensitive to the meanings being made by others, so that when they give advice or help each other they do it in a spirit of comradeship?

Some strategies for finding answers:
- As above.

Stage 5: Evaluating

At the completion of a unit of work it is essential that teachers and children carry out evaluations of what has been achieved. This can be done through discussion and informal reflection as well as by using more formal methods of assessment. Reflection on the quality of what has been achieved is a way both of consolidating learning and of increasing the likelihood of improved performance next time.

Reflection can take in the 'journey', the outcomes of the programme, and the evaluation strategies themselves.

Questions

About the 'journey':

- Review the questions asked in Stage I in order to pose the ultimate question: 'To what extent did we achieve what we intended to achieve?'
- What did we achieve that was initially unforeseen?
- How valuable was this?
- What were the best and worst features of this unit of work?

About products and skills in using media (assignment, performance, artifact, etc.):

- Did the products and skills have features above and beyond the initial expectation?
- Did the products and skills convey what they were intended to convey to those for whom they were prepared?

- Did these products compare favourably with acknowledged quality products from other similar groups?
- Which aspects or features were most successful, and which would need improvement next time?
- Are the products and skills likely to continue to be valued and, where appropriate, used?
- How do these products compare in quality with those made last time?

About the knowledge acquired:

- Are the children able to talk with more understanding about the concepts and ideas upon which the work was based?
- Can the children explain what they know, to me, in talk, in writing or in some other medium?
- Can the children explain or teach someone else the ideas and concepts that they set out to understand (or that I set for them)?
- Have they shown that they can transform the ideas into their own language; and conversely, have they internalized the meanings of newly acquired words, labels, definitions, etc.?
- Can they apply what they have learnt in new situations?
- Can they transform the meaning from one medium to another (e.g. from talk to enactment)?
- How do their understandings compare in breadth and depth with those of a similar group (past or present)?

About attitudes:

- Am I giving students the opportunity to be critical of my values?
- Are they growing in their ability to articulate and be consistent according to their own values?
- Are they growing towards the stated and implicit values of the school?
- Are they growing towards the attitudes that I consider valuable?

Some Strategies for Seeking Answers

About products, skills and knowledge:

- Informally reflect on quality between teacher and class, teacher and group, and teacher and individual student — according to shared criteria.
- Informally observe (over time) the attitudes of children towards their products, to see if they are continuing to use or value them.
- Invite parental and other community evaluation, either formally or informally.
- Show the products (by performance, display etc.) to a wider audience (from another class through to the public), and seek the evaluation of the audience.
- Exchange products with another class for mutual evaluation and sharing of criticisms.

- Formally and informally diagnose the strength of particular skills in a context where they are being used.
- Formally test, by grade, an assignment (in writing, on audio tape, on videotape, in talk etc.) according to established criteria for valuing the knowledge (by teacher, students or outside agency).
- Formally evaluate assignments according to a checklist of established criteria (by teacher, students or outside agency).
- Conduct one-to-one discussions with students.

About values:

- Formally compare behaviours observed before the program with those observed after the program (presently and over time), according to a prepared checklist of indicators likely to suggest the holding of an attitude (by teacher, students or outside evaluators).
- Get the students to fill in a questionnaire.
- Simply ask the students to tell you where they stand.
- Seek formal and informal evaluation from other students, other teachers, parents and people from the wider community.
- Observe the students in contexts outside the classroom and the school.

Evaluating Stage 5: A checklist of questions and answers

Questions about evaluation strategies:
- Are the strategies helping me to be a more effective teacher?
- Are the strategies helping the students to become more effective learners?
- What new strategies are needed?
- Which of the present strategies need modification?
- Which strategies are non-productive or counterproductive?

Some strategies for seeking answers:
- Write a formal evaluation, and submit it to your own (or others') critical scrutiny.
- Reflect informally with yourself or with your class.
- Invite a formal evaluation of your evaluation methods by an outsider.
- Compare your evaluation methods with those of others.

Note

1 Much of this section evolved in work with the South Australian R-12 Drama Curriculum Committee. I wish to acknowledge the help of Ms. Jo Ingram, a member of this committee, in formulating the evaluation questions. The framework and questions have been incorporated in the book *Images of Life: A Handbook About Drama in Education*, Education Department of South Australia, Publications Branch, Adelaide, 1981.

Part B

Cases

INTRODUCTION

A central argument we are making about negotiating the curriculum, as it is been theorized and explored in this book, is that it is not, and ought not to be, envisioned or applied as a rigid or static set of techniques. Rather, negotiating the curriculum is a set of theoretical principles of teaching and learning. Nowhere in this volume is this more in evidence than here in 'Cases'. In the playing out and enactment of negotiating the curriculum, we're given the opportunity, by being invited into the classrooms of reflective negotiators, to gain the greatest understanding of how teaching and learning actions are derived from theoretical principles. The multiple voices which narrate these case stories demonstrate a range of meanings and provide us with pictures of the various possibilities which curriculum negotiation might hold for transforming teaching and learning.

Demonstration is a powerful way from which to learn. In 'Cases', we see teachers and learners doing. And what they *do is framed and driven by* the theoretical principles of teaching that are negotiating the curriculum. Given that the reflective negotiators in 'Cases' have not applied negotiating the curriculum as a predetermined regime, we should not be surprised that what we will see going on will be varied and various ways into and ways of reflecting the teaching and learning theory of curriculum negotiation. Differences in application exist, we would claim, for the following two interconnected reasons.

1 How we read the word and the world
Because negotiating the curriculum is set within a social constructivist view of the world (its theory of teaching and learning is also derived from such a view), it follows that those of us who attempt to build our practice around it, will inevitably 'read' it (interpret it) in light of our past and current experiences, beliefs, and values about teaching and learning, the contexts in which we are working, the colleagues with whom we work, the books we have read, and so on. In other words, who we are inevitably shapes how and what and why we see. And this accounts for the different results, the range of meanings, and the various possibilities we will see in the cases which follow.

We would argue, however, that the ultimate goal is to build shared interpretations and communal ways of seeing and reading curriculum negotiation, and that it is on the level of theory that collaborative views can best be achieved.

2   How we practice

In 'Cases', we will see a variety of teachers and learners grappling with negotiating the curriculum. We might call some of them apprenticed negotiators, while others might be seen as practised negotiators. This is not a distinction of expertise; nor is it a valorization of the myth that practice makes perfect. Rather, it is a way of distinguishing those who are new to curriculum negotiation and those who have been working at it for a longer time. We will see that all the negotiators in these cases are learners. It is the focus of their learning which seems to shift when the negotiators have had more experience, more incidents to reflect on and to learn from, and it is the focus of learning which we wished to bring to your attention.

And along with shining a spotlight on the focus of their learning, we wanted to represent a range of negotiator voices. We were particularly sensitive to ensuring that the voices of the apprenticed negotiators be heard. Much of what we read in our professional literature seems to come from those who sound pretty sure about what they think and do. The writing is polished, the thoughts neatly organized and laid out. While this may be the result of publication demands, it still leaves us with a void. How do we sound when in the midst of learning? How do we sound when confronting dissonance in and discomfort around our teaching? How do we sound when we are just not sure about what is going on and why? What is valuable about hearing these learning voices is just that: We learn what learners sound like. And this can help us to learn how to respond and build meanings with them.

The Cases

In attempting to begin to transform their theories of teaching and learning, the apprenticed negotiators focus their learning on confronting head-on some of the myths of teaching and learning which have grown out of their experiences and which comprise, at the time they had begun to enact curriculum negotiation, their current theories of teaching and learning. Among some of these myths we may count: teachers are experts; students are empty vessels; knowledge is a commodity; motivation can be developed from the outside-in; teachers are sole authorities and wielders of power in the classroom. What we will see, then, is how the apprenticed negotiators 'read' their new curriculum negotiation situation against their current theories.

In chapter 12, Christine Cook continues to wrestle with her power and authority in the classroom. She has not yet been able to work out co-intentional learning. The chief challenge to her is to understand the connection between how students act and why they act the way they do; or as Eleanor Duckworth (1987) says, 'giving students reason'. That is, is it possible to separate intention from behaviour? At the time of this writing, Christine seems to have settled on the conclusion that behaviour is independent from intention and this conclusion forces her back into a position of power and authority that is inconsistent with curriculum negotiation. It is crucial, however, to see how she struggles towards a deeper understanding of these issues. Even though she is still poised on this precipice, she is also still willing to explore the dissonances between her competing theories of teaching and learning, particularly those having to do with the construction and control of knowledge.

In her reflections on a chronicle of a jointly taught interdisciplinary course (chapter 13), Chris Louth, with the additional insight that distanced reflection can provide, begins to critique the whys of negotiating that she and Doug Young, her co-author and co-teacher, employed. What Chris seems to be wrestling with is the difference between applying curriculum negotiation as a theory of teaching and learning rather than a mindless set of predetermined steps. Her mostly fruitless search for why and how students might have learned differently from the ways they had traditionally learned in her's and Doug's chronicle of their team taught curriculum negotiated course illuminates the theoretical core of curriculum negotiation. Further, it enables Chris to identify a critical aspect that was missing from their understanding of negotiating the curriculum as they enacted it which, in turn, heightens Chris' discomfort. The discomfort, like Christine Cook's dissonance, will propel Chris to deeper understandings and enactments of curriculum negotiation.

Stephanie Siegel's and Ellen Skelly's apprenticed negotiator stances in chapters 6 and 8 pivot around still another issue: Outside-in versus inside-out motivation. Because they are working with mostly disenfranchised students — students who, because of their colour and/or language, have been politically, socially, and culturally denied equal access to quality education — Ellen and Stephanie attempted to use curriculum negotiation as a device to motivate these students to learn. They grapple with two critical parts of these contradictory inside-out/outside-in principles of motivation: (i) 'coming clean' with their students about what they are trying to do; and (ii) distinguishing mere choice, that is, choice among teacher-decided options, from genuine intention to learn. The value for Stephanie and Ellen of making these issues explicit and 'talking' them through with an experienced negotiator (chapter 7) is that they were able to examine and revise the issues with the goal of reconciling their theories of teaching and learning.

We have, with Jo-Anne Reid's and Susan Hyde's chapters, 'Negotiating Education', (chapter 9) and 'Negotiating Mathematics', (chapter 4) respectively, two historical artifacts. Both chapters were in the 1982 version of *Negotiating the Curriculum*. Both chapters were read by all of the other negotiators in this section. Jo-Anne and Susan provided the first demonstrations of curriculum negotiation which guided the practical experiments of the other negotiators in 'Cases'. Interestingly, Jo-Anne (in chapter 10 with Betty Thwaites) and Susan (in chapter 5) build on their respective 'historical' chapters to tell their new stories. The case reports in chapters 4 and 9 reflect a rich understanding that negotiating the curriculum is a theory of teaching and learning which leads Susan and Jo-Anne to integrating curriculum negotiation more productively into their classrooms.

What seems to be the common thread in the remaining cases — Susan Hyde (chapter 5), Garth Boomer (chapter 7), Jo-Anne Reid (with Betty Thwaites) (chapter 10), Nancy Lester (chapter 11), and Cynthia (Cindy) Onore (chapter 14) — is that all of the authors are teachers of teachers in various teaching/learning contexts and, thus, working side-by-side with other practitioners to enact and reflect on curriculum negotiation.

There are two important common strands running throughout these cases. First, from both what they say and from what they do, all of these experienced negotiators seem to have shared interpretations of and to have come to communal agreement on the teaching and learning theory of negotiation the curriculum.

Secondly, while they argue for this current conception and enact its principles, none of them stops questioning, inquiring into, or critiquing that conception. This means, of course, that there is room for them to transform their current conceptions. By engaging in the acts of teaching teachers, observing teachers, and writing to, with, and about them, and then reflecting on these experiences, these more experienced negotiators have presented themselves with and in a situation which talks back to them and, as a result, might, indeed, lead to transformation. The experienced negotiators in these cases focus their learning on attempts to push the 'meta' envelope on how we read the word and the world of curriculum negotiation.

Susan writes in chapter 5 unashamedly in the mode of one who is passing along insights and advice gleaned over many years of reflective practice in negotiation. At the same time she offers advice, she is open about her own neglect of this advice in her moment-to-moment teaching. One of the most crucial 'meta' focuses for Susan is how she sets out to reconcile the micro-events of her classroom with the macro-forces of schooling and the wider society. She recognizes that curriculum negotiation has created the context for these forces to arise; now she is intent upon using curriculum negotiation to work on and work out contradictions and injustices.

Garth's writing to Ellen and Stephanie is a way for him to talk about how he now conceives and thinks about negotiating the curriculum. He is, however, forced to look at and reexamine the theory in a new and, to him, unfamiliar context of two inner-city schools and with two apprenticed negotiators who are at a crucial juncture in their own understanding. By having the familiar made strange, Garth is given the unique opportunity to see his vision of curriculum negotiation recast, with the possibility that he will create enriched versions that will inform us about how we can think about and act out curriculum negotiation in twenty-first century classrooms.

Jo-Anne wants to reconstrue curriculum negotiation within a framework of action research. As action research, negotiating the curriculum may support teachers not only to think and reflect-*in*-action and think and reflect-*on*-action, but support teachers to reconstrue themselves in the process of that thinking, reflecting, and acting. Jo-Anne attempts to 'reread' and 'rewrite' curriculum negotiation in order to broaden the insights negotiation might contribute to the wider social, cultural, and political school life of teachers.

In the context of a university teacher education course, Nancy focuses mainly on assessment issues in curriculum negotiation. She pushes to understand, redefine, and transform the direct cause and effect relationship students make between 'getting an A' and learning. The battle to demystify the teacher as sole expert and examiner continues to be waged here, and while there is still no definitive set of answers, the context in which this case takes place gives us new insights and raises new questions to inform our conversation and push our collective understandings of the role curriculum negotiation can play in providing alternative ways of being.

The insights we might gain from being an observer, a noter, a 'fly on the wall' in a colleague's classroom are invaluable as Cindy shows in her case. By sitting in and watching and listening to Mrs Gillis and her students' enactments of curriculum negotiation, Cindy not only gains understanding about Mrs Gillis' understanding, but she is able to assess how young children learn in a negotiated context as well. This 'double vision', if you will, allows Cindy to enrich her current conception of curriculum negotiation from the perspectives of teachers of teachers, teachers of young children, and learners — whether they are children or experienced teachers. When all of these perspectives converge, as they do implicitly and explicitly in this case, they have the potential to create a new mixture and, thus, new ways of looking at, critiquing, and envisioning curriculum negotiation.

Invitations to Inquire

1 How do you see the reflective negotiators' concepts of curriculum negotiation? What do they think negotiating the curriculum is?

2 What role or roles does reflection play in these teachers' concepts of curriculum negotiation?

3 How do you see the learners' concepts of curriculum negotiation? What do they think negotiating the curriculum is?

4 How would you relate the learners' stances to their concepts of curriculum negotiation?

5 What kinds of teaching/learning principles are enacted in each of these cases of curriculum negotiation? What beliefs and values do the teachers have about teaching and learning? What beliefs and values do the students have about teaching and learning? Are the students' and teachers' views compatible? Are they in conflict? What does the answer to these last questions have to say about enacting curriculum negotiation?

6 Do you see any impediments to curriculum negotiation in these cases? Are the impediments personal? Are they institutional? Social? Cultural? Political? If we can define what the impediments might be and where they come from, how might that help us to understand and push through them?

7 What are the conditions which enable curriculum negotiation to be enacted? Are these personal? Institutional? Social? Cultural? Political? If we can define what conditions need to be in place in order to enact curriculum negotiation, how does that help to understand them and to create them?

8 Why does curriculum negotiation succeed when it does? Why does it fail when it does?

9 When does curriculum negotiation come off as a technique in these cases? How do we know it is not a technique from these stories? In what ways does the 'technique' of curriculum negotiation impinge on these stories?

10 What kind of support would each of these teachers need to develop?

11 How do you prepare your class before you actually negotiate? What factors need to exist prior to curriculum negotiation, if any?

Cases

12   In what ways do we get in our own way and undermine our students' participation in curriculum negotiation?

Reference

DUCKWORTH, E. (1987) *The Having of Wonderful Ideas and Other Essays on Teaching and Learning*, NY: Teachers College Press.

Chapter 4

Negotiating Mathematics

Susan Hyde[1]

When I decided to negotiate the curriculum with my Year 8 mathematics class, I had already had experience with the model in teaching science. I had also experimented with certain teaching strategies appropriate to the model in the mathematics classroom. Before I discuss these I want to consider what negotiating the curriculum implies in the light of teacher and student experiences of learning and teaching.

Effects of Curriculum Negotiation

Negotiating the curriculum is not an alternative teaching strategy or a way of breaking the monotony of second term. It involves the development of the teacher's understanding of the learning process and of how to provide conditions in which learning can best occur. It is a curriculum design that is developed by students and teachers in the classroom.

One of the basic attitudes in this design is teachers' confidence in their students' ability to learn and make informed decisions about their learning. We know that people know *how* to learn, because people learn to speak a language from ages zero to five, not to mention walking, eating, dressing themselves, drawing etc. They may have help, of course, but not in the form of formal instruction or prescription. However, by the time most people enter secondary school they have had seven years' experience of being told how to learn. In my experience this has a variety of effects, which manifest themselves when I offer a negotiable curriculum to my students.

Student Reactions to Offers of Negotiation

• Firstly, there are those students who are *thankful and amazed* when they realize that at last they will be able to learn in the way they know they can learn. They are pleased because I am treating their self-confidence with respect. They react responsibly to helping to make decisions about class activities, and they help others to stick to the decisions. These are usually students who are interested in learning what is offered at school — who have put up with teacher direction

53

because they have been very, or reasonably, successful at passing tests and achieving standards (and because they feel that they are powerless to change teachers' attitudes, or even to suggest it).

• Other students view the offer with *suspicion*, because they don't really think that I will go through with it. They don't trust me. They approve of my attitude, but their experience of teachers allowing them to make decisions about what they will do is not vast. They think that I am 'conning' them. These students involve themselves reservedly at first, but once they see that I am serious their involvement becomes more enthusiastic. They need encouragement and react well to praise. They are quick to react when I *do* tell them to do something and, justifiably, demand reasons for my direction. They react well to my inquiries about how they are going about their learning, but I have to be careful how I word any suggestions about how they might do it better, because they often interpret this as a direction and follow it out of habit. These students usually have been 'turned off' to the degree of accepting that what happens in the classroom is likely to be boring. They have mostly experienced inconsistent success with tests and grades, depending on how bored they have been with the topic. They are usually cynical and either quietly go through the motions expected by the teacher, with their 'brains in neutral', or become disruptive, determined to thwart the teacher's plan of action.

• There are also those students who are *dismayed* at the whole idea, because they can't understand how they will learn anything if I or someone else doesn't tell them what to do. If left to themselves they will flounder in confusion and never get anything done. Some refuse even to start. These students need a lot of attention, and certainly more guidance, until they become more confident in their abilities. Above all, they need help in starting to learn a new 'topic', because they can't trust their own judgements about what they already know about the subject. I try to help them by involving them in discussions about what interests them and what they have experienced. This helps them to realize what they know, so they can choose a starting point. I try to help by offering a limited set of alternatives to make their choice easier. Once they have chosen a starting point they need attention and encouragement right through the learning process. These students usually have experienced a lot of failure and have little self-confidence. They have either become very dependent on prescription or learnt how to avoid schoolwork as much as possible.

• Finally, there are those students who react with *contempt*. In their opinion I am shirking my responsibilities by not giving the class a prescription for learning (the teacher is the expert) and allowing students to help each other (after all, that is cheating). They resent my attitude of encouragement to the disruptive persons in the class, and criticise and complain about the 'discipline' in the classroom. They want me to be more judgmental and to compare students with each other. They are continually asking 'How much is this worth?' or 'What grade will I get for this?' They refuse to help, or resent helping, other students. Understandably, these students are not usually popular with the rest of the class, and therefore their influence is not very great amongst their peers. However, they can influence me because their attitude can plunge me into paranoia about doing something different. Their expectations of me are those which I am trying to avoid and indeed unlearn, so I oscillate between outright confrontation or reasonable persuasion when dealing with these students. Interestingly enough, they may be bright, competitive students, super-confident from being so successful, or they may be those who have been so turned off by failure and humiliation that they criticize my attitudes and actions simply because I belong to that hated class of people — teachers. They are very often boys, and their attitude is often partly sexist (women are not to be taken seriously). They often approve of the competitive and prescriptive atmosphere in which they usually learn at school and have learned to succeed at the expense of others.

The Need for Confidence

I have written at length about this because I want to emphasize that negotiating the curriculum implies that the teacher has confidence in his/her students' ability to learn and make decisions about their learning. It is important to realise that the majority of students have not had this experience. In fact they have been learning quite the opposite for most of their school life. This conditioning can cause a lot of problems and barriers for a teacher who is attempting to make his/her classroom open and collaborative and means that students will be at different starting points.

Another reason I mention this is because students have to be confident of their own ability to learn. In some cases this takes quite a while to develop, depending on what experience the student has had. This is why I insist that a negotiable curriculum results from an attitude that has to be shared and developed by teacher and student. It is not a teaching strategy or method, and it is not just an interesting way to approach weather or graphs. It is a long-term, continuously developing and improving relationship between teacher, students and learning.

Planning the Course Together

During 1979 I was one of a group of teachers at Banksia Park High School involved in what we called the *classroom-based curriculum study*. Essentially, we decided to get our classes involved . . . in planning their year's courses in mathematics, science and humanities.

During the first few weeks of the term, we involved our classes in discussions about the learning process, the nature of the subject and learning that subject in the classroom. We did this because we believed that these discussions would focus their attention on the learning process, as well as· giving them a more informed basis on which to make decisions about the content and skills to be learnt in the particular subject areas.

At first I was rather apprehensive at the thought of students planning a mathematics course. However, they coped with planning this subject very easily — in fact, often more easily than with planning the other subjects. I was amazed at how much they knew about mathematics and how easily they could justify learning about the topics they chose. Really, this is not so surprising, because they had already experienced seven years of learning mathematics (which was certainly more than they had experienced of learning science).

Once we had planned the course we then used the book with which they were provided to find appropriate exercises (Franklin and Preece, 1973). In reality the basic content of the course was not really negotiable, because they were limited to a certain extent by the graded exercises and concepts covered by the book. However, it was understood that the content of the book could be (and was) added to, rearranged, rewritten and left out according to the needs of the course that we had planned.

Planning the Topic Work

At first I planned the exercises for the class. I gave them a set of exercises and discussion topics to be finished with the time we had planned for the topic. I did this because I wanted to show them how the book worked, and to give them a model for a plan. The work that I set was negotiable in that they could change the plan for their own needs. For instance, they could negotiate to leave out certain exercises if they already knew how to do the problems well. They could also ask for extra ones if they were finding them hard to understand. They responded very well to this. Both fast and slow learners took advantage of it. (The class was a mixed ability group.) Each student had to negotiate with me before making the change. In almost every case the student's judgment of his/her understanding of the exercise and whether he/she needed to omit it or needed more practice was right. It certainly made me realize that there must be quite a few students who either sit in mathematics classes being bored by doing many exercises in which they don't need practice, or rarely have the satisfaction of knowing that they understand how to do a type of problem, simply because teachers refuse to trust students' judgments about their learning.

After a couple of topics, I asked those students who had finished their work before the time limit whether they would like to help set the next topic work instead of doing extension work. They did this and produced an excellent topic for the class. Gradually, more students became involved in this, some working as a group to plan for others. Others planned their own topic work, and sometimes a group of friends would work on a common plan.

It was very interesting to see how the students actually planned their own work. The number of students who did this varied with each topic, depending on how confident they felt with the subject matter. By the end of the year, most students were planning their work for each topic, and if they didn't plan their own work they had several versions from which to choose: mine, their friends' etc.

The way in which they sequenced the work was varied also. I think that we take it for granted that mathematics must be learnt in a certain sequence, and in some cases it is necessary to know about one concept before another can be understood. Most students accepted the sequence that the book offered. However, it is most significant that some students varied the sequence according to what they knew or didn't know. Others varied it according to interest. For instance, during a topic called 'Decimals, Fractions and Percentages', some students sequenced the exercises so that they learnt about decimals in relation to percentages, decimals in relation to fractions, fractions in relation to percentages etc. In other words, they chose a bit out of one chapter, then a bit out of the next, then dropped back to the other chapter for a few exercises and so on.

This all sounds very rosy and easy, but for some students the experience was traumatic at times. Primarily, they were faced with the realization that they had to take the responsibility for the amount and quality of their learning. In a conventional mathematics classroom students depend on the teacher for set work, and thus can complain if the work is too hard or too easy. Some students set their work too hard, confident that they could complete it with understanding, and faced disillusionment when they could not cope with it — especially if I had advised them that this would happen. In most cases they needed a lot of encouragement to continue to direct themselves. Some other students set work that was too easy for them. They then had to face the realization that they were underestimating their ability, and this also affected their confidence to direct themselves. 'I can't do it', they would say. However, some students persisted in playing the game of 'bludging', mainly because they were afraid to fail again. They then had to face confrontation with me about responsibility and taking advantage of the power that they had agreed to use properly.

You see, a negotiable curriculum is not just a wishy-washy attempt by a teacher to let students do what they feel like. It is a process by which the teacher can help to develop students' confidence and self-direction, often against all experience and conditions of both teacher and student. This process is ongoing and is based on the developing relationship between teacher and student. This relationship must be based on honesty about confidence, ability and personality, and is therefore filled as often with confrontation and disillusionment as it is with warm feelings of cooperation and friendship. Students find this traumatic at times, because usually they are not used to being granted responsibility for decisions that affect the quality and quantity of learning. The teacher has to be sensitive to all of this and to know when to relieve a student from the responsibility until his/her confidence is regained, and when to insist that the student does not try to opt out of making decisions.

It helps, and in fact is essential, for the students to be aware of this developing process. This is why I consider it very important to involve students in discussions about the learning process, and about what self-directed learning implies for them. These discussions should continue throughout the process, and should help the students to rationalize some of the strong emotions they are feeling.

Collaborative Learning Atmosphere

The relationships between the students in a classroom are also very important if the classroom is to be open and collaborative. The basic idea is that learners collaborate and share ideas and information to help each other to learn. In mathematics it is as important as in any other subject that students have plenty of practice in explaining verbally what they know, what they mean or how to do something. Teachers, especially, are familiar with the experience of increasing their understanding of a particular concept or method through having had to explain it many times.

In the classroom the teacher has to allow this to happen. Students, of course, always help their friends to do mathematics when sitting next to each other — that is, if they are allowed to talk in class. But the traditional mathematics classroom is very quiet and orderly, so it is not surprising that the value of students talking about mathematics and helping each other is very underrated by most mathematics teachers.

The competitive atmosphere in the traditional classroom also does not encourage students to help each other. Why should they? They may be helping other students to get better marks. I was very surprised when I realized that often the seemingly brightest students in a mathematics class have a very poor ability to explain what they know.

In my classroom students could help each other, as well as get out of their seat to find someone else to help them if their neighbour could not. At other times, when everyone was working and lots of hands were going up for help, I would organize a student or two to aid me in giving help to those who needed it. Several students in the classroom spent one lesson per week helping another student.

The discussion that follows (from a tape transcript) is part of an interview conducted by a colleague with some members of this class:

Interviewer:	Someone said the kids help. Is that very common?
Mandy:	Yeah.
Bridget:	Oh, sort of, like my friend didn't know how to do fractions, so I had to sit down and help her.
Stephen:	Yeah, she sometimes picks people that know what they're doing to help the others that don't.
Michelle:	And if they've finished it and they know what to do and they've got it all right and that.
Interviewer:	Have any of you people helped someone else?
All Students:	Yeah . . . I have . . .
Interviewer:	All right. Well, what do you get out of helping someone else? Doesn't that interfere with . . .?
Students:	(interrupting) Helps us too.
Interviewer:	How does it help you?
Michelle:	Well, by saying it to them we're learning the same too, like we're learning more.
Stephen:	No, we're not. We're learning the same, but we're just sort of revising it over ourselves with other people and they know what to do.
Interviewer:	What do the other kids think of having a kid help them?
Bridget:	Oh, they don't mind. The kid talks to them in sort of their own language or whatever you like to call it.
Mandy:	Yeah, with the teachers, they might go too fast and they might not understand it.
Bridget:	They might say, oh, 'these denominators', and that, and some kids don't understand what they are or something.
Scott:	If the kids don't understand, when a teacher says it, they sort of . . . They say it, they explain it to you, then you say, well, you don't know how to do it and they go mad at you. But when a kid does it, they explain it through a couple of times.
Interviewer:	You reckon kids are better at that?
Students:	Yeah.
Mandy:	That's if they know what they're doing.

Bridget:	Oh, teachers can do it too, but you know, other kids . . .
Interviewer:	Don't you think that's the teacher's job?
Students:	Yeah.
Scott:	But kids can do it better.
Bridget:	But kids can understand . . . like kids that have got problems understand kids better than they can understand the adults.
Interviewer:	Why's that, do you reckon?
Bridget:	I dunno, they sort of talk the same . . . I dunno, the teachers talk bigger and longer words that the kids don't understand.
Stephen:	Yeah, and probably they don't understand, and so when other people [kids] help, and that, they understand what they are saying.
Interviewer:	Mmmmmmm, all right.

Some teachers became rather worried when I mentioned that my students helped each other, because they were afraid that the students would not teach each other properly. This fear is well founded in classrooms where students are not allowed to help each other. One of the most crucial discussions that students should have before they do this on an organised scale is how to help someone best. They also need to be aware, as were the students involved in the above discussion, of how it helps the person doing the explaining as well.

Teaching Strategies

There are certain teaching strategies that I found appropriate to the negotiation model in the mathematics classroom. They were adapted from those that I use when teaching science. They included brainstorming, class discussion, group discussion and offering a range of audiences for writing and information presented by students for other class members to learn. They were not distinct entities, because a combination could be used in any one lesson. They were based on the principle that learning should be an active process, involving the learner's prior knowledge and language as he/she comes to grips with the language and concepts involved in the new information. Two factors were basic to the success of these strategies:

• There must be an *emphasis on meaning* in the mathematics classroom. Students must know that mathematics is about *understanding* as well as getting the right answer. It is possible, and I've seen it many times, that students know how to get the right answer but not be sure about why they get it. All they do is to memorize the steps to get that answer. However, memorization of method is much easier when it is rooted in meaning — then the student understands what the steps are about. I think that we owe more to our students than a promise that when they get to Year 11 they will understand the steps they are doing in Year 8.

• The teacher must give the class (both students and teacher) *time to develop class and group discussion skills*. The students have to learn to share their ideas, ask each other questions and, above all, feel confident that what they say is seen as a valuable contribution. The teacher has to learn to help these discussions to continue without interfering with the students' flow of thought. In particular, the teacher has to learn new responses to students' explanations that are partially incorrect, in order to encourage the students to be more explicit, instead of telling them that they are wrong. This latter response encourages the 'guess the answer in the teacher's head' game, which is prevalent in many classroom discussions in schools.

A lot more could be said about how these skills are developed in the classroom. However, the main point that I want to emphasize is that it takes time for both teacher and students to adjust to the different roles involved. The payoff in the quality and involvement of the students' learning is well worth the time.

Writing Mathematics

Writing rules, definitions and explanations of methods is excellent for giving students the opportunity to make meaning in mathematics. Every now and then my mathematics class had what we called a *writing lesson*. They chose a rule, concept or method that they had been working with, and tried to generate the definition, rule or method for themselves. We usually *brainstormed* the idea first and then took the ideas to *group discussion*, where they worked out what they should write. After that the *groups reported back*, and we discussed the writing.

The following definitions were generated by group discussion about factors:

Factor definitions (First attempt)
Factor is a number that will go in another number.

Factors are whole numbers that can divide equally into another number.

Factors are a set of numbers that divide evenly into one another.

Factors are whole numbers which can divide evenly into any whole number like: 15 — the factors are 1, 5, 3, and 15. The factors of a number are whole numbers that go into another number.

Factors are numbers that can be divided into a certain number, like 4.

When the Year 8 students saw what the other groups had written they began to discuss the adequacy of the various definitions. They continued this in group discussion with the aim of improving their own definitions. During these discussions I spent my time going around, asking sticky questions to encourage them to be more explicit. When the groups reported back their definitions were more explicit, and some of them quite adequate:

Factor definitions (Second attempt)
The factors of a number are whole numbers which will go into this number equally.

Factors are whole numbers which divide evenly into another number evenly: e.g. factors of 10 are 1, 2, 5, 10; the factors of the number 16 are 1, 2, 4, 8, 16.

Factors are a set of whole numbers that divide evenly into one whole number, e.g. 30; 1, 15, 2, 5, 6.

Factors are numbers that can divide into a certain number.

At the end of this lesson, students were feeling very pleased with themselves, because they had worked out for themselves what factors are, written some mathematics, talked a lot of mathematics and read a lot. Mathematics was making sense.

A similar sort of strategy was a very efficient way to teach mathematical method. At the end of the discussions and writing, the students could explain in their own words why and how to do each step in the method involved. It was certainly a more efficient and rewarding way for most learners to come to grips with both the concepts and methods of mathematics than just listening to me practising my explanations with a piece of chalk in my hand.

A very important aspect of this writing was that the students were writing for themselves. I wanted my students to value this and to know that they *could use writing for learning*. One way to demonstrate this to them was to get a student who was not sure how to explain what he/she was doing actually to write it out. This helped the student to understand what he/she was doing as well as to memorize the method.

The most powerful aspect for me when the students were writing for themselves and for the other students, was that I got to see their writing in the formative stages. (This is not usually possible when students are writing to me as examiner.) I found it an excellent opportunity to introduce new terminology or to help them to understand a particular concept when it was relevant and meaningful to them.

Rewriting the Textbook for Other Students

My students also wrote mathematics for each other, and they enjoyed doing this. The writing involved dividing a particular section of work amongst groups of students. During the group work they examined the text to decide whether it needed revision of the explanations and/or exercises. This approach was particularly suitable for geometry, where the textbook that we used approached geometry in an abstract way that made it particularly indecipherable for students.

It is important for students to be given direct experience with the language of mathematics. The language of mathematics is very accurate and descriptive, and if one is familiar with the concepts and terms involved, it is a very useful and meaningful language. Learning to be able to articulate the meaning of certain concepts involves the development of language that can best describe the concepts involved. This is especially pertinent to mathematics. Everyday language is useful for understanding many of the experiences and concepts that we use to live our lives. However, it is not very useful for describing and understanding many of the concepts involved in mathematics.

For instance, in the textbook we used in Year 8 the following definitions are offered for points and lines:

Susan Hyde

Undefined Terms

A point
- has no dimension
- marks a position in space
- is usually denoted by a capital letter

A line
- has one dimension
- is an infinite set of points
- extends indefinitely in both directions
- Only one straight line can pass through two given points
- A *straight* line is usually denoted by the names of two points on the line

A model of the line PQ (or 1):

1   •   •

<----------------------------------> (page 48)
P   Q

After this set of definitions (the book goes on to define a set of lines, a plane, space), the students are asked to answer a set of multiple-choice questions based on understanding the concepts. Not surprisingly, most students cannot do this.

The student who reads these definitions cannot understand them unless he/she understands the meanings of the words 'dimension', 'space', 'denoted', 'infinite', and 'extends'. The definitions will not make sense unless explained in everyday language. Okay, I could do that — give them a lecture about what the definitions really mean. However, I consider the strategy to be fairly inefficient, because it does not actively involve the students. A more efficient way is to get the students to try to explain and understand these concepts in their own terms. This means talking to each other about them and trying to explain them in their own writing. This can be done on a classwide basis. However, doing this so that students can explain the concepts to other students adds interest and purpose to the discussions.

A group of students who worked on this section offered the following definitions to the class.

A dot

A dot is not like a point, it is a mark on the page. If you want to show a point you do a dot, for a point is invisible. A dot is a model of a point.

A line

A line is not a line, it is an invisible thing between two places, it cannot be seen. If it is drawn, then it becomes a model of a line. A model of a line is visible. A line goes on forever.

These definitions were well received and promoted a lot of discussion amongst the students, who were subsequently able to do the exercises with ease.

In the next example the students decided that the textbook definitions were too exact.

Definitions

Concurrent lines have a single point of intersection.
Collinear points lie on the same straight line.
Coplanar points (or lines) lie in the same plane.
Parallel lines are coplanar lines which do not intersect.
Skew lines are lines which are not coplanar and do not intersect.
A line is parallel to a plane if they have no point in common. (page 53)

The students rewrote some of these definitions and used examples and diagrams to illustrate what they meant.

Concurrent lines: are two or more lines which intersect (cross over each other) at one point and continue away from each other.

Collinear points: are two or more points which lie on the same line as each other, e.g.

A   B   C   D

Coplanar points or lines: lie in the same plane as each other.

Parallel lines: are two lines or more, which as long as they go they will never join because they are the same distance apart all the way. They are coplanar.

These students also rewrote the exercises provided to test the understanding of these concepts.
    Sometimes the students completely rejected what the book had to offer and made up their own explanations and exercises. The following is an example of part of what one student offered his classmates for work on measurement.

Measurement

The whole idea of measurement is to be exact. For example:

This line is exactly $31\frac{1}{2}$ mm long, not 30 or 31 but exactly $31\frac{1}{2}$ mm.

The measurement of the blackboard in height is 115 cm or 1 metre and 15 cm. The width of the blackboard is 1 metre and $15\frac{1}{2}$ cm.

Now I have set some work for you to measure, the same way as I have done.

1. The mobile trolley is ____ wide and ____ long and ____ in height.
2. The shelves on the wall are ___ in depth and ___ long and ____ wide.
3. A clock is ____ round as in [___] and ____deep.
4. A teacher's collection box (orange) — the type the P.E. teachers use for log cards: it's ____ deep and ____ on the bottom and at the top from the top of the side to the other side is ____.

This work should help you with your measurement.

Gavin

When the groups of students had finished revising their section, and had it checked by me, I then had their work printed, or they prepared it on overhead transparencies.

Each group then presented its work to the class, gave time to discuss the explanations and then set the appropriate exercises from the book, or from what they had prepared, for the students to finish during the lesson and for homework. These lessons were a great success. The students enjoyed being 'teacher', and other students enjoyed being taught by students. Presenting information to other students in this way helps students to be more articulate about what they have learnt and gives them experience and confidence in explaining their ideas and learning to other people. Students openly admit this, and I'm sure that other teachers who have used this approach would support me in this claim.

Conclusion

After two terms of working on the course that the students and I had planned, I examined the amount of work done from the textbook in comparison to the amount of work done by other classes in the school. I found, to my delight, that we had covered the same amount of work as the other classes, although, of course, in a different sequence. We finished the year's work with most students covering the set Year 8 course, and some covering considerably more. I was very pleased with these results, and so were the students. I felt that, because the students and I had shared the responsibility for planning the course and topic work, we were more able to cope with the individual abilities that were present in the class. As I teach in a mixed ability situation, I found this result both remarkable and satisfying. In my opinion most students — fast, slow or average learners — benefited from being able to use their own judgment about their learning and to use this judgment to negotiate with me what and how they learnt in mathematics.

A Note on Barriers to Change

When a teacher offers a negotiable curriculum to students, he/she is sharing power with them. The teacher recognizes the basic democratic principle that people should have the right to help determine the activities in which they will participate. Over how much the students will have control is the negotiable factor and is determined by the teacher. By convention it is the teacher in whom control and authority within the classroom are vested. Because of this convention there are pressures within the conditioning of teachers, and within schools (and, indeed, within society), that act as barriers to a teacher's confidence in sharing that power.

Most teachers have been conditioned by their own schooling (primary, secondary and tertiary) and perhaps their teaching experience, to consider that in the classroom the decision-making input of the teacher is high while that of the student is low. Teachers traditionally make the decisions that concern learning, use of space, use of time, use of equipment, tone of behaviour and so on. The teacher who negotiates with students about these matters faces considerable amounts of rethinking in his/her attitude towards the relationship with, and responses to, the students.

Pressure from the school coincides with these conditions. Firstly, the decision-making model offered by the teacher may be in direct contradiction to the model recognized by the school. Industrial democracy is still fairly unusual within the administration of schools. The hierarchical nature of curriculum decisions still exists within schools, so the teacher may be faced with restrictions to, or disapproval of, negotiations he/she is undertaking with the students.

Secondly, the reactions of other classroom teachers to a teacher who is attempting to make changes within the classroom are varied. Some teachers, of course, react with interest and generally give support to the teacher. However, others react negatively because all that they hold important within the classroom is threatened. They are alarmed and critical of the change seen in the negotiating teacher's classroom. This group of teachers needs not to be large to cause, in various ways, considerable doubt in the teacher's mind about what he/she is doing.

• A lot of comments are made about the *noise level* of the classroom (this is what often attracts other teachers' attention first). The necessity for a fair amount of group and class discussion means that the classroom will be noisier than the norm at the time — especially when the norm is thirty still, silent students doing mathematics or whatever. Not all teachers recognize the value of talk in learning.

• There are sometimes undertones of criticism in these comments, because a noisy classroom is often considered indicative of the teacher's *'lack of control'*. Other objections are raised because of the question of who is in control of the classroom. In fact, the teacher who is negotiating with his/her students has an equally varied opinion about who should be in control of what happens in the classroom as those teachers who won't negotiate.

• When a teacher is seen *not to sequence* the content — that is, not to offer a certain prescription for learning, something by which all students *have* to learn — he/she will be criticised by those who don't recognise that people learn in different ways. It bothers them when they realise that the students are not performing uniform exercises, because they worry that the teacher cannot be maintaining 'standards'.

• Some teachers disapprove of the *less formal relationship* they see developing between the teacher and students in question.

I have described some of the objections that can be raised by other teachers because sometimes they are not made in the open. Traditionally, a person who has different ideas from most and tries to put them into practice comes across a lot of criticism. These criticisms need to be considered carefully and answered by using the theory on which the teaching is based. In fact, a teacher who is faced with these objections and is given a chance to explain him/herself, can use this opportunity to strengthen his/her articulation about teacher-student negotiation. The teacher can gain confidence in answering the issues raised by discussing them with teachers and others who support what he/she is doing. I found that discussing my ideas with the Curriculum and Learning Unit staff and with other teachers at my school was very important in helping me to develop confidence in practising the negotiating model, as well as in coping with barriers to change that arose in the classroom and the school.

Note

1   At the time of writing Susan Hyde taught science, mathematics and music at Banksia Park High School, South Australia.

Reference

FRANKLIN, J. and PREECE, K. (1973) *New Mainstream Mathematics*, Book 1, Melbourne: Longman-Cheshire.

Chapter 5

Sharing Power in the Classroom

Susan Hyde

I believe that sharing power in the classroom which, in turn, will help students to become more powerful and independent learners, rests on teachers challenging aspects of classroom practice that maintain the authority and power vested in them by the system. Naturally, this can be a stressful process for students and teacher but power sharing can be achieved over time.

When I first began to negotiate many years ago, I jumped off the cliff and did it all at once. My students and I rushed headlong into the stresses, excitement, confusions and doubts that were generated by letting go all of the structures at once. I remember some hair-raising, noisy and confusing times as we learnt how to cooperate, to share, how to discuss and negotiate, but I can also remember the students running down the stairs to science lessons and the way they learnt to become articulate about how they learnt. It was an exciting time that I have documented elsewhere (chapter 4 this volume; also Cosgrove, 1978, 1981).

However, since then I have developed collaborative strategies more slowly with other groups of students, letting them into it carefully, building up their skills and letting their trust in me develop until the point that they take it for granted that they should share the power in the classroom.

What follows is a distillation of some of the things I have learnt and describes some of the work I now do in my school.

Whether we jump right in or gradually move to collaborative power sharing, the challenges we face include: assessment, valuing students' knowledge and experience, developing negotiation skills (rather than directing skills), developing collaborative skills (sharing, discussing, group work), and establishing less rigid roles for students and teachers.

Becoming Theoretical and Political

Since I began negotiation with my students I have refined my practice and my understanding of my practice in several ways. The process of action research has been vital to this development. On the practical level, I have learned how to manage the collaborative classroom learning more effectively. My classrooms are a good deal more ordered and systematic than they were when I was beginning my development and when I was somewhat younger! Through continuing action research, I have refined the kind of teaching set out in chapter 4. The most powerful part of my developing understanding came when I broke though the euphoria of working in an exciting classroom atmosphere to realize some of the political implications of working in a collaboratively negotiated context.

My naivete had been challenged when I realized that some of my colleagues were feeling threatened by the different power structures in my classrooms. Then I realized that the decision-making process in the classroom was at odds with the way schools are organized and, in fact, the whole society. I began to be interested in action research as a systematic way of improving my practice, to change my practice to something better — better in that I could help my students collaborate more effectively, help them to question their lives, and work out ways to improve them.

By the time that I got around to reading about the different theories about how society is organized (Giroux, 1981) and about how existing inequalities in society are maintained, I was already steeped in classroom practices that were designed to help my students question and learn in in a collaborative way. I was already democratizing my classroom. My practice helped me to develop my theoretical understandings about society, power, ideology, schooling, privilege, inequalities, labor power, and about how society is formed and transformed. And my theoretical understandings have helped me to refine my practice and the way I interpret what goes on in the classroom between students and teachers, in how the school is administered and the effect of different teaching resources and curricula.

I have also developed theories about how the school is administered and how different teaching resources and curricula have different effects. Giroux (1981) helped me to understand the significance of sharing power in classrooms. He says that we need to develop a 'pedagogy which helps students to link knowledge to power and human interests' and which moves away from classroom content, structures, and processes which maintain the students' powerlessness. What I interpret it to mean is that we must examine these aspects of classroom experience in the broader context of how society operates and how schooling maintains the power structures of that society. For instance, maintaining a gender balance in classroom interactions and working to discourage and expose sexist behavior in the classroom and school, especially my own, will help girls to challenge their powerlessness and help to break down patriarchal power relations which, in turn, help to maintain economic inequalities in our society.

Critical Reflection

Giroux and others call this type of thinking and connection 'critical self-reflection'. It is an empowering process and it is what I try to model to my students. Using action research is to recognize my own need to learn and, because I must involve my students by collecting their feedback on the process, then I model the process of critical self-reflection for my students. Over time, the investigation through action research will help teachers see their development and this acts as a basis for increasing self-confidence and for developing theories from practice.

I have learnt, as a teacher, the power and utility of 'action-research' by which I mean documenting what is happening in my classroom reflecting on the action recorded and then modifying my approach and so on in a never-ending cycle. The advice I have to offer in this chapter comes as a result of my personal reflections and practice. It is not to offer sure-fire tips but rather to indicate a way of 'being in the classroom'. This is how I do it. Readers have to find their own way.

I am always learning through my version of action research or 'reflective practice'.

For instance, I recall an anecdote that occurred with a Year 10 Science class whom I had been teaching for about twelve weeks. We were using work required assessment (Johnston, 1985) and had just finished a topic called *Physiology Questions*. I had decided that they were ready to negotiate the constraints surrounding the new topic of *Acids and Bases*. In a class meeting, I explained how the faculty generated the work required statement and showed students what we came up with. I then asked them to modify the statement. They made their suggestions, voted on them and I included them in the final draft of the work required statement. The following is a note from my journal:

> Today I presented them with the work required statement and went over it point by point. They were obviously surprised that I had included the decisions that they had made in Friday's class meeting. They are starting to trust me and can see that I want them to take more control over their learning. I nearly blew it though. We were discussing how to find, design and order experiments. They were all looking a bit perplexed (I thought) so I said to them, 'If you like, I'll order an experiment that the whole class can do tomorrow, one which will show you how to tell the difference between acids and bases, then you can see what the experiments are like'. There was dead silence. They were looking at each other sideways and I could feel them thinking, 'Oh, yeah, so she is going to take over'. Quickly, I said, 'No, no that's a silly idea, Forget it' I said it. 'I'm only interrupting again. Go ahead with your planning'. The students went back to their discussion, the trust had been restored, if a little tenuously. I nearly blew it, but I learnt something.

Assessment: Non-Competitive vs. Competitive

In the early work on negotiation in South Australia, too little attention was paid to the overriding determining power of assessment systems. Without changes to what is valued and how we evaluate, negotiation regimes will be constrained and undermined. As I developed theories about society and schooling, I could see the assessment issue in a wider context. There is a good deal of literature that demonstrates that grading in schools, while being supposedly unbiased, is based on a value system that advantages more privileged students and, therefore, perpetuates inequalities in class, race, and gender that exist in our society. It encourages and legitimizes competition as a way of sorting out what is seen as success and failure and, indeed, is an important ideological factor which underpins the way society and its economic structure is organized.

My reflections have led me to believe that this is one of the key aspects of negotiating the curriculum which is often overlooked or underplayed. I suggest that until teachers learn how to make explicit and to negotiate what is to be learned and how it is to be assessed, they will be negotiating in a context where the ultimate power, the power of judging success and failure, remains the hidden controller. I therefore wish to discuss this in some detail.

This understanding helped me be more articulate about why I use non-graded assessment. As well, it has caused me to question how my values impinge upon my classroom practice and how my students' values can be valued in the classroom.

I moved to non-graded assessment when I began developing collaborative strategies in my classroom. I could see that in a collaborative classroom, marks and grading would be a major obstacle in encouraging the students to collaborate because of the competitiveness inherent in graded assessment. As well, I wanted to encourage self and peer evaluation hopeful that it would help students take more responsibility for the quality of their learning and increase the confidence of the less confident students. Graded assessment sets up a power structure within the classroom, with the teacher possessing the rights over the allocation of grades and students allocated to various levels in the pecking order in accordance with the way that they compete for grades. Other pecking orders exist in classrooms that often run in opposition to that generated by graded assessment. By removing grades and sharing the evaluation power with the students, I removed some of the reasons behind some of my more reluctant students' decisions not to participate in classroom learning. I experienced considerable resistance from the more competitively successful students who realized their loss of power in the classroom.

The development of work required assessment has been very helpful in making my assessment procedures in the classroom more systematic. Work required assessment, sometimes called goal-based assessment, refers to a formalized approach which requires the teacher and the students to reach agreement on an explicit work contract in which required processes, assignments and assessment criteria are already documented and understood before work on any unit begins (Johnston, 1988).

One of the main problems in my collaborative classrooms was the issue of varying degrees of participation and quantity of work attempted by the students. (This problem also exists in competitive classrooms, although the problem is often expressed as one of quality.) The work-required statements, as negotiated by the teacher and the students, make participation in class activities necessary to completing the work successfully. Before I used work required assessment I was much too fuzzy about what could be regarded as a fair amount of participation, as it was usually an individually negotiated factor with the more reluctant students and this was often seen as unfair by other students. In my experience, students appreciate the work-required statement because it makes clear what is fair participation as well as what can be negotiated.

What I appreciate most about work required assessment is that I can build collaborative processes into the required participation in a variety of ways. I can build in negotiation, group work and sharing as well as individual study. I usually discuss with the class the sort of activities that they and I think fair and interesting and then devise the Work-Required Statement around that. The process also acknowledges their questions as valid and worth pursuing which helps to build their self-confidence and worth.

Work required assessment also acts as a rigorous evaluation of the teacher's own practice. Through using this assessment approach, I have refined my recording procedures to make my negotiation with students more systematic. This has helped me develop a better understanding of the negotiating process as well as to concentrate on the various factors which need to be negotiated, especially quality of work.

In summary, I find work required assessment a systematic way of developing a collaborative atmosphere in the classroom and a powerful process by which to empower students as they negotiate their participation in their own learning. The work requirement statement as negotiated by the teacher and the students provides a clear statement of expectations for the student and, thereby, the decision to succeed rests with the student.

However, I am aware that some teachers work in schools where they have no choice about grading students when it comes to the end of the course. I have worked in such a school and while there I developed ways to negotiate the grades with the students, thereby increasing their responsibility over their own evaluations and sharing the power that I had to assign the grades. It was a compromise, but at least I was making students aware of the ways in which competitive assessment affected them.

I always maintained non-competitive assessment throughout the courses and this generated plenty of discussion about grading and competitive learning. In one class, when it came to the end of the course, I ran a class meeting and asked the students to generate criteria on which we could assign grades. The students then agreed to write down what grade they thought they should get with the appropriate reasons. The next day we discussed each person's assessment and assigned the A's to U's accordingly. We even attempted to follow the normal curve and achieve gender balance! The students thought the whole process was very fair and had a say in the process as we developed it.

I am convinced that collaborative learning cannot be developed in classrooms that revolve around competitive grading. It certainly occurs in them but usually as a resistance to the competition that the students find themselves in. This, I find, is particularly true for girls and particularly in science and mathematics and it usually consists of a form of cheating where students copy each other's work if they can't do it. If a teacher believes in sharing power in the classroom, then she needs to seek ways to include non-competitive assessment into her practice. This certainly means taking risks for those teachers in schools which are heavily into competitive structures like grading and tracking/streaming.

Valuing Students' Knowledge and Experience

Part of the power structure in a teacher-directed classroom is that the decisions made about what and how to learn are made by the teacher. This rests on the assumption that the teacher is the only one in the classroom who knows the subject matter and knows the best way to go about learning it. Indeed, one transitional barrier that students raise when resisting collaborative learning is that the teacher ought to know and ought to tell the students what to do. 'That's what she's paid for, isn't it?' is often heard in this regard. The students know about this power and many of them, especially secondary school students, expect the teacher to wield the power.

There are several strategies that I use to share this power. Firstly, when setting up the collaborative student-centered classroom, I encourage students to learn from each other. This is the basis of group work and I encourage students to discuss problems together and then consult me if they need to check their understanding. On occasions, a whole group of students can work out an understanding which is at variance to the standard explanation. I use this as an opportunity to negotiate further about their version as compared with the official version. I build regular teacher contacts into the Work-Required Statement. Usually this contact occurs with the group of students and I am able to help them clarify their understandings at that point. With regular encouragement, students can become less dependent on the teacher's knowledge or the authority of the teacher's knowledge and learn to respect their own and their peer's abilities to solve problems. This is sharing the power.

Secondly, I always try to build into the beginning of the topic a session where the students discuss and recall what they already know about the topic. At the moment I am teaching a year 10 topic called the *Laws of Motion*. The following is an extract from the Work-Required Statement. The knowledge generated by the initial discussion about what the students know has led to the week's lessons of experiments and sharing.

LAWS OF MOTION:
Work-Required Statement

1 Participate in generating a class list of what you know about motion.
2 Write your own definitions of words identified in the discussion.
3 Develop a glossary of technical terms (new words) that you come across in this unit.
4 In consultation with the teacher, design or find an experiment that tests one of your existing ideas and share your findings with the class.
5 Generate at least two questions about motion in negotiation with the teacher:

  • doing at least one experiment
  • using a textbook or resources from the Resource Center

6 Solve problems set by the teacher.
7 Rewrite Newton's three laws of motion in your own words and illustrate your understanding by referring to at least two experiments for each law.
8 Participate in a weekly lesson where the teacher answers questions set by the class. The questions must be submitted at least one lesson in advance.

In this case, I had a student teacher working with me and he managed the session which began the process. He encouraged them to think of examples and then explain what they thought was happening. They then spent the rest of the lesson in group discussion. At the class discussion next lesson, each group shared and explained their idea to the whole class. Most groups had begun with an example and then attempted to generalize in the explanation. I wrote it all on the board. Here is a note from my journal:

Once I had all the group's contributions on the board, I was going to suggest that we group the statements into relationships. Turning to the Work-Required Statement, I explained that if they could define some of the ideas on what they knew then they would have a clearer idea of the one that they wanted to test. 'Well', said Prue, 'What we should do is all write an example to each point because then we can see if we really understand it or not'. Not exactly what I had in mind, but the rest of the class were in total agreement. Well, they are the ones learning it, and it's obviously the wrong time for generalizations now.

And that's what they did. It took them about a lesson to work on that in groups and to write it into their books and by the end of that lesson some groups were looking through books or designing their own experiments. We had soda bulb rockets, inertia experiments, parachutes, ticker timers and collisions going on for several lessons. Once they had finished, most of them spent about a lesson discussing the experiment and writing it up. We then spent a lesson on class discussion sharing their experiments and discussing their original ideas.

The point that I am making with this example is that by starting with what they knew and building on that, the students had begun to learn about the laws of motion. I hadn't said very much about what I knew at all. As well, they were learning to respect the power of what they and their peers knew.

Thirdly, I encourage students and then insist that they do not copy second-hand meanings from books. Teaching students to value their own understandings and become less dependent on expert (book and teacher) meanings is a process that takes time and requires patience. In my experience, most secondary school students need to be taught how to do this. I use the following activities to develop this skill:

a   I do a lot of questioning when I recognize second-hand meaning written in students' books and try to persuade them that it is pointless to copy things that they don't understand without translating it into their own words.

b   I show them in a one-to-one or small group situation how to write down their meanings as they say or discuss them. Many students don't realize that they can write their spoken language onto paper and then refine the meaning from there.

c   I model how to take notes from prose by doing it on the blackboard in front of them, thinking aloud as I go. I then rewrite these notes into prose, using my own words.

d   I run rewriting exercises where I use a statement from a book and then get them to discuss it in group discussion. At the end of the group discussion, they collaborate in a class discussion and refine their understandings back in the group situation (see number 6 of the *Laws of Motion* Work-Required Statement). The teacher has to be careful not to rephrase statements that the students make into the formal language of the discipline. They have to develop the language themselves, just as a child learns the spoken language.

e   I try to vary the audience for student writing. Generally this is for their peers to be used for class presentation and sharing times or to go into a booklet for the school library. However, where the opportunity exits, younger students, family members and wider audiences (magazines, newspapers, newsletters) can be sought. Faced with this situation, the students know that the writing and explanations must be comprehensible for their audience.

Only after I have modeled the processes that they can use to write their own meanings can I expect them to do it. Students need a lot of encouragement to become confident to make, use and learn from their own meanings rather than relying on the teacher.

Negotiation

Developing the appropriate negotiating skills is essential for managing collaborative student centered classrooms. Whilst I have had plenty of practice, I still haven't actually worked out what it is that I do and what factors affect the development of these skills. This is the focus of my action research at the moment.

Through journal writing and focused observation, a group of teachers with whom I work is investigating the development of our negotiation skills with our classes. We have identified four areas to investigate: levels of negotiation, issues raised during negotiation, type of interaction during negotiation, and feedback from students. We are interested to reflect on our behavior as well as the behavior of the students as we develop student centered learning in the classroom. For instance, we are interested to see if the students will increase the number of times that they initiate negotiation at all levels as they become more independent learners. I have already recorded this on the individual level and at the class level in two Year 10 Science classes.

Negotiation at the class level requires patience and persistence to develop, particularly with students who commonly resist learning in schools. The teacher cannot resort to traditional control behavior, which rests on the assumption that the teacher is responsible for controlling the behavior of the students. The collaborative student centered classroom is based on the assumption that the teacher and students share this responsibility, because the behavior of students, individual and in groups, can influence the learning atmosphere in the classroom especially as the success of the strategies of group and class discussion depend on students listening to each other, not interrupting, asking each other questions and helping each other to learn.

I use several strategies to develop an atmosphere in which class discussion can proceed.

a   *Developing shared and individual rules for classroom behaviour*
This is best done at the beginning of the year (semester or module). It involves discussion about why and how to share the responsibility of classroom behavior and then brainstorming the types of behavior that are appropriate or not appropriate to the classroom in group discussion. Once the students have shared their lists then each point is discussed and a decision made whether to include it in the rules. After the rules have been established, then students can discuss what will

happen if the rules are contravened. At the school where I am teaching at the moment, this is a school policy and we have found it particularly successful for helping students to reflect individually on their behavior as well as encouraging the awareness that students can do something about the types of behavior that interrupt their learning in the classroom.

b   *Holding regular class meetings that deal with teacher and student concerns about the management of the classroom and behavior.*
I usually hold one of these at the end of each learning topic. At the lesson before I give out a feedback sheet to students and then use the collated results to give stimulus to the discussion. The following is an example of the questions I asked recently. I modify the feedback sheet to fit each topic.

YEAR 10 SCIENCE   **RPHS**

Feedback about the Laws of Motion
1   What was the best thing that happened in Science in the last unit?
2   Write down one important thing you have learnt.
3   How do you feel in Science classes at the moment?
    (Circle the words which apply to you.)

interested	relaxed	worried
successful	confused	clever
happy	bored	rushed

    Write your own word/s.
4   Which Work-Required Statement helped your learning the most? Please explain why.
5   Do you have any concerns about your learning at the moment?
6   Are you getting enough help from the teacher?
    (Circle.)

         YES   NO

    Have you any advice or comments about how the teacher manages the class?
7   On a scale of 1–10, how did you enjoy the unit?
    (Circle.)

    NO 1   2   3   4   5   6   7   8   9   10   YES

Thank you for your contribution.

According to the comments made by the students, I can negotiate constraints, behavior and methods of learning with the students. For instance, statement number 8 in the *Laws of Motion* Work-Required Statement referred to earlier was the result of an idea brought up by a group of students during class meeting. On other occasions, students may identify the behavior of a student or a group of students that is causing concern and then the class can discuss what we can do about it. I have also brought up my own ideas or concerns for discussion.

With time and patience, the students will get more confident about bringing up their concerns. The teachers must develop their trust by taking their ideas seriously and by making an obvious effort to include their suggestions into the classroom and by not using the class meeting for a complaining session. The students can appreciate and respect the responsibilities that the teacher has towards the school and their parents and can accept that suggestions have to fit in with certain conventions. For instance, they cannot decide to spend lessons listening to a tape of their favorite rock group and not doing any learning about the subject for which the lesson is designed.

c *Insist that students listen and share their comments during class discussion*
I will not tolerate inconsiderate behaviour during class discussion. While the students are learning to conduct themselves during discussions, I chair the meeting and I will interrupt any speaker to deal with students who are talking amongst themselves or talking over the speaker. This can be really frustrating at first, for the students and the teacher, but, in time, the offenders realize that it's not worth the attention that they get from the behaviour. I have one class at the moment who take it in turns to chair the class meeting. I notice with amusement that they have learnt the same tactics as I use to keep the attention of the class. This class has a rule which excludes any student from the meeting on the third reminder.

I build into the class meetings time for students to discuss ideas with one another. This is useful when there is a lull in the conversation or when students are obviously excited about something and need to talk about it all at once. Then I say, 'Talk about that idea with your neighbours for two minutes'.

However, some students will continue to resist. Why tolerate it? Arrange for them to go elsewhere while the class meets, rather than put up with their inconsiderate behaviour. In fact, I have a class of year 11 boys where until recently most of them couldn't cooperate together to have a class meeting. I have spent a lot of time working on this one and with help of consistent effort from their other teachers, reading the 'riot act' and other tactics, I have achieved enough reasonable behaviour to hold some class discussions. As mentioned, the control is mainly my responsibility and I believe that it will most likely be fairly short-lived. These students have resisted for so long, it is an uphill battle to persuade them to share the power. I keep trying though.

It is worth the time and effort to establish the atmosphere where a class of students can cooperate to hold a class discussion. Apart from being a useful medium to develop the shifting of responsibility, it is also a powerful way for students to learn through talk and sharing.

Negotiating with individual and groups of students requires other skills. Whilst the main issue for negotiation at the class level is about classroom management and organization matters, the issues raised with the individual student or a group are more diverse. So far, I have documented the following: helping students to realize their interests and decide the direction of their learning, depth of understanding, helping students to generalize from their experiments/research, individual/group effort, group interactions and involvement, use of resources, time lines, finishing times, planning, completeness of work, neatness, written expression, editing, redrafting, final presentation, making your expectations clear, use of time. I have no doubt that this list is not exhaustive.

In Conclusion

If I had to provide advice to teachers about what to do on the basis of my experience, I'd say that, first, the teacher needs to have good communication skills, those of listening carefully, friendly body language, not interrupting, etc. This, of course, is supported by all that I have read about the nature of language and learning. As well, the teacher needs to be able to judge how much withholding of teacher intervention is appropriate in different situations. For instance, withholding teacher advice is important when students are grappling with new concepts or when a student wants to copy your knowledge second hand. In the former case, I ask questions of clarification that will be helpful for the students in their understanding, and in the latter, I direct the student to find out for herself. However, when I am aware that the student has really tried to understand or has searched carefully for information, then it is not appropriate to withhold information that will help to relieve the student's frustration and develop her understanding.

The most important skill, however, is the ability to encourage the learners and to build up their confidence to go on learning. Certain groups of students often girls in my experience in the teaching of math and science because they have been constructed to view themselves as likely to fail these subjects, need constant encouragement. This does not mean that the teacher oozes with praise; it means recognizing low self-confidence or discouragement and helping the students to recognize what they have achieved so far.

Students need to be able to conduct collaborative group discussions by themselves. I make this issue a matter of regular discussion and encourage groups to reflect on their process regularly. I have had some groups tape record and videotape their group process so that they can see ways of making it more efficient. As well, students need to be well organized. Some students need more help with these skills and they are mostly boys, I find, perhaps because they, too, have been socialized, and thus, constructed into thinking that organization is a feminine skill. Students who are not well organized are the most dependent on the teacher.

I have tried to illustrate how I have progressed as a reflective practitioner in the complex and contested contexts of my school. I continually generate knowledge about how to effectively share power with my students. It soon changes, shifts and expands as I look more deeply into what I am teaching and how my students are learning.

References

Cosgrove, S. (1978) 'Some thoughts on learning' in *Language Across the Curriculum Project*, **3**, Adelaide: Education Department of South Australia.

Cosgrove, S. (1981) 'Using action research in the classroom and school: A teacher's view', *AARE 1982 Conference Papers*, **3**, pp. 627–34.

Dwyer *et al.* (1984) *Confronting School and Work*, Sydney: George Allen & Unwin.

Giroux, H.A. (1981) *Ideology, Culture and the Process of Schooling*, London: Falmer Press.

Johnston, B. (1985) 'Work required assessment', *The Australian Teacher*, **14**, pp. 11–16.

Johnston, B. and Dowdy, S. (1988) *Teaching and Assessing in a Negotiated Curriculum*, Australia: Martin Educational.

Chapter 6

An Open Letter: New York to Adelaide

Stefanie Siegel & Ellen Skelly

Dear Garth Boomer:

What is it about a letter that helps one get over the uphill struggle for a beginning? Does the audience suddenly become accessible enough so that one can grasp the right tone to use? Anyway, for whatever reason, a letter seems to be the right format for us here.

We are new teachers who came to teaching as a second or third career. In other words, we have both had previous experiences in the work world, experiences very different from teaching. In fact, there has been nothing in our lives that has previously prepared us for the positions we now hold except for our own backgrounds as students and the education courses we have taken with Cindy Onore at City College.

Stefanie has just completed her third year of teaching. It is the first year she has remained in the same school for two consecutive terms. All the shuffling around has greatly curtailed her growth as a teacher. When she decided to try teaching and received her temporary *per diem* or provisional certificate, New York City's answer to the teacher shortage, she was lucky enough to investigate City College's secondary education courses first, in order to fulfill the education requirement and discovered Cindy. By the time our methodology course met for the second time, she was employed at a Brooklyn high school teaching ninth graders English.

This is Ellen's second year of teaching. She entered the profession in a somewhat more front door way than did Stefanie. After two graduate education courses, she student taught and then obtained her temporary licence. Now, in her third high school, she continues her adjustment to the system and to different sizes of schools, different populations, and different administrations. Especially tough is the fact that none of these schools has had an appointed principal.

The schools where we teach are generally those read about in the newspapers and not academic journals or books. They are in a state of horrible disrepair and neglect. Their student populations reflect the surrounding neighborhoods: 90–100 per cent minority, often the newest arrivals to the city. The majority of students at Erasmus Hall High School, where Stefanie works, are either African-American or from the Caribbean or Latin America. At George Washington High School, where Ellen teaches, the majority of students are from the Dominican Republic.

These neighborhoods are overcrowded, poor, and in a state of disrepair and neglect. (As seems to be the case so often today, poverty is preyed upon by drugs and crime.) The police precinct which encompasses George Washington High School had the highest murder rate in New York City in 1989. In addition to this harsh environment, our students struggle with a new culture, a new language, a new set of expectations from school and society. Not all of our students become victims of these circumstances, but all these problems take their toll on them, on teachers, and on the school as a community.

Both Erasmus and George Washington have been labeled 'failures' by the New York State Board of Regents because of low results on standardized tests. Each receives special federal government funds for remediation programs, which although changing, limits how classes can be taught, adds mountains of paper work, and restricts the credit value. Our stories are about our struggle to understand the reality of our students, to involve them in our attempts to make the system work for all of us, and to bring change.

In George Washington, two hundred or so seniors graduate every June. Yet, they had entered the school four years previously with approximately 1,000 other students. Ellen's students for this past year have been ninth and tenth grade honors kids. In her school, this means that almost all of the students read at or above grade level according to the New York City-wide examination called, Degrees of Reading Power (DRP), a cloze-test. The idea behind the program is to offer enrichment in the form of two English classes. The program is well-funded (ironically in part by federal funds for remediation), and the teachers are told repeatedly of the money available for books and trips. The trips have occurred, but the books took too long to arrive and many had not reached school by June. Consequently, they had to rely on the very limited selections available from the book room of the English Department. The major problem of the program is that there is no curriculum (written or suggested) for English. It's impossible to adapt the curriculum of the English Department because there is no curriculum there, either.

Up until four years ago all of what Ellen said about her school could have been said about Erasmus. But changes in the curriculum and the attitudes toward students, primarily due to the efforts and dedication of one administrator, are gradually starting to make the school work. Four years ago Marcia Lyles became Assistant Principal of the Communication Arts Department. At that time Erasmus had a drop out rate of 12.6 per cent and a passing percentage of 45.9 per cent on the Regents' Competency Test (RCT), a writing exam which requires students to write in three different genres. This school year the drop out rate was down to 5.1 per cent and the percentage passing on the same test up to 84.86 per cent.

During her year at Erasmus, Stefanie has taught mostly ninth and tenth graders either first year English or reading. She had been trying to get a position at Erasmus for the past two years, just to work under Marcia Lyles. Her position opened up this year because the neighborhood around the school continues to grow. There were five hundred plus 'Over-the-Counter' students (those who enter after the term has begun) admitted fall of 1989. Often these students are classified without the help of their school records. The general rule seems to be, if you haven't taken a DRP, you need reading. Newcomers are taught by a newcomer.

So, Garth, we are new to the profession and to the idea of negotiation; and we ask your patience with our näivete and unanswered questions. We first came into contact with the idea of negotiating a curriculum in our first graduate education course at City College with Cindy. It is probably safe to say, if it weren't for her, we wouldn't know each other and there is a good chance, given the state of teacher education in New York City, we wouldn't know about your work either.

Through this course, we came to realize many things about education and the role of negotiation in it. At every class session, by working in small groups, choosing the focus of our discussions, and deciding how and what to share with the rest of the class, we negotiated our learning. We learned that at the heart of this process is the belief that the materials used in class will expose students (and teacher) to various ideas, but the impact of the ideas will vary from individual to individual and from class to class. And the impact these ideas have and the form they take cannot be predicted or plotted out in advance. As fully active members of that negotiated methodology class (how can one be a passive negotiator?), we learned far more than in any traditional classroom where the content was laid out ahead of time and delivered according to a rigid time line.

On Beginning to Negotiate

While Stefanie participated in this negotiated classroom as a student, she felt strongly attracted to much of what she encountered. However, she didn't know what to do with this concept in terms of her own classroom. She was too confused, inhibited, and, in many ways, too intent on observing all of the new things around her. She couldn't stop and digest the theory she was learning, make it part of her own teaching. But looking back at her first teacher-researcher paper, Stefanie discovered surprisingly that negotiation was one of the first things she attempted after loosening up enough to try and put things into a larger picture than just getting through from day-to-day.

Her first attempt to negotiate involved classroom rules. Agreeing on the rules went well; reinforcing them was another matter. A matter partly indicative of the ongoing nature of negotiation. And also of the fact that negotiation aims to get at the broader picture of the philosophy and atmosphere of the classroom. Negotiation is less about agreeing upon rules (a mechanics issue) than about the idea of what rules are for and then what can be done to achieve an atmosphere of respect for ourselves, for others, and for the work that goes on in the room.

The rules that Stefanie negotiated were particular to the structure of her school but had more to do with fear of getting in trouble (for all parties concerned) than setting up a working environment. We have come to think that rules must evolve out of the desired learning environment. In order to do this, members of the class need to explore together how they learn best and under what conditions. In other words, the first step is to negotiate an image of a positive environment and, then, the necessary rules will evolve out of a shared understanding of what the particular community of learners needs to work effectively. If this were the case, then the job of reinforcement would be a shared concern.

Ellen's first attempt to negotiate came the following semester as she student taught. She negotiated with her students the selection of short stories for a project. On a superficial level, the negotiation was successful. Stories were chosen and read. Groups produced written and oral projects based on the stories. No groups failed to do the work and some of it was, indeed, fine. The real problem was the way Ellen framed the questions and activities for the groups: the students' concerns and questions about and responses to the stories were not included.

So, Garth, from the start of our teaching careers we tried to negotiate. Now, two and three years later our questions still abound: What does it mean to negotiate a curriculum? Or more specifically, how is it possible in the traditional urban high school classroom? What will negotiation look like, and how will we know if we are successful?

Despite (and maybe because of) our questions, we still press forth with negotiation knowing that what makes negotiation a vital part of the classroom is that it is the means for everyone to gain ownership and choice. Both of these are necessary steps in taking charge of your own learning.

Our model for the negotiated classroom, as always, was our methodology class with Cindy. So taken with our own learning there, we perhaps didn't closely analyze it enough so that we could grasp the underlying structure involved. We believed the class to be 'free form' because its structure differed from other classes we knew. Cindy did not talk at us for an hour and a half. We moved; we talked; we wrote. The high level of participation and the noise generated by the groups perhaps could make observers see chaos where truly there was order.

When Ellen read *In the Middle* (Atwell, 1990), she thought she found another model of a structured, negotiated classroom. Atwell teaches her rural, junior high school students two periods per day (for English and for reading) and sets up writers' and readers' workshops. Students choose their own topics, write, confer, and edit all year long in writing workshops. In reading workshops, the students read self-selected books and write letters to one another and to Atwell about their reading.

Ellen learned about structure and the role of choice in negotiation when she tried to follow the Atwellian model of reading and writing workshops. These are her observations about what took place:

One day my tenth grade class just exploded. They were sick of what was going on in class and were not going to stand for it one more minute. They told me things that day I already knew: the class was too unstructured for them on a daily basis; that there was no group cohesion; and they had no idea why we were doing this stuff. In addition, there was too much predictability on a weekly basis. Monday-Wednesday meant writing; Thursday and Friday meant reading.

My students told me that what I believed to be rudimentary negotiation was so unstructured as to be unworkable. At one point during this dialogue, I commented that I could be flexible (as to what came next) and Adam replied, 'That's your problem, you're too flexible'.

What I failed to communicate to my students was that I believed this broad structure and my flexibility served a purpose. I thought that choice would help them to become immersed in reading and writing. Through the development of their own ideas for writing and through conferring with others, they would become better, stronger, more interested, and more interesting writers. I believed the same for reading. By choosing books that spoke to them personally, the students would be drawn into the world of words that I wanted for them. But the real life concerns of these kids were never addressed in class. In our dialogue, they mentioned: SAT prep, RCT prep (without which they cannot graduate), learning about their classmates, spelling, vocabulary, and grammar. They were concerned that writing in other subject matter would be affected by their lack of proficiency in these other areas.

This would have been the place to begin negotiating the curriculum back in February — not with the open-ended, 'What do you want to do this semester?' as I seemed to be saying every day when I walked in that room. It's no wonder they began to write a letter of complaint about me. I acted as if I either didn't know of these concerns or I believed them to be invalid. What really was going on in my head (which I didn't share with my students) was that these concerns could be addressed in other ways other than tackling them head on. I also believed that choice equaled negotiation and that Atwell was about negotiation. My students taught me that those were fallacious assumptions and that I was as unsure of the curriculum part as I was about the negotiation part.

Stefanie, too, made the mistake of equating choice with negotiation, thinking it was the key to motivating her students into an involvement with formulating the concerns and day-to-day life of the class. This is her story.

During the spring semester of 1990 I began teaching a new reading program at Erasmus High School in Brooklyn, New York. It's called the Literary Center. The goal of this program is to provide our students with the opportunity to appreciate the benefits and rewards of reading rather than remediation: to read for enjoyment, for information, and for insight about the world around them. A special environment is being created for this purpose. Basically the Literary Center will be a room without bolted down desks in rows but filled with conference tables, individual work areas, book cases filled with all kinds of books and magazines, and video and computer equipment.

At the semester's end the room had yet to be transformed due to the slow arrival of money, furniture, and books, as well the insufferable red-tape involved in the simple act of trying to remove bolted down school desks.

After mid-semester, I was finally able to fill one of the book cupboards in our room with a selection of books from the English Department bookroom (usually off-limits to reading classes, one of those strange school paradoxes: no real books for reading classes) — probably twenty titles in multiple copies numbering from three to ten. After much deliberation I decided to open up the cupboard and invite my students to 'swim around' and choose a book. The one requirement was to ultimately find a way to share their reading of the book with the rest of the class. They were also given the option to use the book they were currently reading for English or another subject area class, and they could work together on the presentation or sharing activity.

In each class we set up a schedule for independent reading time and as everyone settled into a book, I continued to discuss ways to share these individual readings with the group. But something was wrong; there wasn't any natural impetus to share and students would repeatedly tell me they didn't understand what I wanted them to do. I continued to talk about book discussions but I didn't model one. I felt like any discussion of a text I shared with them would be interpreted as more intellectually intimidating talk.

One student, obsessed with Ninja turtles, told us about the book, which she had read ten times, and the movie, seen about that often. She went on and on with all of these details which made little sense to the rest of us unfamiliar with the film or the book. I kept thinking to myself, 'What is going wrong here?'

Atwell's (1990) premise behind reading workshops is to try and recreate lifelike dining room table discourse about books. And surely some of the most powerful out of school book discussions we have are those that arise spontaneously when we read a book that connects and makes us want to share that connection. But don't we tend to share that excitement with someone we know will be empathetic, either because they have had a similar experience or know us well enough to perceive the connections we are making?

Choice definitely seems a key element in making classroom activities work. But we think it has to be choice that acknowledges the likes, dislikes, strengths, and weaknesses of all the participants: the whole student and the whole teacher. And it must be choice that revolves around discourse and challenges all those involved. The choices must be at both the problem-posing and problem-solving levels.

Just allowing for choice, whether choice of book or topic to write on, is not negotiation. We now believe that it is not choosing that matters. It is what students do with their choices. This is where intention comes in. Choice without intent means nothing. Books will be unread, and stories unwritten if choice were the only component of learning. Choice is a means of expressing the intentions the learning community decides are important.

On 'Coming Clean'

Garth, you mention the 'eternal triangle of education: the teacher, the child, and the curriculum', in chapter 1. This is an important key to understanding the leap you make from language across the curriculum to negotiation. Another key is understanding that language development is not just about learning to read, write, and speak a language but about learning itself. As you say, the most important questions a school must consider when embarking on change must be: 'How do we learn?'; 'Under what conditions do we learn most effectively?'; and 'Do we all learn in the same way?' (p. 4). But most importantly, the only way schools can solve these questions is through negotiation which results when teachers 'come clean' with students about their own theories of learning. Students then can test these theories out for themselves, a process which will eventually enable them to develop their own.

The situations we have described get at this issue of change and the role of negotiation in it. Traditionally, schools never openly consider the 'eternal triangle'. Teacher-curriculum-student seem to be writ in stone. How can negotiation take place under such circumstances? Any attempt to do such a thing would entail a battle with either one or both of the other two sides as we have seen. If the triangle is static and not in constant flux, there really is no reason for schools to explore the issues involved in negotiation which are the individual's learning process and the conditions which best promote learning for everyone in the classroom. In order to negotiate, there has to be a strong understanding of your role as a teacher, a curriculum which invites inquiry, and knowledge about your students and an understanding of their role as fellow inquirers. And the traditional school structure does everything it can to prevent students and teachers from coming to know each other in a way that facilitates learning for all concerned.

When a teacher makes assumptions about learning that are based on the supposition that we all learn differently, her classroom will look chaotic to those who believe that the traditional teacher-centered classroom is the only picture of learning. Unfortunately, our students have been bred on the traditional system. The reality of this makes it all the more important to 'come clean'. But we are working within (no matter how much against) a system that never comes clean. Why should we be believed?

Garth, we both have had problems coming clean with our students. The reactions have ranged from 'So what?' to eyes glazed over, to 'Who is she and what does this have to do with me; I just want to pass'. Stefanie's comments about her problems with this are pretty typical of both of us.

When I think about your insistence on the need for teachers to 'come clean' with their students about what theories of learning lie behind their curricula, classroom activities, as well as attitude towards them, it makes perfect sense, yet we have both received negative receptions when we tried to reveal the intentions behind our practice. Often it felt like no one was listening or, at least, shortly after we began this mode of talk everyone put on their 'listening to a sermon look' and promptly tuned the teacher out. Maybe this is just like the many other activities which when tried go over like a lead balloon and end up being recast in another disguise. But how can you recast 'coming clean' in another disguise and remain honest? Maybe I'm not really coming clean, but making a confession; how do I do the real thing?

Obviously not the way I did it this semester, which brought all work to a halt. Early on I partially realized a huge obstacle against anyone doing any sustained meaningful work in reading classes. But this semester I clearly saw all of its ramifications. Reading classes are only worth half a credit, but it isn't a credit that figures into the requirements for graduation. That fact in itself is a strong argument for cutting reading class. One response to this dilemma for the teacher is to say, 'Okay, fine. But you have to pass this class in order to get out of the reading requirement which is taking up a valuable block of your program'. However, this isn't true. The only real criteria for getting out of reading is your DRP score, if you're a ninth or tenth grader, and your RCT reading score, if you're an upper classman. And, meanwhile, if you have a reading teacher like me who tells you CLOZE exams aren't reading tests — well the absurdity must be too much to bear.

So, consequently, after my students took the DRP in early May (most of them being ninth and tenth graders), all incentive for work disappeared. All of the reading we had done together wasn't there for them as proof of what reading is really all about. I hadn't negotiated the curriculum with them; we hadn't figured out together why they weren't readers and what it would take to turn them on to reading. The only reality about the class, for them, was the TEST.

Traditionally in reading classes, reading is treated as if it were a separate subject matter not an activity for learning. I was trying to give them a curriculum of readings I thought would help them find their own need for literacy. This didn't happen. But we never negotiated together what would help them find this. I came clean about the reading test but I never gave them a chance to come clean on what they needed to learn about reading.

On Students' Responses to Negotiating

In chapter 1, you succinctly explain what happens when only one or two teachers are trying to make changes within the confines of a traditional school structure:

For example, where individual teachers wish to change the emphasis from teacher as examiner to teacher as collaborative evaluator with the students, they act in a broad context quite inimical to their intentions: students socialized for years into seeing the teacher as judge, a school system geared to external reward for effort, and a society based on competition. Depending on their own personal charisma, teachers may begin to succeed in winning the confidence of some students, who may then feel aggravated by their other teachers; but the more usual result is that such teachers are devalued as soft or even slightly crazy. It is therefore very difficult for teachers to share their power with students, because society and schools are not based on such a philosophy. (p. 7)

Both of us have encountered the problem of being perceived as 'soft and slightly crazy'. Ellen's students rebelled because the class was seen as uncontrolled, undirected, and lacking in purpose. Because our intentions and practices are different from most of our colleagues, our students don't see us as representing school. In addition, as teachers we don't have models of negotiation in school — although we negotiate all the time in life. If we feel the void of role models, how can our students not feel the same? There is no evidence to them that our version of the school game is any better. And if we can't guarantee that, why not just stick to the rules as they are now?

Perseverance in the face of feeling absurd is often a new teacher's biggest obstacle. It is easy to throw things out too quickly or abandon ship without a lifeboat. Stefanie has suggested one image of her three years of teaching would show a sea of abandoned shards from many a promising ship. Many of our feelings, we think, have to do with knowing well those you are expected to teach, being able to determine when someone is digesting new information, not quite trusting the situation enough to reveal their interest, or have already rejected all possibility of engagement, and, perhaps, most importantly, not being paralyzed by the seeming gaps between teacher knowledge and student knowledge. It is usually past the mid-semester point when we could say we know our students well. But if their questions and concerns had been incorporated from the beginning into what made up our day-to-day activities, we wouldn't be the one doing all of the guess work.

Not surprisingly, Stefanie found that this semester the class she had been most successful with was the one where she shared a majority of students with a teacher who also tries to negotiate the curriculum and create a student-teacher partnership.

I was lucky enough to take part in four workshops for teachers and students, held by this same English teacher. Even though the workshops were held after school, eight of my students took part. The workshop leader is an unusual man. He has taught for twenty years in a variety of schools and has been a teacher trainer for the New York City Writing Project at Lehman College. The theme of the workshops was change — in the world and the self. Our work culminated in trying to find ways to change our learning experiences at Erasmus.

Mickey introduced this project by having us look at three pictures of learning: the traditional fountain, an African market, and a swimming pool. We looked at these pictures in small groups of students and teachers and were asked to choose the one which represented our view of learning. At first the students in my group inclined to choose the fountain. But when they were prodded to explain their choice, it came about from familiarity more than anything else. I think it was confusing at first to even be asked what learning looks like, but when the questions got more specific, like, 'What is your favorite or least favorite class?' and 'What happens in that class?', some interesting things happened.

The three students in my group generally had difficulty in classes where the teacher held a tight rein over the curriculum, where they had no input or influence on what got covered and how. They had to spend a lot of time at home going over the notes they had spent the period copying off the board. It just didn't make much sense when they were 'taking it in' and there wasn't time to work it out in class. By the end of our discussion, all of the groups chose the African Market (with some of the Swimming Pool thrown in) as their preferred image of learning.

I know these workshops provided a special non-school-like atmosphere which encouraged the students to get engaged in the topic. Students, who often enough seem like one of the greatest obstacles to change, are really very adaptable in the right environment. The desks were movable, food and drink was at hand, and there was plenty of time — time to work, gossip, stretch, and eat. Learning was more like life than school.

I spoke with my students who shared the workshop with me about the differences between what went on there and in our classroom. Calling teachers by their first name, working in groups with both teachers and other students, sharing food, all contributed to the enthusiasm they showed for the workshops. But also it was a no threat situation: no tests or accountability except to the self or the group. There was homework and projects to be completed but they were given time to take form. No forty minute bell.

In our initial interest in Atwell, we were both taken with the 'dining room table' metaphor for book discussions. We know the power of sharing with someone what you have read. Atwell seems to have made this connection between life and school in her workshops with her junior high school students and carried that spontaneity into school. We have yet to make such a transfer. But both Atwell's and Mickey's workshops leave the question in our minds of, 'What is the connection between life and school?'

We both are coming to believe that school and life are different and should be different. While we want to capture the naturalness and excitement which generally comes with learning in the real world, we know that we do not operate under the same circumstances. In real life, learning generally does not occur with a group of thirty-five people who meet on a regular basis with the agenda set by only one of those people. If we have as a model of learning the African Market, then some aspects of the connection involves choice, purpose, meaning, and pleasure. But an African Market, while lively and exciting and chaotic is not without structure. We have been struggling with and avoiding the role of structure in schools because of frustration with the structure that is in place. We were perhaps becoming anarchic educators.

By the end of this semester, we were both beginning to understand why Atwell's model doesn't work (or isn't enough) in high school. Atwell is not political. Her method is not inquiry and it is not negotiation. While her students explore their own individual literacy, they never discuss, debate, argue, problem pose and problem solve the societal issue of literacy. School is something more than the heated discussion of books around the dining room table. Or high school should be.

We need to prepare our students for the pressures of urban life in all of its complexity. It is extremely crucial that they understand they must struggle to own the power of their own literacy or someone will take it away from them. It is crucial they understand that the power of their own learning lies in their hands, that no knowledge exists without a knower, and that living a full life is about the struggle to know this.

It is in the curriculum where we can prepare and empower our students for the modern, multicultural, urban world in which they live. And it would seem that now the third side of the triangle — curriculum — would be the easiest to get a grasp on. After all, it is not alive. But as each of us has discovered with our various attempts to create it, curriculum is not easy to pin down. Curriculum is not an approach (à la Atwell) and it is not what you do from day to day to get you through. As you hint at in the very phrase 'negotiating the curriculum', Garth, it is an exploration, an inquiry into ideas to find answers (and maybe even some more questions).

As young teachers with few education courses to back us up, it's been hard to define curriculum from our situations. We hear from our more experienced colleagues that the curriculum is the book list. As we have found out in the course of this inquiry into negotiating the curriculum (which started out as an independent study course), this is not so. We have learned so much that goes beyond the book list. We have followed such related issues as teacher directions; the nature of New York City reading programs; student and teacher passivity; how groups work (and don't work); the role of dialogue in learning, and more.

On Growing Into Negotiating the Curriculum

Despite our problems and misreadings, we've had success negotiating the curriculum with our students. Stefanie had preplanned a curriculum for the Literary Center. The semester would be divided into three, six-week units under the broad theme, *The American Experience*. The units would be: *The Black Experience*, *The*

Immigrant Experience, and *The Native American Experience*. For each unit, students would be responsible for completing three different types of reading experiences: reading a book with the whole group, reading a book in a smaller group, reading a book independently — all on a different aspect of the theme. The 'book' selection would be varied and would include newspapers, journals, and magazines. Students should choose readings from a variety of genres. Reader response journals will be kept for each unit and would be shared, especially during group reading activities where writing back and forth to each other about the book will be part of the course.

In organizing all of this, choice was foremost in Stefanie's mind, not negotiation. And actually choice or making a selection of materials for the students was the hardest part. If she had allowed them to find their own questions at the the beginning of a unit, those questions could have framed her search for appropriate materials. By the time we hit *The Native American* unit, a subject of study Stefanie knows very little about, it was easy to blame the class disinterest and confusion on her own lack of knowledge.

Stefanie found that one of the most powerful learning experiences took place when the students' questions were the focus of the discussions.

> A small group of students and I unraveled one linguistic puzzle today. I have been trying to introduce the topic of *Native Americans* for the past few days, using some writings by same on the predicted coming of the white man. My students immediately picked up on the contrast between the people who were speaking and the White man, establishing a racial conflict. But every time I used the term 'Native American' there seemed to be a problem. Of course! To them I was a Native American so they couldn't figure out who I was talking about because a contrast between light and darker skinned people had been established in the prophecies we read.
>
> Luckily, I had managed to decorate my room with maps and I was able to show them Columbus' 'mistake' and the problem with calling American Indians, Indians, once historians recognized this misnomer. All this is further confused by the people labeled 'coolies' or the East Indians who have migrated to the Caribbean and those peoples who were native to the Caribbean who share the ancestry of Native Americans. There we were stumbling along together trying to work all of these connections out.
>
> This discussion happened after we had brainstormed a list of all the things we knew about Indians or Native Americans. But I hadn't followed up with the next part (as I hadn't in the earlier units) with an opportunity for the students to discover what they needed or wanted to find out about Native Americans. I had brought in about twenty books on the topic for them to explore, and with minimal directions — find something that interests you and share what you learned with the class. And once again, predictably, they lost interest, became confused and bored. I never allowed them to find a shared context for their search — the questions and concerns the classroom community formulated about the topic. Consequently, there was still a major linguistic confusion present which luckily the maps helped us straighten out.

Ellen found similar things to be true about the importance of listening to students' voices during her classes' inquiry into *To Kill a Mockingbird*. The students explored wonderful ideas and issues and engaged in mostly meaningful talk about the book and their reactions to it when the 'teaching' centered around the students and not the text. She could not have predicted the way the students' learning would occur. Nor, after witnessing the work they did, would she want to!

I found many of the assertions about negotiating the curriculum to be true. The quantity and quality of student talk (including questioning) was wonderful. From the beginning of the inquiry the students made demands to know the text. They questioned Harper Lee's beginning to the novel. Many asked, 'Why is the Finch family history in the book?' I realized that I didn't quite know because I glossed over it as an uninteresting tidbit before the good meat of the story. From the start, they asked about the title. And they were all taken with the fact that Atticus is not called 'Dad' by his children. These issues might have been ignored by me in my desire to 'get through' the book.

I found that by listening, I became more aware of my students as readers and learners. For example, I know that the initial difficulty with the book had to do with the fact that they are not readers. The family history put them off because it was boring and they did not know that readers sometimes have to wait for rewards. I also learned that at times I became obsolete. As I eavesdropped or listened to the tapes, I found that many of the groups worked quite well and that discussion and questioning flowed, although there were still problems. Some students believed that my voice mattered more, so that when I came to eavesdrop on the groups, I became a hindrance; they directed all their questions to me. In order to get work done, one group banned me and asked to be taped instead.

I think that what made this inquiry a successful example of negotiation was that the framework I created was loose enough for everybody to use their voice. The inquiry focused on reading strategies and how the use of these strategies affected the students' interests in the reading and what they learned from the book. So, the students asked their own questions about the text and then tried to answer them (individually and in groups). They put themselves into a character's shoes and tried to figure out who these people were and what made them tick and what their role was in the book. And finally, after getting into the book and being the focus of the learning, the groups then studied sections of text in order to analyze their importance to the book. The analysis went into greater depth, I believe, than if we had started out trying to explicate text from the start.

And so now we've come to the end of our stories Garth. We don't want to sign off in the usual way. We don't think we need a typical, tidy conclusion because, by reading this chapter, you will know what we have learned through our struggles to negotiate: Choice does not equal negotiation; negotiation is about learning and about people's relationships to learning and to their fellow learners; structure is important in negotiation; negotiation is inquiry; dialogue is important in negotiation; and the relationship among the parts of the 'eternal triangle' must be constantly evaluated and negotiated.

And by reading the chapter, you will realize what we still don't know: What does negotiation look like? What must we do and how must we change in order to truly negotiate curriculum with our students?

We shared our tales with you, not in the hope that you will rush to the States in September to guide us as we begin to negotiate again. Rather, we share these stories so that you will know the seriousness which we (and other negotiators) have taken your work. By writing this, we have learned so much about teaching, negotiation, and ourselves.

The work we have done this semester, both as teachers and students, has cleared up some of the mystification we had about negotiating the curriculum. One thing we do understand now is that negotiation is much more than an approach, or a method, nor is it just a process. It is a frame from which to view human interaction within the school structure. Or it is one way to answer questions concerning means to structure learning. What school is supposedly all about.

In chapter 1 of the 1982 *Negotiating the Curriculum*, you quote Richard Campbell commenting that with negotiation 'a framework is being offered by which teachers can take the lid off the learning saucepan and show students what is involved — how learning is a matter of choice followed by collective and personal actions' (p. 7).

That seems to be an appropriate summary to what we have learned through our action-knowledge inquiry and of what we hope to share with our students.

Sincerely,

Stefanie Siegel
Ellen Skelly

References

ATWELL, N. (1990) *In the Middle: Writing, Reading, and Learning with Adolescents*, Portsmouth, NH: Heinemann.
BOOMER, G. (1982) 'Turning on the learning power: Introductory notes', in G. BOOMER, (Ed.) *Negotiating the Curriculum: A Teacher-Student Partnership*, Sydney: Ashton-Scholastic, pp. 2–7.

Chapter 7

A Response: Adelaide to New York

Garth Boomer

Dear Stephanie and Ellen:

Your letter has massaged the inside of my head. Thank you. It gives me the opportunity to think again about negotiation and reminds me that negotiating the curriculum must never become an 'it'. 'Itness' in education is the hardening of the categories which precedes death. Long live the Stefanies and Ellens around the world who pursue ideals in the jungles of conflicted practice!

You bring a new dimension to my imagining of classrooms. While in Australia we have some very 'difficult' contexts, I doubt that we have the full intensity and overlay of the challenges to be met at Erasmus Hall and George Washington. One way to look at your situation would be to see attempts at negotiation as a kind of pedagogical suicide, taking on kids who are street-wise, alienated, self-destructive and, no doubt, highly skeptical about the motives and commitments of teachers. One would expect that most students would 'smell a rat' if a teacher purported to be willing to accommodate their concerns. Even if the teacher succeeded in establishing a *bona fide* willingness to negotiate, the class would simply move from cynicism to pity for a teacher who was crazy enough to be 'soft' — a response that you have both experienced.[1]

Another way to look at the challenge is to deduce, logically, that negotiation is the *only* way to go, the only option, if you want to bring about radical change and get students learning in these schools rather than enduring them or subverting them. There is a sense in which the relatively powerless tend to collude in their own oppression. Socialized into a low opinion of themselves and alienated from the middle classes, they will either actively reject access to middle class know-how or deem themselves incapable of understanding it. And so they ensure that they will fail, thereby reproducing the cycle of oppression and ignorance that no doubt kept their parents entrapped.

It seems that the choices facing both of you, Stefanie and Ellen, reduce to a stark alternative. *Either* conform to the *way teaching has always been* and face the consequences of most students going through the motions or rebelling *or* radically move to a negotiation regime risking rejection and ridicule on the one hand while opening up the chances of real learning engagement on the other.

As I read it, you have, in fact, no alternative. Your hearts and minds have already rejected 'the transmission model' of instruction and embraced the notion of students as collaborative/constructors of knowledge, or rather 'knowing'.

So even as you adopt the time-worn 'teacher-as-head-stuffer' stance, you will be subverting and mocking your own incongruence. In the thick of old structures and habits you will not be able to contain or dismiss your deep-seated, strongly theorized conceptions of learning and teaching. Even when you don't negotiate, you will, at a more subtle level, be negotiating. You will look for moments, fissures in the facade of common-sense teaching, for uncommon-sense intervention; opportunities for acknowledging the world and orientation of students; ways of connecting your abstractions with the lived reality of those compelled to be in your classes. Why subject yourself to the pain of pretending to be like most teachers? Better to come out and have a go; be authentic; be courageous. And that's what you are doing. Pushing out the pedagogical boat; putting your very being on the line; showing yourselves as strugglers towards understanding and, in so doing, teaching, above all else, *yourselves*, what you are, what you stand for, how you think people should behave towards each other. You suffer buffeting, miscues, rejections. You find moments of engagement. You construe and re-construe, read and re-read, construct and de-construct what is happening to you and your charges. You are learning to be a post-modern teacher in a largely modern world. You take your place with Neil Armstrong in making one small step.

And I have trouble in how to speak to you. My first instinct is to want to 'help'. I've spoken with hundreds of teachers who have set out to negotiate and who return from the front-lines to tell me stories similar to yours. I think I know ways of coping that will be of assistance.

But then, I've written elsewhere (1989) about how 'the helping hand strikes again'; about how help given when not commissioned is patronizing, de-powering and downright offensive (/) (I thereby condemn so much teaching!).

Are you commissioning ideas and information from me? Do I have your permission to tell you some things that I know which may make life easier and better?

My own theory says that we learn most in areas of our greatest 'anxiety' (in the sense of disequilibrium rather than paralyzing fear). You are both healthily 'anxious' about negotiation. Your act of writing to me I construe as an invitation to dialogue, if not help. I therefore rationalize that I can treat your letter as a series of questions, hypotheses, interim formulations, reflections and wonderings which I may, provided I adopt a similar stance of vulnerability and speculativeness, engage with. Let me then imagine that I am providing ideas which you will take up or not take up as you seek to allay your anxieties and learn to negotiate the curriculum in your own way.

This is not your friendly guru. This is not he-who-knows-better. This is a fellow wonderer, probably a bit wiser about the politics of education, a bit more hard-bitten after thirty years in the game, and a lot more remote from the business of teaching in schools.

Please do not take it unkindly if I say that you are both engaging much more with what you are doing and thinking than you are with the students or the educational system in which you work. How could it be otherwise? Whenever we struggle with new techniques and behaviours we must go through a self-conscious, egocentric or at least technocentric phase where we foreground and render problematic our practice. You are in a sense at a stage of negotiation within yourselves rather than with the students as you fight the oscillating battle between what you'd like to do and what you have been socialized to do and are being reinforced in doing as a teacher. At this stage the students are very important agents in your drama and 'the system' also is a 'grey eminence' but the up-front action is to do with your planning, your dilemmas, your compromises. You are researching yourselves. As you do this you are having insights into the art and craft of 'negotiating'. You are critiquing the unfolding 'texts' of your own teaching.

If I asked you both the first of Cook's four questions (chapter 2) about negotiation at the moment — 'What do you know about negotiating?' — you would, extracting from your letter, produce a very long list containing at least the following:

- it is hard to do, especially in inner city, impoverished schools;
- it works for us as learners;
- you can start negotiation on a small scale (e.g. rules);
- negotiation is about student choice and ownership (I'll come back to this one);
- student choice is not a sufficient condition;
- students' agendas are often different from the teachers';
- negotiation needs to take account of the whole class not just individuals choice;
- negotiation involves teachers 'coming clean' about their theories and intentions (I'll come back to this, too);
- negotiation involves consideration of teacher, student and curriculum 'agenda';
- students often do not appreciate 'negotiating' methods (e.g. 'coming clean');
- students often have a very pragmatic and 'correct' assessment of where the 'crunch' value is placed (e.g. tests, examinations);
- negotiation is enhanced if more than one teacher is doing 'it';
- learning is social, interactive, collaborative and 'various';
- schools are 'unnatural' institutions;
- negotiation involves setting up structures;
- negotiation is a way of teaching life, not just a method.

I'd say that this is a very impressive list. What you now want to learn is how to do it better, presumably without going out of your mind or collapsing through nervous exhaustion.

I'd also say that armed with a little more political and strategic *nous* you are now ready to begin foregrounding your students and their learning rather than yourselves and your learning. Your letter is exciting to me because of the way the students, in your text, have intruded themselves. This means that the theory is working. Your orientation *allows* students to reveal their resistances and constraints. It allows them to derail your trains of thought. Painful as it may be, you have had the privilege of uncovering some of the usually unspoken worlds and fears and hopes of your students. You now realize that you cannot take middle class notions of dining room conversation about books and transport them into schools like Erasmus and George Washington. You know that students will see methods which seem not to meet their pragmatic goals (to pass the valued tests) as frustrations if not betrayals. You know that students do not necessarily appreciate choice and flexibility.

Let me now add to your critique of yourselves. Overall, I'd say that you over-value the notion of 'we all learn differently'. Cook's chapter, I think, could be seen as saying that when we learn deliberately we all learn in *the same way* (i.e. from intending to learn something, gathering what we know, forming plans, designs, hypotheses, trying things out and reflecting on how well we did). Of course, because we construct what we know out of our unique constructs, *what* is learnt will always differ across individuals. We can't legislate that all children will learn the same thing but we can get groups or whole classes learning in the same territory in relation to common questions.

My own reflections on negotiation suggest that we can overdo 'individualized learning techniques' in negotiation. In chapter 3 on curriculum composing, I suggest that we should generally try to have the *whole class* working on common territory, with groups and individuals negotiating assignments within an agreed whole class venture. Classroom organization will change from whole class, to small group, to individual work but always it will come back to consolidations of learning with the whole classroom community. In relative emphasis, I'd say that the whole community is more important than any one individual. I take from your letter that you may wish to argue with me. Concentrating on individuals may lead to an owning of private learning property. Concentrating on the whole community should lead to 'owning' each other and sharing the public knowledge property.

With regard to choice, let me put a different perspective. What difference would it make if, while valuing choice, you made your *first* focus as planners on where there will be *no choice*? What is it that you as teacher have no choice over; what is it that you *will not be diverted from* by your students (at least without a long fight); what learning processes (knowing how children learn best) will be insisted upon? Once you have clarified this for yourself, you are ready to go to the class and, 'up front', state your non-negotiables. This is what we will be learning about. This is what will be assessed. These are the non-negotiable processes. Now, how are we going to do this? Let us negotiate within these constraints.

I favour this approach because I believe that, whether stated or not, teachers have very firm *designs* on students. (What they want them to learn; how they'd like them to learn.) Better then for teachers to admit these designs to themselves and declare them as non-negotiables to the class than have them working as crypto influences.

I'm not saying that the teacher having declared non-negotiables should never deviate. I've quite often found halfway through some teaching that I had come to it with a wrong head-set. But if the teacher takes an explicit stand, then there's clearly something for students to come to terms with. If they don't like it and can't change it, at least they are forewarned and can develop their own coping strategies. If 'designs' are coming at them implicitly it is harder for them to be powerful in relation to those designs.

Stating clearly the *no choice* is a way of delivering the kind of structure and security that students seemed to be demanding of Ellen during the Atwellian experiment. This leads me also to state what might seem obvious. You can have *tightly* framed negotiation and *loosely framed* negotiation. In general, I'd advise beginners to begin with fairly tightly framed negotiation. The reading class may have responded better if Ellen had made it quite clear what she wanted them to learn and how she would be checking to see whether they'd learnt some of the things she wanted them to learn.

A strong part of teaching children how to become powerful is giving them experience in dealing with *no choice*. If you as a teacher are, for good reasons, laying a course on students, you can still be a 'radical negotiator' by rendering this teaching text problematic; by putting this course itself on the curriculum. 'This is what I'm laying on you. Let's talk about how you can cope with it'.

I hope you can see that negotiation is more about how to deal with power and authority and how to handle power than about choice and doing your own thing (an illusion anyway, since no one is autonomous). Romantic notions of Rousseauian 'natural learning' as the spirit takes you have no place in my pragmatic radical scheme of things. Schools are 'unnatural institutions'. Let us try in the long run to make them better places but in the meantime let's explicitly teach students how to deal with them.

I guess what I'm saying here is that rather than seeing yourself negotiating in some classes and not in others, you should, in my view, see yourselves negotiating *all the time* within more or less constraints. Ironically, the word 'negotiation', I realize, can seduce one into getting the wrong slant by foregrounding the 'what' of negotiation rather than the 'whether' or the spirit of negotiation. Negotiation is not the end. Powerful learning and know-how is. I've seen too many teachers being spuriously or cosmetically democratic in essentially undemocratic schools. Kids get mixed messages. Better to draw attention to the school's contradictions than to make believe that all is rosy and cozy.

Another area in which I'd like to offer some critique is in regard to a deafening silence in your letter. You don't mention what you seek in terms of *learning outcomes*. For better or worse you will only survive in schools if you *deliver* valued learning. Sadly, value is often represented in reductionist tests and assignments but the kids know this (as you learnt dramatically) and expect the teacher to collude with them in helping them to meet the tests. Now if you want the students to try for something richer than the tests, you need to make clear to yourself and then to the students what you are going to demand and expect. This needs to be explicitly signaled and *shown* also to the school (especially to the school principal). Negotiation has too often fallen into a hole in classrooms in Australia because it has been strong on process and fairly bankrupt in terms of *content* and *demonstrable outcomes*. Politically, 'negotiators' must show that they can not only get kids to do better on the conventional tests but that in addition they can go far beyond the tests.

'Negotiation' is the learning value-added regime that will save America and Australia from entering a new dark age! Let's trumpet it and show that it works! Anything transmitters can do, negotiators can do better. When it comes to learning outcomes, negotiators need to be beyond reproach in rigour, explicitness and *evidence*.

Two more areas of critique and I'll close. 'Coming clean'. A nice notion, but as you have learnt, highly problematic. 'Slide evenings' tend to be very boring. The one who has adventured wants to come clean about all the places he/she has been, indeed in frightening detail. I've argued that we need to take kids behind the facade of our teaching to reveal our theories, strategies and magical ploys and I still hold to this as a desirable and highly significant part of negotiation. *But* slide evenings are not likely to grip unless you as audience/viewers have a vested interest in what is being shown. Are you about to go, or have you been on a similar journey? Are these slides giving you information that will help you do something which you need/want/have to do? I made this analogy because it probably explains why students were turning off/tuning out when Stefanie was trying to unburden herself of information about herself and her intentions. If students see no purpose or have no anxiety about the territory being revealed then they will put their minds into neutral or think about things that are on their minds.

'Coming clean' generally makes human beings feel better whether they are Ancient Mariners or supplicants at a confessional. It can, however, be an intrusion or unnecessary burden on the 'confessees'. We need to be very clear about the functionality of what we divulge. What we provide needs to be *functional* for the students in helping them to do what they have to do and they must recognize this functionality. 'Coming clean' therefore is not an undifferentiated spilling of guts. It should be a carefully considered selection of what students need to know about my 'secrets' as teacher which will be functional in helping them cope with schools, with me and with the curriculum. Part of my fear is that this book may be a non-functional 'slide evening' for many teachers even though it is a whole-hearted 'coming clean' on negotiation.

I suspect that as students realize that they are genuinely being invited to be teaching apprentices if not co-curriculum planners, they will become more and more interested in the mind set and tricks and theories of the 'master magician'. Until curriculum and teaching/learning itself becomes a fascination for them it will be fairly pointless to 'come clean'.

Finally, a few words on the system (the grey eminence). Luckily, Stefanie has Marcia Lyles, a key administrator who is supportive and empathetic. But Marcia, herself, like all of us, is contained within a wider system within which there are powerful hegemonic forces; embedded values, sanctions, accepted myths and legends, economic imperatives. Within education we have to realize that a pedagogy based on behaviourist psychology and a view of knowledge as trans-mittable stuff permeates schooling and is reinforced in the wider society as an accepted view of what happens and should happen in schools. The learning theory and democratic principles underpinning 'negotiation' are at war with these em-bedded forces. Marcia and Stefanie and Ellen and I need to know our enemy in as much depth and with as much subtlety as we can muster so that we can nego-tiate and carve out room to operate within the containing structures and beliefs. We need to be politically strategic, cunningly empowered ourselves so that we in turn can pass on strategies to students. We are on about changing the ruling discourse and paradigms of education.

In this we are not alone. Allies may come from unexpected quarters. Busi-ness and industry, for economic reasons, need to bring about a similar revolution in factories. There is scope, despite some of our value differences, for us to get together.

Having this macro-system perspective, Ellen and Stefanie, you are also freed from some of the guilt that may accrue if you think that negotiating successfully is simply a matter of your skill as a teacher. You may be brilliant and still fail in your own terms because of the way that education is framed.

There are things we can do now and things that we will only be able to do when the governing frames have been changed.

Enough. If we judge our contribution to a conversation by what it provokes in 'the other' then, Stefanie and Ellen, you may conclude that you have certainly started something. You have well and truly pressed my buttons.

I can't wait to read your reply. Have I pressed any buttons or have I been soliloquizing?

With very best wishes.

Yours sincerely,

Garth Boomer

Note

1 Since writing this, I've had further talks with my New York colleagues. What I write here is a form of presumption. I am guilty of stereotypical depiction from afar. These students are individuals with multiple and varied intentions and anxieties. In many cases, though often hidden, they have a fierce desire to learn and a hunger for knowledge and know-how.

Reference

BOOMER, G. (1989) 'The helping hand strikes again?': An exploration of language, learning, and teaching', *English Education,* **21**, 3, October, pp. 132–151.

Chapter 8

Postscript

Stephanie Siegel and Ellen Skelly

Dear Garth:

After receiving your response, it was difficult to avoid writing our own response of some kind, although we felt as if we had already taken up enough of the book and your time. But you have massaged the insides of our heads. You gave us so much to reconsider, and by reconsidering we realized that we had already moved far beyond the stories in our first letter. We remain confused over which issues are the most pressing for the readers of *Negotiating the Curriculum: Educating for the 21st Century*, but there were some things too pressing for us not to say to you.

Although it may not have been clear in our original letter, we do realize that we're telling our stories, researching ourselves, and not focusing primarily on the stories of our students. But more and more as the students come to take center stage, we see how researching ourselves must be transformed into researching the zone where our intentions and those of our students must interact. Not surprisingly, it is as often difficult to unearth our own intentions as it is to reveal or tap into our students'. (We're not sure what verb to use here because knowing how to do this remains a mystery.) And we see ourselves as individuals against a system. So, separateness is a big issue for us.

We would also like to comment on your concern that we might be over-valuing the notion that 'we all learn differently'. Ellen believes that her:

> focus on the individual in my first attempts to negotiate (and indeed, teach) stemmed from my desire to see students as distinct individuals, not as an anonymous, unified group. My students each have a story to tell (as I have a story different from this one Stefanie and I have colla-borated on). Each student has unique needs, problems, and strengths. It seems easier to offer 'help' to one person that you know well than to view a group and offer 'help' that will benefit all.

In a system where the transmission view of teaching is so thoroughly en-trenched, our students often lose their identity. School has so little to do with who they are. They've learned early on not to bring themselves into the building. But how can we teach those whom we do not know? Another aspect of our emphasis on the individual might be a result of the institutionalized racism of American society. The schools we teach in are segregated because they're 'zoned schools' that reflect the population of the segregated neighborhoods in which they're situated. It's part of our political and moral stance to try to bridge the gap between the privileged life of the predominantly white teaching staff and those whom we teach. So we think there might have been a confusion between what's basically our attempt to welcome our students into school and your concern about our overemphasizing the individual.

But, in looking back on our own best educational experiences, it is true that our most exciting, most important learning occurred in groups. We learn best when we read, discuss, argue, write, reflect, and reread. So, another thing we have learned about learning is that it is social.

Both of us have a contradictory relationship to authority; we're either searching for it or pushing it away and never acknowledging fully the authority of our own voices. This problem heavily influences our problem with determining learning outcomes. We both wonder how external forces, like when teachers set up predetermined learning outcomes, act upon the intentions to learn of our students.

Our problems with asserting learning outcomes is complicated by not knowing an appropriate language or how to stage a learning outcome. The New York City school system has been dominated by the development lesson plan which uses the language of behavioral psychology to describe learning outcomes. The students 'should' or 'will' accomplish these objectives by the end of a forty-one minute class. What happens if the objectives are met sooner or later? What if the objectives are inappropriate?

In her further explorations of negotiated education for her Master's thesis, Stefanie has focused on learning outcomes more.

> I'm very reluctant to say what anyone else should or should not (or has or has not) learned. Shouldn't learning outcomes, too, be the result of shared intentions, collaboration, and reflection? But, perhaps this very take on things is a learning outcome? Intending to learn, something that's a stickler for me — how does one 'find out' those intentions? Just offering choice doesn't necessarily uncover this. What will?

> I think this matter of getting 'out' or 'into' intentions is a more complicated process than the negotiation success stories detail. Isn't investigation of the learning process key here? Where is their engagement with the choice? On what level is choice connected with intending to learn something? How things went this past semester really makes me doubt they're connected at all.

> When students withhold their intentions, classroom productivity suffers. Should I perhaps spend a lot of time on the learning process first before going to Cook's four questions (chapter 2)? The context of the questions needs to be shared too!

> I realize that when Susan Hyde says in chapter 4, '. . . we involved our classes in discussions about the learning process, the nature of the subject and learning that subject in the classroom' (p. 55), I don't have a clue as to what she did to engage students in this very difficult activity!

Garth, as we write this postscript, we begin another semester. We have clean slates which both excites and frightens us. New ventures signify hope. Beginnings can mean endless possibility. But, as we must fill the slates ourselves with our students, the prospect daunts us. We're beyond the 'just getting through from day-to-day stage'. But we're not yet at the stage where closure comes naturally. That's tied to our earlier hesitance regarding learning outcomes, our uncertainty with and problems we have had with the last of Cook's questions (chapter 2). 'How will we know, and show, what we found out when we're finished?'

After Ellen's students read and performed *Summer and Smoke*, she asked her classes: 'How can we show what we've learned?' and was silently stared at. Earlier in the project she had tried to have students reflect in writing at the end of class. Her students would have none of it. Ayisha said, 'How can we reflect on something when we're in the middle of it? That's something you do at the end'. After several days of having no one write during reflecting time, she gave up. And now we're back to Stefanie's sea of abandoned shards from many a promising ship. Following through with negotiated education demands more of students than does transmission. And without time, students and teachers find this too difficult to continue. Despite knowing that learning outcomes cannot always be accomplished in forty-one minutes, despair can ensue when one realizes that a succession of forty-one minutes also seems to 'produce' nothing.

> I think we failed at formulating a plan for showing that we've learned because we never answered the question: 'How will we go about finding out?' It seems to me that is the most engaging question of the four questions. The other three can be adopted by teachers and used as a way, for example, to generate writing topics. And in my attempts to answer, 'What do we want, and need, to find out?', with my students, the answers were so predictable as to make negotiation seem like a futile exercise. But, by intending to learn something, gathering what we know, forming plans and designs, hypothesizing, trying things out, and reflecting on how well we did, students become our apprentices. And learning becomes not just information to be spit back on the test. Learning in school becomes more like learning in 'real life'. And I guess because this is so new and complicated and difficult, much time must be spent on ground work.

Yours sincerely,

Stephanie Siegel
Ellen Skelly

Chapter 9

Negotiating Education

Jo-Anne Reid

Now that our course has ended I'm grateful and sad; grateful because without this course I'd probably still be in the dark about most things; sad because it is over and because now we'll be back to just students, not students with something to look forward to and be proud of, but just everyday students.

Donella

The idea of negotiation between teacher and students about what is studied in classrooms is not, of course, a new one. Like many teachers, I had often tried to give students a say in what they were doing in my classroom, as I believed that this had a lot to do with motivating the students to do the work I had planned for them around whatever topic or theme they selected. Although waiting to consult students about *what* we would be doing meant that I couldn't program in advance, this always seemed a minor problem when compared with the improved attitude of classes whose suggestions were taken into account before I commenced preparing a program for them.

Then, during the 'language and learning' conference in 1979, I came to realize that negotiating *what* students would study was not really such a worthwhile activity if, as I had been doing, the negotiation process stopped there. I found out that there was a way to negotiate also *how* students would work. Moreover, it was simple. Jon Cook (now in chapter 2) suggested four questions for teacher and students as collaborative curriculum developers:

1 What do we know already?
2 What do we need/want to find out?
3 How will be go about finding out?
4 How will we know and show that we've got there?

I decided to test it — to try to implement and evaluate this negotiation approach to curriculum development.

The Situation

As an advisory teacher I did not have any classes of my own to work with, and I had only one day each week that could be used for a project of this kind. But I was able to borrow a year 9 English class, which luckily had a double period on the day that suited me, even though I was limited to only eight weeks. There were thirty-four students, and I had sixteen periods in which to work with them. Thus this report does not deal with a 'normal' classroom experience, where students and teacher have had time to generate a relationship of trust and understanding on which to build.

I considered the following factors to be most important in preparing the project for this class:

- I did not know the children.
- They did not know me.
- They had no experience with small group work in English classes.
- Their teachers were interested and enthusiastic about the project but realistically unsure of how the students would react.
- Time was extremely limited.
- The school had a fairly extensive collection of resources and was close to community centres and other schools.
- I would not be available for 'between lesson' consultation or follow-up.
- The students were not academically 'successful'.

The time factor seemed all important, and I decided that to enable us to make the optimum use of the eight double periods available (i.e. to start work immediately) I would not negotiate the topic of our investigations with the class. The topic I decided to use was 'Kids in Schools', selecting this on the assumption that it was one situation that everybody in the class would:

- have had direct experience of
- have formed personal opinions on
- be able to relate directly to him/herself, and therefore
- find a non-threatening area to examine with a stranger.

The aims of the unit (in the International Year of the Child) were 'to allow the students to think, talk and write their way to understanding the purposes and workings of schools, and *their place* within them'.

Negotiation

How they were going to go about it had to be negotiated; and although I prepared a fairly detailed program of what I thought was going to happen around the four questions for curriculum negotiation, what *I* thought the students would want to learn was in fact astonishingly different from what *they* decided they wanted to learn.

I went out to see the class on the day before the project began, and explained to them what my intention was, why I had already chosen the topic, why I wanted to do this unit and how I was hoping it would be carried out, along with why I considered group work to be important. The students had never worked in small groups in English before, so I thought it necessary to do some preparatory activities (listening games) to establish 'rules' for successful small-group work. At the end of that introductory session, I asked students to decide whether they wanted to work on the project, and (probably because listening games are fun) all of them did.

Next morning the project began, with a tightly structured lesson to explain the curriculum negotiation model and begin the work. The students each received a handout sheet on group discussion, and a checklist of 'What happened' for them to evaluate their group's success at working together. The first question, 'What do we already know about kids in school?', generated a list of opinions (e.g. school is for learning, making friends, keeping us occupied, keeping us out of trouble, socialising, helping us get a job) through small group discussion, and this was stuck on the window for future reference. After this, students were asked to write individual lists of what they didn't know about school and what they would like to find out, and then to discuss these in their groups with the aim of making a list of things that the group *would* find out.

It is interesting to see how group discussion changed or refined the questions that individual students had written. Karen wrote:

Here is a list of things which I don't know about school:
1   Is it really worth it?
2   Do any teachers have nervous breakdowns?
3   Would any teacher ever hit a kid in school?
4   How often do they clean the toilets?

Karen

After discussion between group members, Karen's group decided that they would find out:

* How are we marked and graded?
* What does the principal do?
* How important is our schoolwork for getting a job?

In another group Fiona wrote that she didn't know:

* What other people in other years do.
* Why teachers have a special staff room.
* Why some people get good grades and others don't.
* What teachers think of me.
* Why teachers act differently towards different people.

Fiona

Her group's list of things they were going to find out was:

* What do teachers really expect from us?
* Why are facilities for teachers better than those for students?
* What do year 13 students do?
* What are schools like in other places?

When all groups had formulated lists of things they wanted to learn, they shared them with the rest of the class, and a composite list was drawn up:

What We Want to Find Out

Why do teachers treat people differently?
What are other schools like in different countries?
Why do teachers get all the luxury and the students don't?
Why isn't smoking allowed in schools?
What marks do we need to continue study?
Why should we work for an achievement certificate when we know there
    won't be many jobs when we leave school?
Does the principal do what he is paid for?
What do teachers really expect from us?
Why do we (or who makes us) change class every forty minutes?
What use is social studies?
What do students in years 11 and 12 do?
What do teachers think of us?
Who makes the decisions in school?
How have schools changed over the years?
What problems do students of today face in schools?
How are we marked and graded?
How does the principal react when a student is in trouble?

This, then was what the students *wanted* to find out. I was astounded at the differences between what I had anticipated the areas of study would be and what the students themselves decided they needed to know. On consideration of the questions they had generated, I was forced to admit that they did *need* to know much more of what they asked than of the 'study areas' I had devized. I reminded myself that my aim in planning this unit was to 'allow the students to think, talk and write their way to understanding the purposes and workings of schools, and *their place* within them'. It seemed that their questions were more likely to achieve that aim than the ones I had prepared 'for them', and that they were therefore more valid.

The next step was to implement the third part of the negotiation model: 'How do we go about finding out what we need to know?' The negotiation of the 'how' meant that the students (and myself as a newcomer to the school) had to be aware of what constraints or limits needed to be taken into account. I learnt from a whole-class discussion how the school bureaucracy worked (notes for being out of school; classroom, library and borrowing equipment, etc.). We decided that time was the most important constraint after the problems of actually moving out of the classroom.

Following this, the students went back into group discussion to work out a program for four lessons that would enable them to answer the questions they had set themselves. A transcript from a tape recording of one group's discussion shows that the boys not only were aware of the constraints within which they would have to work, but also had the ability to achieve what they wanted within them. They were also aware of the resources that were available to help them find the knowledge they were seeking, and of the need to organize *themselves* so that they could accomplish what they'd set out to do. Although they had little experience with small group talk in the classroom, they seemed to realize that the important thing was 'getting on with the job'.

Brett: Hey, wait, wait! The first one is, 'Why or who made us change classes every forty minutes?' (pause) Why don't we assign it to, say, two kids in the group? They go and do the research for the week, right, and find out what they can, and then when we come back, meet again on Friday, in this, we explain to the, um, rest of the group what we've found out.

Laurie: Yeah, that's a pretty good idea, that one.

Craig: How we gonna find it out, y'know, who, who we gonna ask?

Laurie: Yeah, well, those two people can work it out between them, but they'll have to let us know too.

Brett: But they'll have to ask somebody, you know, how did it come about. So who would they ask?

Craig: Well, you could, um ...

Laurie: You could, um ...

Brett: A topic like that would take a lot of work at home, right?

Laurie: Yeah, but it would also take, like, asking the senior masters of English, maths, social studies and science, 'cause they'd all know, y'know?

Craig: (in background) And the education department.

Brett: That, that'd be nothing ...

Laurie: And, and the education department ...

Brett: Yeah, you could contact the education department.

Laurie: Yeah, you could ...

Brett: (fast) They could, they've probably got records and everything.

Laurie: All we have to find out is ... um, yeah, oh no, oh sorry ...

Craig: Change classes every forty minutes, yeah, that'd be the education department. Or Mr Carlson [the principal].

Brett: See, yeah, they'd know. They'd have to. Somebody's bound to ask them that sometime.

Laurie: (louder) Or Mr Carlson.
          (pause)

Brett: Yeah.

Laurie: And what we all will be doing, the group together, is 'What 11th and 12th years do'.

Craig: Yeah, we can all do that.

Brett: Yeah.

Craig: All of us. You can ask Kainey, your brother Kainey.

Laurie: Kainey, yeah ...

Craig: Yeah, we could maybe, like, find out what one period they've got when we've got English today.

Laurie: Yeah, I'll find out, yeah. Find out.

Brett: And see if we could fix it up with the teacher and that, to get the video in there.

Craig: Yeah!

Laurie: Yeah. Get the video, and for, say, English, maths, social studies and science . . .

Craig: Yeah, we could film it. We could film them doing what they do.

Brett: Yeah, if they wouldn't mind. (pause) We'd have to get the whole class's permission though.

Laurie: Yeah.

Brett: Me and Craig . . .

Laurie: (despondently) That'd be a bit hard to do.

Brett: Me and Craig could . . . yeah, and, um, me and Craig could fix that, because we um, we both do media and we could book the . . .

After the small-group discussion a time for journal writing followed, to allow the students to reflect on what they had been doing. Laurie wrote:

Today's Work

A good day's work no-one interrupted; we're on tape. It's a good idea about videoing 11th and 12th Years 'cause I've always wondered what they learn. But I wonder if they'll act stupid (I know some that will). I wonder what the education department will think of us. I hope they'll help us. Does anyone ever use social studies? That's what we have to find out. If we do go to the education department we'll have to write out an interview so we know what to say.

Laurie

So, after only a short space of time the students, working in small groups, had generated their own programs around the topic and had begun the more involved task of organizing how to implement them. It seems apparent from Laurie's comment that the 'intention' to learn had already taken hold.

Implementation

At this point my planned and tightly structured lesson preparations had to be abandoned. Working things out in my journal that night, I wrote:

They understand that the onus is on *them*, which is great — and they all seem extremely keen to 'get on with it' — so much so that I'll have to adapt what I've already planned . . . What I think I'll do is leave the final part of the curriculum negotiation model — 'How will we show/know that we've learnt what we set out to learn?' — until they have the material they've collected to work with . . . On Friday, I think we'll have to spend about one period at least organizing what we need to gather of the information they're seeking.

As I look back, it was at this point that the 'intention to learn' became most apparent in the students, and I began to see that the process of negotiating the curriculum had created much more 'motivation' than I'd ever encountered before. After the next lesson I wrote:

> When I arrived, I was met by two groups that were already organized and ready to start the business of finding out what they want to know. The group that is researching what happens in years 4 and 5 had organized video equipment, teachers and classes, and was all ready to film. Fantastic! So much for all my organizing of what they were going to do today — the momentum had gained strength, and they were away — leaving me for dead! Anyway, the planning won't be wasted — it's just got to be reorganized a bit . . . So much seems to be going on, that I don't know whether I'm doing very much to help them at all.

That feeling, 'Am I helping them with their work, like a good teacher should?', was one that plagued me during the next two sessions. All I seemed to be doing was writing 'permission to leave the school' notes, checking that the four boys who were going to interview mothers in the shopping centre would not scare too many of them away just because of their appearance, driving a girl to the local primary school to arrange a survey of its students, talking about what they'd discovered so far, and wishing all the time that we had more time. I was afraid, too, that I was losing control of just *what* was going on. With the students working so much on their own, I had to rely on their once-a-lesson journal entries for much of the information I wanted:

> Last week [Friday 12/9/79] we went to the Cloverdale Primary School to interview grades 7, 6, 5 and 4 classes with handout sheets. What we set out to do is find out from other people, adults and children, what they think about school, and compare their opinions.
> It wasn't very difficult to organize it. All we did was give handout sheets to the students when we went to interview them in each class, and we went in town with a camera and tape recorder and interviewed some of the adults.
> Everything turned out good because all the people cooperated with us and were very helpful — and I think the students at the primary school enjoyed it, because they didn't mind getting out of schoolwork.
> From all the different things we found out . . .
>
> *Tanya*

As most groups had diverging interests (although the question of unemployment after leaving school worried a considerable number of groups), I found these journal entries a valuable record not only of what had gone on, but also of how the students had implemented the programs they'd drawn up for themselves:

19 October, 1979
Well a lot has been happening since the last time I wrote, which was about three weeks ago. The groups have had permission to go out of the school and try to find out things they didn't know before.
The first week our group went to Vic Park where we interviewed some people about jobs.

The next week we went into town and talked to managers of firms and just people in the street.

Then last week we went to the unemployment office and we wrote down a lot of jobs that were available to the public.

We are hoping to go to Belmont Forum, because they have set up an unemployment bureau in the centre of the shopping centre.

During the week I'm going to ring some unemployment places up and talk to them.

Wendy

Because of the time restraint, even though I knew that some groups had not completed all the tasks they had set themselves, I was compelled to cut short the time for research, so that the final part of the negotiation process could begin: 'How will we know/show that we have learnt what we set out to learn?' At the beginning of the project I had introduced the negotiation model in full and discussed each of the four questions, including this final one, in a general manner. At that stage I had suggested that one avenue for showing what they had learnt might be telling year 7 students at the nearby primary school.

Such is the innate power of teacher suggestions that already, before we'd even begun the sixth lesson, the students were saying, 'When do we go to Cloverdale?' and 'How much longer till we visit the grade 7s?' However, to give direction, and to emphasize the negotiation *process*, we went through with the task of organizing the responses to the fourth question, beginning with the problem I considered most important: 'Where are we now?' To help to solve this, I asked the students to write a brief statement that would help them to answer a further question: 'Where do we go from here?' Donella wrote:

The weeks have been interesting, and we all have expressed our will to learn. Our group has been very cooperative in working together. We, in our group, reached one conclusion and set out to find others' views on education, combine it with our own, and come to one main conclusion.

Setting out on the second week of our programme, we were determined to find out from people their views, if any, on what we learnt and how we learnt it. Most people reasoned that schools were like factories, mass-producing average-level students with no experience in how to handle interviews and attitude. This is something which all the workers agreed, not only them but the shoppers as well.

They agreed with us that the whole education programme should be changed to suit different types of students with different ideals for their working career to come.

Donella

Donella's attempts to use the knowledge she had gained to make her own thesis 'Most people reasoned that schools were like factories...' can be seen when her statement is compared with Karen's, from the same group:

First of all, we set out to ask people what they thought of school (mainly adults), asking them questions like:

1 Have you any children?
2 Do you think schooling is better than before?
3 Could it be improved? And so on.

We also took a trip over to K Mart and went into different stores, asking people with jobs how they got them. We asked them questions.

1 Did you need your Achievement Certificate for getting a job?
2 Is your work satisfactory, such as good pay and hours?
3 What questions were asked?
4 Do you think there should be a special course for jobgetters?

We organized a special set of questions for employees and a special set of questions for parents or adults. Then we took a trip across to K Mart and asked questions. We stopped adults and went into shops. The response was very good and the questions were answered very nicely. All in all, we found out this:

1 The majority of jobs didn't need the Leaving or Achievement Certificate.
2 You did need experience.
3 Grammar did help get a job.
4 Work was quite satisfactory.
5 There should be a special course in education in getting a job.
Karen

This activity also served the purpose of focusing the students' attention on the job they were doing, so that their next small group task, that of organizing how they were going to present their findings, was not overly impeded by the fact that it had been a week since they'd last worked on the project.

The fact that I was not there all the time was a problem I found increasingly irksome over the eight weeks of the course. Although the teacher I was working with, Laurie Crouch, had planned the first four lessons of each week around the topic (study of a novel, short stories and work on improving group discussion techniques) the gap between lessons and the short time available within lessons made me realize how much better I could have handled things had I been a 'regular teacher' and not a 'once-a-week visitor'.

However, the students' intentions to learn and their continued interest were more than compensation for this. After the fourth lesson I wrote:

... once again they amazed me. Laurie says they're wonderful during the week now ('so well motivated'), that he's become very excited about the project too. And he's great — he's organizing an excursion for them, and helping them to prepare for their investigations during the week — running off things they need etc.

Presentation

The students were also very aware of time limitation, particularly now that the project was drawing to a close. I had blackboarded a list of 'things to be done' by the groups to organize their presentations, so that they knew what I anticipated would be achieved by the end of the lesson. I had given each group a scrapbook, just in case it was needed, and discovered that six of the seven groups felt the need to use it. In discussing how they were to tell the year 7 students what they'd been doing and what they had learnt, these year 9 students decided that, in case of nerves 'on the day', they would like to have something on display if their oral presentations failed them:

> In our presentations to the kids at Cloverdale Primary, we'll have a scrapbook, in which this will include pictures, writing and a few bits which are a bit hard to explain in just talking. We shall also have a separate part for each person to talk to the kids. This talk will include what we have been doing, the things we have found out and what we have learnt altogether. Each person will be able to tell of these things and how they went about it and the experiences they have had.
>
> Then after we have presented the kids with the scrapbook and our separate talks, we will have a separate section for the kids to ask questions.
>
> *Karen*

A couple of enterprising groups, predicting their nervousness, solved the problem in another way:

> ... but now it's Friday — and we are all working out what we are going to do next week when we present our project to the kids at Cloverdale Primary. Our group has decided to make a tape and just hand the book around. Jackie has been picked to talk, but we are all going to work out what she is to say. One thing the group has decided on is to try to tell the kids how important it is to get a good Achievement Certificate. 'Cause a lot think it doesn't matter. We are going to ask questions like:
>
> 1   What do you think school is for?
> 2   What is their idea of high school?
> 3   What job would you like when you leave school?
>
> *Wendy*

Their ingenuity seems to have impressed Dany:

> We hope we can tell the primary school students exactly what we have done and researched into. Some of the kids are going to put all the information they have collected onto a tape and play it on the tape recorder to the primary school class, instead of having to stand up in front of the whole class and tell them what they have done. Our group has got a scrapbook in which our info is.
>
> *Dany*

Leaving the selection of what they would put in their scrapbook up to them resulted in this entry in my journal that day:

... they seem excited about what they've done, as well as enthusiastic about getting it ready to present. It's good to see them taking pride in what they're doing, too, even though it is 'only' in a scrapbook. I felt in such a good mood this morning that I was a little disappointed that they didn't seem to 'need' me much at all. Sure, a few groups had questions to ask every now and again, but most of them just go on with their work without any assistance from me — in fact I probably disturbed some groups by asking questions myself!

The way in which the students viewed their purpose in talking to the year 7 students (and beyond that) interested me.

Next week is our debut at Cloverdale Primary. Our group is going to try to give them the benefit of our experience over the past six weeks, try to get them to understand just how important education and attitude is when applying for a job when you know you have to get one. We'll have a group discussion and let them ask as many questions as time will allow. Our group has definitely benefited from our past experiences and we hope that we are capable of getting the point across to them — but our work isn't finished. When these eight weeks are through we are going to see if we can get a new course added to the subjects in school about attitude and experience, so that they have some idea of what to expect when they go for an interview. We may not get a chance to benefit from the course but our experiences have helped us to see the problems which face us when we go out to secure a place in the work force.

Donella

My main job that week was the organization of the trip to the primary school: revisiting the headmaster, checking out rooms, noting what equipment was needed etc. I wrote that night:

There are two grade 7 classes, so we'll halve the groups so that one lot goes to one room, one to another, and then swap at half-time so that they'll have 'two showings'. I hope that will work out. I rang Claudia [the librarian] and have booked all the video equipment, two tape re-corders, extension cords, double adaptors etc., so I don't think I've forgotten anything important. It's up to the kids now to produce the goods. The group who were interviewing Mr Carlson [the principal] this morning had great success according to both them and him, so I'm pleased about that. I hope that they don't expect to play it all to the year 7 kids — it may be a bit boring for them. The boys are so enthusiastic that I feel they might — they were quite anxious this morning that they might not have enough time to do it all with the primary kids. Perhaps they could be on their own in one room and all the other groups together might make up the same time in the other room! (And I don't really think I'm joking!)

During that week I worried about Friday, but apparently the students didn't. The problem of a child who had been suspended from school and then returned to class the week before, and was consequently 'out of things', was solved by giving him the task of compiling a questionnaire to present to the audience after the presentation, so that the groups could judge how effective they'd been. Each group formulated one question to evaluate itself; he collected and compiled these, adding an introductory comment. His job in the proceedings was to explain and distribute the questionnaire. However, they were nervous. My journal says:

> Arrived at school at 8:15am and the video boys were already there, asking if they could go over to the primary school and get the equipment all set up for their show . . . [The class] had five minutes of last-minute preparation/ fear, and then we set off.

The two-room set-up worked well, with Laurie and me able to be with one or the other half of the class. By sheer good luck the timing was perfect, with each group being able to present its speeches, tapes, scrapbooks, charts or videos; ask for immediate comment/questions from the class; and then, after each session, move among the year 7 students while they answered the questionnaires, 'to help them' and talk about the scrapbooks:

> . . . last Friday [2 November] we went to Cloverdale Primary School to express all the work we've done to two grade 7 classes. All the grade 7 students seemed to enjoy it, as well as cooperating with us. The ideal school Denise and I designed became a big interest to students. Many questions were asked as the scrapbook went around the class to other students. At first we were scared to talk about the work we've done in the scrapbook, but when the second class came we got the hang of talking to them. The students asked many questions about the high school. As we were at the front we all took turns of speaking to the students, but the words just ran out of our mouths, and we were saved from embarassment.
>
> *Tanya*

They had had no time to rehearse their presentations, so I consider Tanya's comment about its being better the 'second time' to be very valuable.

Evaluation by Students

Through the project, I was anxious to 'teach' the students the value of preparation: that a lot of work often needs to be done to produce a final product that is satisfactory to both ourselves and others. Many of the activities the groups carried out required redrafting of written materials to suit a particular audience, such as:

- letters to the principals of the primary school and a nearby secondary school to request permission to survey students
- questions to primary school students ('Will they understand words like "Achievement Certificate"?')
- questionnaires for use in the local shopping centre, among teachers at school and among students of their own age group

- preparation of speeches for the 'presentation'
- summaries, news reports, personal remembrances etc. for inclusion in the group scrapbooks, again for year 7 students.

Because of the nature of the exercise, I found the students very willing to attack the tasks of redrafting and perfecting these pieces of writing. The reasons seem obvious: there was a purpose for their writing, and it had to be good enough to serve that purpose. It may even be significant that almost no student commented on the amount of preparation, writing and redrafting that took place. It did not seem like 'work' to them because they were involved. The only student comment related to this came from Ritchie, who wrote:

It was pretty easy because we did our work beforehand and we knew most of the answers to the questions.

Ritchie

The writing of a journal as a record of what they were doing with their programmes was not considered an onerous task either, even though it was teacher imposed. In her evaluation, Donella wrote:

I think that all the work we did was interesting and good, the thing which amazed and frightened me was that Miss Reid got me to write journals when that's what I most hate about English. I think it's because there was so much happening and I could only express myself by getting it down on paper. Now I'm finding that I don't hate it, maybe just the opposite.

Donella

Most students took it as a matter-of-fact occurrence. They were writing mostly for themselves, so that they would easily remember 'where they were', and at the same time they knew that I would read their journals if they decided to give them to me.

Some students used their journals for personal writing outside the course ('I'm not s'posed to be writing now, but I've had a terrible week . . .'), and others (most) merely used their ten minutes per lesson for factual recall of what they'd done. However, when asked if they liked having the time to think about what they'd been doing, and to organise their thoughts on paper, *all* the students responded positively.

Here again, ten minutes per lesson was not, I found, enough time to gain the full value from a journal entry. I found myself writing with the class for ten minutes, always aware that I couldn't follow through things I was thinking about and writing down, because I wanted to use the ten minutes as efficiently as possible. So I was not able to explain the points I was making. I had too much to say in too little time. I feel that this was reflected in the students' writing also:

I think that it was a good experience and idea. I'm sure that I've learnt a lot about unemployment, things I never knew before. I thought it was good the way we were able to go places and do things we usually can't do. I only wish we could have more time to be able to go places. During

this last week we tried to fix up the scrapbook, and discuss the questionnaire and do the questionnaire. I'd rather do what we've been doing
than write essays all the time and do what other classes are doing. I just
think that the last eight weeks was well worth it.

Mary

As I read this journal entry/evaluation, and others like it, I was faced once again
with the realization that if this project had been conducted by a teacher and class
who worked together all the time, not just once a week, the students would have
been able to spend more time reflecting and writing for themselves, and would
probably have gained more from these very important activities. However, even
in this limited form, I consider that the exercise was valuable. Students showed
that they understood and enjoyed the process by which their work was generated,
where they were actively involved in the learning process:

... and I think that it has been very good for me in the way that instead
of being dished up a lesson by a teacher that has been explained and
then we've been told to do it then it all turns out the same. We have to
go out and do it on our own backs.

Fiona

Their involvement also meant other rewards, mostly on a personal level, for
me as well as them. I learnt that trusting students to 'do the right thing' without
my supervision was not something that came easily to me. I was not prepared for
(although I had been told about) the dedication or commitment to a task that
arises once a learner *intends* to find out. I was skeptical of plans to 'go to town
to the Unemployed Workers' Movement' in a car driven by 'Vicki's brother'. I
believe that I had a right to be concerned, and to make my concern felt, but I am
grateful that the students recognized that concern for what it was, and did not
abuse their 'freedom'. In Kellie's evaluation of the project, she echoed these
feelings.

Today is the last day of our eight weeks. I enjoyed it as well as learnt
from it. We have worked hard and have received good results. I really
enjoyed how we were trusted to go and do things by ourselves, e.g. Fiona
D. and I and two other girls went into town by ourselves with about a
thousand dollars' worth of equipment and did some filming.

Kellie

If students are made to feel that they are trustworthy — that they are able,
through perseverance, effort and availability of resources, to achieve what they
set out to achieve — then they *can* actively control their own learning. Their sense
of achievement and pride in the work they have done are their own reward.

The overriding feeling that came from reading evaluations of the course was
a positive sense that students found the work they did to be valuable to them:

Well, finally it's all over and to tell you the truth I'm really glad to have
been able to do what I've been doing as I've really enjoyed it a lot. I
think that in these past lessons I've learned more about my school and

other people than a lot of the time I've been here. I hope that in the future other students have the same chance to do this activity as if they learn half as I did the teachers and parents should be really proud of them.

Fiona

Evaluation By Questionnaire

The positive comments made by students after reflecting on the course were, of course, very pleasing, but to enable me to evaluate the negotiation process I decided that something more was needed. In evaluating the preplanned programme, I had usefully applied Garth Boomer's checklist for evaluating planning (chapter 3, p. 38). I now adapted this, preparing forty questions for the students in what I hoped was appropriate language.

Begging another two lessons with the class, I gave each student a copy and asked them to discuss the questions in their groups for one lesson. Then I called for volunteers (one from each group) who would like to complete the questionnaire in writing. In this way I considered that the whole class would be involved, while no individual child would feel threatened by having to fill out a questionnaire of the length (and bulk) of the one I'd prepared.

Although the recorders' responses to some questions indicated that my transformation of the questions into language that could be easily understood by the students was not particularly successful, I feel that their comments did reflect on the quality of the curriculum we had negotiated. The following examples give an indication of the student response:

Q: Were you able to recognize what you were going to do?
A: Yes, that also was very clear from the word go.
Q: Did you understand why some things (e.g. the topic) could not be negotiated?
A: Yes, certain restrictions were ahead and we planned around them.
Q: Were you aware of the constraints you had to work under? Can you think of some of them?
A: The time wasn't very much, how far you could go, who you were permitted to see. Yes, probably the most important was time, time was very short.
Q: Were you allowed to share what you already knew about the topic early in the program?
A: Yes, we frequently had inter-group discussions about this topic.
Q: Were you able to tell stories or memories about the topic to other students?
A: Yes, most of my friends knew exactly what we did from week to week. Yes, you were permitted to tell that in your journal.

The question of children's being able to share what they already know has been dealt with earlier in my report of the project. Looking back, I feel that the students did not have *enough* time to indulge in exploratory talk before getting down to the business of achieving their aims. Although time for exploratory talk (and writing) was given in the early weeks by the class's English teacher, I consider that the 'unnatural' situation of working with a visiting teacher was a disadvantage in this area, particularly to me, as I was not able to share in a part of the learning process that I consider to be extremely valuable.

Q: Did you feel that anybody in the room was more important than another?

A: No, never, that we all had equal rights etc.

Q: Were you encouraged to seek help and support from other students?

A: We were encouraged to seek help and support from whoever we wanted.

Q: Did the teacher act as 'manager' in the classroom — organizing time, how the lesson went etc.?

A: Yes, she did, but we organized ourselves sometimes.

Q: Did the teacher share in and do some of the tasks you were asked to do?

A: Yes, when we wrote journals she wrote too.

Q: Do you think the classroom 'atmosphere' was made better by working in this way?

A: Yes, 'cos everyone worked together.

Q: Would you like to work like this all the time?

A: Yes, because I think that you learn more when you're doing things yourself.

The question of a 'teacher who is a trusted adult, co-learner and senior curriculum planner', not just the disseminator of information, was one that struck me as very important. The role of teacher as 'model' cannot be underestimated, in both encouraging and extending students. While I strongly believe that curriculum negotiation has an extremely important role to play in educating students to become independent (and ongoing) learners, I feel that it is important to stress here that there are some things that *cannot* be negotiated, in any subject discipline. It is the teacher's job to make these professional judgements.

Looking Back

Now, after describing how things happened (and in the process also of describing what actually happened), it is time for me to ask myself: 'So what? What does it prove? What does it mean?' I consider that the success of the project, considering the limitations of time, says the following things.

• Students are responsible and trustworthy people who, if allowed to use their sense of responsibility in a meaningful way, do become independent learners, capable of generating and following through a quest for knowledge and understanding that will prove intrinsically rewarding.

• Once students have become active participants in their own learning, the role of the teacher must change. No longer is the teacher able to be the One Who Knows, from whom students, in return for polite respect and good behaviour, will (somehow) glean the Knowledge that the teacher deems important. When students are devizing their own questions, and using their own powers of reasoning and attack to find the answers to these questions, the teacher's role finally becomes one of Educator, that of leading the students further on their way of understanding.

• This does not mean that the role of the teacher becomes less 'important' in any way; in fact the duties and responsibilities must increase. Not only must the teacher act as Facilitator (helping students find information, suggesting alternative directions, providing experiences or materials of which the students are not aware etc.), but he/she must also act as Enricher and Extender of the resources and experience, aiming always to improve the *quality* of both.

• For students to become involved in the learning process, there seems only one real necessity: that they perceive a sense of purpose in what they are doing. Aimless activity, whether planned by teachers or students, is merely a waste of time. As I mentioned earlier, writing and talking to real audiences for a real, understood purpose appears to be an excellent vehicle for improving the quality of students' work.

• The importance of evaluation cannot be ignored. Feedback, in the sense of 'how I'm going', is important in the learning process. Again, the purpose and quality of work must be taken into account. Students communicating with real audiences will receive 'real' feedback; they can judge the success or failure of their efforts from the reactions they receive. Work that is carelessly or hurriedly prepared will just not do when it has to serve a purpose other than being submitted for marking and comment by the teacher.

• While this may result in what appears to be less formal 'marking' by the teacher, it does not mean that the teacher's role in the evaluating process is diminished either. The teacher needs to be continually evaluating and assessing — his/herself and the teacher's role, the program, the students' attitudes and output, the quality of the experience — and the teacher's professional judgments on these will determine his/her actions. (Is more structured input necessary? Is there enough variety in the activities? Are certain tasks beyond the capabilities of the students? Are the less able students experiencing difficulties? Is there scope for more demanding work to extend the more able students?)

• Reflection and allowing students time to reflect upon what they have learnt are important. The process of reflection, reviewing and making sense out of what has been done is essential if real learning is to take place. Providing students with time and a means of reflecting upon their experiences (such as a journal or an evaluative questionnaire) gives them not only a method of understanding what they've done and of making it a part of themselves — their knowledge — but also a basis from which further learning can develop.

In conclusion, it must be stressed that the importance of a 'controlled', businesslike atmosphere is paramount. The learner's surroundings must be conducive to learning. If this is the case, the attempt to help students become active participants in their own learning will be rewarding to both the students and their teachers.

Chapter 10

Negotiating the Curriculum: Action Research and Professional Development

Jo-Anne Reid (with Betty Thwaites)

Introduction

When chapter 9 was completed ten years ago, I was convinced that the only real educative work I had done in my career as a teacher had taken place with that particular class, but that it had been in some way out of bound or abnormal — not acceptable within the institutional practices of secondary schooling, as I knew them. But it was 'liberation pedagogy' for me as a teacher — because for the first time I had felt the satisfaction of self-initiated professional development. I want to focus this present chapter on the question of professional development. I want to explore the experience of the *teacher* involved in negotiation and the role of classroom action-research as a means of organizing and validating the experience of teachers' learning within the constraints of the institution.

Looking back over a decade now to the time I wrote that chapter, when I worked on the texts I had collected during my action-research into negotiating the curriculum, it is clear that the task of representing my experience as a teacher in a new textual form for other teachers to read became the site for my learning and professional growth. More than just 'being there' in the classroom, it was the act of writing — the selection, review and critique of what I had experienced and the construction of a version of that experience for others — that helped me come to understand what had happened. The texts I had to work with — the students' journals, my own journal, their scrapbooks, letters, video and audiotapes, as well as my lesson plans and program — were all in themselves *representations* of the lived experience we had undergone; they were not the experience itself. The text of chapter 9, the representation I made public at the time, was therefore already a reconstruction of these representations of reality. It was a site of reflection, a site of growth; it was my learning time, and it was only the fact that this site for learning was available to me that I did come to advance my understanding of what it was I was doing and would continue to do in classrooms to improve the quality of the educational experience on offer there.

Traditionally, as I did, most teachers who want to engage in what is recognized and valued as 'professional development' do so outside of the schools in which they teach — often returning to their schools to research their own experience as part of the requirements of outside agencies. It was just in this way, in 1989, while pursuing part-time postgraduate studies in educational research, while herself at Belmont High School, that Betty Thwaites encountered the text of chapter 9. Intrigued by the coincidence and strangeness of her professional reading relating directly to the school in which she was currently teaching, she decided to test the idea of negotiation once again as action-research into her own teaching in the same school ten years later. The opportunity to 'replicate' the earlier experiment and examine these two experiences (even though differentiated by time and the obvious changes it has brought to the social and educational climate of the school) presented itself as an exciting way in which to review and evaluate the idea of 'negotiating the curriculum' within the framework of the action-research literature she was studying. Betty contacted me in the hope that I would have some further information about how the original unit had been planned, structured and developed and devized her own project around those original lesson plans. I was equally enthusiastic about the project; but as I too have been made different by the last ten years, reflection on Betty's paper now leads me to suggest that investigating negotiation in classrooms can, and ought perhaps, be seen as a pedagogical imperative — for teachers as well as students' learning — as a means by which the bounds of our own development can be expanded.

This chapter provides my construction of Betty's report on curriculum negotiation as I now read it, from a particular and of course 'partial' position as interested outsider. It begins with a brief description of, and Betty's own reflections on, her project reproduced from the report of the investigation which *she* presented as part of the requirements for her course of study. Following this, I then want to work with Betty's text in a deliberate attempt to highlight the value of reflecting on and rethinking existing representations of classroom practice in the service of our own professional development. To this end, purposefully 'playful', I actually *reconstruct* Betty's report. This is, I work with her text, rewriting it in such a way as to generate a set of potentially new readings which allow us to look at it in a new light in order to examine the implications of curriculum negotiation for our own classroom life and labor. The particular concern of the reconstructed text is for the place and development of the teacher as 'professional' within the context of negotiated classroom action and the associated area of classroom action-research. For you, the reader of this chapter, the invitation therefore is to negotiate your own reading *between* the two texts offered — one a version of Betty's classroom experience as she read and reported it; the other a deliberate intervention in and reinvention of the classroom experience. My major concern is to provide a reflective account of how teachers might be able to negotiate the slippery path of professional development along which, all too often, we are left to lurch.

The idea of negotiating the curriculum is at base an invitation to lay one's pedagogy, the teaching 'self', on the line and in so doing watch it *change*, perhaps, as a result of one's response to the intervention of influences 'other' than the teaching self. In the same way, classroom action-research provides the teacher with a means of scrutinizing her existing practices and systematically modifying them in the search for a better understanding of the inventions and interventions of classroom discourses and actions. Both these practices obviously involve the teacher in a certain amount of risk. With negotiation, the risk may lie in the threat of the unknown — a latent potential for disruption and chaos. With action-research, it may lie in the threat of the unknowable — a possibility of uncovering without understanding what it is we have found, or are doing, without being able to define what it is that we have produced.

But with both action-research and negotiation I suspect that it is this very risk that enhances the quality of the classroom experience for the teacher: It's the tentative pushing at the 'outside of the envelope' that gives an adrenalin surge of terror/pleasure long enough to satisfy our personal and professional need to step outside the bounds of everyday experience and test ourselves against our own ideals. In other words, it may well be addictive! One can get high on the thrill of negotiation and the pleasures of collaborative action-research. And such rewards are also addictive, in that the increasing awareness of one's own teaching behaviors and action-knowledge of the classroom arising out of these communal enterprises results in a conscious and spiraling development of expertise and effectiveness. 'Professional' development, then, becomes very much a source of 'personal' satisfaction. Action-research and negotiation together make for professional development that is both powerful and pleasurable for all of us concerned with developing a reflective and critical approach to our own teaching/learning practices. In addition, the practices of the institution generally are also brought into question through such a critical reflection.

Reading/Writing: Negotiation as Action-Research

An illustration of the reciprocal benefits arising out of systematic classroom investigation of our efforts at curriculum negotiation can be seen in the following account of Betty Thwaites's work at Belmont High School. Betty's research aimed, in most respects, to replicate the project reported in chapter 9, although she chose to work with a group of fifteen year 8 students who were streamed into Belmont's 'Educational Support Unit' — a special class for learning disabled, low-and under-achieving students — and who were withdrawn from mainstream classes for the major academic subjects.

From the outset, therefore, there can be no question of simply comparing the two projects in terms of 'results'. Using the same topic and working from the same program around the four collaborative curriculum development questions outlined by Cook (chapter 2), Betty's attempt to negotiate 'education' for 'kids in schools' was, like my own, primarily action-research designed to examine whether a negotiated curriculum would be an effective means by which she could improve her students' attitudes to, and outcomes from, small group learning. Betty had a wider purpose, though; she was also hoping that such an intervention into their usual classroom processes might help to improve students' confidence in taking risks, in learning by their mistakes, and in involving themselves in collaborative work projects. The aim of her research was to effect change in the areas she considered desirable — to improve the working conditions of the classroom she shared with this group of educationally disadvantaged students.

Betty's overall plan of action followed the earlier study closely. She began with a brainstorming session for the formulation of responses to the question of 'How do we learn best?' and then divided the class into groups to write their responses on wall charts. The students, combining their group findings into one class chart, concluded that 'communication' was the key to how they learned best and placed a major emphasis on 'asking questions'.

Then, using a similar format of group discussion, the students compiled a chart of responses to the first negotiation question, 'What do we know already?' and went on to write individual lists of what they didn't know about their school and would like to find out. These were discussed as a class and a new list, this time of 'questions for investigation', was compiled. The class decided that they would have to make some sort of presentation of their evidence and conclusions in order to respond to the fourth negotiation question, but that they would wait to see what they would find out before making any final decisions about presentation. Betty initiated journal writing for herself and her students to allow for systematic reflection on what they had done as well as to plan each new stage of their research. After reflection on the questionnaires they had developed to use with each of the groups they wished to interview, the class made modifications to both the wording and order of some questions.

Their questionnaires were prepared in order to suit what the students saw as four different groups of respondents, each of which seemed suitable to provide answers to the questions the class had posed about high school and the transition they would have to make, eventually, into paid employment. The students decided to use the questionnaires they had prepared as the basis for these interviews recorded on audio or videotape for later analysis. Betty noted, in relation to this, that:

When they then realized that three of our members could not read well enough to ask the interview questions from the prepared sheets, it was decided that these students begin as 'technicians' and operate the tape recorders whilst listening to the questions being asked. This way they built up confidence and eventually asked if they could ask the questions. Their backup person on the tape recorder would be there to help out if they got stuck with a question.

They all decided it would be best to begin on home ground, at school, for the first set of interviews. It seems they were far less worried about making mistakes in front of teachers than in front of students from other classes. Then, with their confidence built up, they decided it was time to begin asking [other] students. They began at their own school, went on to Cloverdale Primary School and then were ready to take the big step into the unfamiliar territory of Kewdale High [a neighboring school].

They were very nervous when we went there with the video camera and a tape recorder for backup. We waited there for a long time looking for the teacher who had forgotten we were coming. Great groans of agony and disappointment — but soon fixed up when we made another appointment for the next day. All went well the next day; we arrived at Kewdale's Educational Support Class and the students were relieved to find a class very similar to our own.

Reflecting on this later, Betty made the following comments:

The questionnaires were used to keep some sort of uniformity within each group. The taped responses were used as backup as the students knew they would be unable to write quickly and wanted to keep the flow of the interview going. Three of the students would not have been able to write any of their responses because their writing skills were so poor. No one was to feel disadvantaged in any way and after acting as 'technicians' helping the more able interviewer a couple of times, these less able students felt confident to 'take the risk' of being interviewer and reading the questions (backed up by a more able student in case of need). The outcomes of these exercises in terms of confidence builders were enormous. The students enjoyed taking the risk, learning by mistakes, in a non-threatening atmosphere. These exercises . . . finally [extended] to interviewing the public at the shopping center.

The responses to the interview questionnaires were collated for each group where possible. The cooperation and collaboration among students that had become apparent to Betty during the 'finding out' stage of the project continued back in the physical environment of the classroom itself as the students shared the task of preparing their information for presentation.

Her reflection at the end of the project that her students' experience of small group learning had previously 'been almost nonexistent, partly because group work had [in her previous experience] usually meant working with someone at the same academic level', shows a marked shift in her own professional knowledge as a result of this action-research.

This was often difficult to organize as these students were at such vastly different levels and their lack of confidence and experience meant that if they were put into groups they would often allow the more enthusiastic or more able students to do all the work. The motivation created by the knowledge that this was their own research to learn what and how they wanted, around the set topic, was enough to let them relax and form work groups according to their interest in the particular task at hand. They quickly understood that it was up to them how to find out what they had all decided they wanted to know. The fact that teacher and students were able to negotiate the curriculum gave them the freedom and the impetus to plan, organize and act upon their ideas.

It would seem that for the students, at least, the experience of *collective* endeavor towards a communal goal within the social and situational context of the school as they already knew it was in many ways a new experience — and one that had the potential to change their perceptions of themselves as 'students' within the school.

The taking of risks was certainly a major step in these students' lives, and when they came through this experience unscathed, their confidence rose. Mistakes made were discussed openly with the group and solutions, or 'how to do it better' strategies were worked out between them. Their enthusiasm for this work never faltered and they would often begin a session in class with 'What's next?' or 'Where do we go from here?'

They were already thinking about how they would show what they had done. They also wanted to ask questions to evaluate themselves and find out how effective others thought they had been in what they had done.

Just as 'my' group of students had done ten years previously, this group decided to present their findings to audiences other than the teacher. Betty's class chose a much wider range of audiences that 'my' group had been able to and were thus in a position to judge the results of their efforts on a number of different viewers:

Cloverdale Primary School was the venue for our first showing of our video and posters explaining the responses gained from asking questions of other people. The students set up the television monitor and the video player and set things rolling. The primary students were pleased to see themselves on television, keen also to see others and to hear their responses to questions the same as [those they had answered].

The presentation visit to Kewdale High School took a very similar form to that at Cloverdale except that the students were now presenting to a peer group [who] were interested in the overall aspect of the survey and in the results — particularly, answers to questions they had not known themselves. They were interested in what we had been doing and how we had been able to do it, expressing an interest in doing something similar, as there were some things they wanted to know about their school and their 'transition to work' prospects. [Like the Cloverdale students], they were also asked to complete evaluation forms.

[These showed that] many thought the students researching this topic could benefit from it because they learned from it; others thought they had benefited because they got to do interesting things like going to shopping centers and videotaping people. These respondents thought that all students could learn something from the class's presentation, though answers to the question of what they had learned were varied and were often related to peoples' jobs that they did not previously know about. Most thought the students 'did quite a good job' even though 'they acted nervous', but [the members of this audience] 'were sure that they had enjoyed it'. . . Some were quite sure they would like to do something similar with their [own] class but others were just as sure they would be too nervous.

'Now for our own school' was the slightly nervous response when the class reflected on what was next. It seems when trying things out for the first time they felt more comfortable within the known area of the school, but when the testing time for their presentation came they preferred to go first to the younger 'unknowns', then peer unknowns as practical confidence builders . . .

The presentation to [members of the Belmont] staff had to be done in very small groups around the television in the staff room. These teachers enjoyed the video — they had not been a part of video interviews. They were amazed at the confidence with which these 'Special' students had handled the whole thing. They had not seen behind the scenes when some students had realized that they could not read well enough to conduct an interview alone. They did not see the students practising and memorizing questions from a key word helped on by a more capable partner, the tape recorder technician. They were able to see how the group had grown together as cooperative members.

Reflecting on this feedback later with the class was an important part of Betty's plan and allowed the students' own understandings of the learning process to be considerably enhanced. At the same time they were able to articulate the feeling of satisfaction with their own efforts and success that is so vital as a foundation for further efforts and their perception of themselves as learners.

Most [of the class] later agreed that this was because they were working on 'their own special survey', they were finding out what they wanted to know and going about it how they thought best. The ESU group were motivated because they realized the responsibility was theirs, that it was part of being independent. They were made to feel that they had been trusted to carry things out properly. . . .

It is not possible or appropriate to calculate to what extent the 'success' of this study compares to that of the original study. The process by which the students obtained the survey results is far more important than the results themselves. The students have demonstrated that they are capable of independent learning, able to decide what and how they will learn — as active participants towards their goals. They have shown by their teamwork that they are capable of collaborative learning. Their attitudes, in this particular respect, have improved tremendously. With these improved attitudes and the support of team mates in their risk-taking experiences, their confidence levels have risen significantly. They are able to learn from their mistakes and devise strategies for not making the same mistake again.

Feedback is important in any learning process. The students were working for a real purpose — to present to a real audience who would give real feedback. During the study they used each other for feedback: 'Do you think this sounds OK?' or 'Will the primary students be able to understand our questions?' Reviewing what they had done after each major step was a new experience for most of these students. They were able to sort things out in their own minds, thinking aloud, writing it down. This was a sounding board for what had been done or had to be done again (properly this time) — and how. Time was limited so this precious time was rarely wasted.

Here, then, is where this summary of Betty's written description of her project concludes. The focus at this point is clearly on the *students*, and the benefits she saw for them in the process of negotiating the ways in which they would cover the demands of their language and literacy curriculum. I now want to turn to my own project here and work with the representation of the classroom she presents in this text; to shift the focus from student learning to *teacher* learning and, thereby, highlight the emphasis there has been from the very beginnings of the international project for curriculum negotiation in schools on teachers *writing*. It is only through the reflective representation of action in textual form, as evidenced in all of the accounts of classroom negotiation available to us today as well as in this volume, that the writers of those accounts have been able to make them intelligible to themselves as well as to us, their readers. Through the critical selection and arrangement of their descriptions and comments on classroom experience, these teachers have written the 'reality' of that experience as they have come to understand it, so that we, too, can learn from it.

Rereading the Writing: Negotiation for Professional Growth

Although Betty's reflections here are focused primarily on the degree to which her study has fulfilled its 'professional development' aim of researching the idea of negotiation as an effective and efficient classroom practice, her broader, underlying, and 'professional' aim of effecting positive change in the students' experiences of school and learning governs the way she reads and reports her project. It is obvious that, for Betty, in reading the students' progress and products as the teacher of the class, there has been little question of the value of negotiation as a teaching/learning process. What she saw 'behind the scenes' convinced her enough to make her want to convince her readers of the gains and benefits accruing to these young people as they experienced another way of being students in their school different from the ways they had already lived and learned. However, what I see as I read Betty's report and reproduce it here for a different set of readers is an opportunity to construct, from her materials, the potential of another way of being *teachers* in our schools.

There is a very real and growing sense in which teachers' work in schools today parallels students' work. Prescribed content material must be gotten through in a particular time, teachers have little control over what and how it is to be done. In educational terms. Michael Apple's (1986) notion of the *degradation of labor* suggests that where outside forces have control over both the planning and evaluation of what is to go on in classrooms, we as teachers tend slowly to lose what little control we do have over our work.

> As employees lose control over their own labor, the skills that they have developed over the years atrophy. They are slowly lost, thereby making it even easier for management to control even more of one's job because the skills of planning and controlling it yourself are no longer available.
> (Apple and Jungck, 1990, p. 230)

As professionals, the thought of this deskilling process is anathema to most of us, and, yet, we can recognize, as we hand out the 'teacher-proof' photocopied worksheets and compare 'our' students' results on the latest battery of tests with those of our colleagues' students, how our 'accountability' to the system is replacing our ability to account for our professional knowledge and action. What we are also losing, though, is basic job satisfaction; our sense of ourselves as *teachers* rather than technicians. If we are to counteract this tendency, if we believe it ought be counteracted, we might well heed Jean Rudduck's (1985) view that:

> . . . research liberates curiosity and generates excitement. And now more than at any other time the teaching profession needs, as a counter to increasing bureaucratic demands, a sense of professional excitement that can draw attention back to the professional core of schooling — the mutuality of teaching and learning as an interactive process. (p. 283)

When teachers become excited about the work they engage in and begin to gain personal as well as professional satisfaction from their actions, there is little doubt that their students, their colleagues, and their schools also benefit. Bill Green (1982) reminds us, though, that it is up to *us* as teachers to determine the kind and quality of such professional action:

> There is much that *can* be done, despite constraints of all kinds, provided we are prepared to assume responsibility for our own emancipation. It's no use waiting for others to help us; we must, and can, help ourselves. Indeed, as 'experts' in our own realm, the classroom, there is a strong sense in which there is simply no alternative to doing just this, *if* learning really matters.

How, then, are we to liberate ourselves?

Rereading/Rewriting: Negotiation as Teacher Learning

In exactly the same way that Betty reports her students benefiting from their experience with curriculum negotiation, I now want to argue that *teachers'* classroom understandings are similarly enhanced when they work this way. Using statements from Betty's report reproduced above and focused there on *student* learning and self-image, I want to show how these apply equally to ourselves as teachers — people who need positive and rewarding classroom learning experiences just as much as our students do, if we are to find other ways of being teachers in our schools. In particular, 'the close and necessary connection between personal development, professional development, and curriculum development' (Green and Reid, 1986, p. 6) brings into sharper focus the question at issue here: action-research and the critical significance of classroom studies.

> Teachers investigating their own teaching practices will also find themselves confronted with the problem of authority and the play of power within the classroom . . . and [need to] learn to let go of [their] own ('natural') inclinations to *tell* , to keep control through performance and recitation, and to distrust any learning that did not come about directly as a result of [their] own interventions.
>
> (Green and Reid, 1986, p. 12)

Negotiating the curriculum, as I mentioned earlier, is a risky business for us who are used to the experience of school as a place where, like T.S. Eliot's 'latest Pole', we *transmit* the curriculum 'through our hair and fingertips'! Do we dare?

Because for most of us, learning really does 'matter', I think we can readily see our obligation to provide good models for the students we teach. When we rethink teaching as a potential model of good learning behaviour, rather than a virtuoso performance to be admired, a sense of the *need* to take risks in our efforts to increase knowledge and understanding in our classrooms is apparent. Garth Boomer (1988) has suggested elsewhere that right from the start of their schooling, children too should be helped to make decisions about their learning:

> From the earliest times children should be helped to compose the curriculum. They should therefore have a good curriculum read to them every week so that they begin to internalize the patterns, rhythms and structures of the 'story'. Shared curriculum composing and reading is also a 'good thing'. After the writing or the telling of a curriculum story, it will assist development and learning if students are encouraged to talk about its strengths and weaknesses, its high points and its troughs. (p. 158)

Action-research, by its very nature, encourages us as teachers to tell and retell the stories of our classrooms and curricula and, as we transform these stories by reflection, so too we can reflect on them and seek to transform them — in effect, rewriting and rereading them — so as to lessen the risk by increasing our own power over the 'patterns, rhythms, and structures of the story'.

So here then is a *new* story, every word of which you have actually already read before, as presented above, but which you may not at first recognize, because your first reading involved much more text than the precis I have constructed; and also because I am now asking you to read this text *differently*. Betty's report positions us, as 'readers', to read it as a collegial enterprise, as 'experts' who can share the validity of the experience presented there. The new text, which is simply a reconstruction of selected, ordered words and sentences from Betty's original, asks to be read now as a fantasy, a 'representation' of her reading; and it positions us as potential actors in something like a 'choose your own adventure' story. If we add 'ourselves' to the title I have given to this chapter and read this text as if it was a representation of the experience of a different set of learners from the students Betty wrote about, we see that, instead of our students, it is now ourselves as teachers who are in theme here. This story, although lacking polish like any newly reconstructed artifact, can now be read as a story about *teachers'* learning rather than students' learning; and about the excitement that curriculum negotiation generates for 'us' as well as 'them'.

Teachers Negotiating the Curriculum:
Action-research and Professional Development

The teachers decided it would be best to begin on home ground. This way they built up confidence and eventually asked if they could ask the questions. Then, with their confidence built up, they decided it was time to begin asking students questions. They were ready to take the big step into the unfamiliar territory. No one was to feel disadvantaged in any way and after acting as 'technicians' . . . they felt confident to 'take the risk' of reading the questions (backed up, in case of need). The outcomes of these exercises in terms of confidence builders were enormous. They enjoyed taking the risk, learning by mistakes, in a non-threatening atmosphere. The motivation created by the knowledge that this was their own research to learn what and how they wanted, around the set topic, was enough to let them relax and form work groups according to their interest in the particular task at hand. *The teachers* quickly understood that it was up to them to find out what they had decided they wanted to know. The taking of risks was certainly a major step and when they came through this experience unscathed, their confidence rose. Mistakes made were discussed openly and solutions, or 'how to do it better' strategies, were worked out. Their enthusiasm for this work never faltered and they would often begin a session in class with 'What's next?' or 'Where do we go from here?' They also wanted to ask questions to evaluate themselves and find out just how effective others thought they had been in what they had done. [Others thought] they had benefited because they got to do interesting things. *The teachers* were motivated because they realized the responsibility was theirs, that it was part of being independent. The process by which they obtained the results [was] far more important than the results themselves. Reviewing what they had done after each major step was a new experience for most of them. They were able to sort things out in their own minds, thinking aloud, writing it down. This was a sounding board for what had been done or had to be done again (properly this time) — and how.

In this new narrative, we now can see, or imagine, ourselves as the learners — us as 'them' — and for the first time something of the difference of experience that teachers aim for in a negotiated curriculum is becoming apparent in its application to ourselves. Certain insights into teachers as reflective practitioners emerge for our consideration from this writing — insights that have been made intelligible for us and, importantly, for me as writer through the act of *(re)writing*.

Mutual Learning

When we read this text more closely, we can see that what is happening here, as the teachers take the risk of placing themselves in a position of vulnerability while they research their own act of learning, is that they are now positioning themselves to need the students as much as they have previously been positioned to be needed. No longer are the students merely 'cooperating' with each other and their teacher in the well-known 'rules of the game' of school. There has been a qualitative shift in the nature of these relationships towards a more dialogic collaboration — a necessary collaboration simply because they are 'all in the same boat'. As teachers, we cannot learn how to improve our teaching unless we work in collaboration with our students: We have to find out together, because *all of us* don't yet know 'how we will find out what we need to know'. There will be a different result of this collaborative endeavor for each of us as individuals, of course, yet there is likely also to emerge a collective understanding of new and different ways of potential action, reaction, and interaction in the classroom.

This develops in and through the experience of negotiating, yet it can only be fully realized if the opportunity for critical reflection provided for in the process of action-research is utilized. Carr and Kemmis (1986), arguing for the necessity of this critical process, claim that:

> The action-researcher in aiming to improve practices, understandings and situations is therefore aiming to move more surely into the future by understanding how her or his practices are socially-constructed and historically embedded, and by seeing the situations or institutions in which she or he works in an historical and social perspective. (1986, p. 182)

Reading, and Rereading, the Curriculum

It is probable, for instance, that you, or I, or Betty herself, will derive differing understandings and aims for our future moves from our different readings of her experience as a teacher negotiating with her students. These readings, and the understandings that result for us, derive from our own histories of schooling and the school curriculum; histories that have constructed us as 'individuals' in different ways. Accordingly, the decision to attempt to negotiate the curriculum is a decision to rewrite the curriculum in effect. It involves all members of the classroom in a conscious and critical process of reading the written curriculum. This is because the decision to make changes to existing modes of classroom action and structure in the interests of negotiation means that we are critically deciding for, or against, already-inscribed curriculum content and action. And as we critique these existing practices in this way, we are, at the same time, able to see, and read, our own teaching and learning histories *as they have already been written* by that curriculum.

Just as I have *re*written the text of Betty's report, constructing a new story by a conscious selection of significant components fixed together with the cement of my intention to subvert the first collegial reading of it for a new and different purpose, Betty's report is itself a conscious rewriting of the action text of the classroom. That rewriting caused her to choose for presentation to her readers those components that emerged from her reading of the classroom action as significant for herself and her students collectively. My reading and rewriting enables me to see the significance of this collective understanding for the development of teachers' professional understandings more generally. Your reading, negotiated between the two of ours, will be rewritten, perhaps, in your own future action and research decisions, but it will always arise out of your own context and history as each of ours has arisen.

Learning On Home Ground

In the reconstructed text, for instance, I chose to include Betty's comment that for her students the decision to begin on 'home ground' was important. In the initial 'Negotiating Education' project, Belmont High was selected as the site for the testing of the idea of negotiation for two reasons, only one of which is alluded to in chapter 8. I had been teaching at this school for two years previously and felt secure in the knowledge that both the staff and students regarded me as a 'good' teacher. Even though I was only borrowing a class for the duration of the research study, that class was not selected at random — it was regularly taught by a close friend with whom I was unafraid of losing face and who I knew would support my actions even if he was skeptical of my rationale for them. Similarly, the class Betty chose was not just 'any' of her classes; it was the one she felt the closest personal affinity with and affection for. We both began on *our* chosen preferred ground.

Further, at the time of commencing these projects, each of us had already begun a course of inservice professional development which required us to engage in classroom research as a facet of our program; and each had read and become enthused about the potential and possibility of negotiation as a means of enhancing student learning. We had both felt challenged by what we had read and discussed and took this challenge personally — as a test of our own abilities to accommodate and succeed with 'new' and critical approaches to teaching. But as with any test, we could not predict the outcomes with confidence and, therefore, we needed a secure base from which to take the first step into the unknown. It can of course be argued that by choosing classes where our propensity for failure was minimized as much as possible, we were also minimizing the risk involved. It is clear, though, that without the security that starting 'on home ground' provided, there would have been considerable reluctance to take that risk at all. Historically, for each of us then, the context was 'right'.

Finding the Questions/Reading the Curriculum

'Eventually' then, as the story says, we were ready to 'ask if we could ask the questions'. I found this a fortuitous formulation in Betty's original text as it captured, for me, a sense of the tentative quality of the first steps towards the notion of teachers and students, separately and together, as independent and collaborative learners in the classroom. Were we able to 'ask the questions'? Did we have the confidence to give it a go? What if the students said, 'No'? Or, worse perhaps, what if they said nothing and just let us get on with it? At bottom therefore the question we have to address in relation to our own learning becomes: How do we read *our students' readings* of the classroom we all inhabit? In our attempt to rewrite the curriculum collaboratively, as we compose each new text of a negotiated classroom, we are all 'writing ourselves anew — but always on the basis of the available readings of our histories. Reading my own history now in the text of chapter 9, alongside Betty's new story, I see how my construction of 'teacher' and 'student' ten years ago was simply, in hindsight, unreflective and worked against the notion of negotiation as a true collaborative and constructive process. At that time, however, I could not have made this reading.

For instance, the idea that 'my' students should be free to make alternative suggestions for possible choices of audiences to whom they could present their work was impossible for me at that time. Indeed, to be honest, it was actually unthinkable. I was still learning then how to incorporate into my teaching practices various notions of 'real audience' for student work that were in themselves a risky step into new territory for me. The students were also, I suggest, unable to read the classroom in ways that would make it possible for them to contribute alternative suggestions. This was because for all of us, teacher and students, there was simply nothing in our teaching and studenting histories that would allow us to redraft our newly composed curriculum in this way. Alternative readings/ rewritings were not available to us. The 'power of teacher suggestion', as I referred to it then, was essentially unproblematic and unquestionable. The students simply 'co-operated'.

The passage of ten years has meant that students are no longer unaware of the role and value of 'real' audience to whom their work can be presented. Such ideas are no longer 'new'; both we and our students have lived with them and internalized them as part of our knowledge of ways of being in classrooms. Indeed, it was almost unremarkable for Betty, in writing her report, that what is now such an obvious difference in conventions of what might be termed this particular 'curriculum genre' (Christie, 1984) should have been available to find its place in their negotiation. The students in Betty's class, in their first year of secondary schooling in 1989, would almost invariably have received their primary school language instruction in a system that placed emphasis on Donald Grave's notion of 'the writing process' and the range of real audiences available to children in schools. These students had learned different things about 'publishing' and presenting from the students of the previous decade.

As they move through their schooling experience, children are being progressively socialized into the culture of schooling. This means learning how to 'read' and 'write' the genres of schooling — and it is important to see this as pertaining not just to written and spoken texts but also to 'action-texts' as well. (Green and Reid, 1990, p. 85)

In this way we can see how the 'unwritten' curriculum of school and class-room can also be read in our composition of the negotiated classroom experience. As so much of the existing literature on negotiation clearly suggests, the range of genres of classroom activity available to students, based on their knowledge of *possible* ways of being and acting in the classroom, is, at any particular time, both limited and limiting. Our tentativeness in 'allowing' students the 'freedom' to write their own learning agendas indicates as much about our own construction as subjects of the discourses of school and the curriculum as it does about our students' potential for refusal or disruption. There has been no room, for instance, in a teaching history of curriculum that has been 'handed down' to us so that we can 'operationalize' it in our classrooms for us to learn how to plan and act any differently. We *know* how to 'operationalize'. Taking the first step towards a negotiated curriculum ('asking if we can ask the questions') can therefore be seen as our own disruption or contestation of the institutionalized practices, organizations and discourses (Kemmis, 1988) that have shaped us, firstly as learners and then as teachers. Destablized, we have to struggle to find our footing again — and when we do, it is never in the same place.

Changing Practice/Changing Ourselves

And although each of our first steps is tentative, it is paradoxically the very 'safety net' provided by our students' own construction *as students* in the school system that permits our reading of the results of this first step to be, as was noted at the start of this chapter, 'liberating'. Just as our histories as teachers working within the curriculum structures we already know have shaped us into the teachers we are today, so have our students been shaped by their learning histories. The readings they are able to make, therefore, of the possibilities for action that are available to them parallel our own. Their understandings of life in classrooms are constructed from the experience we provide. Although we may not articulate this to our selves or to others, it is only our knowledge that we can rely on them to behave and think 'as they always do' that provides us with the security of a 'known variable' with which to work.

This may, in fact, be what underlies our words when we talk about choosing our 'good' classes to try out our first attempts at negotiation. They may not necessarily be good 'learners', but they appear to us to be, in Green and Weade's (1990) terms, well socialized into 'the classroom as culture'; they are good 'students'. Our students *enable* us to 'take the big step into the unfamiliar territory' and rewrite ourselves as teachers, in fact, simply because we know that they are always unable to rewrite themselves first! Unless we make the effort to change our own organization, language, and action in the classroom and 'assume responsibility for our own emancipation', therefore, we can have no effect at all on our students' perceptions of and participation in classroom life. They will continue to 'co-operate' with us, within our limitations, never coming to know, through experience of an alternative, the possibilities that collaboration with us might extend to them.

Collegiality and Critique

When we do assume this responsibility, though, we cannot expect to do it all on our own. Just as Betty reported it for her students, it may be that it is only after 'acting as technicians' — going through the motions of reproducing and paraphrasing other people's ideas and tests and rehearsing with our students the necessary components of this 'rewritten' classroom and subject curriculum — that we are able to feel 'confident to 'take the risk' of reading the questions' (our *own* questions) against the grain of our established practice. As the reconstructed text tells us:

> the motivation created by the knowledge that this was their own research to learn what and how they wanted . . . was enough to let them relax and form work groups according to their interest in the particular task at hand. *The teachers* understood that it was up to them to find out what they had decided they wanted to know.

Without this 'relaxing', this information of 'work groups' within which our experience can be safely reviewed and examined, the potential for us to reread and, perhaps, rewrite our histories is curtailed; we remain co-opted, co-operative members of the institution. We need, and benefit from, the support of critical and interested colleagues just as much as our students do. In writing this chapter now, for instance, I am not working alone. Apart from Betty's obvious presence in this text, there is a small group of other people who have read it and read me writing it, stage by stage, as it develops. It develops only because they do *not* 'co-operate' with my writing. In Betty's classroom research she had the critical support of her college colleagues and her supervisor, as she followed her research interest. In my classroom research, I had the support of the members of the original Language and Learning Project team — other readers, other writers, whose own teaching and learning histories provided me with other texts to draw upon as I rewrote my own. But it is always up to us to determine what we need and want to learn, thus generating challenge, motivation, and, importantly, satisfaction and pleasure in our efforts and in our work in schools as professionals.

Beyond Technique to Critical Reflection

Simply 'co-operationalizing' a mandated curriculum, without researching and negotiating our own and our students' positions in relation to it, must lead, in Apple's terms, to the 'de-skilling' of both parties. Henry Giroux (1983) argues, too, that 'there is a growing amount of research that points to the increased use of prepackaged curriculum materials that accentuate delivering instruction while at the same time removing conception and critique from the pedagogical act' (p. 138). The teachers in our story, working to carry out 'their own research', are working to counteract this deskilling process through improving their *professional* competence in a process of collaborative review and critique of their action. According to Carr and Kemmis (1986):

> Professional development is a matter of teachers becoming more enlightened about the ways in which their own self-understandings may

prevent them being properly aware of the social and political mechanisms which operate to distort or limit the proper conduct of education in society. Professional competence, therefore, requires a capacity for continuous deliberation and critical discussion by the teaching profession as a whole of the way in which political and social structures relate to and influence educational aims and practices. (p. 32)

Just as we have seen above, like the students who 'also wanted to ask questions to evaluate themselves and find out how effective others thought they had been in what they had done', we were motivated 'because [we] realized the responsibility was [ours], that it was part of being independent'. Without this sort of critical 'sounding board' our histories are compelled to repeat themselves simply because we cannot rewrite our teaching selves unless we know what it is we are learning — and know what it means for us as teachers. Jean Rudduck (1985) claims that:

as we have come to realize through various analyses of attempts at educational reform, a common phenomenon is 'innovation without change' — where surface realities have been cosmeticized but the basic structures and values remain unchanged. (p. 288)

I strongly suspect that 'negotiating the curriculum' may have the potential to be seen as just another brand of educational mascara, for teachers and for students, unless the lived experience of this as an alternative curriculum genre does serve to instill, in *both* parties, an internalization of what Garth Boomer (1988) describes as, the 'patterns, rhythms and structures of the story'. The outcome of this, Boomer suggests, is that you become, 'like the audience at a Brechtian play', a healthily estranged enquirer,

who knows that the curriculum is a performance generated by the school's culture, a demonstration with palpable designs on you. It is no longer a *given*; it is a way of *taking* now that you have learnt to act upon it. (p. 158)

The necessary reading, re-reading and re-writing of the curriculum that I have argued here is an integral aspect of 'negotiation' for students and teachers alike working together to construct the curriculum in its relation to themselves as learners and provides the potential for such enquiry to make the curriculum, as performance, 'strange'. But at another level, for the teacher, it is the act of writing *about* the negotiation experience that actually realizes this potential. In constructing a textual representation of the curriculum processes and products involved, from the 'evidence' of the classroom teaching and learning texts that were generated 'along the way', the teacher is necessarily *re-presenting* her experience for review and reflection; and in this manner re-writing both her experience and her history.

However, the full potency of such enquiry cannot be fully realized, I suggest, without the sorts of connected critical reflection on practice that is involved in the process of action-research. There is quite obviously little incentive for us as teachers to re-read and re-write the texts of our classrooms in isolation, if we feel ourselves to be 'de-skilled', laboring alone at our work stations on the production line of school. If we enter into the critical community of action-research, though, there is not only a reason, but a real incentive, to 're-skill', through reconstructing and re-writing the representations of classroom life that we gather in our research of negotiation.

While I consider that curriculum negotiation may indeed be a 'pedagogical imperative' for students in our classrooms today, systematic investigation of the practices associated with such a pedagogy is equally necessary for ourselves as workers accountable to (and for!) the technology of the educational institution. We need to help ourselves; to take from our experience in classrooms all that we can to develop our sense of ourselves as 'professionals', who can and do work for education on the basis of our knowledge and accumulated experience. Action-research, then, with its emphasis on collaboration with others who share our interest in the issues we are investigating, though not necessarily either our problems or our perspective on them, both parallels and enhances the practice of classroom negotiation in important and obvious ways. Because we are not alone, we do not depend only on ourselves, but become interdependent — collaborators in our learning — learning as we teach, yet significantly, teaching as we learn. Professionally, we are enabled to push ourselves beyond where we presently are into the space we want to reach and negotiate our position there before we take our next 'small step'. Personally we are flying high.

My emphasis throughout this chapter has been on 'negotiation' as an instance of the relationship between action-research and professional development. I have made much of the notion of 'writing as learning', and the negotiation of the reading and writing of classroom experience as the site for teachers' personal and professional growth. In stressing the value of the sorts of textualization of classroom experience that action-research investigation implies for the teacher as researcher, I have argued not so much for its use as received information for analysis and critique by external readers, but as a heuristic for the teacher herself. Negotiating the curriculum is always a process of critical reading and re-writing of the classroom; but in the sense in which such critical action enables the teacher to read and write herself as a professional, it has the added propensity to effect much wider and long-lasting change in education generally by returning to the teacher a felt understanding of her position as a powerful agent for her own development as a classroom practitioner.

References

APPLE, M.W. (1986) *Teachers and Texts: A Political Economy of Class and Gender Relations in Education.* NY: Routledge.

APPLE, M.W. and JUNGCK, S. (1990) 'You don't have to be a teacher to teach this unit': Teaching, technology, and gender in the classroom', *American Educational Research Journal*, **27**, 2, Summer, pp. 227–251.

BOOMER, G. (1988) 'Reading the whole curriculum, in GREEN, B. (Ed.) *Metaphors and Meanings: Essays on English Teaching by Garth Boomer*, Adelaide: AATE, pp. 151–167.

CARR, W. and KEMMIS, S. (1986) *Becoming Critical: Knowing Through Action Research*, London: Falmer Press.

CHRISTIE, F. (1984) 'Curriculum genre and schematic structure of classroom discourse', in HASAN R. (Ed.) *Discourse on Discourse*, Applied Linguistics Association of Australia, Occasional papers No. 7.

GIROUX, H.A. (1983) 'Ideology, culture, and schooling' in *Theory and Resistance in Education: A Pedagogy for the Opposition*, MA: Bergin & Garvey.

GREEN, B. (1982) 'Of meaning and magic: Negotiating the Curriculum — a review essay', *English in Australia*, **16**, 2, November, pp. 19–24.

GREEN, B. and REID, J.A. (1986) 'English teaching, inservice and action research', *English in Australia*, **75**, March, pp. 4–21.

GREEN, B. and REID, J.A. (1990) 'A curriculum framework: Teaching for powerful learning', in BRUBACHER, M. PAYNE, R. and RICKETT, K. (Eds) *Perspectives on Small Group Learning: Theory and Practice*, Oakville: Rubicon, pp. 81–97.

GREEN, B. and WEADE, G. (1990) 'The social construction of classroom reading: Beyond method', *Australian Journal of Reading*, **13**, 4, November, pp. 326–336.

KEMMIS, S. (1988) *The Action Research Planner*, 3rd Edition, Geelong: Deakin University Press.

RUDDUCK, J. (1985) 'Teacher research and research-based teacher education', *Journal of Education for Teaching*, **11**, 3, October, pp. 281–289.

Chapter 11

Learning to Negotiate/Negotiating to Learn

Nancy Lester

A Purpose: Debunking the Myth of Teacher as Expert Transmitter

As I began to think about and prepare for the language and learning course in which the experiences I describe in this chapter occurred, I realized I was continuing to wrestle with the differences between being a school-based teacher educator and a university professor. I'd been accustomed to working with teachers who were pessimistic about the possibilities for change and healthily skeptical towards me and school-based professional education. I wasn't prepared, as I look back on it, for the quite different response that greeted me in university courses. The students saw me as an expert transmitter, a 'lofty' university professor, who would spread her pearls of wisdom about and expect them to be consumed and regurgitated. Resistance was uncommon. Compliance, especially in the service of receiving high marks, was the norm.

Interestingly, however, compliance to an authority turned into a form of resistance I'd not yet experienced in my own teaching: Resistance to take on a critical stance toward learning. I saw negotiating as a way to enable the students to question their assumptions about learning and teaching and to confront the contradictory theories they'd adopted wholesale as a result of receiving transmissions from experts, since negotiating the curriculum provides learners with the means to rehearse and test out their independent, critical voices. The four questions around which a negotiated curriculum is built (chapter 2) provide opportunities for students to exercise their intentions to learn and to construct knowledge both independently and collaboratively.

My intention for choosing to negotiate this course was, then, to promote an alternative process of teaching and learning; a process opposing transmission — a teaching/learning process that would be constructive, collaborative, and critical. My larger goal, since this was a course for new as well as more experienced elementary teachers, was that the experiences of the course would influence their pedagogy. I wanted these teachers to question the value they placed on transmission teaching and to be immersed in a negotiated, constructivist context. It was this combination of critique and alternative experience which I believed could contribute to their being different kinds of teachers in their own classrooms.

The Content for Negotiation: Selling the California Artichoke

How and what would we negotiate? I began to think about what was so powerful for me in Hyde's and Reid's chapters in the 1982 *Negotiating the Curriculum* (which now appear in this volume as chapters 4 and 9 respectively), and I remembered how a seemingly remote, circumscribed area of study held a myriad of secrets, questions, possible connections, and paths. So my first thought was that I would have to narrow whatever topic was chosen; make it specific; make it have boundaries. I chose the 'Selling of the California Artichoke Across the US' as the curriculum content for our negotiation. It was narrow enough; and, because I was attempting to set up a structure in a university classroom which would mirror certain institutional structures of K-6 schools (those in which these teachers were or would be teaching) without patronizing the students or the structures, this topic, like other topics in 'real' schools which often constrain teachers and students, had the characteristics associated with constraint: imposed from without and seemingly unconnected to students' knowledge and experience.

The processes of immersion — hands-on engagement in learning — and distancing — critical reflection on that learning — would allow us to enact negotiation as well as reflect on it (Lester and Onore, 1990). We would negotiate the curriculum during immersion classes. And during distancing classes we would explore and reflect on language, learning, and negotiation.

Constraints Within a Negotiated Curriculum

I ordered four books for the course (Appendix A). Everyone was required to read Frank Smith's *Comprehension and Learning: A Conceptual Framework for Teachers* (1985), the one I considered to be the core book. Based on their interests, they were to make their own choices as to which chapters/sections of the three remaining texts they wished to read and respond to in their learning logs.

With the goal of having a reading experience common to us all which might show how there could be a range of responses to the same text, I was also attempting to provide choice in the context of constraint. Diverse reading experiences with the remaining three texts would mean students sharing what they read with their peers, encouraging them to see each other as authorities.

Learning logs containing written responses to readings, class reflections, and reflections on the students' teaching were another course constraint. Since one of my expressed goals for this course was that students learn to become critical readers of teaching and learning, the unique and crucial benefit of learning logs is using writing to learn — writing which is thinking and exploring ideas on paper — which discourages copying and parroting. Students are provoked to challenge the author, to question what has been written, to connect in personal ways through sharing personal experiences, and/or to rewrite difficult or dense passages in their own words as a way of clarifying their understanding. Initially, many students are uncomfortable with this process. They've been used to taking verbatim notes out of books, copying down highlighted points, or parroting points of view. But questioning or disagreeing with the published writer, the authority in print, has been virtually absent in their experience.

Of course, negotiating the curriculum itself was a constraint. We were going to try out the process in as much detail as we could and we were going to reflect on it to learn about its hows and whys. At the end of each immersion class, students were asked to write in answer to the questions: 'What did I learn?' and 'How did I learn?' Their responses would be shared during distancing classes as one of the focuses for small and whole group discussions.

Negotiated Assessment

Learning logs, engaging in small and large group reflective conversations, negotiating the curriculum, and end-of-semester 'performances' of learning were the required work areas on which students would be assessed. In previous courses I had come away somewhat disappointed by what I did, or, rather, didn't do, about assessment. I left the discussion of grading until too late in the semester to do it well, and so, in the end copped out and gave the students a choice of grading schemes: all A's, a grade of A–F negotiated collaboratively by each student with me, or the more traditional grade of A–F where I made the decision without negotiating with students.

I knew that I needed to work on assessment for this course. I read Johnston and Dowdy's *Teaching and Assessing in a Negotiated Curriculum* (1988) and from that constructed my own 'work required assessment statement'. The four processes of learning and the work required for each that I decided on prior to the first meeting of the course follow. Each student would receive an 'A' in the course if all of the work was successfully completed (if all the criteria were met). If they did all the work, but didn't satisfy all of the defined criteria or if they didn't complete all of the work, they would receive an 'IP', an Incomplete Pass which, according to university policy, they could make up within a year.

Process	*Work Required*
Reflection on language and learning.	Keep an on-going learning log of both in-class and out-of-class language and learning endeavors.
Collaborative negotiation of learning.	Actively engage in small group problem-posing/solving activities.
Participation in whole group discussions.	Demonstrate, through active sharing, your understanding of and questions about your reading.
Presentation of learning.	Each small group will present to the rest of the class an appropriate product of their learning for the semester.

My principal goals for learning in this course — active engagement in using talking and writing as ways of learning critically, collaborative peer group learning, negotiating the curriculum — were reflected by these assessment areas. They are vague at this point. How does one reflect on language and learning in a learning log? What does it mean to actively engage in small group activities? How can one demonstrate understanding in a whole group discussion? The vagueness was deliberate, however, since the students, in collaboration with me, were going to build the criteria which would guide each assessment area. I knew that if they participated in defining the assessment criteria that would guide their own learning that experience would help them to question their attitudes towards teacher as sole judge of what students have or have not learned.

Snapshots from Negotiating the Curriculum

To begin our journey together, I asked students to share their experiences of schooling and to compare those with the experiences they were going to engage in this course. The latter were laid out in introductory material I prepared and handed out during the first evening of class (Appendix A). The characteristics of school teaching and learning which emerged as a result of some collaborative talking and writing activities contained the following items:

- homework
- teacher at front of room
- teacher gives grades
- quiet
- rows
- blackboard with homework on it
- detention
- red pen
- No talking!!
- multiple choice tests
- grades
- US History: every year
- writing bad poetry; bad essays; first draft = last draft
- stay in line — get in line

As we began to discuss the differences, the students began to articulate, as this list reflects, that their schooling experiences were dominated by learning that was teacher-centered and teacher controlled. From the materials I shared with them, they noted that the goal of this course was to put them in the center of their own learning, to validate the knowledge they already possessed, and to encourage them to take responsibility for their own and their peers' learning, especially in the area of assessment.

My intention here, and one of many I shared with them on that first evening, was to get us to reveal up front our assumptions about schooling, built through our experiences of teaching and learning, so that as we began to experience an alternative process of teaching and learning, we'd have benchmarks from which to compare the new experience with the old, and perhaps, by the end of the semester, alter some of those earlier assumptions. Ideally, we'd go back during distancing classes to this list of assumptions and read them critically through the lenses of our new experiences. Some of the questions I'd hoped we'd address and which I hoped would eventually help the students to 'rewrite' their assumptions were: (i) If the teacher is not up in front of the room all the time, what is her role and what new roles do students then play?; (ii) Can students learn in a classroom that is not quiet (purposefully noisy) and not arranged in an orderly fashion (not in rows)?, and (iii) What role does writing, which is not graded or marked up by a teacher, play in learning?

These were questions which placed *their* experiences at the centre of our learning and which I believed would provoke them to question what and how they learned.

Students formed small groups during the second class meeting and together began to write and think about the assessment criteria. Each individual student free wrote on the work required for this course: learning logs, small group collaboration, whole group discussion, and final presentations of learning. They were asked to write about what each area of work demanded of them as learners and what they thought they needed to do to meet the demands made by each area of work required. They shared these pieces of writing and collaborated in formulating composite small group lists of criteria for each area to be assessed.

We then came together as a whole group to begin developing the criteria for assessing the learning logs. The students had written logs once and I had shared my log with them, so that they were able to build criteria on some genuine practical immersion experience. The criteria for assessing the effectiveness of learning logs that we developed were:

1 Logs to be handed in every two weeks for response.
2 Logs to contain responses to readings and class discussions.
3 Logs to contain responses which evidence coming to understandings and/or insights through:

    (a) arguing with points made,
    (b) questioning points,
    (c) restating texts in one's own words, and/or
    (d) making personal connections to illustrate arguing with points, disagreeing with points, and/or questioning points.

4 Logs to be shared with and responded to by peers.

I, too, wrote my own list of criteria for each work required area. As the students shared their criteria for assessing learning logs, and as we negotiated the validity, practicality, and wording of the emerging criteria, our intentions seemed to begin to gel and coincide. My feeling, however at this point, given students' view of me as expert, was that my list was more influential in determining this final list of criteria for assessing learning logs than with later criteria we developed.

What was important for me, though, and what I think the students needed to feel me out on or test me with, was whether I would genuinely engage with their ideas about and rationales for criteria. So, while this final list of criteria was more mine than theirs, the process of coming to that product, negotiating the reasons for establishing these particular criteria as opposed to others, was, I believe, collaborative and demonstrated my commitment to validating a genuinely cointentional teaching and learning context. While it was too soon to expect them to revise their view of me as professor/expert, it was certainly the appropriate moment — from the start of the course — to demonstrate my commitment and willingness to be some other kind of teacher and how in action I would do that.

Our first whole group distancing discussion on the third night of class centred on learning log responses to articles by Lindfors (1984), and Boomer (1988) and to Cook's, 'Programming for Learning' (chapter 2). Here's my end-of-class log reflection on that evening's class:

> This discussion began slowly, which seems natural, given that this was our first experience with whole group discussion and using what we'd read as the basis for that discussion. Did we really talk about the readings? Yes and no. Obviously, the discussion had roots in the articles, but it will be interesting to see what focuses people chose to write about in their logs. [I hadn't read their logs on this reading assignment yet.]
>
> Listening is a very important component of group discussion. If we don't listen to one another CAREFULLY, then we can't carry the discussion through fully. By interrupting others in mid-sentence or mid-thought, because we want to make *our* point, we don't 'hear' what others are saying and can't respond to them valuably. Eye contact needs to improve. I can't be the only one that's always addressed. We need to learn to use each other as resources. We will, I know, it takes time.
>
> Didn't these kids ever get theory in their program? Hasn't anyone helped them learn that theory underlies curriculum testing and practice? We'll have to get back to this.

I can hear my frustration in this response, but I also recognized that new learning is not automatic or immediate and that time will help to promote change. I was also beginning to build my own criteria for whole group discussion.

Despite the fact that we'd already met three times and still not begun to negotiate the curriculum, *per se*, that time was not wasted, nor unintentional. Students were learning how to work in small groups, how to talk with one another, and were, in fact, engaged in implicit negotiation. In their small groups, students had to negotiate one list from five individual lists of criteria for assessment. These small group lists then had to be negotiated to produce one class list of criteria. And the students had also had to negotiate with me throughout all of this.

One of the crucial lessons to come out of this experience for me was the necessity of giving time to learning how to learn. Students' experiences of learning in school, as their earlier list indicated, had given them very few chances, if any, to learn how to talk with one another, to make decisions on their own, or to collaborate in decision-making with their peers and teachers on teaching and learning issues. Just as they needed to see me demonstrate the teacher as master craftsperson/negotiator/collaborator, so, too, they needed to practise, as apprentices, those kinds of learning strategies they either never had engaged in or were uncomfortable with.

These early days of the course served as genuine practice for students into new ways of learning with and from each other and me. Had they not had these opportunities to practise, I believe their negotiating the artichoke curriculum would not have been as successful as it was. By noting the absence of conflict and confusion in the descriptions that follow, a clearer indication of the results of how such learning how to learn facilitated their negotiation and promoted ownership over learning emerges.

The fourth night of class was terrifically interesting. We continued to negotiate the criteria for assessment, moving to whole group discussion. Here are the criteria for assessment that the students developed for a large group discussion:

1 By the end of the semester, each person will contribute ideas regularly to whole class discussions.
2 Soliciting opinions from others to encourage interaction by all class members.
3 Allowing participants to express their ideas completely/fully.
4 Conversations need to piggy-back.
5 By the end of the semester, eye contact will be equally distributed.

My own criteria, represented by numbers 3, 4, and 5, were also criteria the students themselves had included on their personal lists. Piggy-backing was a term given to us by one of the students and, along with number 3, refers to the concern I voiced in my end-of-class log reflection, quoted earlier, that conversations needed to be continuous. This list looks all neat and finished here, but the process we went through to arrive at this point was messy and hard. My end-of-class log response contained the following reflection:

> This stuff is really difficult. We take it all for granted. Such common-sense definitions for whole class discussion, for example, are seemingly in our heads, but when we're asked to be explicit, to publicly share our meanings, to define what it is we're trying to look at and achieve, it all gets, not so much confusing, but the 'of course, you do this and then this' becomes much less smug, more unsure. I think Wendy's probably right about cautioning us not to get overly conscious about how we converse, but on the other hand, as I said, we're always complaining about how kids *can't* do this stuff and we need to teach them how. Well, how do we do that? We must at least explore the boundaries, send up the trial balloon, test out our assumptions and beliefs to see what they are, where they go. Otherwise, we remain in the dark.

This challenge to take risks and question assumptions that I was so eager to have us all meet soon began to dissipate during the days following class. I started to question the validity of the required work I was asking them to engage in: Was there such a process as 'whole class discussion' in the first place? We were having so much difficulty trying to come up with criteria, could it be that whole class discussion was an artificial process? Did 'whole class discussion' happen only within a school context, and was it, therefore, only a school-type learning configuration? Did whole class discussion ever happen naturally in a natural language context? These were the questions that floated around in my head and which I discussed with colleagues during the week between classes. As a result, I decided I needed to share my questions and concerns with the class and, so, I made these notes to begin the discussion for our next meeting:

1 Bringing to consciousness things/methods/ideas we've taken for granted and/or think we know how to do actually reveals the complexities and subtlties of these processes/methods.
2 Maybe whole class discussions can't be done because whole group discussions are unnatural/a school phenomenon?

I shared these concerns with them and, in response, they began to argue the need they had for learning how to talk fluently and effectively in large groups. They pointed out that as teachers they would be required to speak at faculty meetings, at parent-teacher gatherings, and potentially they might have the opportunity to speak at conferences where large numbers of people would be in attendance. All of these were large group situations demanding large group discussions. Therefore, they argued, large group discussions do occur in natural language and learning contexts; they are not an artificial device of schooling. Further, they felt they needed to practise how to talk effectively in such settings and that having explicit criteria by which to assess themselves provided them with the means to evaluate their present abilities and to assess their progress. They convinced me that we needed to continue to have whole group discussions.

I was impressed. Students were beginning to exercise their critical voices and share their expertise and knowledge with each other. This class was one of the most exciting I've ever experienced because it was one of the few times that I've ever genuinely felt equality between teacher and students in ownership and knowledge.

We're now at the sixth class meeting of the course and haven't yet touched on the constraint topic of the California artichoke. Tonight is the night!

Each student wrote up an individual list of what she knew or assumed about selling the California artichoke. What follows is the collaborative list of their knowlege, beliefs, and assumptions:

1 Selling the California artichoke throughout the USA is part of the course curriculum that cannot be negotiated.
2 This topic is a typical curriculum topic.
3 The artichoke is a vegetable.
4 Artichokes contain iron.
5 Artichokes, by themselves, are low in calories.
6 Artichokes can be prepared and eaten in many ways, hot or cold, with or without sauce.
7 You can eat part of the leaves (the bottom), heart and pulp of the artichoke.
8 Artichokes are green in color.
9 Thorns must be cut off an artichoke in order to eat it.
10 Artichokes are common in California.
11 Artichokes are sold in restaurants.

At the same time that students wrote up and shared their 'knowns' with one another, they also listed and shared their questions about selling the artichoke and what they thought they would need to find out about the topic in order to learn about it. Here's what the whole class came up with:

1   Where (states, restaurants, etc.) are artichokes sold?
2   To whom are artichokes sold (age, sex, economic status, educational status, culture: retail sales)?
3   How do artichokes grow? (insecticides?)
4   Who grows artichokes? (migrant workers?: raises questions of unionization)
5   Costs (shipping, to grow, to sell, to market, competitive prices?)?
6   Where are artichokes grown?
7   What potential use other than food do artichokes have?
8   What is the nutritional value of an artichoke (calories, vitamins)?
9   What are the possible ways of preparing artichokes for eating (recipes)?
10 Who/what is/are the artichokes' competition?
11 What is the artichoke's shelf life? Home life?
12 What is the best way to sell the artichoke?
13 How should artichokes be shipped? (Are they fragile?)
14 Are artichokes seasonal?
15 Can you mass produce artichokes?
16 How much crop is available throughout the year?
17 Who discovered the artichoke?
18 How did artichokes get their name?
19 What is the image of the artichoke?

One of the assumptions I had about the artichoke topic before we began this process was that most of the students would have eaten artichokes. As you can see from their questions, however, there was a great deal of interest in learning about the artichoke as crop and as product to be consumed because only two or three of the eighteen students had actually cooked and/or eaten artichokes. If I'd proceeded more traditionally to teach on the basis of my own knowledge and assumptions then the class emphasis would have been on the campaign to sell the artichoke.

And had I proceeded in that way, my speculation is that the students would have done a pretty lousy job on selling their product because they would have had no idea what it was they were selling. Instead, their current knowledge and their questions gave them the opportunity to both learn about the artichoke itself and then to build a selling campaign based on what they'd learned, ensuring, I think, a more successful learning product. Clearly, this experience demonstrated for me what happens when students' knowledge and intentions are at the center of teaching and learning.

Our next step was to decide, based on our questions, how to form learning groups and how to go about investigating and answering our questions. This was another fascinating learning experience for me. I had no preconceptions about how we were going to do this, because I didn't know until this moment what our questions would reveal about how and what we would need to learn. All of us sat staring at this list of questions for what seemed like a very long time, but was probably about ten minutes. There was very little conversation and, possibly what made the time seem so long was that we were all tolerating the quiet, something that's rare in the classroom. We didn't need to fill up the quiet because the quiet was purposeful and palpable: you could 'hear' the wheels turning.

Then Susan B. spoke out. She said that it looked as if there were three or four general categories into which all of the questions seemed to fit: Marketing, Finance, Production, and Artichoke as Crop, giving us the conceptual and organizational framework under which we would proceed. The class as a whole nodded and voiced agreement to these categories as Susan illustrated their connection to our list. I literally felt relieved: I, the expert, didn't have to have the answer.

We went through the list item by item and here's what we ended up with: (The letter to the left of the question stands for each of the categories: M = Marketing; F = Finance; P = Production, and A = Artichoke as Crop).

M: 1 Where (states, restaurants, etc.) are artichokes sold?

M: 2 To whom are artichokes sold (age, sex, economic status, educational status, culture: retail sales)?

P: 3 How do artichokes grow? (insecticides?)

P: 4 Who grows artichokes? (migrant workers?: raises questions of unionization)

F: 5 Costs (shipping, to grow, to sell, to market, competitive prices?)?

A: 6 Where are artichokes grown?

A: 7 What potential use other than food do artichokes have?

A: 8 What is the nutritional value of an artichoke (calories, vitamins)?

A: 9 What are the possible ways of preparing artichokes for eating (recipes)?

M: 10 Who/what is/are the artichokes' competition?

P: 11 What is the artichoke's shelf life? Home life?

M: 12 What is the best way to sell the artichoke?

P: 13 How should artichokes be shipped? (Are they fragile?)

A: 14 Are artichokes seasonal?

P: 15 Can you mass produce artichokes?

A: 16 How much crop is available throughout the year?

A: 17 Who discovered the artichoke?

A: 18 How did artichokes get their name?

M: 19 What is the image of the artichoke?

Because only one question seemed to fit the finance category, the students decided to place it under the marketing category. We ended up with three learning groups: one would investigate Marketing, one would work on Production and the third would study the Artichoke as Crop.

The next class (seventh) brought us to the mid-semester mark of the course. I chose this evening and the following one to schedule individual mid-semester assessment conferences with each student. These would be brief — ten minutes per student — but would provide enough time because they were oral, not written, to make contact and share what had gone on so far and what directions needed to be taken for the second half of the course.

While I held conferences in my office across from the classroom, the students met in their learning groups deciding how they were going to find out the answers to their questions and proceeding with their investigations. I scheduled conferences to end fifteen minutes before class ended so that I could bring all three groups together for a learning up-date and to do a reflective piece of writing. It was during the up-date discussion when I could get a feeling for where the groups were (were they all proceeding at a similar pace and intensity?) and they could tell me if they needed me to do anything for them. Other than these fifteen minutes, however, the students were on their own, independently collaborating and learning together.

Each student came to the conference having filled out her copy of the Work Required Assessment Statement for the learning log and whole group discussion areas, these being the only two we had built criteria for at this point. I had my own copy of the form with my assessment for each of them in these two categories as well. The conferences were noteworthy for the amount of agreement and similarity that was exhibited between the students' self-assessments and my assessment of each of them. This was due, I believe, to having built the criteria for assessment together, so that the students not only knew and understood what the criteria were, but as constructors of the criteria themselves, they had genuine personal commitment to them.

I wouldn't want to paint a picture of placid agreement and capitulation to the course philosophy and intentions. There were a few students who weren't comfortable with the course as it was designed, with the philosophy it was generating, with me taking the role of negotiator/master craftsperson, and with the assessment process. But the conferences provided these students with an opportunity to voice their dissent and discomfort.

One student, Amy, was particularly outspoken against the kind of learning and teaching we were engaged in. While she claimed that her experience teaching in a pre-school Montessouri system and its philosophy were similar to what she was doing and learning in this course, she denigrated such student-centered learning and teaching for herself in a university graduate program.

She wanted me to tell her things, so she could write them down and take them back to her school and into her classroom. She was particularly uncomfortable writing her opinions out in her learning log, as her experience had always been to respect the author and the authority's point of view. She showed very little patience, as well, in the large group discussions. She explained to me during our conference that she didn't trust her peers as knowers, and that their stories of teaching and learning were just stories; that stories had no intellectual rigor and that she'd rather hear what I had to say. (Were my stories more rigorous, then?)

The best I was able to do with Amy and with those of her classmates who viewed the world of our course in similar ways, was to reiterate my commitment to hearing and engaging in their critiques of it. I insisted, however, that while they continue to critique their experiences, they also make as best a commitment as they could to the *doing* in the immersion classes. I was confident that, even if in the end they rejected teaching and learning in the ways we were attempting to enact them, that the experience of doing it would enable them to be more informed and educated professionals.

The class in between the two conference nights (eighth) was devoted to a whole group distancing discussion on our responses to Frank Smith's chapters on language and learning. I asked the group if we could focus our discussion on the intersection and interaction among language, thought, and learning, since, for me, this was the central conceptual focus of the course, both as the object of our learning (the focus of distancing classes) and the experience of our learning (what we did in immersion classes). Here is my reflection on what and how I learned that evening:

Language, thought, and learning: did we really talk about this? Yes. I guess we did. Not in the 'intellectual' way I might have preferred — *á la* Smith — but, on the other hand, we did implicitly share our thoughts about all three areas and had some major insights about them and the relationship between/ among them. Politics of schooling, principles of learning, teaching versus learning, productive language use, second language development and acquisition, learning from workbooks versus learning in real contexts were the general areas of our discussion.

One of the greatest contradictions I've discovered in my own teaching is my expertise. This is, of course, ironic given how students want to see me. The contradiction plays itself out in these two questions: (i) How do I share what I know without transmitting it, and, thus promoting regurgitation of what it is I know, not what students necessarily understand or have learned?; and (ii) How do I validate what students do understand and have learned without expecting them to have achieved the same level of expertise that I have?

Negotiating the curriculum constructively was a context in which I could experiment with an approach to teaching and learning where learning wasn't taking on someone else's language and adopting someone else's understandings without building or constructing — without really learning — any of it oneself. Not only is this short-circuited learning (in the ear and out the pen without connecting to the mind), but it's short-lived learning and uncritical learning. It requires no genuine practice of the ideas being 'learned', nor does it embrace and engender reflection on the ideas, the crucial part of the learning cycle which encourages learners to critique and revise what they've learned. In this course, students did practice and did reflect and, so, were building and constructing knowledge for themselves and with each other.

While my reflection after this class continues to exhibit my frustration with all of this, I'm beginning to separate my own level of competence and conceptualization of theory and practice from that of the students. I was crediting them for the depth and breath of their understanding and recognizing that it needn't match my own level to be valid. Many of them had commented in their logs and in the discussion how this course was a living example of Smith's theories. They were beginning to acknowledge how they could teach reading and writing by having students use their own language to learn through reading and writing because that was what they were doing themselves. Such understandings were quite sophisticated given what the students knew and believed at the beginning of the course.

While the students and I were in assessment conferences, the three learning groups met independently to answer their questions and explore how they were going to present their findings to the rest of us. This work in small groups gave the students the personal experience they needed to be able to state their criteria for assessing effective small group work. It was, then, at the eleventh class that we shared and developed the following list of criteria for assessing small group work:

1 Encourage participation/show consideration and respect for each member of the group.
2 Contributions equally shared and active.
3 Exhibit listening etiquette (piggy-backing).
4 Engage in direct eye contact with fellow members of the group.

5 Define and refine individual contributions to group goals through supportive communication (be open/come clean) and continue to share and reflect on individual/group dynamics.

This turned out to be quite a spirited discussion, the end result being the inclusion of criterion number five. It took almost the entire class period for one group to share that they were having some problems. What seemed to be at the heart of their inability to work together successfully was that not all members of the group were contributing equally to the workload. Those who felt they were doing all or most of the work were resentful. They hadn't been able to come up with a strategy they felt comfortable with that could communicate to the non-working members of their group that they must take on their individual responsibilities to the group.

Whether the students are in year three or thirteen or studying to be teachers, the problems in getting each individual in a group to contribute equally seem universal. The basic question the discussion seemed to come down to was: How can we tell our fellow group members they're not doing their work without offending them personally? Criterion #5 gave the small groups an official guideline for talking openly about and assessing individual participation in the small groups.

Coming to this understanding and formulating the criterion with just the right wording was a bit tortuous. From my reflection, I think you can see that I was feeling somewhat at the centre of this discussion, a bit uncomfortable at the controlling role I was taking, and not satisfied with the way I was orchestrating the whole event:

> I don't like teaching standing up. It hurts my back and it hurts my brain and it makes me appear to be the centre of attention and the repository of infinite wisdom and authority. Do I let people go on and on too long? Do I not nip lengthy B.S. stories in the bud quick enough? I still haven't learned how to do this very well, have I? But, boy, wasn't it great how others jumped in to argue with and defend one another, giving each other support and food for thought?

Yet my final note suggests that the students pretty much ignored what I thought was too much me controlling them. I often find that these reflective notes are quite reliable indicators of what actually occurred. Written in free-writing form, they often reveal unexpected insights on the events. In this one, a contradiction is presented to me: I began with my inner feelings of what I thought was happening and ended with an observation of what the students were actually doing. If, in fact, their behavior indicated they were involved in and had control over the class, then I need to question my own perceptions about how I seemed to control them. These notes, then, provided me with new assumptions to question and test out through continuing to reflect on my own teaching.

What Some of the Students Learned

At the last class I asked students to reflectively evaluate the course. In their own words, here's what some of the students wrote:

Susan A.:   The readings, especially the chapters in *Comprehension and Learning* and throughout *Learning to Write/Writing to Learn*, in conjunction with my experience in the class, have emphasized and made clear to me the connectedness of all learning. Growth and confidence in one area supports and almost lures growth and confidence in another. Talking and writing in all its forms are a mode of making our knowledge known to ourselves.

Anonymous: The readings and the classroom experience that I had this semester taught me about cooperation rather than competition in the classroom. I was also thrilled with the experience that we all shared from going from an experience of unknowing to an experience of knowing.

I plan to use this approach in my classroom. I want to make my class a team, a troupe, a company. I really want to use the resource of students helping other students learn things that they already know.

Wendy: 1   I found this class to be both exciting and infuriating. I learned so much from this class's curriculum, but most of all I learned how difficult and long a journey it will be to make others understand the concepts of holistic reading, writing, education, etc. I can easily connect this to Frank Smith's book and [*Learning to Write/Writing to Learn*] because as much as I think I know about using language as a basis for learning how to read and write, I learned something new with every chapter. The reading and class discussions were easily interrelated. After I would do the reading, I had the chance to play it out in class as best I could. Fortunately, I can take what I've learned here and build upon it with further research and practical experience.

2   I will definitedly use this negotiating the curriculum in my class. Of course, I will have to consider my age group and the activities being taught, but I believe there is ALWAYS some degree that children should and must negotiate the curriculum in order to own their education. The entire concept is crucial in and out of the classroom.

Pat: I think this class was very important to me in my growth as a teacher. One of the most critical things I learned was that you must *use* language to learn. I enjoyed negotiation and feel it has an important role in some ways in the classroom. Many of the activities and classes in special education in high school are all teacher oriented. Sometimes there is very little time to have discussions and verbalize new ideas about what we are actually doing. I do make an effort to try to include language (discussion — not just teacher giving lessons) in every lesson now. I am so much more aware.

Anonymous: The class wasn't anything like I expected. I expected a class that instructed you how to help children learn to read and write. Maybe I had the wrong impression.

I enjoyed the readings. They were informative and interesting, but I didn't get much out of the class discussions. It seemed that just a few people dominated the discussions with their own personal experiences.

Learning about artichokes was interesting, but I don't see how it applied to the class other than how you would go about learning something. I feel all I really learned this semester was everything about artichokes that anyone could possiblly learn.

A lot of the ideas discussed in Frank Smith's book I feel could be applied to my actual classroom. I'm sure I'll eventually attempt implementing these into my class curriculum.

I can't say I honestly enjoyed the class because I feel I didn't really learn anything new (other than information about artichokes).

I enjoyed getting to know the people in the class and hearing their views and ideas on topics but other than making new friends I don't feel as if I gained anything from the class.

I don't hold anything against you as a teacher of this class. I know it was a first for you too, a learning experience as it was for all of us. I guess the class was disappointing because it wasn't about what I had expected, but it was still a learning experience.

Maryann: I have always believed in collaborative learning but this experience has helped me process the experience first hand. You gave me the strength to stand up for my convictions and believe in myself.

Marta: Even though the readings were very informative, I felt I learned more from the discussions with both the small and large groups. The interaction allowed me to understand the readings more clearly. And if I had questions, they were usually answered.

Kim: The readings all emphasized the need for developing and using language in order to incorporate new knowledge into existing cognitive structures. Participation in class discussions allowed me to formulate new ideas or revise old ones. Often, with discussion — really delving into a topic — I found my opinions changing. The class emphasized the importance of respecting my students' existing language and building on it.

Susan B.:   Presumably the learning I did in this class will enable me to understand the process of learning as it is being undertaken by students I would work with. It also made me much more aware of the concept of *active* learning, particularly the learning logs. I don't mean learning *about* it, but the *doing* of it. This sounds vague: What I mean is, I learned more about the concept of active learning *by being engaged in it myself*. The artichoke idea did this, also, but brought the point home to me in much less dramatic fashion than did the learning logs.

However, I must admit that I still feel somewhat fuzzy about the language basis to all of this. I think we should have done more, but I'm not sure what. Perhaps more discussions of the readings? One connection/ implication I can make has to do with *patience*. Teaching by process takes a long time, and one has to have a certain amount of faith that it will all 'work out OK'. This is very different from weekly lectures, assessment, drill, whatever, where there is a *superficial comfort* level in 'teaching knowledge'. As an example of this, I was somewhat skeptical about the artichoke project, but I was willing to suspend judgment until we made our presentations. The fact that all learned from it, that it all came together in a number of ways, made we understand the value of doing it. (Hence, the value of patience in teaching: don't be looking for 'quick fixes' or easy 'tricks to teaching'.)

What I Learned

Scattered throughout this chapter are inklings of some of what I learned about negotiating the curriculum and teaching and learning. What stands out for me is the continuing conflict I see — in our actions and in our reflections — between transmitting and constructively negotiating.

This came out most vividly in the final performances of the three study groups. My response to the presentations was that, in general, the groups had fallen back into a didactic, transmission mode of teaching. I'm still not sure why this happened, although I suspect that there was a great deal of factual information the students discovered which they felt they needed to tell to their fellow learners.

Even though we'd enacted a very different kind of pedagogy in this class, there still seemed to be, for many of the students, a need to teach in another way when teaching factual content. The Production group, in particular, were unable to come up with any alternative to telling and giving us a set of facts about each phase of artichoke production. Even their drawing of the production cycle — their central visual aid — ended up being redundant as it depicted graphically what they transmitted aloud to us, even though it might have been used in some other more engaging, collaborative way.

For the last ten minutes of their presentation, one member of the Artichoke as Crop group lectured us on the general history of the artichoke and how to cook it. This information was contained in the first page of the cookbook they'd produced for all of us, and therefore, like the Production group's display, seemed redundant as well as didactic. This group was definitely conflicted, however. The first part of their performance was a clever enactment, involving the entire class, of a restaurant which served only artichokes dishes; dishes we all actually got to sample. But, for whatever reason, they, too, felt that the factual content implicit in their performance had to be transmitted in order to be 'taught' and 'learned'.

The Marketing group, on the other hand, was able to integrate the facts they thought they needed to share into their reflections on their learning, into a story of their exploratory research, and into the presentation for marketing their new artichoke product.

What continues to fascinate and provoke in all of this is what is implicit in the students' reflective evaluations: What each individual student learned (and thus valued about the learning experience) is somewhat different from what other students in the class learned (and valued). In a constructivist, negotiated context this is a natural outcome of teaching and learning. This is very different from what is supposed to occur in a transmission context. If all students memorize and regurgitate the same information equally well, then all would have seemed to have learned the same things. Little tolerance of and even less validity is given to students who learn different things from what is transmitted.

And when I look back at the students' reflective evaluations more closely, I find evidence that a certain level of consciousness has been reached in validating a teaching and learning context which supports students' intentions and recognizes that learners are knowers.

Talking and writing in all forms are a mode of *making our knowledge known to ourselves.*

I really want to use the resources of students helping other students *learn things that they already know.*

There is ALWAYS some degree that *children should and must negotiate the curriculum in order to own their own education.*

Many of the activities and classes in *special education in high school are all teacher oriented. . . .* I do make an effort to try to include language (*discussion — not just teacher giving lessons*) in every lesson now. [My emphases].

And the student who wrote in her reflective evaluation that 'the class wasn't anything like I expected. I expected a class that instructed [me] how to help children learn to read and write', but 'it was still a learning experience' is, even if she doesn't know it, pointing to the contradictions and complexities inherent in the conflict between transmission teaching and learning and constructive negotiation.

Comments such as these will not, in and of themselves, resolve the conflict and the contractions which the students demonstrated by their actions. But they do suggest that while the transmission model of teaching and learning may still be embedded deeply in the minds of these teachers, as learners they now have a growing model of constructivist negotiation as a viable competitor.

Appendix A: Course Introduction
Course Processes

Negotiating the Curriculum

Among the central learning experiences of this course will be to enact and engage in the purposes and processes of negotiating the curriculum. What this means is that we will decide collectively exactly what we will do together, how requirements will be handled, and so on. The goal is to base what we do on:

1 what we already know
2 what we want to know
3 how will we learn it
4 how will we show what we've learned.

Because of the central role of the negotiation process in determining the details of the course, much of the following is necessarily vague. With luck it will gradually become clearer as the next few weeks unfold.

Immersion and Distancing

I have planned this course, as you will see on the attached class activity schedule, to offer you two interrelated learning experiences. Although they are seemingly independent, I hope we will connect them as we proceed, because I believe that the learning cycle is not complete unless we engage in both immersion and distancing and reflect on their connectedness.

The 'immersion' process is another way of describing hands-on learning; in other words, it is enactment. In this part of the learning cycle, we will engage in a curriculum topic which I have selected and which is our content constraint. That is, you have no choice of topic other than the one I have chosen, which will be 'Selling the California Artichoke Throughout the USA'. However, everything else that you decide to do and learn under this topic will be negotiated collaboratively. Since I cannot anticipate what this will be until we begin our negotiation process, I will say no more.

The 'distancing' process is a way of learning which entails reflection, on both our immersion activities and our required reading for the course. Each immersion and distancing part of the learning cycle will be alternated throughout the weeks of the semester, so that we have the time and the hindsight to reflect productively. I have chosen required texts (another content constraint for this course) which I believe will connect to our hands-on activities as well as giving us broader perspectives on them and the whole purposes of this course which is to learn about using language to learn.

What I am attempting to achieve in this course is a model of what I consider to be the goal of teaching and learning reform in our schools. I hope that by engaging in this kind of teaching and learning ourselves we will be better able to understand what this kind of teaching and learning might look like, how learners and teachers behave within this kind of teaching and learning context, and that the experience will give us the necessary expertise to apply this kind of teaching and learning in other contexts, in your classrooms, for example, should you be teaching now.

Work Required Assessment

Because I believe that alternative forms of assessment from those we now use (mostly norm-referenced) need to be developed in schools (K–Graduate School), especially if the teaching and learning reforms we will be enacting are ever to take effect, we will attempt one kind of alternative form of assessment for this course. 'Work Required Assessment' has been developed and used in Australian schools for several years now, and it is this model of criterion-referenced assessment upon which we will base our assessment for this course. A 'statement' of work required assessment is attached to this material. In it,

I have delineated four processes of learning to be assessed and the work re-quired for achieving them. What is not yet included are the criteria by which the assessment will be made. Those criteria will be developed collaboratively by all of us during our first and second class meetings. However, I offer below a general summary of what my notion of each process/work requirement might be.

Reflections on Language and Learning

The one on-going, throughout the semester, writing requirement will be for you to keep a learning log. This log will contain your responses to your reading, your class discussions and reflections, and anything else you deem essential to your learning about how language is acquired, how it is developed, and how it is related to learning. Learning logs are intended to give you a continuous map of your own learning and to provide sources for ideas on classroom applications. They are an example of one way to use writing as a way of learning, and my hope is that they will provide you with both a personal experience of this kind as well as serve as a potential language as learning activity in your own classrooms. Learning logs are serious records of learning and will be considered so by me.

Additional writing may be generated by you as part of the negotiated cur-riculum of the constraint content. At this point I cannot predict what that will be; in fact, you will determine that yourselves.

Reading and Required Texts

John Mayher, Nancy B. Lester, and Gordon M. Pradl *Learning to Write/Writing to Learn*, Boynton/Cook (Heinemann), 1983.
Margaret Meek *Achieving Literacy: Longitudinal Studies of Adolescents Learning to Read*, London: Routledge and Kegan Paul, 1983.
Frank Smith *Comprehension and Learning: A Conceptual Framework for Teach-ers*, Richard Owen, 1975.
Gordon Wells *The Meaning Makers: Children Learning Language and Using Language to Learn*, Portsmouth, NH: Heinemann, 1986.

The Smith book, *Comprehension and Learning*, is the only text we will all read in common in its entirety. You will make your own choices as to which chapters/sections in the remaining three books you want to read for each two weeks' assign-ment. This will depend on your interests, of course, but you should consider dipping into all three remaining texts so you can have the opportunity to sample each one in case you might want to read further in it at some later time. The goal, here, is to engender a rich, diverse discussion of our reading when we meet as a whole group to share our responses. My assumption is that you will be reading different things and will be able to inform your co-learners, as well as the discussion, with particular examples from what you have chosen to read for that week's discussion.

At this point, not knowing what your individual and group learning goals will be, I cannot predict how much more you will need to read on the 'constraint' topic of this course. We will read a few xeroxed articles together for our third class meeting, so you can expect these in addition to the list of books required. Of course, you are welcome to read anything else that comes your way and which you might wish to share with the rest of us during our whole class discussions of our reading.

Collaborative Negotiation of Learning

Much of what I will be encouraging in this class is collaborative learning. Although each of you will be able to pursue your own learning goals, some of which may be naturally collaborative, you will also be encouraged through group talk and planning to work with one another and support each other. If we decide that talking to learn and collaborative learning need to be part of what we learn to do in here, then we should consider this another area for negotiation.

Participation in Whole Group Discussions

We will do a great deal of talking in this class, in small groups, but also as a whole group at times. Since it is my belief and understanding that talking is an active way to learn, I will encourage you to talk as much as I can. My expectation, then, is that everyone will attempt to take an active talking role in their learning. I understand and accept that some will talk more than others, and that there will be times when we may have to stop people from talking. It is important to keep in mind that if you don't pitch in, if you don't contribute your two cents, then you are denying yourself a voice in what goes on in here. That would be too bad, since this course is attempting to encourage and engender your ownership and responsibility over it.

Presentation of Learning

Everyone will be required to make a final presentation of their learning at the end of the course by sharing and showing their learning to the rest of the members of the class. I anticipate that these presentations will be made mostly by small groups, but that is not a requirement.

Summary

Part of the reason I have written all of this out is to give you a sense of who I am and what my expectations and beliefs are. My overall goal for this course is to make it a model for the kinds of classrooms which will result if we implement language and learning. In other words, I am trying to offer you an experience of what it means to use language as a way of learning as well as what a classroom which uses it will look, feel, and sound like. Using language to learn necessarily changes the roles that learners and teachers play, and it is these new roles which I am attempting to foster and have us reflect on. Some of you may be more familiar or more comfortable than others with classrooms like this. But no matter how you feel, although it will be important for you to share your responses along the way, seeing this classroom as an experiment in learning would be an attitude which could help you experiment, take risks, evaluate, and reflect. These are the most important things, I think. If at the end you reject this model of learning and teaching, you have at least gotten a chance to experience it.

Work Required Assessment Form

Name:_____

Process	*Work Required*
1 Reflection on language and learning	1 Keep an on-going learning log of both your in-class and out-of-class language and learning endeavors.

Criteria:

Assessment: _____

2 Collaborative negotiation of learning	2 Actively engage in small group problem-setting and problem-solving activities.

Criteria:

Assessment: _____

3 Participation in whole group discussions	3 Demonstrate, through active sharing, your understanding of and questions about your reading.

Criteria:

Assessment: _____

4 Presentation of learning	4 Each small group will present to the rest of the class an appropriate product of their learning for the semester.

Criteria:

Assessment: _____

Assessment Categories:
S: Work successfully completed: Grade of A
NS: Work completed, but does not satisfy all of the defined criteria: IP
NC: Work not completed: IP

References

BOOMER, G. (Ed.) (1982) *Negotiating the Curriculum: A Teacher-Student Partnership*, Sydney, Australia: Ashton-Scholastic.

BOOMER, G. (1988) The amazing literacy machine. Unpublished address delivered to the Ontario Council of Teachers of English, Annual Conference, Toronto, Ontario, Canada.

JOHNSTON, B. and DOWDY, A. (1988) *Teaching and Assessing in a Negotiated Curriculum*, Australia: Martin Educational.

LESTER, N.B. and ONORE, C.S. (1990) *Learning Change: One School District Meets Language Across the Curriculum*, Portsmouth, NH: Boynton/Cook-Heinemann.

LINDFORS, J.S. (1984) 'How children learn and how teachers teach: A profound confusion', *Language Arts*, **61**, 6, October, pp. 600–606.

SMITH, F. (1985) *Comprehension and Learning: A Conceptual Framework for Teachers*. NY: Owen.

Chapter 12

On Beginning to Negotiate

Christine Cook

In the last five years of my thirteen-year career as a teacher of English to 12–17 year old students, I have tried to negotiate with students. What has made me reconsider how I have been teaching during these years has been the impact of my reading (*Small Group Learning in the Classroom*, 1990, and *Negotiating the Curriculum: A Teacher-Student Partnership*, 1982, are among the most significant) and my observation of the education of my own children. Five years ago, my own children were in kindergarten and junior primary school classes. I had regarded myself as a good teacher in the past, but came to realize that my students at school were missing the vigour with which 'kindy' kids approached their learning. I could see that many good kindy teachers used small group learning and elements of negotiation for most of their lessons and I started to question: Why wasn't I?

My students were not experiencing the learning opportunities that small group learning and negotiation seemed to offer, and somewhere between kindy and high school they had lost the zest for learning. I felt that small groups and negotiation might offer a way to hold onto teenagers' zest. I thought it was high time I tried these ideas, hoping to make my students as interested and keen as kindy kids seemed to be and give them the chance to think about what, how, and why they were learning and to share those ideas with me and other kids.

I wanted to give kids the chance to share their thoughts without being intimidated by me or the whole class; to have a say in what they might read, talk, or write about, and how we might do it; to see why sometimes we had no choice about what we learn; to think rather than be spoon-fed; to decide on aspects of their learning and be responsible for them; and to be excited about learning. I wanted kids to use talk to explore, analyze and reflect on texts, ideas and concepts much more than I had previously allowed through the way I controlled classes. Exploratory talk is an essential and imperative learning activity before kids present an oral or written product. Small group work is a perfect forum for kids to thrash out, rehearse and perhaps present their ideas and their products.

I know that students can teach and learn from each other. In fact, students seem to listen better to points made by their peers than points made by a teacher. I don't have to be the only teacher in the classroom. Therefore, I think it's important to give kids the opportunity to be able to share their knowledge. Small group work is a medium which allows for this.

Putting small group work and negotiation into practice has caused changes in my teaching which have been an improvement for both me and my students. The learning that now occurs in my classroom in relation to students' interests and what they achieve has improved. I enjoy teaching more because of the changes. This paper deals with the way I now teach students, some of the problems I encounter, my reflections and the improvements I have come to recognize need to be made in the future.

Problems With and Benefits From Small Group Learning and Negotiating the Curriculum

Small Group Learning

When I started teaching at my present school three years ago, I seemed to be alone in setting my class up in groups because students were used to rows of pairs or individual desks, or long benches for subjects like science. Although every activity in my class wasn't conducted in groups, students could swing into a class discussion, with desks placed diagonally facing the front, into pairs, or into individual work. I found the ideas and strategies in *Small Group Learning in the Classroom* a great help when I was working out classroom structures.

When kids first start with me, they need time to adjust to the class setup. However, it doesn't take them too long to observe the benefits of being able to share their ideas and work comfortably with a small group of peers without feeling pressured by whole class or teacher-dominated discussions and expectations. They have even become outraged if I change the desks into single files after a period of time working in groups. Some English teachers have followed my practices which makes teaching this way easier. Although the kids enjoy the way I teach, they also need to see that this kind of classroom structure is acceptable to other teachers. They had to do less adjusting to different classroom practices. Fitting my way of teaching into the approaches of the whole school was difficult, but my students' responses to small group work has bolstered my confidence about using these strategies.

One student, sixteen year-old Sharon, in her reflections on a unit on advertising, indicated the benefit she considered the group work to have:

> I think the way that we handled the television advertising unit was great, as we weren't repeating things that we already knew or were skipping things we didn't. When we do things in groups or orally I seem to learn more and concentrate for longer.

Brad, from the same class, reflects on his learning:

> I feel as though this unit has been beneficial because I understand how advertising companies use different methods to brainwash people. The way in which it was studied was good as it made me think for myself rather than relying on the teacher, and this gives you self-esteem when you succeed in your given role or task.

Group work has been a beneficial way for students to make known what they knew, what they would like to know, and how they would like to find it out. They didn't seem to be as inhibited as I remember in my first years of teaching, where only a few students actively participated and those few were guessing what they thought I wanted. They assumed in the past that my reading of the context, whatever it might have been, was the right and only one. I like the idea of students realizing there are many readings of a situation or text.

Negotiating

Initially, I found it awkward sharing the power that had always rested in my hands. I was no longer the centrepin in total control or the star of the show. Previously, I was always the only one to know what the next lesson or set of lessons would be or what had to be studied and why, and, even, for how long. I had to become used to sharing these decisions with students.

There are three problematic aspects to negotiating. The first I noticed when I started negotiating five years ago. I failed to give students enough information or explanation about the learning we were encountering: the what, why, where, and for how long. It's very difficult to plan lessons with students without them having knowledge of these components. Specifically, I didn't give enough guidance to students in the type and range of activities which could be used to explore texts, processes, and concepts. When I didn't give enough information students were floundering with the choices I did give them; and balked when I said to them something very general without much guidance, like: 'This is the text, process or concept we're going to do. How do you want to do it? What are you interested in doing in relation to this unit?' Although there may be points negotiated throughout a unit, it's mostly at the very beginning that it's hectic. The thinking aloud about what we're doing and the energy that that necessitates has its rewards for me in the way students become more engaged and interested in learning, the increased sharing of ideas, the improved products, and the happier atmosphere in the classroom.

The second aspect is accommodating and listening to students' contributions, ideas and interests. The students don't misbehave, but my skill in group management, especially when students report on their group discussions, is tested. Kids are brimming with ideas and I have to ensure that a rule of one person talking at a time, either in groups or whole class discussion, is enforced.

Allowing sufficient time to explain and inform a class about the non-negotiables is the third aspect. I have found that students need time to understand information I have given them about a course, for groups to share their ideas, and the class to come to consensus about a negotiated aspect. I've tended sometimes to worry that we're wasting time, but the talking, persuading, and note-taking which are involved in a negotiating process facilitate language and communication. Also, the amount of incidental learning is considerable.

Taking the time to help students obtain some understanding of the framework of their curriculum, which, in turn, gives them more knowledge about what is non-negotiable and what can be negotiated is worthwhile. It gives them a chance to see some of the small parts which make up the larger picture. They have the chance to understand the constraints under which I work. For example:

the texts to which we're limited; the expectations of the syllabus (including texts and processes which are prescribed or recommended, and any flexibility of units within the course); the school expectations regarding timetabling and assessment policies (including percentage weightings recommended, assessment criteria, and a range of possible assessment modes and audiences).

Adjusting

Some students indicate they've never experienced teaching practices like these before and are unfamiliar with the demands being made of them and the information being given to them. I ask them to think and talk about aspects of their learning which are usually spoon-fed to them. I think they expect me to work out and plan all the aspects of their learning I want to negotiate with them. And why not? That's what they're used to. They're not familiar with negotiation. Some teachers negotiate on a small scale, like giving kids a choice about alternative essays to write, but few use it on the scale I am attempting. Therefore, students find it different in my class because most other teachers don't ask them to write their own questions to a poem; or frame their own essay about a novel after considering the syllabus and their own interests; or work out ways to explore a text or concept. Students find it hard to work in this unfamiliar territory because my class may be the only one in my school trying to negotiate with students.

Learning

As an experienced teacher I have found that small group work and negotiating with students allows for more oral contributions and, therefore, students have a chance for wider exploration before they produce further written or oral work. Their written work shows more detail and understanding. They become more articulate. I think my reflection on the unit of work on advertising shows this.

> The essay products that most students completed exhibited sound structure, content, and understandings. They showed that some students had grasped comprehension skills of analyzing television advertising relating their views to the cultural context in which we live. Most students showed an understanding of the need to explain their interpretation of television ads in detail using specific points of analysis and illustration to explain their ideas. Most could acknowledge people's needs and desires to which advertisers play, the role and number of gimmicks advertisers use, and an interpretation of the effect of them. The knowledge/learning shown by students, in contrast to Day 1 of the unit, had significantly changed.
>
> Was it worth negotiating for a one-week unit of work? The turn around in the level of interest for the majority of the class and the higher standard achieved in work products than before the unit of work when little negotiation occurred made it worthwhile.

I think students appreciate the chance to negotiate even though they may not immediately take up the opportunity. Students know that some of their interests have been considered, and they know what external restrictions, demands, and expectations are placed on them. They are rejuvenated in their learning. They want to participate because they have ownership.

Contradictions

I find some contradictions between wanting to share power and authority with students while at the same time wanting to control and discipline student behavior. I want to explore some of those contradictions and think aloud about how I might resolve them for the future negotiating I hope to do with my students.

Noise and Discipline

[Negotiating] can be a frantic time because the compromises that are reached need to be worked through. I had to reestablish classroom rules of listening, which students had forgotten. This took patience and energy.

I want to reflect on this journal entry. Should I try to *make* students listen? I could discuss with them a code of behaviour and set up a framework for this aspect of the classroom as a non-negotiable. Certainly, in most classes I have I 'come clean' about what my conditions are — conditions which I have made non-negotiable for classroom behaviour. This may not be the ideal way of predetermining how students should behave. Time is a constraint for me; I rationalize my laying down a code of behaviour to classes as a pragmatic move. However, this could be a negotiated aspect of their curriculum, and considering the importance I place on this precondition in the classroom for negotiation or any other learning, then perhaps I should allow time for us to decide democratically how we should behave.

A desirable classroom is one where students listen to each other and the teacher. Achieving this in a class is necessary. I don't think a teacher can negotiate unless this occurs. Achieving and managing a situation where there is respectful listening while allowing students to contribute their ideas doesn't mean that the teacher has given up all the power over learning. It just places the teacher in a role of facilitator for negotiation to occur. With classes who are experienced in negotiating, this role could be allocated to them.

Our school has a code of behaviour to which all students are exposed and there's a whole school approach to managing student behaviour. I make these clear to students when I first meet them. I explain my rules and how they fit in with the school's. The school's code is no different from mine, because it requires that students have respect for other people's learning. This could be used as a starting point in negotiating rules for our classroom. Measures taken against recalcitrants could be debated in the class with consideration of school policies in this matter. I need to continue to remember that a classroom full of people contributing and asserting their ideas as negotiation occurs in small groups and as a whole class is bound to be noisy. It can be hectic accommodating input as I pointed out earlier when discussing some of the problems with negotiating.

Trusting kids and not underestimating their abilities is related to students taking responsibility for their behaviour as well as their learning.

Sharing Control

How much power over learning do you give kids? I've tried to say how hard I find it to share power with students. Most often kids take up the spirit of sharing and want to put their stamp on what's going to be studied. They want ownership. Sometimes, when a class is unused to contributing in this fashion, all has been deadly quiet and they acquiesce to anything. In this situation, it's hard not to dominate the class with ideas about how and what we should learn. To ameliorate this in the future, I would make sure students have plenty of alternatives about their learning from which to choose.

The fact that I have more knowledge about lesson preparation and teaching strategies gives me power. Students need to be informed about these things thus empowering them to be able to give ideas and help make decisions. Students have a bank of latent talent about the 'what' and 'how' of lessons. Their ideas are interesting, worthwhile, and fun. The decision for me of how much guidance to give them about the negotiable aspects of the curriculum would depend on how much knowledge I thought they had about lesson planning. It is my responsibility to share this aspect of my knowledge with them.

I think the focus in teaching should be on students' needs in their learning. Being flexible and accommodating those needs is vital. Flexibility includes sensitivity to the school context, to students both in terms of where they are in their learning and their experience with negotiation, and the intentions of students and teachers. This snapshot from my classroom comes from a journal entry I made on the second day of negotiating with the class I've used throughout this chapter as an example:

> From that point, individuals asked if I would analyze the ad and model to them what was enough. The whole class came to consensus about this and about my idea that they take notes as I talked. They agreed with me that they could not write at length about TV ads at this stage. They were revizing the knowledge they thought they had and felt that more exploration and input from some source was necessary. Most realized that their questions about the unit were different from the previous day.

After students become more familiar with how I teach and with the idea of negotiating, they are less inclined to allow me to dominate. When I consciously try to step back and allow us to take risks (even with non-negotiables taken into account), I sometimes find it intimidating. As students and I recognize that our interests and needs can be met, and when this is accompanied by success in meeting syllabus requirements and other non-negotiables, our confidence builds allowing me to be more flexible in my negotiation and students to contribute more freely.

I don't think sharing power comes easily. It's important that students see that I'm prepared to acknowledge their input and that I'm prepared to change or rearrange according to the consensus of the class or because of a persuasive point made by a group or individual. I should be able to use my professional judgment to advise, persuade, argue, cajole students into following a type of learning that I think is preferable. More importantly, I should also be able to justify the why to them.

Thoughts on the Future

Reflecting on the past often helps us to understand where to go in the future. I can see that there's a philosophy of teaching in all of my classes which is sharing learning. I continue to make blunders and oversights in many areas of negotiation, but learn from them. As my learning increases, so does my interest level. I'm openly more accountable to students. They respect me for sharing learning with them and giving them a clear idea of where we are, what we have and what we're expected to do. The rest of the school community including teachers, principal and parents seem to respect me because they observe the interest my students have in their English classes and the high standard of work that's produced.

Considering that negotiation and small group work have been around for at least ten years. I'm astounded that there aren't more teachers trying them out. Is negotiating with kids too hard or just too different? Why am I willing to work with kids in these ways while so many teachers don't want to give it a go? Is the element of risk too high using small group work and negotiation? Are teachers fearful of trusting students? Perhaps the contradictions and dilemmas associated with the struggle over power and authority, control and flexibility make 'safe ground' seem preferable for so many of my colleagues.

As I work through those struggles, I realize I can become more relaxed about the 'risks'. If students accept responsibility for the activity and clearly understand what that responsibility is and means, then surely this creates a more confident context for my risk taking. Can students frame suitable questions? I think students can undertake many activities, detailed organization, and complex thinking which we assume they can't. My expectations of the kids have increased and as they increase, kids meet them. I think, in the future, I will expect more!

References

BOOMER, G. (1982) *Negotiating the Curriculum: A Teacher-Student Partnership*, Sydney: Ashton-Scholastic.

REID, J.A., FORRESTAL, P. and COOK, J. (1990) *Small Group Learning in the Classroom*, Portsmouth, NH: Heinemann Educational Books; Toronto: Irwin Publishing.

Chapter 13

Negotiating Interdisciplinary Teaching and Learning in Secondary English/Social Studies

Chris Louth and Doug Young

Editors note
This chapter was written collaboratively by Chris Louth and Doug Young.
Almost a year later, we asked them to reflect some more, since we thought
the distance from this first experience might have prompted additional
insights. Chris decided to respond. Her continued reflections on this first
attempt at the negotiating of and in an interdiciplinary team teaching context
are deepened by the fact that she and Doug are team teaching this course
again. Her reflections are printed in italic type and we think they help us
to see the power of continued reflection over time and through continued
actions.

In the spring of 1989 our principal, Sherry King, approached us with the idea of piloting a 9th grade interdisciplinary English/Social Studies course.[1] It wasn't a surprising proposal. In many ways, it was a logical next step for us to take considering the work we'd done together over the previous three years. We'd both been involved in a district-wide school-based education program referred to as 'The Writing Workshop', facilitated by Nancy Lester and Cindy Onore. This program had prompted us to reconsider dramatically the way we viewed teaching and learning.

Because of that programme we'd both been struggling to enact the roles of teachers as researchers in our own classrooms. We talked together and with other teachers frequently — both through the official framework of the writing workshop and in the snatches of time we could grab in our hectic schedules — about what happened when we observed in our own classrooms and then tried to respond to those observations. We wrestled together with issues ranging from small procedural minutia to broad theoretical concerns.

We both wanted to support our students in reading the curriculum and thus taking greater ownership of their own learning. As a result, we often hashed over successes and frustrations as we negotiated with students, encouraged them to look at learning as a process rather than as an exercise in regurgitation, and tried to demonstrate the roles of teachers as coaches and co-learners. One of our continual frustrations in all of our attempts was that we were often asking students to function in ways that ran counter to something they had learned very well: the structured, commonsense way school is 'sposed to be'.

I also realize that we had to engage in creating such problems before we could fully sense just how difficult it is to construct a curriculum that has real meaning and purpose for all of us and to help students read that curriculum and see the depth of the meaning, the purpose, the possibilities for themselves. To continually pull myself back from being a 'traditional commonsense' teacher — and to collaborate with others to do so — is hard enough; add to that a myriad of institutional and political constraints.

What follows is the chronicle of our work: the planning, the reflections, the frustrations, the replanning, as we attempted to negotiate with each other and our students toward real learning. We hoped that as we consciously exposed our processes — to each other, our students, and our colleagues — we would come to a greater understanding of genuine learning, which we defined as learning how to learn, and what that looked and felt like admidst all the constraints of an institutional setting. Initially, we'll discuss what happened with the planning and first month of school chronologically in order to give the flavor of our processes. From there, we'll step back and take a more focused look at several key issues that we struggled with throughout the year.

A Brief Chronology: Teachers as Negotiators

Once we decided to take the plunge and to team teach, some immediate questions needed to be answered related to scheduling: Which students would take the course? How could our time with them be increased beyond traditional forty minute blocks? Would we have enough planning time during the course of the day and the year among ourselves?

All of us, including Sherry, were in agreement that the course should be heterogeneous, so it seemed logical that students be computer-scheduled into the course at random. Social Studies and English were scheduled so that they could meet in an eighty minute block of time. This would give us at least one period of planning time together each day. With these 'basics' established, we requested summer workshop time from the District to begin building the framework of the course itself. Because the social studies curriculum in New York state is rigidly driven by a Global Studies Regents Examination which students take at the end of 10th grade, and whereas English content requirements allowed greater latitude on the part of the teacher, we decided to set up the course so that it would be driven by the social studies curriculum.

On a very simple level, the double-period (eighty minute time block) combined with the opportunity to have two teachers in a classroom to coach eighteen students made a noticeable difference in the students' chances to reflect about their own learning. Simulations didn't have to be broken over two or three days. Instead, students could be immersed in an activity that allowed them to experience or recreate 'real world' situations and still have time to distance themselves and reflect on the significance of the activity through writing and discussion with peers. The same held true for extended work with their writing. Students had chances to see

demonstrations of some aspect of the writing process, followed by immediate op-
portunity to try out that strategy, through work with peers and teacher conferencing.
And again, they would have immediate chance to pull back and reflect on how that
strategy had or had not been helpful for them.

We went into our summer planning work with mixed feelings of enthusiasm
and uncertainty. We asked Harold Zabitz (the art teacher) to join the team.
Harold's contributions do not figure into this report, but were nonetheless important in the overall planning process. We felt that without question the direction
we were heading was the right one. We also knew from our previous work together that our beliefs about teaching and learning were compatible. We had
instrinsically the same goals for our students: that they become inquiring owners
of their learning and see us as partners in learning, not distributors of some
commodity called 'knowledge'.

Accordingly, we knew that we wanted to demonstrate active learning with
students allowing time for reflection about what went on. Negotiating would also
be crucial — between the two of us and with the students. However, in spite of
a firm scaffold of like philosophy, we felt uncomfortable trying to merge the skill
and content requirements of two courses. We had seven days in our summer
workshop to try to negotiate a broad plan for the year and a much more specific
plan for the first quarter of the year. In addition, we were worried about translating
our ideas into a 'linear' curriculum that could be published for the Board of
Education and parents.

We both believed that teachers are learners, so we knew that we would be
learning as we went and, therefore, constantly changing any stated curriculum,
once we reflected on what we'd observed about our students and each other. We
devised a working solution to this by deciding on broad activities over the course
of the year that we thought we wanted students to be immersed in. Through these
activities, they could experience the distancing, reflecting, and questioning that
would comprise the heart of the course and which we believed would result in
thoughtful learning.

In a 1989 article in Educational Leadership, *Grant Wiggins advises educators*
to accept the fact that students will leave high school not knowing a lot. What they
do need to leave with, Wiggins asserts, are '... the habits of mind and high standards
of craftsmanship necessary in the face of one's inevitable ignorance' (p. 45). In my
mind, interdisciplinary study should enable students to develop and see the im-
portance of the habits of mind I believe Wiggins is speaking of: the continual
inquiry and thoughtfulness with which we try to answer some questions just as we
move on to new ones. I believe that our first year with an interdisciplinary course
indicated that potential for interdisciplinary work, just as it uncovered its complexities
and problems.

Because we had come to see writing as an integral part of learning and
negotiating, from the initial steps of finding out what we already know to the final
steps of reporting for an audience what we had learned, writing would be used
frequently. In addition, we wanted to use a writing project that Doug had been
developing over the previous four years. Doug's 'Adopt-a-Country' project asked
students to choose to research one third world country for the entire year and
report back on their findings in several papers that looked at increasingly complex issues.

These projects were designed to help students develop their abilities to write expository papers while, at the same time, learning more about the third world. Students are asked to present their findings in a personal, narrative style as they deal with basic cultural diversity in early drafts and then in successive revisions to expand their focuses to issues involving conflict and human rights. Chris had worked in her English classes with students as they researched, wrote, and revised their papers, and so this seemed to be a perfect focal point to start with. We also were aware that many demonstrations would come in here, for we planned on writing the same papers that we would ask students to write. In addition to using a great deal of writing, there seemed to be obvious links with literature, particularly literature dealing with racism, prejudice, and discrimination.

My goal for student learning in English can be stated directly: I want my students to have extensive experience in making purposeful meaning. I really believe that if students can see that the writing, reading, and talking they're doing all relates to their constructing ideas which are important to them, then the sort of intensive thoughtfulness needed to write, read, and communicate with power will develop from successive practice.

I know, of course, from experience that finding those things that will be meaningful to students and providing the balance of structure and freedom that will help them discover what is important to them often feels like a never-ending juggling act. I know that students need the chance to make the same choices that readers and writers make all the time in the real world, choices which include deciding what they want to read and what they want to write. I believe that the more often that they're asked to look carefully and respond thoughtfully to something they've chosen to read or write, the more likely they are to make that sort of 'close looking' a habit whenever they work with a text for a purpose that's clear to them.

I can't think of any more powerful experience in a classroom than students responding thoughtfully to each other's writing or students engaging in extended discourse about a novel to which they've made a personal connection. And so I do find myself 'juggling', trying to listen to what they say is important and compelling and interesting and trying to respond to what they're trying to do, and then building an ongoing classroom experience with language from forty minute blocks of time that is only one-eighth what they're asked to focus on each day!

I had hoped that through the interdisciplinary class we would be able to simply extend the opportunity that students had to look thoughtfully at their own texts and those of others, so that they would see what was asked of them in English as a universal habit in dealing with the printed and spoken word. In both my English class and the interdisciplinary course, however, freedom of choice got too mixed up with required curriculum. I often feel that what I originally intended as something for students to make critical choices about got bogged down in content choices made by the teachers.

As we tried to convert these constraints into a workable schedule for the year, we fell into a pattern of 'brainstorming': pose questions, research, build tentative answers. We would talk about what we wanted to do, break to do it, then come back together to work out a solution. Doug noted later that he saw our summer work as being

> ... immersed in constant negotiation ... which is seldom done by teach-
> ers because of difficulties resulting from divergent views on what educa-
> tion should be and consequent varying styles of teaching.

Proceeding in such a fashion we devised a 'working outline' of the course, which we thought of as a framework for future negotiations. We met with Sherry in July and shared our initial draft with her along with some concerns we had about funds we might need and the potential for parental complaints, since only a quarter of the freshman class would have the chance to be involved in the course. We emerged from that meeting with Sherry's support and promise to take the heat from any parental problems. This seemed to us to be the kind of administrative support that's necessary when teachers are attempting to try out new ways of teaching and learning.

However, there were also questions gnawing at us that we suspected would continually surface throughout the year. At the top of our list was the feeling of dissonance over having said we wanted to leave plenty of room for negotiation and then turning right around and creating what looked like a very concrete, commonsense 'To Do List'. In trying to give ourselves a sense of comfort with the course were we engineering and contriving too much, eliminating the possibility of ownership by the students, or any chance to really negotiate with them? Would we be tempted to fall back on our 'curriculum' and 'follow' it once the ongoing pressures of the year began to erode our good intentions of being reflective practitioners? That question, of course, immediately led to another one: How would we ever find time to plan all the things we had left up in the air, not to mention the time to carefully process and document what we were doing?

As I try to look through the lens of our interdisciplinary experience to help me see what I've learned about negotiation, I feel the greatest frustration. So many things are bumping up against each other. It's difficult to begin sorting them out. After scratching out page after page of starts, stops, and restarts, it just ain't simple.

We wanted to negotiate with each other and demonstrate the learning that results from such negotiation to our students. We did that on occasion, but it was never the driving force of our practice. Much of our negotiation was behind closed doors and there, I believe, too often we dealt pragmatically with our negotiating our way through the content of the Social Studies curriculum and trying to make tenuous links to English content, rather than focusing on what I am now coming to see as the real questions at stake in teacher collaborations. 'What habits of mind do we want students to practise in this course? And what will they do to show that they are developing them?' What if our negotiations started there and students were given the results at the beginning of a course along with chances to respond and have real input to the possibilities of how such learning would be uncovered in the course?

When Grant Wiggins explains his teacher as coach metaphor, he talks about sending players right out to play the game, not having them first memorize the history of the game, take quizzes on game technique, and write essays about game theories. I wonder, were we ever clear in our minds with what the game — the final performance — in the interdisciplinary course was? Or did we simply negotiate the curriculum with ourselves in the same sense that one 'negotiates the rapids' — gets through the next set of currents, worrying about the ones after when, and if, we get there?

Getting Started: Teachers as Reflective Practitioners

Teaching with someone else is exhilarating . . . really cuts the feeling of 'me-ness' which can be so defeating and isolating.

Chris wrote those words in her learning log toward the end of September, but they reflected our growing awareness about the task we were undertaking. Thus far we were having a good time and so were the kids!

The initial work for the course focused on concepts and terminology which were non-negotiable constraints of the curriculum. During our first joint session we wanted students to have the chance to begin making some personal connections to these concepts. In the first half of the eighty minute period, students worked in groups to share what they knew about articles they'd found at home which were produced in the third world. They discussed their findings and then presented their conclusions back to the whole class, using maps to point out the various countries. During their presentations we took the opportunity to question and respond both to them and to each other. Early on, we wanted to demonstrate ongoing inquiry between the two of us, hoping students would view it as an underlying habit of mind.

In the second half of that first period, we demonstrated how to brainstorm to select our country. By the end of the class, everyone had generated, via brainstorming, possibilities that they were considering and had shared those choices with the entire class.

In reflecting on our first session afterward, we were amazed by how much had been done in eighty minutes. Our sense of starting something, working it through, and reaching a natural conclusion was very strong and contrasted starkly with our normal feeling of truncating something, then trying to resuscitate it the next day as is often the case in forty minute time blocks. Doug's observations of his other classes confirmed our feelings. He wrote in his log:

I felt frustration when my other classes were asked to make choices. It took three to five days to get everyone finalized and often they were simply responding to my suggestions, not generating choices of their own. Without the extended demonstration, I had no vehicle to engage them.

In another session shortly after, with a simulation we were calling 'The Global Village', students were asked to work in continent groups to discuss their knowledge and feelings about their situation in relation to other continents, their assessment of causes of unequal distribution of wealth, and their recommendations for solutions. Their task was to present their findings to the whole group in a creative fashion, such as a poem, skit, rap, etc. While students conferred with each other, we acted as consultants. But, we felt that the most important learning that took place during this time was learning what took place without us, learning what was going on when the students, in their roles as spokespersons for their continents, had to negotiate, threaten, and plead for recognition.

We reflected together again the following day on what had happened. We especially wanted to be sure that students began to look at what we were doing as part of an ongoing learning process, not just a series of neat activities. Accordingly, all of us wrote about what was beneficial in what we'd done and shared what might have been done differently. When asked to list areas for improvement, students focused on both themselves and us as teachers. For themselves, they talked about a need to be more 'creative, forceful, and prepared' in their presentations. For us, they talked about needing more time to prepare presentations for the group.

Looking back now at what happened early in the year, we still can feel the initial enthusiasm that we and the students felt. However, with the more critical eye that distancing can bring, we also wondered if we did do enough of bringing the students behind the set. We'd briefly discussed with them why it made sense for disciplines to work together, but in our enthusiasm to cut to the chase, so to speak, we hadn't really asked them to do much exploration of our reasons nor had we assisted them in reading the curriculum that we'd set forth. Certainly our bringing them in on evaluating what had happened so far in class was a step in the right direction, but was it enough?

It's clear to us now that we were still the ones working behind the scenes, not exposing our struggle, much less bringing them in on being authentically involved with posing the actual questions to be answered. Going back to our logs, it appears to be the juncture where we were really starting to look closely enough at what we and the kids were doing and to begin to act, or at least question each other, on the basis of what we were finding. Chris wrote in her log after one session:

> It took us a whole period to come to a solution. We had to really work with and then dump our original idea to get to a workable one. How often do we 'allow' kids to experience working through a bad idea in order to get to a good one? (Or of seeing us or their peers do so?)

I think we were able to ask students more consistently to extend their thinking to more abstract levels and to push themselves and each other beyond the obvious connections and conclusions, a habit of mind we tried to prompt each other to do as well. In essence, we were attempting to establish an ongoing demonstration of thoughtfulness.

Perhaps the fact we were together made it more than likely that we would thoughtfully respond to the students. Our roles were altered by the interdisciplinary environment, too, not only in terms of our immediate in-class responses, but maybe in a more subtle sense, in the very way we perceived our roles. Is it possible that since we'd removed ourselves from a traditional classroom set up that we were less likely to fall back on typical 'teacher as teller' roles? We knew we always had the other one watching, not in a negative sense, but literally as a reminder of certain expectations, as mutual checks for each other.

This possibility clearly speaks to the power of collaborative teaching that, for me, is inherent in interdisciplinary work. Just as it encouraged us to enact different roles within the classroom, it increased the likelihood that we would ask each other questions outside the classroom about student learning that we might otherwise overlook.

Demonstrating: Teachers as Learners

As we've mentioned, we wanted to act as demonstrators through the course, encouraging the kids to look at how we approached something, not just what we said about it. We really saw demonstration as being the most critical piece in enabling kids to view us as coaches. We attempted from the very first sessions to make our interactions in front of the class demonstrations of questioning strategies between us. We started to see examples of kids picking up on such approaches, even our language. Students would stop us and each other now and say, 'I really don't understand what I'm being asked here', just as we'd questioned each other earlier on.

We looked at the students' Adopt-a-Country papers as an opportunity to show our own writing processes, hoping to get the students to look more critically at theirs. Since we were going to demonstrate, we were, of course, going to write which meant we would be completing the research too. So, like the students, Chris started requesting articles. After she'd been working with them for a few days, she noted in her log:

> When I first read that article on Nigeria and the International Monetary Fund my eyes literally crossed . . . but since then I've stuck with it, kept digging, and kept organizing. Kids need a scaffold to do that and time and support, and we have to give them that along with a model of how to do it.

And Doug noted at the time:

> As teachers we take it for granted that our students have the research skills to do a paper. They do have the ability to use a biography or an encyclopedia, but what we're asking them to do is on a higher level. They have to focus on a broad issue which means merging a lot of research material from different sources and then writing about in it a narrative style.

It was from these realizations about what we were asking our students to do that we designed our first demonstration session on writing the papers. We wanted their papers to be learning tools, not just evaluative exercises. We hoped that they would see them that way if we emphasized and demonstrated our own learning through writing. Chris was the writer and Doug was her coach. We built a framework by demonstrating how exploring certain questions could lead to new thinking and new writing. After this demonstration, all students responded to these same questions: 'What do I already know about my country? What do I need to find out?'

After observing this demonstration, students were asked to recreate our discussion in their own groups by talking to and questioning each other in order to find an organizing format. As we circulated around the room to consult, we noticed that the students who were sitting in groups according to the area or continent their country was located in were picking up information and ideas from each other. Also, problems with research were beginning to emerge. Students seemed involved in authentic conversations about what problems they were experiencing and how they needed to proceed. By the end of the period, students had clearer ideas of what they wanted to do, but we could see they needed more time and scaffolding to be able to get there. We designed our next session to reflect this need. Students were asked to continue their research and to try a first draft before we came back together again.

In the next session we again began with a reflective piece of writing around the following questions: 'What have you done? What do you need to do? What's frustrating you?' The period was set up to be a workshop where students would conference with each other and us and begin additional research. We had a chance to conference with every student. Chris's log on the session reflects what happened.

> Kids had a really strong sense of what they needed to do. Lots of bog downs on research, having trouble knowing what articles to request. In our conferences, there was way too much teacher talk — our telling them rather than letting them talk through the possibilities. That was partially a time problem, but we can't fall into this trap if they're going to own their writing.

This reflection shows us struggling with a problem that would continue to bother us. We'd clearly worked to set up a framework where kids could own what they did, but as veteran teachers, it was so easy, so comfortable, for us to slip back into the roles of 'tellers', telling them how to solve a problem or what to include in their papers, rather than coaching them through a reflection on their writing where they might find the answers themselves.

Writing Processes: Teachers as Collaborators

Demonstrating ourselves as researching writers was just one form of practising what we had been preaching. When we asked students to do a performance of what they'd learned from a field trip to the UN, we also designed, negotiated, and performed as well. We successfully demonstrated collaboration: We set up peer review conferences, used guiding questions, and experimented with fish bowl techniques. All of these strategies involved us in immersion — we did peer review, we conferenced, etc. — and distancing — we reflected on what, how, and why we had done what we did.

The following were typical of the students' written comments when asked to evaluate how these strategies affected them:

- I was able to find out a lot of what I need to add and what wasn't clear to Liz.
- Renato helped me to clarify the government sections which I am trying to do right now and Emily asked me to go into depth about the day-to-day life of the Haitians.
- I was told mine sounded like an encyclopedia which I wasn't sure about, but reading other papers made me see better that it was.
- In having a peer edit it makes me feel that I'm writing for more than just a teacher, but for my friends. Emily really gave me a great guiding start to my paper.
- I think I helped Kate to find areas in her paper that needed smoothing out. She knew though what she needed to do, so I think I just helped her to sort it out. She helped me with a part in mine that I was doubtful about.

We were struck as we moved toward late winter and as groups worked together in a variety of ways on many different activities, how adept they'd become at working together. There were heated arguments about what was going on, and they were much more likely to really push for a resolution to a problem within their group than to ask us for help. In reflecting on how they worked in groups, they showed a great awareness about their individual roles in helping and/or hindering group functioning. They were also quite sophisticated in articulating the purposes for group work. We also noted that their comments illuminated the idea that negotiating with others is an intrinsic part of moving toward greater understanding. Here are some of the students' reflections:

- *Carol*: We could do better by getting deeper into the whole idea. Someone said we should just answer the question and that's it. That's too easy. They said forget creativeness and just get it done. That's not good.
- *Emily*: I know if I was doing this alone I wouldn't have done as effective a job. The other people in the group make you think more.
- *Wendy*: I added some ideas on government, food, fire, etc. I didn't, however, agree with all that was mentioned. I feel I shouldn't totally degrade what someone says because I didn't like it, rather try to build from it more.

They made more abstract and divergent connections that hadn't typically come out in their reflections earlier in the year:

- *Becky*: All we really did was copy the US government on a smaller scale. To us, there's really only one government that's ideal. The other forms (communist, dictatorship, etc.) weren't even considered.
- *Wendy*: I kept relating this project to *Animal Farm* and *Lord of the Flies*. Possibly if we discussed these two books and how they related to what we were doing, it could give people a better perspective.
- *Liz*: You have to have the respect and knowledge of others to live in a community. That's why education is so important.

Seeing the students move naturally and independently to immersing and distancing themselves to a higher level of thinking made us feel that what we'd been focusing on all year was becoming a habit of mind with most students. We saw analysis, synthesis, and, most important to us, evaluation that we didn't feel was often typical for 9th graders.

Two months into a new year of interdisciplinary work, still struggling with the issue of content coverage versus learning about learning. The difficulties we are having this year are at least helping me to see more clearly what I learned from last year's experience. I believed then and I still think now that we gave students opportunities to learn about learning. What I'm now able to bring into sharper focus is that these opportunities were never clearly fitted by students into a picture that had real meaning for them. While we can cite very specific examples of students being more independent, of their more thoughtfully dealing with each other's and their own work, of being able to engage in more thoughtful collaboration, I'm not convinced that students saw the value in what they did and, so, I doubt their ability to connect their experiences and build on them in a new context.

What I finally arrive at is the knowledge that my learning takes place over years. *It's a long series of making messes and then seeing what I know now that I didn't know before as well as what new questions I have. To expect students to make great leaps toward such real learning in one year would be to contradict what I know about myself. (That's not to say that stating such a fact will enable me to shed years of commonsense expectations about 'student growth'!)*

In any case, perhaps now I can at least begin to move toward being more comfortable with trying to facilitate students' purposeful learning and meaning making in as many ways as possible given the constant constraints of a traditional school and curriculum. Then hope that, as students have similar experiences with other teachers in other classes, some will come to see themselves as continual learners as I do.

Evaluation and Future Planning: Teachers as Negotiators

We hope it's obvious that we'd been questioning and reflecting on our observations and decisions throughout the year. So many of our conversations seemed to start or end with this comment: 'Next year we need to think about. . . .' As we prepared for summer workshop time to rethink the second year of the course, we knew we wanted some very explicit information from the students. On the last day of class students were asked to do a written evaluation which asked them to comment on their perspectives on various aspects of the course.

In summary, many students said if given the choice, they'd want to participate in an interdisciplinary course next year. They cited various reasons from, 'It was new and interesting', 'It keeps things from dragging', to 'We learn more', 'It's a good change from lectures', 'It broke down walls between classes', and the honest response of 'It was fun'. Asked to follow-up on this by commenting specifically on their learning, several students felt the program increased their learning in Social Studies. Many spoke of increased learning because of the chance to make personal connections, act things out, gain real life perspectives, spend more time and go into greater depth, and talk to each other rather than be lectured to.

Looking at their learning in English, however, half the students felt that the interdisciplinary class was mostly focused on the Social Studies content. Therefore, 'English often got lost in the shuffle'. Several students thought more time should have been spent on their personal writing. Those students who felt they did increase their learning in English cited the Adopt-a-Country papers or the writing process in general as helpful here.

Another question asked about the sense of community within the class compared to students' other classes. All but one student said there was a strong sense of community in the class. They referred to the class as a home base and a family. They mentioned the values of talking more, being open with each other, getting more involved as the year went on, and having to work together in order to get things done.

We asked students to specifically evaluate the double period, two or three teachers working together, and double grading. Almost all the students saw a benefit in having time to expand and not having to 'stop in the middle'. All students saw a value in several teachers working together, mentioning most often that we clarified things for each other, gave them a chance to see several perspectives, and improved accessibility for conferencing.

We were also curious as to whether the class set up changed their view of the teacher. Several students thought so. They responded that we were 'more casual' or 'more human'. They also mentioned that we tended to lecture less and be more likely to let them figure things out for themselves. The majority of the students said, however, quite bluntly that 'teachers are teachers', which we interpreted to mean the experts and dispensers of knowledge.

As we now face the troubling and challenging task of combining our own evaluations with students' to plan for next year, we can't help feeling that we're going on to a next level of negotiation. And so we ask ourselves: 'What do we know?' and 'Where do we go from here, acting on what we've learned?'

In looking at what we know, our answers are, of course, many and varied. However, there are clearly some which are most compelling and at the same time most problematic. These areas are where we'll focus as we set about planning for next year. Early on we'd worried that time would be one of our greatest problems. And, no surprises here, it was. Saying that seems too obvious and almost begs our skipping over it. Yet, it proved clearly the root of the most frustration during the course of the year. It influenced our pedagogy more often than we feel comfortable with. Simply finding the time to meet and reflect and plan together became more and more difficult as the year went on. As we had feared early on, in the second semester it sometimes triggered reversion back to working more on our own than as a team. We also ended up abandoning key projects and strategies that we'd hoped to use.

Unfortunately, there don't appear to be any simple fixes here. We're probably provided with as much time as we can hope for at the moment. During the past year, our principal encouraged us to use substitutes for class coverage whenever we needed to do extensive reflecting and planning. This is a luxury which would probably not be provided in many districts and again shows the power of this type of administrative support to encourage teachers' learning and change. We can hope that as we become more familiar with what we're doing and as we develop more course activities/resources to have available, we'll be able to spend more time reflecting together. Reflection time is clearly what goes by the way side when times gets stretched. We can also simply acknowledge the difficulty of never enough time along with the likelihood that there are always things we won't get to.

However, this certainly does raise a question which must be dealt with in the school reform movement: 'What sort of class loads and summer research time are appropriate and necessary for teachers who are involved in changing a school?' The answer demands a chapter in itself, at least, but it's a chapter that must be written and followed if serious reform, not just more passing fancy, is to take place. We're fortunate enough to be working with an administrator whose typical response to a request is to say, 'How can I help?' But, she also, of course, is limited by budget and political considerations. The kind of reform effort we're talking about demands serious rethinking at all levels of the school community.

We also know that in spite of time frustrations and strategy and content abandonments we do have success to build on. Our student evaluations confirmed what we'd sensed about the simulations we often used. They provide experiences and connections that kids definitely pick up on. We also have evidence that our demonstration and coaching were strong beginnings, from the students' use of questioning techniques in their group and class discussions, to their more thorough peer responses and revisions of their writing and their increased independence in collaboration and negotiation with each other as the year progressed.

In examining students' Adopt-a-Country papers and their English portfolios at the end of the year, there's no question that they learned to exert greater control as writers. They were much more likely to question their own techniques and to utilize writing strategies we'd discussed to make their writing more powerful. We see their increased independence as a strong sign that learning about learning really happened. We intend to build on these starts by bringing in students as the demonstrators more often, both through the use of their writings and the use of fish bowls we only really started this year.

We are troubled, but not surprised, by comments on student evaluations, as well as during the year, about 'too much reflection'. We had hoped for students to see reflection as the hallmark of real learning. Perhaps the fact that they continued to reflect in depth even as they complained is a positive sign. Perhaps we have to remind ourselves that, after all, these are 9th graders for whom the expedient is most often the rewarded way of life. One student remarked on her end of the year English evaluation that, 'All this deep thinking is hard work. It gets tedious'.

We knew going in from our work with previous classes that sometimes it's the best students who fight the hardest against uncommonsense teaching and learning. This is a phenomenon that's been documented in recent works by both Mayher (1990) and Lester and Onore (1990). True to form, two of the brightest girls in the class were the ones who were most likely to say, 'You're not teaching us'. Yet, they did continue to reflect with us and both of them achieved two of the highest grades in the entire 9th grade class in their Social Studies final exam. While we wouldn't agree, they would probably suggest that the key to their achievement had nothing to do with the reflecting we continually asked of them, but rather that they would have achieved on their own, no matter what. Are they right? We, of course, don't believe so, but realize that their view is simply a commonsense reality we're going to have to live and come clean with them about as long as what we're asking of kids is more the exception than the rule.

One of the reasons it's likely to remain a reality that's hard to swallow, however, is that we're impatient for students to see the value in the very type of experience that has proved so powerful for us. Without a doubt, both of us see our coaching and negotiating with each other as the single most important element in improving our teaching and learning. Because we continue to ask thoughtful questions to each other about our practice, we've found that we're much more likely to look at students' questions, objections, and confusions as prompts to us to rethink what we're doing, rather than annoyances to be ignored. In short, we believe that in learning with each other, we're much more likely to learn with and from our students.

However, we weren't together all the time, but usually only for one or two classes out of six, and so what we saw as consistent practice when we were together was quite possibly for students just another piece in a puzzle whose central picture was none too clear. Given both input from students and continued reflection on my own learning, I'm also now looking at the idea that the view of learning that we hoped interdisciplinary study would uncover isn't necessarily learning that students and teachers value.

We're bringing into conflict an alternate view of knowledge with ingrained expectations about school and knowledge. Students have been taught well that knowing content, knowing facts, is important. As a result, they could readily point out connections they saw between Social Studies content, which they were tested on in standard ways, and the content we often focused on in interdisciplinary sessions. Not often in the course of their total schooling are students asked to focus on their learning processes or to really habituate thoughtfulness. So, they missed linking their continual reflections about their writing and reading in English class with the same processes requested in the interdisciplinary class.

Or, more likely, a link that I see so clearly simply isn't there at the level I think it is. If I logged all the time we spent with students on experiences that were clearly reflective or collaborative, where they were really building on their own ideas and making their own meanings, and then compared it to the time they were asked to spend in more traditional ways including the methods through which they were evaluated, the final message we sent had to be that it was really the traditional activities and assessments that held the most weight, as they always seem to do. The other stuff is really 'extra', nice, fun maybe, but certainly not covered on the test.

Our greatest hope, perhaps, is that students come to see serious reflections with each other as a way to raising and starting to answer their own important questions. This hope brings us to continuing to look at our use of negotiating the curriculum. Clearly, the bulk of our negotiation this year was between us as teachers. We have much to build on there, as we continue to struggle with the problem of Social Studies driving the curriculum.

We obviously didn't utilize any wholesale negotiating of curriculum with students. However, we frequently negotiated grading criteria with them, due dates, class procedures, and approaches. We're not about to suggest a full-scale negotiation of curriculum for next year — the New York State Regents system precludes that at present — but we believe that having more explicit discussions with students about our goals, the goals of the course, and their concerns — implicit negotiation itself — will lead to more frequent explicit negotiation of class procedures and evaluations, with a consequent greater understanding on the students' part about their own learning. And that will be only a beginning, because as we ourselves learn first hand the power of posing questions and working out answers which often lead to more important questions, we realize that student questions must play a central role in our curriculum, even with the current constraints of a state course of study. We can't help thinking back to our first class sessions in September. We launched right into the curriculum with only a few passing words about the why of interdisciplinary study. It's no wonder that at the end of the year, students saw English as taking a back seat. We hadn't confronted directly our view of English as using language to make meaning.

And so ultimately the potential we set up for students coming to learn habits of mind couldn't be fulfilled as long as the bulk of their experience fell much more into traditional, expected schooling. I'm starting to see though that we're much more likely at least to help each other break through the traditions of common sense when we coach each other on learning new roles. If we continue to do so, the likelihood of our extending those roles into more areas of our teaching and helping kids to read how those altered roles relate to their learning has got to increase.

We've written so far almost as though our work took place in a vacuum from the rest of the school. In some ways it did, in others it didn't. In either case, it certainly is a final issue in this chapter that needs to be addressed as it's very much tied to where we go from here. Changing practice and the ever-present reluctance toward change will become even more a focal point for all of us. Our particular concern is how we bring other teachers in on the power of collaborative teaching without appearing to be the missionaries who've seen the light and now wish to be sure that everyone else sees it too and in exactly the same intensity and color as we do. We realize that such a perception would likely prove as fatal for us as it has for other missionaries! However, most important, we hope we can make our struggles and frustrations more public, so that more than just a few people can help each other learn. Ultimately, we know that the more teachers who struggle with us, the less likely it will be that students will view reflection and negotiation as things that don't or shouldn't happen in schools.

In the end, informed choice, in answering questions and solving problems through continual collaboration, reflection and negotiation is what we believe we're working toward for ourselves and our students. We've learned from each other that learning doesn't end in having all our questions answered, but rather results in our posing new questions. Our being comfortable with and even seeking such a spiral must be apparent to our students if we wish them to view teaching and learning in a similar fashion.

I don't necessarily see that what I've written in these reflections is getting me any closer to what negotiating the curriculum is or ought to be in an interdisciplinary course. But I'm starting to have a very clear sense of what it shouldn't be:

For Students: *It shouldn't be an insertion that happens once in a while in a course. It becomes then just another gimmick with which kids are all too familiar and to which they'll simply respond by giving teachers exactly what they think the teachers want to hear or by trying to negotiate the least amount of work possible.*

For Teachers: *It shouldn't be just another planning session in how to engage students in small bits and pieces of curriculum content, ignoring what ought to be the real curriculum of the course, the answers to the questions: 'What is learning across these two disciplines?' And, 'How can we facilitate students' work toward that?'*

Last, I'm reminded of Nancie Atwell's plea to make revision a way of life (In the Middle, *1990). Just as revision in my writing helps me to create what will not work in order to get at what may, my seeing what to avoid in negotiating the curriculum gives me a good chance of creating a classroom where it may begin to work, so that I may 'resee' once again.*

Note

1 Sherry also asked the high school as a whole to consider joining the Coalition of Essential Schools, a national organization of reform-minded schools headed by Ted Sizer at Brown University. Sherry's previous school had been a coalition school and she was enthusiastic about the promise of interdisciplinary collaboration as the key to lasting school reform.

Chris Louth and Doug Young

References

LESTER, N. and ONORE, C. (1990) *Learning Change: One School District Meets Language Across the Curriculum*, Portsmouth, NH: Boynton/Cook-Heinemann.
MAYHER, J.S. (1990) *Uncommon Sense: Theoretical Practice in Language Education*, Portsmouth, NH: Boynton/Cook-Heinemann.
WIGGINS, G. (1989) 'The futility of trying to teach everything of importance', *Educational Leadership*, **47**, November, pp. 44–48, 58.

Chapter 14

Negotiation, Language, and Inquiry: Building Knowledge Collaboratively in the Classroom[1]

Cynthia S. Onore

Teachers are all the time teaching about talk. We can't avoid it, since talk is our medium of exchange. When teachers tightly control the flow and the topic of talk, students learn that talk — at least talk in institutions such as schools — is disembodied from the world of meaning. When teachers share control with students, students learn that talk is a means for constructing knowledge. The scary thing is that when students do learn about talk as a vehicle for choice and for negotiating what will be learned, then teachers discover that their classrooms are full of twenty or thirty other teachers. Then you have to rethink what it means to teach. That's the scary thing, and that's the exhilarating thing when you do a good job of teaching your students about talk.

Conversations reveal much more than they literally say. The nature of entire contexts can be exposed by the kinds of conversations that take place within them. Clues about the relative status of the participants, the nature of their relationships, and the purposes they have for talking with one another are revealed by the forms and functions of the conversational language. Read the dialogue below and see if you can determine what the context is and who the speakers are:

S1: Who are these two people?
S2: A woman and her maid.
S1: What kind of relationship do they have?
S3: Friendly.
S2: They get along.
S1: Is that all?
S3: Well, it seems like they're friends.
S1: Yes, but, do employers and employees usually have relationships like this? Are they usually so friendly?
S2: No.
S3: Yes.
S1: Well, we have two different answers here. Does anyone agree with Sandy? Terry, do you agree?

S4: No. I don't think they're friends.
S1: OK. Now, how does the Inspector treat the maid?
S3: He's OK.
S1: Really? What does he say to her?
S2: He wants to know why she wants to learn to drive.
S1: Does the Inspector treat the maid with respect?
S5: No.

I think you'll agree that the clues in this conversation point quite clearly in one direction: this is a class 'discussion'. I have reproduced here only a small portion of a seven-minute segment of this high school literature lesson during which the teacher posed twenty-two questions, all of which were rapid-fire and required only factual recall through short answers, or yes/no responses. All of the teacher's questions and her automatic evaluations of each student's response communicated that there was one right answer to every question. A few students dominated what interaction there was while the rest either whispered to one another or sat quietly, looking bored. All the while, the teacher worked very hard. She was animated, enthusiastic, and energetic.

I have shown a number of people this excerpt of classroom dialogue without identifying the context or the speakers and have asked them to tell me what they think the context is and how they know. And whether or not the guessing-game players are educators, they easily recognize this context as a classroom because it captures something very familiar to anyone who's ever been a student. The dominance of one person over all the others through controlling the substance and form of the conversation, the not-so-subtle evaluations of each answer, the insistence on one particular point of view, and the attempt to force a consensus about the topic at hand all convey the essence of 'schooling'.

Certainly, this teacher could have been a more skillful discussion leader. She could have varied the kinds of questions she posed so that students might have been encouraged to interpret and analyze rather than simply recall information. She might have also used strategies for supporting students in posing questions of their own. But as long as the purposes the teacher had for this 'discussion' remained to test the students' recall of the story, or to guide the students toward one way of seeing the story they had read, the amount and kinds of talk the students would engage in would resemble the dialogue I have reproduced. Such so-called class discussions may in fact do more to limit learning than they do to support it. And the better teachers are good at orchestrating the manner in which students swallow the bitter pill of learning, the harder it is to get beneath the surface of classroom talk and examine the structure of knowledge in which students and teachers are participating together.

Without fundamentally altering the messages the students were receiving about who has the knowledge, who determines what kind of knowledge is legitimate, and how to go about getting knowledge if you do not have it, the teacher and her class would have been locked into a 'discussion' which is really a thinly veiled lecture about the one valid meaning of the story, the teacher's meaning.

My point here is that the way the teacher conducted this discussion is only one aspect of how language is being used in this classroom. This class discussion, I believe, raises larger questions about language use in the classroom. From the perspective of the relationship between language and learning, and how language and learning connect to issues of knowledge and control, there are deeper issues for exploration. For example, what is the nature of school knowledge in this classroom? What kinds of messages about school knowledge are students receiving from the classroom talk? These are the questions I will attempt to explore in the remainder of this paper.

The Nature of School Knowledge

In the classroom discussion I have described, learning is a process of reproducing the contours of the teacher's thinking, knowledge is a commodity consisting of single, correct answers, and the teacher is the sole transmitter and evaluator of learning. In other words, knowledge is in the teacher's full and individual control. Such a knowledge structure will profoundly affect and ultimately control what and how students learn, not just what and how they will talk. That, at any rate, is the principal assertion of this paper.

Based on such a small sample of classroom talk, my conclusions about teaching and learning may seem unfair. But this is exactly the composite picture of school knowledge that Michael Stubbs (1976), a British sociolinguist, draws after reviewing numerous studies of classroom talk. Stubbs's conclusions are supported by the findings of Goodlad (1984) and Sizer (1984), to name just two of the many recent critics of public schooling here in the United States. Here is Stubbs's description of knowledge in a typical classroom:

> Classroom knowledge consists of strings of short answers which can be individually evaluated. Classroom knowledge is therefore essentially closed, not open-ended. All questions have correct answers. Teacher-pupil talk is effectively a monologue with the pupil supplying short answers on demand to contribute to the teacher's train of thought. (p. 99)

Stubbs is suggesting that teachers need to go beyond simply encouraging more language use in the classroom, though that would certainly help some. Classrooms must be forums for students to set and solve meaningful problems if learning is to be open and not closed. Teachers must reconceptualize the kinds of control they assert if students are to be encouraged to negotiate and explore their own lines of reasoning. Evaluation must be tied to the learner's purposes and intentions if assessment is to support learning. All of this implies a thoroughgoing redefinition of curriculum, a new way of defining what classroom knowledge consists of, alternative concepts of power and authority, and new roles for teachers and students.

That was what the British researchers who studied classroom language, and whose work was the spur behind the American 'Language Across the Curriculum' movement, intended. But, as Garth Boomer (1988) has pointed out, when these researchers' ideas have been translated into classroom practice, they have become a way to develop students' reading, writing, speaking, and listening abilities rather than an approach to reformulating the nature of school knowledge. According to Boomer, rather than seeing language across the curriculum as a way to improve students' literacy, the thrust should be, 'Let's improve learning by looking at how language affects and shapes learning. This involves school and faculty policies focused on matters of thinking and meaning and learning' (p. 2).

Cynthia S. Onore

Negotiating the Curriculum[2]

There is classroom talk which can improve learning by addressing 'those matters of thinking and meaning and learning' which Boomer argues ought to be the central concern of language across the curriculum. Boomer (1982) has, himself, developed such an approach to knowledge building which grows out of a classroom saturated with student talk directed toward joint meaning making and goal setting. This partnership between students and teachers is called 'negotiating the curriculum'.

I am going to take you inside a classroom where you will see students engaged in learning which is simultaneously open-ended and the joint responsibility of learners with their teacher. The goals and directions for learning will be collaboratively set in order to satisfy both individual and group concerns. What learners already know will be tapped and extended by building bridges between their old and new knowledge. This is learning which will depend on students' using their own language to learn.

In the course of negotiating the curriculum, the role of the teacher, the definition of curriculum, and the nature of knowledge will be radically transformed as well. You will not just see more language use by students. You will see a language-rich environment in which the teacher is a co-learner, in which students collaborate with one another to build knowledge, and in which students will reflect on and assess what they have learned in order to complete the learning cycle. This classroom will look very different from the one we glimpsed earlier, the one that is so familiar and so easily recognized.

Principles Underlying Curriculum Negotiation

Before looking at a classroom, let me sketch the principles guiding curriculum negotiation as well as the four practical steps to follow in order to negotiate. Jon Cook (chapter 2) and his Australian colleagues conducted hundreds of interviews with teachers and students of all ages and abilities in order to define how people learn best. They found that learners learn best when they are *engaged*, when they are supported through collaboration with peers and teachers to *explore*, and when they have the opportunity to *reflect* on their learning, to stand back from it and assess what and how they have learned. Engagement, exploration, and reflection form the basis for the negotiation process. In negotiating the curriculum, the purposes and intentions of the learners are of central importance, but they must be integrated with the constraints under which the teacher and the institution operate.

Negotiation is driven and organized by a community of learners addressing the following questions:

1 What do we already know, assume, or believe about the subject at hand?
2 What do we want or need to find out?
3 How will we go about finding out answers to our questions or solutions to our problems?
4 How will we assess what we have accomplished? How will we know what we have found, and with whom will we share our findings?

Negotiating the Curriculum: One Classroom in Action

Let's turn now to a classroom of second graders early one November. This heterogeneous group in a small suburban New York classroom is about to embark on a typical November topic — 'The Pilgrims'. Mrs Gillis, their teacher, assumes that Thanksgiving has been a topic for these students in their kindergarten and first-grade experiences, and so she anticipates that the children may respond with boredom and disinterest. Nonetheless, Mrs Gillis feels an obligation to treat the topic. After all, every class in her school will be studying Thanksgiving as well as celebrating the holiday in some way. In order to stave off boredom, her own as well as the children's, and to give the students a chance to share whatever knowledge they already have, Mrs Gillis decides to negotiate the curriculum with her students. Keep in mind that the topic of their inquiry is non-negotiable. What the children choose to learn, how they will go about learning, and how they will share their learning is, however, open to negotiation.

What Learners Already Know and What They Want to Find Out

Mrs Gillis asks the students what they know about the pilgrims. The class is divided into small groups and each group is asked to make a list of everything it knows about the pilgrims. After about fifteen minutes of small group talk, the whole class convenes in front of a flip chart. Mrs Gillis records on the chart what the students already know or think they know. This chart is entitled, 'What We Know about the Pilgrims'. In order to create their small group lists, the students had already engaged in a form of negotiation with one another, using oral language as the mode of negotiation. Some children knew things about the pilgrims that other members of the group did not know, so that part of the seemingly straightforward process of compiling a list involved the knowers in becoming

---

What We Know about the Pilgrims

1 They made up Thanksgiving.
2 They made friends with the Indians.
3 They sailed on the *Mayflower*.
4 They were settlers.
5 When they landed, it was at the end of Cape Cod.
6 The Indians taught them how to plant corn.
7 The king wouldn't let them do what they wanted to, so they left.
8 They didn't have much food on the ship.
9 Some died on the ship.
10 They built houses on the coast.
11 Some got sick on the *Mayflower*.
12 They dug for salt.
13 The kids played games on the ship — leap frog, tug-of-war.
14 They taught each other a lot.

---

teachers of those children who did not know. The children switch roles as knowers and learners with one another quite naturally throughout the small group talk.

This process continues as each group shares its list with the whole class. Mrs Gillis's role becomes that of teacher-as-facilitator. If one child reports on a piece of information that others are not familiar with, Mrs Gillis asks for clarification or elaboration. If there is only one child who is aware of a particular piece of information, she asks that child to keep that item on a personal list of 'Knowns'. Once this part of the negotiation process was complete, the class generated this composite list:

How Old Knowledge Can Lead to New Learning

During the whole group session, questions naturally emerged. Mrs Gillis asked the children to write their questions in their journals as they came out. Then she sent them back to their groups and asked them to decide what they would like to learn about the pilgrims. The children generated their own questions and shared their questions with one another. Like the knowledge the children had, some questions were individual and some were collective. Note how the questions grew quite naturally from the information they had generated and recorded. They were engaging in the process of inquiry by allowing what they already knew to lead them in new directions:

What We Want to Know about the Pilgrims

1   How long did it take to make the *Mayflower*?
2   How big was the *Mayflower*?
3   How many people died on the *Mayflower*?
4   How many people were on the *Mayflower*?
5   How long did it take to get from England to America?
6   What kind of food did they have on the *Mayflower*? How much?
7   Did they eat fish?
8   What was the captain's name?
9   What kind of houses did they have? Who built them? How did the rain stay out?
10 How long did the pilgrims live?
11 How did they get off their boat?
12 How did they become pilgrims? Why were they called Pilgrims?
13 How did they make their clothes?
14 Do they still have the real *Mayflower*?
15 Who discovered the land?
16 Who ruled them?
17 Was the *Mayflower* bigger than the *Titanic*?
18 Are there any Pilgrims living today?

Questions 1, 2, 3, 4, 5, and 8 center on the ship, the *Mayflower*, and the details of the journey, and so they appear to grow from the simple statement (#3) that

'The Pilgrims sailed on the *Mayflower*'. Questions 6 and 7, which centre on food, are related to the statement, 'They didn't have much food on the ship' (#8). Question 9, about housing, is a derivation of statement 10, which asserts that the pilgrims built their own homes, and so on. Contrasted with the question-and-answer session which formed the opening of this paper, this field of inquiry is clearly framed, not by the contours of the teacher's thinking, but by the children's own knowledge, interest, and connection making. They are building on what they already know from inside as well as outside of school. In the context of negotiation, the source of knowledge is not as important as the act of connecting knowns with unknowns. And so the range of children's understandings, even those often deemed irrelevant, intrusive, or tangential, can come fully into play in the negotiation process. Additionally, there is a natural modulation between individual knowledge and collective knowledge and questions. The entire negotiation process sets up a dialectical relationship between individual and collective knowledge. If Mrs Gillis does not dominate the knowledge-building process, neither does any single child.

You will see this process quite clearly operating in question #17, which compares the *Mayflower* with the *Titanic*. Here the students are bringing their out-of-school knowledge to bear on in-school learning. At the time that the children were studying the pilgrims, the *Titanic* had just been located beneath the Atlantic Ocean, and quite a few of the children knew this. The process of collaborative curriculum building created a central place within the curriculum for something that was part of the students' out-of-school knowledge. It allowed them to make a potentially old topic, Thanksgiving, a new one. It guided them in their inquiry, invested them in learning, and simultaneously built upon what they already knew to make new knowledge. In this way, negotiating the curriculum is satisfying two of the principles of learning on which it is built: engagement and exploration.

Douglas Barnes (1986) would probably say that these children were on a 'hot topic'. What distinguishes a 'hot topic' from a 'cold' one is that a hot topic addresses the learner's purposes and intentions rather than only those of the teacher. Hot topics do not require that learners be externally motivated to learn. Hot topics are intrinsically satisfying to learners.

If we contrast Mrs Gillis's classroom, which is enacting a negotiation model of teaching and learning, with traditional curriculum process and content, what Boomer (chapter 1) designates the 'motivation' model, we can see the advantages of negotiation for building school knowledge and for creating 'hot topics'. At the best of times, according to Boomer, in a motivation learning model, the teacher's and students' intentions for learning will overlap somewhat. More typically, however, there is little overlap in intentions, not just between teacher and student but among the students themselves, a factor limiting successful collaboration. The teachers must therefore spend a great deal of time and energy on motivational activities in the hopes of generating some co-intentions (pp. 9–10). But, even at its best, in the motivation model, 'the children's learnings only approximate to the teacher's goals, so the curriculum may touch only a little of each child's key and associated interest' (p. 9).

In addition, asking learners to state what they already know about a topic and what they would like to learn helped Mrs Gillis avoid a typical pitfall of treating school knowledge as a commodity owned by the teacher: telling learners what they already know. John Dewey (1933) calls the process of informing learners about what they already know as 'impertinent interference' (p. 282). Dewey says, 'To pry into the familiar, the usual, the automatic, simply for the sake of formulating it is both an impertinent interference and a source of boredom' (p. 282). Dewey would find much to support in Boomer's model for negotiating the curriculum on this basis alone.

How the Children Learned

Let us return to Mrs Gillis's class to see what and how the children used curriculum negotiation to learn. The students reviewed what was on their list and selected the question about the relative sizes of the *Titanic* and the *Mayflower* as their first investigation. Mrs Gillis guided the class in planning how to go about finding an answer to this question. One child suggested, 'We can read and ask people'. Mrs Gillis asked, 'What do you think we should read?' Another child said, 'Maybe the newspaper tells the size of the *Titanic*'. Three children volunteered to go home that evening and see if they could locate the information in the newspaper. Someone else suggested reading a history book to find how large the *Mayflower* was. Mrs Gillis noted on another chart who would be responsible for which tasks.

The next day, the class had the information they needed to compare the sizes of the two ships. Mrs Gillis suggested marking the length of the two ships on the school playground. The children assembled outside and measured the proper number of feet and made chalk marks on the macadam surface. They were then able to see not only that the *Titanic* was larger, but by how much. Let me point out here that the children were learning about measurement simultaneously, even though this was not the focus of the investigation. Unlike traditional curriculum, where it is assumed that what is learned is equivalent to what is taught, in negotiation it is acknowledged that a great deal of learning is incidental, unplanned, and even unconscious. But is is learning, nonetheless.

The class also decided to go to the library together and select a number of books to help them with many of their questions. One ongoing activity was Mrs Gillis's daily reading from a book on the *Mayflower* voyage. Whenever the children found an answer to one of their questions, they checked off the question on the chart.

One small group of children was particularly interested in finding out if anyone in their town was a descendant of the Pilgrims. Mrs Gillis, a *Mayflower* descendant herself, volunteered to be interviewed by this group, which together generated the questions that would guide their interview, and selected one of their members to record Mrs Gillis's answers. These children decided to share their information with the class through an oral report.

Throughout this process, Mrs Gillis's role was that of collaborator, facilitator, and orchestrator rather than motivator. Classroom talk was not an end in itself but a means for building knowledge. Not only were the children developing their literacy abilities, they were also using language in all of its modes to learn, and they were learning how to learn.

Reflection as a Moment in Learning

The third principle of learning guiding negotiating the curriculum provides that learners learn best when they have the opportunity to reflect on what they have learned. Learners need both to produce knowledge for themselves and to contemplate what they have produced. This reflection on learning may involve self-assessment, sharing the products of learning with peers, and evaluation by the teacher.

I hope it is clear from my description of the learning process in this classroom that learning was not controlled by the teacher's preset curriculum. As a result, the children's learning was largely individual. At the same time, however, there was a core of common knowledge being built.

In a traditional setting, this lack of uniformity of input and output would present tremendous problems of assessment. While I do not wish to suggest that evaluation is not rendered more difficult by negotiating the curriculum, there are distinct advantages. One problem with the motivation model of learning is that when students follow the teacher's line of reasoning, whatever they might learn that does not fit in the prescribed curriculum cannot be reflected upon, and so learning is incomplete. Boomer (chapter 1) has suggested that the motivation model 'leaves a good deal of what has been learnt unexamined and unevaluated, because the teacher, or external examiner, tests only what is set on the curriculum' (p. 9). By contrast, in the negotiation model, the teacher can get a sense of what students have learned while the students are allowed to reflect on their learning. The teacher does not assume that what is taught is exactly what is learned.

Mrs Gillis discussed with the children when they would like to share and assess their work and how the sharing the assessment would take place. In order to help the children assess what they had learned and to help herself evaluate what had gone on, Mrs Gillis suggested that each of the children write about what he or she had learned about the Pilgrims. Here are three children reflecting on what they have learned, or in Paulo Freire's (1987) terms, 'knowing' what they have learned.

Amanda wrote:

> Once there was some people thay are calld pilgrims thay wanted to have there own church. So, thay asked the king. The king said no! So the people went to Holend. But the peoples children were lerning Duch. So, the people went back to England on a boat calld the Spedwell. When thay got back to England thay packed tere things. and thay berded back on the Spedwell. But, on ther way tere was a stom and the spedwell berok. but luchalea there was a nuther boat cold the Mayflower. So thay all boarded on. the pilgrims sald for 66 days. there was a lote of stoms. and all of them brock a bem. but luhaley thay had a big bult that thay were going to use for bilding. So thay useed it to hold the bem up menwell Stephen Hopkins (illegible) . . . a log time after that the people got to America.

Amanda's interest centred on what happened on the voyage itself. Mike, on the other hand, focused his inquiry, and therefore his learning, on what happened to the Pilgrims once they landed in America:

> The pulgrims saild on the Mayflour from Spayn to America. They met two Indins named Skwatow and Samaset. The Indins tautht the Pilgrumes

haw to plant corn and furtilise the corn with fish. And once thay sind a pese tredy so the Indins codnot bring that bo and arow to the pilgrims vilige, the pilgrims cod not bring ther guns to the Indins vilige. Today we selabrate the day the Pilgrims had the first thanksigiving.

Kevin asserts, in a tone of complete ownership and authority, what he has learned about:

I know the Pilgrims journey. It all started at England when the pilgrims wanted to go to a place were there was freedom. They bought a boat, It was the Speedwell. They got half way and the speedwell started to leak. The Pilgrims had to go back and get a new boat. They rented the Mayflower. They got to where they wanted to go. They have Thanks for making it There safecly.

Mrs Gillis's assignment required the children to synthesize and organize what they had learned. Each student's ability to create a coherent picture out of the bits and pieces of his or her learning was affected by a range of factors, including individual development. One child wrote only thirty words. Another wrote 350 words and attempted to discuss all of the following: the reasons the pilgrims left England, what happened on the *Mayflower*, the landing at Cape Cod, the encounters with the Indians, and the first Thanksgiving. You will note, however, that even in the sample of three texts I have quoted, there is some knowledge which all of the students seem to have developed. Even taking individual differences into account, then, what and how the children learned represents both individual and collective concerns and interests. Assessment, then, is both individual and social, and contains both negotiable and non-negotiable elements.

The Nature of the Language of Negotiation

The classroom language used to bring the children to the point of confidence and ownership which they exhibit in these culminating pieces of writing was exploratory, that is 'hesitant, incomplete, hypothetical, directed not to make confident assertions but to explore the range of possible accounts' (Barnes, 1986, p. 73). It is paradoxical that learning through exploratory language use, though this type of language is less controlled and controlling, has more power to generate confident assertions and make connections than does 'presentational' language, which, by contrast, is focused on getting the right answers to teacher-or textbook-generated questions. Language in its presentational function is concerned with 'satisfying the teacher's criteria. It is abbreviated, it serves the purpose of educational control and it brings pupils' statements into line with the teacher's frame of reference' (Barnes, 1986, p. 73). With its implicit goal of control over students' learning, presentational language supports learning which is short-circuited. School knowledge built through the presentational function, then, will tend to oversimplify issues, smooth over potential controversy, avoid obstacles, and exclude anything novel from being explored or discovered (Dewey, 1933, p. 282).

In a recent study, Linda McNeil (1986) places the presentational function of language in a wider teacher context which she terms 'defensive teaching'. According to McNeil, defensive teaching is designed, above all, to control. Unfortunately, one of the consequences of control is that we sacrifice engagement, responsibility, and ownership over learning to create an illusion of harmony and order. That is the central contradiction of a motivation model of curriculum design. The more disengagement, alienation, resistance, and boredom students exhibit, the more tightly we attempt to control them and the curriculum. Boomer's solution to this contradiction is to change the entire structure of control. Increased language use and language of varying kinds will not, by themselves, achieve a change in this structure. Only a partnership in learning can do this. Only when children are supported by the classroom structure and by their own language to 'reorder their pictures of the world in relation to new ideas and new experiences' (Barnes, 1986, p. 73) will school knowledge and its construction come to resemble the purposeful and collaborative learning that human beings engage in all the time in the world outside of schooling.

The Promise of Negotiating the Curriculum

It is reasonable to conclude that so much of what has been described in this second grade classroom depends upon the prior commitment of the learners to learning, on their 'open-mindedness', 'wholeheartedness', and 'responsibility' (Dewey, 1933, pp. 30–32), and that negotiating the curriculum may very well be just another 'irrelevant impertinence'. But if we return to Stubbs's formulation of classroom knowledge, with which I began this paper, we may be able to see that negotiating the curriculum fosters rather than depends upon prior commitment from learners. Once learners are respected for what they bring to the learning situation, once they are allowed to use their own language to learn, once they recognize that uncertainty and questions are the signs of real learning and not error, once they may follow their own intentions rather than be required either to suppress those intentions or to take up the teacher's intentions as if they were their own, then engagement in learning will occur.

Paradoxically, the traditional curriculum fosters dependence by cutting learners off from their needs and concerns. In Australia, where negotiating the curriculum has been institutionalized in many schools, the students who are allowed to negotiate call their peers, who must follow set curricula and conform to teacher-generated goals, 'spoonies' because they believe that their peers must be spoon-fed knowledge. These students recognize that their own learning events are much more demanding, and they feel joy and pride in the amount of trust and respect that curriculum negotiation grants them through its stiff demands for responsibility and hard work.

I would, therefore, suggest that the student engagement we have observed in Mrs Gillis's classroom setting depends upon a context of real inquiry and not on some prior commitment and motivation. Not only is the potential for the individual learner's transformation embedded in the context of curriculum negotiation, but the underlying purposes for education and the nature of schooling are changed as well from individual struggling against individual and the curriculum to a partnership of learners who work together to build joint understandings.

Cynthia S. Onore

The Good and Bad News about Negotiating the Curriculum

Negotiating the curriculum is not just another alternative method or interesting strategy to be used occasionally. On the contrary, curriculum negotiation implies a very different view of learning than traditional methods do. Where the traditional curriculum implies that learning can be given by teachers to students, curriculum negotiation implies that learners must construct knowledge for themselves. Where typical classrooms value single, correct answers, curriculum negotiation develops multiple perspectives and many more questions than answers. Where teachers must oftentimes see themselves primarily as diagnosticians and evaluators, teachers who negotiate the curriculum can view themselves as co-learners and facilitators.

Because negotiating the curriculum is such a powerful way of engaging students in learning, I must add one further caution here. Negotiating the curriculum is not simply a better way to control students and their learning. It implies a very different definition of learning. Without a real commitment to learning which is surprising, difficult to assess, and unpredictable, without a real dedication to helping students become independent learners and full participants in a democratic classroom, negotiating the curriculum can simply become another way to seize and maintain power over students.

I would like you to listen to the voice of the teacher whose classroom I profiled and critiqued at the opening of this paper. She is reflecting on her own transformation which occurred when she became a student in a classroom where the curriculum was negotiated:

> There are lots of questions I have about education and about life, which should be the same thing, and now I kind of like that. I used to be afraid of all the questions I had in my heart and soul (and in my brain, too) because I believed adults should have more answers than questions. But, I've come to see that as fallacy. Too many answers lead to rigidity but the problem-poser looks at life from varying perspectives and by defining the problem, shapes the answer.

In her earlier life as a student, this teacher learned to be afraid of her own questions. She translated this fear into her own practices as a teacher. As a teacher, we saw her pedagogy enacting her belief in single rather than multiple perspectives. We observed her conveying to students that knowledge is a commodity which teachers alone possess. In her former life as a student, this teacher believed that teachers transmit learning to their students, and so when she began to teach, she was a transmitter, not a collaborator. She had learned to distrust her own voice, her own language, and her own questions as a learner, and so she tightly controlled how their students used language. She did not see language as a mode of negotiating meanings.

The reawakening of a natural and purposeful need to know and a desire to learn, and the rediscovery of her own meaning-making capacities was spurred on, developed, and dignified for this learner by negotiating the curriculum. These qualities of learning may be engendered in ordinary, day-to-day conversation in the classroom. Not only is genuine conversation a means to achieving learning, it is the result of negotiating the curriculum as well. When learners are given a voice in their own learning and opportunities to build knowledge collaboratively, their already-present potential for engagement in learning will be tapped. This is the real purpose for encouraging classroom talk.

Notes

1   This chapter has been reprinted with minor editorial alterations with permission of the National Council of Teachers of English from *Perspectives on Talk and Learning*, edited by Susan Hynds and Donald L. Rubin (Urbana, IL: NCTE, 1990, pp. 57–72).
2   I would like to express my deep appreciation to Shirley Gillis for opening up her classroom and exploring with me insights about children's learning. Many thanks to Garth Boomer, of course, for his responses to a draft of this paper and for sharing his ever-deepening perspectives on curriculum negotiation with me.

References

BARNES, D. (1986) 'Language in the secondary classroom', in BARNES, D., BRITTON, J. and TORBE, M. (Eds) *Language, the Learner and the School*, 3rd ed. New York: Viking Penguin, pp. 11–87.

BOOMER, G. (Ed.) (1982) *Negotiating the Curriculum: A Teacher-Student Partnership*, Sydney, Australia: Ashton Scholastic.

BOOMER, G. (1988) 'Reading the whole curriculum', in GREEN, B. (Ed.) *Metaphors and Meanings: Essays on English Teaching by Garth Boomer*, Hawthorn: Australian Association for the Teaching of English.

DEWEY, J. (1933) *How We Think*, Boston: D.C. Heath.

GOODLAD, J. (1984) *A Place Called School*, New York: McGraw-Hill.

McNEIL, L. (1986) *Contradictions of Control: School Structure and School Knowledge*, NY: Routledge & Kegan Paul.

SIZER, T.R. (1984) *Horace's Compromise*, Boston: Houghton Mifflin.

SHOR, I. and FREIRE, P. (1987) *A Pedagogy for Liberation*, South Hadley, Mass.: Bergin and Garvey.

STUBBS, M. (1976) *Language, School, and Classrooms*, London: Methuen.

New Theoretical Perspectives on Negotiating the Curriculum

INTRODUCTION

If theories weren't made of the stuff that they are, new visions for this book wouldn't have developed and the chapters in this section, in particular, wouldn't have been written. What is unique in this part is that the authors have all decided to interrogate their own theoretical positions and assumptions in order to discover both what is reasonable and generative in what they believe and what needs challenging. These efforts are just as Dewey has described them since, according to him, theories emanate from questions and lead toward further inquiries. Theories ought to state what is known, the questions which engendered those knowns, the consequences of knowing and believing as we do, the consequences of not acting upon what we know and the new questions which are raised both by acting and by resisting action.

So, a good place to start in introducing this section would be to state what we do already know about negotiating the curriculum. We know that it is more than a method or technique, that it is a theory of teaching, learning, and curriculum composing. It emanates from questions about authority, power, and knowledge, from questions about the roles of language in learning, from inquiries into the nature of democratic schooling, the kinds of students we want schools to launch into the world, and questions about the relationships among all the members of the school community. Having practiced and researched and reflected on negotiating the curriculum for ten years, we now seek and find new questions, new spaces, new discontinuities in need of exploration. Those are precisely the intentions and issues which underlie the chapters in this section.

These chapters represent a second stage in the development of a new vision of schooling. Our questions and problems are qualitatively different from what they were in 1982. In large part, this is the legacy of our national and international histories; in part, this is a necessity and an essentiality for making progress in the history of all new ideas.

Having come as far as we have in these ten years, we have also unearthed contradictions and tensions. You will see in these pieces much that we have to complain about, things have not gone as smoothly as we had hoped. We found no magic bullet, no panacea, no final answers and many new questions. Read these pieces as cautionary tales: they tell us as much about what to struggle against as they do about what to struggle for.

Here are some of the underlying messages you may discover in the articles in this section:

- watch out for technical solutions to classroom problems; critique quick-fixes and question neat solutions to complex problems (Lester, chapter 15);
- ponder the messages your child's school is sending about who and what it values; don't be content with changes in individual classrooms; support teachers in setting coherent goals for our schools (Cook, chapter 16);
- recognize the complexities of negotiation; be ever mindful of the propensity to ignore and coopt students' intentions; seek the power in collective dialogue; value dialogue and its potential to create thoughtful and respectful relationships between teachers and students (Thomson, chapter 17);
- resist the possibilities of recreating unequal and oppressive social relationships in the classroom; find a fit among why, what and how learning proceeds; strive toward building a community in the classroom; connect the classroom to the lived lives of students (Onore and Lubetsky, chapter 18);
- discover the sorts of students you would like to help develop; interrogate the structures which impede this development; critique the goals of schooling and challenge them as they express themselves in your teaching (Lester and Boomer, chapter 19);
- reveal, whenever you can, your own values and beliefs; continually seek to act congruently with what you espouse (Boomer, chapter 20).

None of these messages is intended as a recipe for success. Each contains unanswered questions, criticisms waiting to be voiced, uncertainty about what schooling will ultimately look like should these visions of negotiation become reality. But these authors do know something about where and how we should launch our challenges against the way things are. These pieces are animated by a belief in the power of collective action and reflection. They invite you, dear reader, to question, critique, and act as well.

Invitations to Inquire

We all want to know more about:

1. How can we teach for independence and resistance to unreasonable authority?
2. In what ways does the stuff of the curriculum change when we negotiate?
3. How can we connect the classroom to the world outside of school?
4. Should students learn differently just because teachers suggest they should? Whether you answered yes or no, think about why you answered the way you did.
5. What happens when we invite students to challenge the authority of textbooks and teachers?

6 Is it possible to create schools and classrooms which do not mirror the inequities of society? How?

7 Will we be able to resist the forces of conservatism within ourselves and forge a vision of teaching and learning based on reciprocity and shared enterprise? How will we resist, if we answer this in the affirmative?

8 Is it ever possible to empower or liberate another person? How?

9 What does it really mean for teachers to be learners in their own classrooms?

10 Are we really prepared to help students set their own agendas for learning? How must teachers and schools change in order to make this possible?

11 What kinds of students do we want schools to help launch? And what sort of twenty-first century world do we wish to live in anyway? Can schools make a difference?

Chapter 15

All Reforms Are Not Created Equal: Cooperative Learning is Not Negotiating the Curriculum

Nancy Lester

The teachers and learners in this volume are working hard at learning together. Through their actions and reflections on and in their actions, they are gaining insights about how meanings are made by individuals, how those personal meanings are shared and developed consensually, and how to use their collective brain power to enhance and enrich each other's learning. Although they have some blueprints to follow, particularly Cook's and Boomer's chapters (2, 1 and 3 respectively), these teachers and learners are mostly cutting their own trails. What they've done is moved beyond the rhetoric of reform to the enactment of transformative education.

While it's been crucial to have had a growing number of voices from diverse educational quarters — such as the US Department of Education, various university consortia, teacher unions and professional subject organizations — call for educational reform and restructuring of a quite similar nature, it's also clear that the time has come for action and active experimentation of alternative paths to teaching and learning. Demonstrations of alternative possibilities gives us new 'texts' to read, respond to, analyze, and critique and makes revision both possible and constructive. This continual cycle of doing/reflecting/redoing creates richer and more complex examples of what learning and teaching might look like if they were reformed or in the process of reform.

The complexities involved in the process of enacting reforms, specifically those having to do with learning from reading these new 'texts' and changing what seems to limit or distort the values we're seeking to demonstrate, should caution us once again about the potential successes we might derive from the 'quick fix'. Historically, each wave of reform has been accompanied by its own set of technical solutions, remedies which seem to patch things up for a while or cover up, with a thin veneer, the deep cracks lying just below the surface but threatening to erupt at any moment. From assembly line efficiency models of education, to 'teacher-proof' materials, and now to cooperative learning, we've been bombarded by, but have also contributed to, the proliferation and application of quick fix reforms.

Whether it's been our lack of power, our feelings of being burnt out, our inabilities to recognize and come to grips with the impoverished commonsense ways of doing school, or, as I suspect, a combination of all of these, we've pretty much gone along on the bandwagon, believing that we could make the problems of schooling disappear by pargiting over the cracks. It's been this last wave of reform which has helped us to look below the surface to the inside of schooling — to the whys as well as the hows and whats of both learning and teaching — and promoted the kinds of reflecting that is evident in the thoughtful descriptions and analyses shared in this volume.

It is the fact, however, that even in our latest efforts to transform schooling there is a quite powerful technical rational quick fix taking hold. It is, as we'll see, couched in language which sounds as if it reflects the same values which underlie a process like negotiating the curriculum. And because it uses language so deviously to disguise its real nature, we are distracted from the essential beliefs and principles of teaching and learning it represents. And we are once again attracted by apparent simplicity, a set of rules to follow, and an orderly and disciplined approach. It seems that we don't have to dig beneath the surface after all, work hard to uncover the problems or the possibilities, because cooperative learning can fix it all up without having to do the hard work. As a result, we fail to question and critique.

In order to resist the temptations that cooperative learning proffers, we have a responsibility to expose the values and beliefs which comprise its core and compare them to those at the center of negotiating the curriculum. I hope a more honest picture of what's really involved in educational reform, both process and product, will emerge through the combination of seeing curriculum negotiation in action in the cases contained in Part B of this volume and the critique that is presented in this chapter.

The Hidden Curriculum of Cooperative Learning

Collaborative and *cooperative* learning have come to be used interchangeably to describe certain learning and teaching contexts. The latter may be distinguished from the former by its association with what has become a popular, educational 'movement', conceptualized, most notably, by Robert Slavin of Johns Hopkins University, Spencer Kagan, formerly of the University of California, Riverside, and Roger and David Johnson of the University of Minnesota. Although proponents of the cooperative learning movement have described their work as collaborative in nature, I make a distinction between learning that is genuinely collaborative and learning that seems by its label to require collaboration, but shows few, if any, signs of being so.

My critique is based on this argument: The teaching and learning that goes on in cooperative groups, chiefly characterized by transmission, memorization, and regurgitation, is no different from the teaching and learning which has traditionally gone on in whole class groups. By using the term 'cooperative learning' as the name for their movement, its leaders seem to be striving for association with values characteristic of joint work, but when carefully examined, their prescriptions for instruction don't seem to embody these values in action. My analyses will show that cooperative learning is too often rote learning done in groups. The tradition of rote learning in American schools hasn't been abandoned, or questioned, or challenged by using a cooperative learning model. It's been fitted into a new configuration of rote groups.

Cooperative learning is the newest technology of instruction on the educational market. And as a technology, it involves controlling time and the pace and sequence of learning. It's highly prefigured and strongly framed. In other words, cooperative learning isn't a model which responds to learners' intentions, knowledge, and questions — it doesn't lead from behind — but, instead, cooperative learning is imposed structure with preset goals and explicitly defined and rigidly adhered to steps for attaining those goals. Outcomes are rarely surprises, but almost always predicated/predicted. But by parading as a neutral technology — not very different from how other technologies wish to be or are seen — a cooperative learning model hides the toxic properties of its approach.

Listed below are the beliefs/principles of schooling which I believe comprise the hidden curriculum of cooperative learning and which I will highlight in my analyses:

- Knowledge is an object which gets delivered from expert (teacher and/or textbook) to novice (student), via transmission, memorization, and regurgitation.
- The models focus more on teaching and testing than on learning.
- Correct answers are valued and rewarded; approximations, guesses, even multiple interpretations are not considered essential paths for learning;
- Competition, although veiled by heterogeneous group structures, persists.
- Students' intentions and, therefore, their ownership of and responsibility for the means and ends of learning are neither valued nor encouraged.
- Power and authority over discipline and evaluation continue to reside solely in the hands of the teacher.
- Traditional schooling divisions of time, content, and disciplines continue to operate.

In addition to these, the cooperative learning model implies a certain attitude and value stance towards teachers. While authority over and control of student discipline and evaluation continue to be wielded by teachers, little else could be said to be. In very real ways, this movement takes us back to the 1970s when American educational research and practice were greatly influenced by those who believed that the less responsibility teachers had over what and how they taught, the greater the possibility that teaching would be delivered equitably and objectively. It's another 'teacher-proof' system.

The Appeal of Cooperative Learning

What seems so surprising to me is the enormous appeal cooperative learning has had for teachers in this time of educational reform and restructuring, where a major focus has been on transforming our conceptions of teaching away from the legacy of the 1970s, away from the dehumanizing, technologizing, depowering, and deskilling of teachers (Smith, 1986; Apple, 1986; and Giroux, 1988). I've been drawn to this discussion by my own research with Onore into redefining teaching by revealing more fully its complexity, its dynamism, and its continual ability to provide renewal and growth for those who practise it (Lester and Onore, 1990). The cooperative learning movement is a reversion to a time when these characteristics of teaching were barely acknowledged or valued, and, sadder still, it seems to appeal strongly to a majority of those who are themselves engaged in this complex act of teaching.

In attempting to discover why cooperative learning has such a widespread appeal, I find myself looking anew at the reform movement and those whom it seeks to 'reform'. Generally, I think, there are two belief systems which reign in our schools and are embodied in teachers' theoretical practice: 'Commonsense' beliefs support teachers to confirm traditional ways of teaching and learning and 'uncommonsense' beliefs promote them to transform traditional conceptions of teaching and learning and to construct alternatives. [Mayher's, 1990, rich, critical descriptions of common and uncommon sense have provided us with a new language and a new set of lenses for looking at schooling.] While these views of the world of school aren't necessarily rigid or static, they characterize comprehensively the competing belief systems underlying teaching and learning.

One key to unlocking cooperative learning's appeal to teachers might be found in its goals. Common and uncommonsense teachers, despite their taking different paths to teaching and learning, more often than not have very similar goals. Robert Slavin, one of the 'founding fathers' of the cooperative learning movement, describes its goals this way:

> It is . . . an alternative to tracking and within class grouping, . . . a means of mainstreaming academically handicapped students, . . . a means of improving race relations in desegregated schools, . . . a solution to the problems of students at risk, . . . a means of increasing prosocial behaviour among children as well as a method for simply increasing the achievement of all students. (1989/90, p. 3)

I think we would all share the goals that Slavin has laid out. To twist Henry Perkinson's (1968) phrase, cooperative learning seems the 'perfect panacea' for America's educational ills. It's the perfect panacea because its goals appeal to both uncommonsense and commonsense teachers. Commonsense teachers can take comfort that they are, indeed, joining in the battle to confront major issues of the reform movement (i.e. at risk students, racism, tracking), while at the same time securing the safety of familiar beliefs, goals, and approaches to teaching and learning. Because, as I will show, cooperative learning doesn't seek to transform any of the latter.

More troubling for me, however is the appeal cooperative learning has had on uncommonsense teachers. While we can all nod in agreement as we read the goals Slavin has articulated, I'm concerned that we aren't questioning the paths on which and from which those goals might be achieved. Have uncommonsense teachers been fooled into supporting the cooperative learning movement by its slick veneer of democracy and pluralism?

While in the rest of this chapter I work to uncover the hidden curriculum of cooperative learning to reveal what I see as its true nature, my short-term answer to this question is 'yes', based on what I see as a political agenda underlying Slavin's goal quote. The quote is from the 'Guest Editorial' of the December/January, 1989/90 issue of *Educational Leadership*, a widely read and respected journal for administrators and curriculum leaders, those officially in charge of reforming/restructuring schools. The entire issue is devoted completely to the cooperative learning movement (except for the 'Contemporary Issues' section which traces the 'corporate influence on schools') and the editorial has been written by one of the movement's founders who's also a consultant to schools on cooperative learning and producer of cooperative learning materials.

Immediately following the exerpt I quoted, Slavin cautions readers that these goals can only be achieved if they're followed slavishly (Slavinly?) and if practitioners get long-term 'training', administrative, and materials support. I would interpret such a caution to be an implicit device for selling cooperative learning to schools, who would have to buy the program so that it satisfied the cautions emphasized. Thus, they'd have to buy one of its gurus (or a close disciple) and plan on long-term training and support, all of which will cost a district a great deal of money and make a great deal of money for the guru/disciple/movement.

My own experience as an inservice educator convinces me that commonsense and uncommonsense educators, alike, will undoubtedly, if not now then sometime soon, find themselves attending an inservice 'training' course on cooperative learning as a result of an administrator reading or hearing about this issue of *Educational Leadership* or following in the footsteps of the school district down the road which has already jumped on the bandwagon. In fact, since I drafted this chapter, just such a scenario has taken place. Cooperative learning has spread like wild fire across the US, up through Canada, and over to Australia!

Collaborative Learning Through Negotiating the Curriculum

I wouldn't be participating in this volume if my beliefs about teaching and learning didn't support a very different model of instruction from that advanced by cooperative learning. Negotiating the curriculum is, as we have seen in the cases told thus far, a cointentional and, thus, *collaborative* process of learning and teaching designed to provide a climate for promoting democratic schooling. It recognizes the need for learners, students as well as teachers, to question and critique the word and the world (Freire, 1970) in order to understand it better so as to challenge and change it. Rather than serving to perpetuate the beliefs about teaching and learning and the structures and systems which have characterized American schooling for over 100 years up to and including today (Cuban, 1984), negotiating the curriculum was, itself, conceived as a way of questioning the status quo (Boomer, 1982). In other words, it isn't a new way of doing the same old commonsense school things we've always done. Negotiating the curriculum isn't a modern façade for a traditional edifice; it's a new kind of building altogether.

Through a negotiated curriculum, a crucial component of a democratic classroom, learners and teachers are taking chances to remake and transform commonsense American schooling. The definition of the 'quiet classroom' as the 'good classroom' where learning goes on, for example, is challenged by the central place that's given to talking to learn in the negotiated classroom. Even talking and writing to learn question the reigning commonsense belief that knowledge is a commodity which resides already formed in the textbook or the teacher's head, since using talk or writing to learn suggests a process of discovery, a process of meaning making where knowledge is constructed over time through collaborative exchanges. Learning in a negotiated climate is no longer seen as the ability to get the right answer because right answers themselves are being questioned as the only valuable way of looking at the world. 'Whose right answer?' is a core question around which critique is built in a democratic classroom.

Maintaining the Status Quo Through Cooperative Learning

I've taken as my task in this chapter to show how cooperative learning is a technology of instruction which provides a practical method for extending and supporting the commonsense educational *status quo*. And by doing so, to demonstrate a process of reading and critiquing the reform curriculum. You'll see in the critiques of the excerpts from the 'Cooperative Learning' issue of *Educational Leadership* (December 1989/January 1990) which follow that the strategies contained in them weren't designed to promote cointentionality, but quite the opposite. Therefore, I see cooperative learning as having as its hidden curriculum what I've come to call rote groups.

This shorthand emphasizes that cooperative learning's claims to innovation must be questioned since traditional rote/transmission teaching and learning is still the dominant feature of the model. I grant that cooperative learning is an attempt to use heterogeneous grouping, an uncommonsense schooling practice. But it's what these groups do finally that defines cooperative learning and exposes it as the heterogeneous small group equivalent of commonsense learning: a traditional pedagogy repackaged. Moreover, from these articles I've concluded that proponents of cooperative learning haven't questioned or challenged any of the reigning assumptions and beliefs about schooling, from how students learn to what they learn.

I selected what I considered to be the most significant and representative excerpts from five articles plus the guest editorial of the 'cooperative learning' issue of *Educational Leadership*. My choice was governed by several readings and rereadings which helped me to determine which of the fourteen major articles demonstrated the essential concepts and practices of cooperative learning methodology. Since four of the five pieces were either written or co-written by or contained an interview with prominent theorists and researchers of cooperative learning, I considered them to carry more weight than the others. I cite the excerpt first and then follow it with my analysis. For easier reading I've *emphasized* those parts in each excerpt I focus my analyses on. Therefore, when not otherwise indicated, the emphases are mine.

Cooperative Learning Supplements Direct Instruction

At worst, *some teachers* hear about cooperative learning and *believe that students can simply be placed in groups, given some interesting materials or problems to solve, and allowed to discover information or skills.* Others may *allow groups to work together to produce a single product or solution. Research clearly does not support either of these uses of the approach.* Successful models always include *plain old good instruction*; the cooperative activities *supplement* [emphasis Slavin's] but do not replace *direct instruction* (what *they do replace is individual seat work*). (Slavin, 1989/90, p. 3)

Slavin argues that 'successful models [of cooperative learning] always include plain old good instruction' which he uses interchangeably with 'direct instruction'. Plain, old, good direct instruction is commonsense transmission/regurgitation teaching and learning (Goodlad, 1984; Sizer, 1984). Instead of individual seat work, students in 'successful' cooperative learning models can now regurgitate in small groups, the unique feature which differentiates a cooperative learning model from the usual commonsense one. Transmissions and regurgitations — direct instruction — are fitted into uncommonsense small groups.

While some teachers . . . [may] believe that students can simply be placed in groups' and collaboration will magically occur, this isn't a position that anyone urging collaborative learning actually holds. It surely is the case, though, that students who haven't been accustomed to learning collaboratively need to learn how to work together productively. We've seen in earlier chapters that students resist learning from one another because they distrust the validity of each other's knowledge. This isn't surprising given the fact that for most of them the only knowledge which was considered valid, and valuable, was that stored in the teacher's head or in the pages of a textbook. Students and teachers, therefore, must learn how to learn in small groups from one another and this type of meta-learning must always be built into the reflective processes of negotiating the curriculum.

However, I strongly question why students could not be given, after engaging in demonstrations and reflections on the processes of collaboration, 'some interesting materials or problems to solve', and be 'allowed to discover information' for themselves. As we have seen throughout this volume, this kind of problem-setting/solving and discovery learning is basic to negotiating the curriculum.

Research may show that discovery learning and collaborative learning products 'don't work' in successful cooperative learning models, but I'm able to construct a different cause and effect argument for this kind of failure. (Actually, Slavin doesn't provide us with the argument; he merely asserts the research conclusion without references.) If direct instruction is the chief means for transmitting information and cooperative learning groups 'supplement' this mode, as they do in the models I'll be analyzing later, then discovering or problem-solving will not only be inappropriate and unsuccessful, but might even prove hazardous, since discovery and problem solving could result in different answers/solutions/interpretations from those transmitted and sanctioned by the teacher or textbook. Cooperative learning groups, as we'll see further along in this chapter, mask what's essentially commonsense accountability: individual assessment/evaluation. Therefore, solutions or projects which are collaboratively produced and don't lend themselves to assigning individual grades couldn't be used successfully either.

Cooperative Learning to Spell

Cooperative Spelling Groups: Here is a procedure we recommend for using cooperative groups to teach spelling.

First, in order to collect data on individual spelling abilities, *teach spelling in a traditional individualistic setting for three to four weeks*. Then form heterogeneous triads including one high-, one average-, and one low-achieving speller. *Triads then work together to study spelling for the rest of the year* in the following fashion:

Day 1 — Pretest. As teams sit together to take the *pretest*, they reach consensus on *how to spell each word*. Teams self-correct their pretests and note any troublesome words.

Day 2 — Spelling games and activities. Teams choose from a variety of activities to study the unit words. For example, if teams 'jigsaw' the words (Aronson, *et al.*, 1978), they divide word cards for the spelling unit equally among team members. *Each student is responsible for studying his or her words and devising a strategy to teach the others how to remember those words.*

Any spelling games or activities are appropriate — as long as the students perceive a group goal. Everyone must learn to spell all the words, and *everyone must understand that she or he will be held individually accountable on the test.*

Day 3 — Practice test. Teams spend five minutes coaching each other in preparation for the test. *Students take the practice test individually*. After the test, teams reconvene (*without pencils*) *to compare test papers*. Teams tutor teammates who have misspelled words, then celebrate accurate papers.

Day 4 — Study or free day. If all team members within a team have *accurate practice tests*, that team earns free time. *If any team member(s) misspelled a word, the entire team uses the time to tutor the student(s).*

Day 5 — Final test. Teams spend five minutes coaching members who misspelled words on the *practice test*. These students *retake the test individually*. After the test, the entire team *reconvenes* (*without pencils*) *to check test papers* and praise each other's work.

Teams in which every member masters his or her required number of words receive a reward. If one team member fails to reach mastery, the team does not earn the reward. This reward system promotes positive interdependence: a feeling of 'we're in this together, sink or swim' (Johnson, *et al.*, 1988). *The combination of peer pressure and peer support creates an environment where students feel accountable to each other* for learning spelling. In this motivated atmosphere, individual spelling scores have always improved in our classes — in some cases increasing from 40 per cent to 100 per cent accuracy. (Augustine, Gruber and Hanson, 1989/90, p. 6)

I find this approach clearly supports a commonsense theoretical practical belief system of language education: direct instruction. I'm referring to spelling lists/tests. Learning how to spell by memorizing words suggests an outside-in (from someone's list, rather than from the learner's intentions), context-free (first learn to spell the word correctly, then use it), bottom-up (learn words, then sentences, then paragraphs, etc.) theory of language learning and development. Under the guise of studying spelling lists together, testing each other, and being responsible for each other's scores lies the traditional commonsense belief that students will learn to spell by memorizing a list of words.

In fact, the chimera of cooperation disappears on close scrutiny: the spelling curriculum begins with students being taught 'in a traditional individualistic setting for three or four weeks'. When students move to the cooperative activities, these are severely limited in promoting genuine cooperation by the goal that's preset by the teacher: 'everyone must understand that she or he will be held *individually* accountable on the test' (my emphasis). In the end, learning is assessed on an individual basis as in the commonsense classroom. We see how a cooperative learning model can only succeed if it continues to rest on individual accountability rather than on collaborative solutions.

Here, too, is our first glimmer of the cooperative learning approach to assessment: a test. It doesn't seem very different from what has always gone on in school. In fact, in this approach there's an awful lot of testing going on. Based on my own experience of being taught spelling in an individualistic setting, there was at least one test a week, so that for the first three or four weeks where the students are taught 'in a traditional individualistic setting' there are three to four tests. Each succeeding week of the program requires students to take three tests a week: a pretest, a practice test, and a final test. We could assume that some of the games/activities could also be characterized as tests, but even if we don't count these, we're talking about approximately 120 tests a year just in spelling!

What's the cooperative nature of the learning going on in this model? Students are directed to feel responsible for each other by tutoring and coaching fellow team members. But if one member doesn't pass the test, all members are punished: Instead of free time they must coach and tutor their peers who haven't passed the test. Team members who don't pass the tests must feel pretty guilty when the rest of their team doesn't get to have a 'free day'. And why are students directed not to use pencils when comparing test papers? Is there a hint here that students might cheat by changing answers? If teachers don't trust students even with their own team members, how are teams to build cooperative spirit and responsibility for assisting one another's learning?

What, if any, long-term learning does this model engender? In this article there's no evidence that students develop an ability to use the words from their spelling lists in their own writing. Being able to use these words productively in a new context is one way of assessing whether students have genuinely learned them. But the goal, as the teachers have defined it in this excerpt, is *accuracy*. A characteristic of cooperative learning here, as well as in the other articles, is teaching for the test itself, rather than for any other purpose. As long as students practise and pass the tests, they've succeeded in 'learning' and so 'learning' is equated with the ability to pass the test. And the test is — almost always — short-term and context-free.

Might we assume from what we know of commonsense schooling that what was 'learned' for the test on Friday has been forgotten by Monday in anticipation of the new week's testing regime? Students' knowledge is not growing richer or even greater as a result of equating test passing with learning. If we want students to be better at passing tests, then this model of cooperative learning would succeed. If we want students to develop a richer and larger vocabulary (I equate learning new words with enriching vocabulary rather than with memorizing correct spellings), then cooperative learning to spell isn't the best way to do so.

A common goal of both cooperative and collaborative learning would be, I think, to help learners develop responsibility for their own as well as their classmates' learning. A true community of learners is established only when we all contribute to each other's growing knowledge and mastery. My argument with the approach here, in light of this goal, is twofold. Students don't seem to have a choice, nor are they given time to develop, responsibility for one another. Instead, they must follow a regime which directs them to teach each other, test each other, and get punished together when even one of them fails to meet the predetermined, nonnegotiable goal. If I were a learner is this classroom I would resent this form of responsibility. If I was one of those who could pass spelling tests easily and successfully, I would grow to feel angry at those in my group who kept me from my just rewards. If I was the one who continually held my group back, I'm sure I would feel (I can even recapture such feelings from my own experience) like a burden to them, even guilty that I was preventing them from their just rewards. I would have no more responsibility for my peers under this regime than I had under one where I was being tested individually. To me, the approach here, is not genuinely collaborative, since it creates all kinds of bad feelings — resentment and guilt particularly — rather than good feelings like caring and support.

Cooperative learning has a really positive ring. Nobody wants to be *unco-operative*. But too often, by overstructuring and overcontrolling whatever genuine collaboration might break out in these 'cooperative' groups, no real cooperation is possible. So what actually happens, as it does here, is either thinly disguised individual competition or inter-group competition. Neither leads to the kind of mutually supporting learning that Vygotsky (1962) recognizes in the 'zone of proximal development' or in the cointentional collaboration among students and teachers in a negotiated curriculum context, although by labeling the 'process' as cooperative, it seems to benefit from the good image such sharing and co-intentionality have. Another indication, perhaps, why uncommonsense teachers might be drawn to cooperative learning.

In an earlier version of this chapter I critiqued a mathematics and language arts/reading model (Slavin *et al.*, 1989/90) in addition to this spelling model. What I found there was similar to what I've analyzed here: tests predominated; skills were practised in isolation and out-of-context; teachers transmitted the only knowledge that really counted; students were passive learners (an oxymoron, I think, since if you are truly learning, you have to be active!) whose chief re-sponsibility was to keep their peers on task and to help each other pass practice tests, and the primary goal of learning was accuracy.

A particularly insidious adaptation of Graves' writer's workshop (1983) was adopted — perhaps to appeal directly to uncommonsense teachers — in the language arts model (Slavin, *et al.*, pp. 26–27). The authors have cleverly used Graves' work to give process legitimacy to their commonsense beliefs about writing learning and teaching. Writing continues to be carried on in strictly limited time periods and direct teaching of grammar, punctuation, and spelling dominates. Unlike Graves' use of mini-lessons which grow out of the childrens' writing and are sensitive to the developing sophistication of that writing (i.e. if children are beginning to use dialogue in their writing, then a teacher may choose to give a mini-lesson on the correct use of quotation marks to those children whose writing is showing readiness for such surface level attention), Slavin *et al.*'s use of mini-lessons appears to be the result of the pre-determined curriculum. Teaching, not learning, is the prevailing focus in all of these models.

Structural Cooperative Learning

Q — Brandt: There are, of course, different formulations of cooperative learning. They aren't necessarily opposed to one another, but they are somewhat different. Will you contrast your approach with those of Roger and David Johnson and of Robert Slavin?

A — Kagan: Sure. The structural approach [Kagan's contribution to co-operative learning] shares with David and Roger Johnson's approach [the spelling approach just analyzed] *the idea of giving teachers new methods so they can teach whatever they want to teach more successfully. It's curriculum free*; the choice of a structure does not involve choice of any particular curriculum or curriculum materials; in fact, the structure can be used from K through University across the curriculum. . . . on the other hand, the structural approach shares with the Johns Hopkins [whose research centre is directed by Robert Slavin] approach an *emphasis on specific behaviours among teachers rather than giving them general principles and leaving it up to them to decide how to structure the classroom.* (Brandt, 1989/90, p. 10)

I'm reminded again by this excerpt of the educational reform proposals of the 1970s which resulted in attempts to create 'teacher proof' materials. In their attempts to control and create smooth running, efficient classrooms both approaches suggest that teachers shouldn't have more ownership over what and how they teach; that teachers are, in fact, better off not having to worry about too many issues, thus reducing decision making. Not involving teachers in any discussion of principles of teaching and learning is a continuation of the status quo status of teachers today. Kagan confirms the popular view that teaching is mindless work, that educators don't care about or aren't capable of engaging in discussion about why and how they do what they do. In a structural approach to cooperative learning, teachers aren't encouraged to question or reflect on their beliefs and practices or on those of cooperative learning which they're being asked to adopt. Furthermore, they aren't encouraged to compare the new approaches to what they've been doing, because, under Kagan's and Slavin's models, teachers' behaviours are more important than the reasons why they behave the way they do.

I'm sure this excerpt creates quite a stark contrast when compared with the chapters in this book. After all, the teachers here who are negotiating the curriculum are constantly thinking and reflecting in and on action and questioning what's going on. The integrity that such mindful processes as thinking and reflecting give to teaching and learning is one of the attributes that attracted me to negotiating the curriculum in the first place. I suppose it's not surprising that teacher-proof materials continue to hold such power in the US as we are a country which looks down on and denigrates education and learning (Gardner, 1990).

Our particular brand of anti-intellectualism sneers at the notion that teachers might wish to act as 'transformative intellectuals' (Giroux, 1988), educators who seek to learn about and change what they do so they might help students change the larger society in which we all live. The phrase 'transformative intellectual', itself, gives rise to nervous giggles which turn into distain as the accusation of it being just another instance of educational jargon is hurled. It may not be the most feliticious of phrases and it may require us to think hard about what it means, but it does have meaning, especially when it's being enacted. To call it jargon is to dismiss it's power in redefining what teachers do. To call it jargon is to demean the process of changing ourselves as well as the schools we teach in, not to mention demeaning the role language might play in this process. All this contributes to creating a snug place for teacher-proof materials to dig in and take hold of teaching and learning.

> The structural approach to cooperative learning is based on the creation, analyses, and systematic application of *structures*, [emphasis Kagan's] or *content-free ways of organizing social interaction in the classroom.* Structures usually involve a series of steps, with *proscribed behaviors at each step.* (Kagan, 1989/90, p. 12)

As we have seen in the descriptions in this volume, one of the cornerstones of the negotiated, uncommonsense, democratic classroom is that content is inextricably tied to form, and so content will direct what form develops or is eventually chosen. When form is determined without attention to content, then Kagan's probably right: 'the choice of a structure does not involve choice of any particular curriculum or curriculum materials'. And as long as the structures are consistently applied and adhered to, learning can proceed. Social studies, biology, and poetry must all be able to fit into the same structures if we follow Kagan's content-free cooperative learning organization.

What this suggests to me is that the structures must be more or less like filling-in-blanks, must rest on the belief that knowledge, and thus learning, in every subject involves transmitting right and wrong answers, which fit into similar looking slots. Otherwise, how else could you learn these diverse subjects if the structures for learning them remain the same? Hypothesis testing through hands-on experiments in science, imaginative creations and recreations of the what-if type in social studies, or a drafting and revision process of poetry writing can't be accommodated in the structural cooperative learning model because the structures which support learning in each of these subjects will vary.

Structural Cooperative Learning Predetermines Outcomes

> When the teacher is aware of different structures, he or she can *design lessons with predetermined outcomes.* (Kagan, 1989/90, p. 13)

Can we always, or do we always want to, predict what students will learn? In the negotiating classroom, teaching and learning aren't equated. Although the hope is that students will learn from teachers and with teachers and that some of what teachers want students to learn will be coincident with generalized learning goals and objectives set for a subject or a semester, learning is more cointentional, and, therefore, the specific outcomes can't be predicted or determined consistently beforehand. This notion of predetermined outcomes smacks of lists of behavioral goals and objectives; lists we've lived with in the US for decades now with some effect on the nature and structure of teaching, but very little effect on long-term learning.

It's certainly consistent with Slavin's discomfort with discovery as a legitimate route to learning, because if a teacher can design a lesson whose outcomes are already determined, then where, how, and why would discovery be applicable? Discovery suggests, certainly at the beginning, that the end is unclear or has yet to come clear. Discovery suggests that there may be more than one end in sight depending on who's looking and how they choose to look. Discovery suggests complexity which seems antithetical to the belief that we can determine the end before we set out on the journey.

If students are genuinely cooperating — as opposed to complying to cooperate in taking in transmissions, in memorizing and regurgitating, and in testing each other — then outcomes will be much harder to predict. Because, even if all groups take in the same transmissions, there's no guarantee that they'll all come out with the same responses. Such is the characteristic nature of true collaborative learning.

Rote Structures for Structural Cooperative Learning

To illustrate the distinct domains of usefulness of different structures, let's contrast Color-Coded Co-op Cards ['Students memorize facts using a flash card game' (Kagan, p. 14).] and Three-Step Interview ['Students interview each other in pairs, first one way, then the other' (Kagan, p. 14).]. *Color-Coded Co-op Cards work well for convergent thinking (knowledge-level thinking), such as when the academic goal is memorization of many distinct facts*; the Co-op Cards promote helping and are most often used for practice. Three-Step Interview does not serve any of these goals well. In contrast, *Three-Step but not the Co-op Cards is most often used for divergent thinking (evaluation, analysis, synthesis, and application-level thinking), such as when the academic goal is promoting thought as part of participation in the scientific, inquiry process or as part of the writing process*; Three-Step Interview promotes listening skills and serves well to provide an anticipatory set for the lesson (*'What would you most like to learn about ...?'* or *'What do you now know about ...?'*) or to obtain closure (*'What is the most important thing you have learned about ...?' 'If we had more time, what aspect of ... would you like to study further?'*). (Kagan, 1989/90, p. 15)

I'm suspicious if any time thinking is divided up into labeled categories, such as 'divergent' and 'convergent'. What such categories tend to do, as they have here, is to promote a separation in the kinds of ways students learn and, even more harmful in this case, to validate 'good old direct instruction'. The 'Color Coded Co-op Cards' strategy is used to promote and test 'knowledge-level, convergent thinking' and might be viewed as an 'innovative' way to memorize and regurgitate expert facts. What's even more ironic is that learning through Color-Coded Cards is called knowledge-level learning, while the Three-Step Interview strategy for divergent thinking doesn't seem to involve knowledge at all. According to this excerpt, divergent thinking involves activities like analyzing and synthesizing. What will be analyzed or synthesized isn't mentioned, but if knowledge isn't in the domain of this strategy, then are we to assume that something other than knowledge will be analyzed and synthesized? We do get the suggestion that learners would apply their thinking through Three-Step Interview. Has what is applied already been memorized through the convergent thinking strategy?

I would argue that all learning involves the activities and strategies described for the divergent thinking category, including the making of knowledge across the content areas. 'Sharing personal information such as hypotheses, reactions . . . [and] conclusions' seems to me to be at the core of genuine, purposeful, engaged, collaborative learning. Once we separate these ways of coming to know (divergent) from the learning of content area facts and information (convergent), we revert back to a passive, transmission model of learning and teaching for the 'real' stuff of school. Because students continue to do school via transmission and regurgitation through the convergent strategy of Color-Coded-Co-op Cards, and because this kind of doing school continues to be separated from the analyzing and synthesizing kind of doing of the divergent strategy of Three-Step Interview, the message that continues to be sent to students is: First and foremost, you must memorize the essential facts and figures that we've deemed important; then, if we have time, you can think about them.

The questions which make up the 'anticipatory set' and 'closure' parts of the divergent thinking category fit quite neatly into the kinds of questions asked in a negotiated context of learning and teaching. On the surface, anyway, this part of the 'structured cooperative learning' model is compatible with negotiating the curriculum. And this may be one of the major attractions of this model for uncommonsense teachers.

But: Are these questions really taken into account when a new unit is introduced? Are students' intentions ('What would you most like to learn?') the basis for what's learned and how it's learned? Is students' knowledge validated ('What do you know now?') and used to guide the pace and depth of the curriculum? The last question — 'If we had more time, what would you like to study further?' — seems patronizing, since there obviously isn't enough time in this type of teaching/learning schedule to continue with the topic, so what use would students' responses serve here? If students responded to the question of 'What was the most important thing they learned?' that they learned that solving quadratic equations were a waste of time, what would teachers do with these answers? How would they effect the classroom climate and what is taught and learned in the future?

Once you bring students' personal knowledge, intentions, and assessments into the teaching/learning context, rigid structures, passive learning, and predetermined outcomes might as well be abandoned. If proponents of structured cooperative learning are ready to abandon their basic tenets, then I would believe that these anticipatory and closure questions are really genuine.

If, in fact, the questions and responses do play a more constructive role than I give them credit for, I wonder whether students sense the contradictions. If they're asked, on the one hand, to memorize and regurgitate a set of facts told to them by the teacher or textbook and, on the other hand, to evaluate, analyze, synthesize and assess those facts through a personally active and constructive process, will students question how they learn and are taught? Will this lead to further disenfranchisement when students begin to question the purpose and validity of school knowledge? [See McNeil, 1986, for more insight here.]

Cooperative Learning of Science: The Hidden Curriculum is Control

Cooperative learning is a central strategy of the [Science for Life and Living] program, for several reasons . . . *cooperative learning helps teachers with classroom management.* Hands-on science requires that students interact with materials; and cooperative learning is structured so that students, not teachers, manage those materials. In a cooperative learning classroom, students help each other with assignments and problems, which *alleviates some of the stress on the teacher to maintain order and to keep students on task.* (Hannigan, 1989/90, p. 25)

Perhaps this is the most revealing of all excerpts as it states overtly the central advantage to the use of cooperative learning strategies: control of students. The argument here is that students will, through cooperative learning groups, take over more of the responsibility for controlling each other's behavior and for maintaining and sustaining each other's concerted efforts on the tasks at hand.

While not explicitly stated here or in the other excerpts I've looked at, wielding control, through maintaining order, appears to be a subtle, but pervasive educational value of cooperative learning. When coupled to the control over teachers that comes as a result of enacting a structural cooperative learning model, my interpretation draws further strength. Like most commonsense schooling practices, the hidden curriculum of cooperative learning methodologies reflects a paradox. Teachers in the confines of their classrooms control their students through the intricate, well-oiled machinery of cooperative learning structures. Because the structures are so explicitly defined and rigid, there's little room (or time) for students to break out into non-conformist behaviour. Moreover, since cooperative learning continues to rest on transmission, teachers gain additional power by controlling knowledge — what's learned, how it's learned, and whether or not, through determining the means and ends of evaluation, learning has occurred.

The paradox emerges as we search for alternative routes for teachers' and students' ownership over teaching and learning. Making decisions about curriculum — what content will serve the learning — about means — how students and teachers will learn the content — about goals — to what purposes will learning be put — about schooling structures — what configurations, from team teaching to altered scheduling to schools within schools, will promote, most democratically, the achievement of the goals — and about mission — why and what schools do — are all decisions which seem to be owned by others in the educational community, but not by teachers and certainly not by students. These are, by and large, intellectual and ethical decisions.

Boomer's metaphor of 'reading the whole curriculum' (Green, 1988) is appropriate here. Although placing the most emphasis in his argument on students — they have the right and must take the opportunity to involve themselves in the processes of deconstructing and constructing the curriculum they're being asked to learn and master if they're genuinely going to learn in school — I believe that the metaphor is just as powerful for teachers. When teachers

start to ask . . . questions of the school's curriculum [or tracking system, or decision making hierarchy, or intentions, etc.], it is no longer possible to believe that it is 'natural'. You have to become like the audience at

a Brechtian play, a healthily alienated inquirer who knows that the curriculum [or any other schooling issue] is a performance generated within
the school's culture, a demonstration with palpable designs on you. It is
no longer a *given*; it is a way of *taking*, now that you have learnt to act
on it. (pp. 156–158) [Boomer's emphases]

Such critical readings of schooling aren't possible when teachers' only source
of power comes as a result of controlling students' behaviour and when teachers,
themselves, are rendered powerless in a structural approach to cooperative
learning. And perhaps that's intentional. Because when I 'read the whole [co-
operative learning] curriculum' what I read is a text with the intention to control
students and teachers by controlling their behavior. This is not an accident; it is
'*constructed*' (Boomer, in Green, p. 167). We must ask of the cooperative learning
movement whether teachers and students are meant not to question schooling
and then we must ask, Why? If cooperative learning models don't make room for
reading the whole curriculum — and there's no sign from these excerpts that they
do or want to — then we must assume their proponents don't value critique
which would lead to transforming schooling, but rather wish to hold on to the
status quo.

A Final Label Warning

Those readers who've rightly expected of a critical essay to hear a discussion
about race, gender, and/or class will have noticed by now that I haven't included
one. In the articles I critiqued, the writers didn't address these issues of schooling
and I, therefore, found a vacuum where a discussion of these issues could or
should have been. These omissions might be themselves an indication that
practitioners of cooperative learning choose to eschew issues of race, gender, and
class in their work.

While it's clear that heterogeneous grouping is a major goal of the movement and might influence the cultural/social/political fabric of a school, I didn't
really know why it was being promoted. I didn't believe it was a proactive move:
grouping students heterogeneously wasn't designed to shake up and transform
the status quo of tracking. I saw it more as a reactive measure: a response to what
has become one of the few reform issues that almost everyone can agree on. One
of the appeals of the cooperative learning movement, as I argued earlier, has
been these integrated groups. But when I examined the make-up of these groups
closely, I recognized that the students continued to be identified as 'at low, middle,
and high achieving levels' (Augustine, Gruber and Hanson, p. 6; Kagan, p. 8, 13;
and Slavin, *et al.*, p. 23). These are surely still tracks, since these levels are determined by test results which continue to measure students in ways which would
identify them as above or below a norm, the same as for tracks. Like individual
rote learning repackaged into rote groups, so tracks have been repackaged from
whole classes into small groups within one class. A critical point of view of tracking built on social, political and cultural grounds, as that taken by Oakes (1985),
makes these seemingly reform-minded heterogeneous groups highly suspect.

I also haven't really dealt with the issue of purpose. I've pointed out that
cooperative learning models don't seem to question or challenge why schools are

the way they are or what gets taught to students and why (their goal seems to be repackaging not transforming). Since there aren't any explicit statements of the purposes of schooling, I can only guess what they might be. My suspicion, therefore, is that the cooperative learning movement would have no quarrel with defining a school's purpose as transmitting, producing, and reproducing society's values, structures, and institutions (Bowles and Gintis, 1976). If I'm right about this, then my criticisms about their use of heterogeneous grouping are further supported.

From my own experience of negotiating the curriculum and from the experiences of my colleagues in this book, we can attest to the fact that the social, political, and cultural issues of schooling, which have long been hidden or ignored and continue to be so in cooperative learning materials, cannot help but emerge under a process like negotiating the curriculum. The moment a teacher introduces the constraints on negotiating, she is beginning to reveal some of a school's intentions. When students share their knowledge and their questions, they inevitably share their cultural milieus and backgrounds. When questions are allowed by teachers and raised by students about who's knowledge is under study or who's decisions guide the study, then teachers and students engage in a political dialogue. It seems, then, that negotiating the curriculum is not only a transformative process of teaching and learning, but a process through which our beliefs about and our enactments in the social, political, and cultural spheres might be transformed.

These issues which surround and pervade schooling should be potentially useful as a basis for critiquing the cooperative learning movement. I would urge teachers and administrators, any in the educational community who are contributing to making decisions about and participating in inservice education on cooperative learning, to question and probe consultants, inservice educators, and leaders about all the beliefs underlying the cooperative learning movement.

I believe it's up to those of us who are committed to transforming schools and enriching teaching and learning to continue to expose the underlying assumptions and beliefs — the hidden curricula — that characterize popular educational movements. Through deep analyses and thoughtful critique, we have a better chance of understanding the complex issues which we as educators continue to face as we develop alternative, transformative, and democratic ways of teaching and learning. It is, as Freire (1970) and Boomer (in Green, 1988) suggest, a process of reading the word, in order to read the world; a process of reading the whole curriculum.

References

APPLE, M.W. (1986) *Teachers and Texts: A Political Economy of Class and Gender Relations in Education*, NY: Routledge & Kegan Paul.

AUGUSTINE, D.K., GRUBER, K.D. and HANSON, L.R. (1989/1990) Cooperation works! *Educational Leadership*, December/January, 4–7.

BOOMER, G. (Ed.) (1982) *Negotiating the Curriculum: A Teacher-Student Partnership*. Sydney: Ashton-Scholastic.

BOWLES, S. and GINTIS, H. (1976) *Schooling in Capitalistic America*. NY:Basic Books.

BRANDT, R. (1989/1990) 'On cooperative learning: A conversation with Spencer Kagan,' *Educational Leadership*, December/January, 8–11.

CUBAN, L. (1984) *How Teachers Taught: Constancy and Change in American Classrooms, 1890–1980*. NY: Longman.

FREIRE, P. (1970) *Pedagogy of the oppressed.* NY: Seabury Press.

GARDNER, H. (1990) The difficulties of school: Probable causes, possible cures. *Daedalus*, **119**, 2, pp. 85–113.

GIROUX, H.A. (1988) *Teachers as Intellectuals: Toward a Critical Pedagogy of Learning.* MA: Bergin & Garvey Publishers, Inc.

GOODLAD, J.L. (1984) *A Place Called School: Prospects for the Future.* NY: McGraw-Hill.

GRAVES, D. (1983). *Writing: Teachers and Children at Work.* Exeter: Heinemann.

HANNIGAN, M.R. (1989/1990).

GREEN, B. (Ed.) (1988) *Metaphors and meanings: Essays on English teaching by Garth Boomer.* Hawthorn, Victoria, Australia: Australian Association for the Teaching of English.

HANNIGAN, M.R. (1989/1990) Cooperative learning in elementary school science, *Educational Leadership*, December/January, 25.

KAGAN, S. (1989/1990) 'The structural approach to cooperative learning', *Educational Leadership*, December/January, 12–16.

LESTER, N. and ONORE, C. (1990) *Learning Change: One School District Meets Language Across the Curriculum*, Portsmouth, NH: Boynton/Cook-Heinemann.

MAYHER, J.S. (1990) *Uncommon sense: Theoretical practice in language education.* Portsmouth, NH: Boynton/Cook-Heinemann.

McNEIL, L. (1986) *Contradictions of Control: School Structure and School Knowledge*, NY: Routledge & Kegan Paul.

OAKES, J. (1985) *Keeping Track: How Schools Structure Inequality*, New Haven: Yale University Press.

PERKINSON, H. (1968) *The Imperfect Panacea: American Faith in Education, 1865–1965*, NY: Random House.

SIZER, T. (1984) *Horace's Compromise: The Dilemma of the American High School*, Boston: Houghton Mifflin.

SLAVIN, R.E. (1989/1990) 'Here to stay — or gone tomorrow?' *Educational Leadership*, December/January, 3.

SLAVIN, R.E., MADDEN, N.A. and STEVENS, R.J. (1989/1990) 'Cooperative learning models for the 3R's'. *Educational Leadership*, December/January, 22–28.

SMITH, F. (1986) *Insult to Intelligence: The Bureaucratic Invasion of our Classrooms.* NY: Arbor House.

VYGOTSKY, L. (1962) *Thought and Language*, Cambridge, MA: Harvard University Press.

Chapter 16

Parents, Teachers, School and System: Negotiating the School Curriculum

Jon Cook

Part A — The Parents, The Teacher and the School

As a parent I reckon it's my right to ask questions about my daughter's school.

Shelley is a thirteen year old student in her second year at a comprehensive high school. The curriculum is essentially composed of subjects: English, mathematics, history, science, computing, health education and so on. Some are compulsory, some electives. With varying classmates according to the subject choices, she moves through a predetermined day of subject periods, about an hour in length each. She goes from class to class and, of course, from teacher to teacher according to the subject for the period. In each subject, there is a syllabus to be covered, assignments to be done; in most there is a test or exam at the end of the term or year and/or an accumulation of marks through completing set assignments or projects. So far so good; it's all very normal.

This is a 'good school'. Shelley and virtually all her peers wear school uniforms, behave according to the standards laid down and expected of them, obey the fair set of school rules, and are fortunate to work with a relatively experienced 'team' of professionally trained teachers in a reasonably well-to-do school system.

Still all is well and recognizable. But I singled out the word 'team'. What does the word suggest? Working together, collaborating and sharing, on the same track? Better still, might it suggest, in an institution as trained and caring and professional as a school, working in complementary ways towards the achievement of agreed goals and outcomes for the school's clients (students and parents)? My description of Shelley's school life so far doesn't seem to quarrel with this deeper understanding of what a team means.

But now let's visit Shelley's classrooms during her typical day as she moves from subject to subject and teacher to teacher.

Period 1: Mathematics with Mr James Harrison
James is a disciplined man. He knows that regular practice makes perfect, and drill is good for instilling mathematical skills. Since maths is intellectually demanding, he demands quiet and concentration. Numbers become lost in noise. The purity of mathematical logic is garnered through personal, almost poetic introspection and external symbol manipulation to an inevitable conclusion. His students sit in single rows and do not converse. They work on their own and he

sets the work. In whole class sessions, he provides direct teaching with students listening and taking notes or he takes the class through the problems they have just attempted. In this, he asks the questions and always knows the correct answer in advance. And there is always a correct answer.

Shelley is a good and obedient student. She does as she is told and passes her rather regurgitative tests.

Period 2: Geography with Ms. Elaine Braden

Elaine is a conscientious teacher, who has been in this school for seven years straight taking lower secondary geography and history. She is tired at the end of her day, but marks assiduously every evening during the week. She doesn't need hassles; she expects her students to get through a lot of work, which focuses on practical activity of the project kind. While she knows that copying maps and coloring them in is limited and hours in the library doing 'research' by copying slabs from texts is restricted in its value, she also knows that it gets through the day, provides plenty of evidence of much work, and demonstrates that the course has been 'covered'. She is quite happy for her students to sit informally together as they do their projects, as long as it doesn't lead to too much talk and stop them getting their quota of work done.

Shelley is a good student. She does her library research and fills notebooks with wisdom and knowledge culled from the recommended texts. She presents her work well and always passes her tests, since she is prepared to work at remembering the facts which arise for the next test.

Period 3: English with Mr Sean Croker

Sean loves literature, gets on well with kids, and loves to yarn and debate with them. Shelley loves to read, and enjoys going to Sean's 'lit.' classes — which hardly seem like work to her or to most of her class — though she notices that some of the students don't seem to do much in group and class discussions. The same few seem to hog the talk time and make all the points. In fact, Sean knows it's a waste of time asking some of the kids to express their ideas about the latest poem in class, since they get it wrong anyway and he has to put them right about proper critical interpretation, drawn from the subtleties of the text's rich fabric. Class is for discussion and the students write essays at home, which they submit for marking on a weekly basis.

Shelley is a good 'lit.' student and does well. She joins in discussions and, in fact, argues about it sometimes on the weekend with her friend Susan, who sits and dreams in class most of the time. Susan thinks it's all a boring waste of time, believing that reading books won't help her get the job she longs for with its guarantee of independence for getting on with her life.

Period 4: Computing with Ms. Joanne Castle

Joanne is competitive about her subject. It is relatively new in the school curriculum and is constantly changing and being updated, since its field expands as technology advances. She explores the application of computing to other fields of knowledge and tries to guard against her enthusiasm for the power of computers letting her forget that the things are merely tools for serving thinking. She expects her students to join in the exploration of applications, uses a problem-solving approach and is always open to alternative hypotheses and possibilities emerging for doing things better. She argues that explanation and understanding are crucial if her students are to have power over the machine.

Some of the students, including Shelley, have difficulty with this. Couldn't Ms. Castle lay the work down for them to do rather than demanding that they work so much of it out for themselves? Other teachers give them notes and formulae. Ms. Castle makes them work their notes out for themselves, then test their ideas out to see if they've got it right, and then argue with each other about whose approach works best! This is hard — but it's sort of fun when you get it right, they suppose.

Period 5: Science with Mr Fred Makin

Fred is second year out of teacher training. His first year was disastrous. He's trying again and it isn't working. He can't control the students; they sniff out instinctively his innate weakness and take advantage of it. His recourse is to the science text. He tries to dictate directly from it, avoids hands-on experiments, and, in essence, lets the students run riot which many are pleased to do.

Shelley used to try to concentrate. It was impossible. Science became boring and frustrating. It was a period in which to dream or surreptitiously to do her mathematics assignments. She didn't learn much science, knew she wasn't, and had no idea of what to do about it.

Periods 6 and 7: Variations on the Above Themes

Shelley goes through the motions, engaged to greater or lesser extent, adapting her learning behavior, or having it adapted for her, according to varying rules and conditions established by her various, idiosyncratically attuned teachers.

During the day, several minor incidents occurred:

- In Mathematics, Shelley became confused; she encountered a problem about the relationship between two trinomial theorems, and in her puzzlement asked her teacher to explain. He replied that they weren't dealing with that topic now and she should get on with her present work. Shelley started to protest that she could see a connection, but James cut her off at 'But . . .'
- In English, Shelley's friend Susan finally became exasperated and protested out loud that 'This is a stupid poem. It makes no sense at all and it's got nothing to do with me'. Several other students groaned, but Sean said nothing, waited until the discussion got going again and sat down quietly, next to Susan. He gave her a challenge: Find a poem yourself that you do think relates to you and write about how it speaks to you. But there's a catch: it's got to be metaphorical.
- In Business Education (period 6), Shelley got tangled up in the differences between competition and monopolies. Her teacher sneered, told her that it was just as well she didn't run a shopping centre, and made her copy out the relevant pages in the textbook as homework punishment.
- On three occasions, Shelley received the following response to her attempts at answers to teacher questions: 'Nearly, Shelley, but the answer I was looking for was . . .'.

- In Science, to students in states varying from hyperactivity to inertia, Fred desperately dictated an analysis of rock strata in spectacularly bare cliffs near Shelley's city, something she'd been curious about for years. But her mind was elsewhere and the geology she'd have loved to understand didn't even register on her.

Several things are pretty obvious about these sorts of scenarios: they are limited and simplistic or even clichéd; there is a lot more that could or even needs to be said to fill the picture out; there are dozens more pen pictures which could be drawn of different teaching and teacher types; there are so many variables which change things in context; Shelley is only one kind of student in a huge range; teaching is difficult, and it's impossible to respond at every minute to every individual student. All, I guess true.

But I'm not satisfied by this; and I'm entitled to some answers. What might Shelley's school say to me in response to these questions:

- What are the consistencies and differences I may expect to find in the approaches my child's teachers are taking throughout the normal day?
- What are the reasons for these consistencies and differences and what learning outcomes may I expect to see emerge from them?
- What are the valued skills and abilities I may expect to see embodied, explored and tested in these approaches?
- More specifically, in delineating these questions, what may I expect in terms of:

  — the development, reinforcement and testing of generic skills (e.g. researching);
  — vertical and horizontal development of these skills (from teacher/ subject, and from day to day to week to year);
  — the kinds of in-class and homework tasks the child is asked to undertake;
  — the kinds of testing the school puts students through and how what is tested connects to what and how things are taught;
  — the higher order, but non-content-specific, skills and abilities and values which employers and governments are demanding of our school graduates (I'd quote any one of the growing number of statements from employer and government groups which define these desired or required skills);
  — the opportunities my child has during the day for engaging in problematic and challenging tasks, involving experience, interaction and reflection?

- What patterns of reporting has the school determined which are linked discernibly to the school's explicit valuing of skills and abilities and behaviors in classroom practice?
- If I have already observed a pattern of inconsistency and incoherence in these terms, I'd be asking questions like:

  — Why is my child required to learn in such apparently contradictory ways during the day and what is the pedagogical rationale for this confusion;

    — What is the reasoning behind the fact that my child is left to make the connections between one subject and another, one application of skill and another, one learning process and another for herself;

    — What attention is being paid in whole school planning (and is there any such thing?) to generic skills and developmental approaches to learning and teaching from period to period, day to day, and subject to subject?

What is the point here? My answer is twofold. Firstly, these are proper questions for parents and systems and school boards and the school itself to ask of the school; questions which, surely, one could reasonably expect are capable of ready answers in any professional organization. Secondly, in the terms of this chapter on negotiation, I believe that satisfactory answers to these questions *can only be achieved through active negotiation amongst the full school staff at the whole school level.*

Regretably, on the evidence of Shelley's teachers and wider observations of schools at work, it is clear that private practice is the norm rather than teamwork. Teachers in western societies are used to accepting and taking into the classroom whatever instrumental paraphernalia they must, shutting the classroom door, and then getting on with things in their personal styles. Classrooms with the door shut are ships at sea, the teachers are captains and power is theirs. Others designed and built the ships, perhaps, and the ocean is uncontrollable probably; but really, so what? 'Others' aren't there, and so teachers easily close out the world and do things *their way*.

Most teachers operate unseen. Teachers in most schools are but marginally accountable, although they are expected to play by the rules: to follow a syllabus, if it exists; to fit into time slots for classes and subjects; to use a limited set of physical resources; to do a bit of testing or even conduct an end-point exam perhaps; to provide reports for parents; to comply with some school rules to do with conduct and discipline. But these are merely the baggage the captain takes aboard. The important things, like the charting of the course to get the ship somewhere, what fuel rate propels the boat, and the actions of the crew tend to be idiosyncratically decided by the captain.

And the school? The school seems usually to be an *ad hoc* collection of captains and crews drawn together by happenstance and circumstance, too often lacking the direction and cohesion which might enable a collection to become a fleet or convoy, journeying together towards planned destinations in which the real comes ever closer to the ideal. Ironically, at a time when big accountability questions are being asked of schools, I think that perhaps the biggest accountability question of all — about the quality of teaching and learning — is being missed.

I have come to what I view as an inevitable conclusion that the greatest single determining factor in producing high quality learning outcomes in classrooms is the teaching-learning process employed within them, the ways and means of classroom action. And method is generated from pedagogy; that is, from the teacher's theory of teaching as it relates to learning, or even the theory of learning translated into teaching.

The greatest determiner of success isn't what the content is; it isn't the wealth of the resources available; it isn't the school's discipline policy: its's *how* things are done in the classroom. It's what you go through and do and how you do it that determines the quality of what comes out at the other end.

However, in most whole school practice we see, in effect, a line of logic that goes like this:

- The school's learning base is the classroom, in which through the pedagogical power of teachers, students may learn well or less well.
- Managing this teaching and learning power towards the best possible learning outcomes for its students is the essential purpose of the school, put into practice through the coordinated collection of individual classrooms which constitutes the school.
- Therefore, the school should let every individual teacher please him- or herself about how to exercise this essential teaching and learning power.

Extraordinary logic, when put like this! But let's develop this argument further.

- The school (or its governing system) should legislate or negotiate the content and structural features of the curriculum and of its social setting; it might even deal at the whole school level with some really important deep features, such as what the school values about how people deal with each other and equity and social justice provisions.
- The school might go so far as to exercise some quality control over new or inexperienced teachers, through the examination of programs or through peer support systems or supervision of subordinates. And, yes, the school or its governing system may use the not-so-subtle influence of tests and examinations for students, to keep teachers up to the mark in the various ways we all know about. Exams might ensure that teachers will work harder and stick to the written-down curriculum.
- But should the school address the crucial quality control factor of *how* teachers teach towards improving the quality of their students' learning outcomes? No; that's the personal-professional domain of every individual teacher and is not to be tampered with.

The more this line of logic is developed, the more outrageous it becomes! Yet this seems to be what happens in reality. Frankly, I think it's what happens in the vast majority of schools I've ever seen.

Again and again, I've been informed that the greatest determiner of success with any approach to classroom practice is teacher attitude. The ultra-constrained classroom can work well, and so can the most open — it all depends on teacher attitude, so I'm told. I remain unconvinced by this strange notion. Work well at what? Producing what? It can make no sense to me that all ways of working are equally good or powerful or productive, and merely attitude makes them so. I cannot accept that all methods are capable of producing equal outcomes. To the contrary, under examination what seems evident is that different methods will produce different outcomes. Whether the differences are equally valued is another matter. I do accept, however, that teacher attitude is crucial in any approach being given a decent go. I am confident that if a teacher doesn't want something to work, then it won't — so all the greater reason to negotiate!

Although we know that, like attitude, reflection is a crucial part of powerful learning, at the whole school level it is rare that all the staff members come together to reflect on their teaching approaches and the impact they have on students' learning throughout the school or to analyze what patterns and messages are emerging for the students as a result of the various ways teachers do things with their students throughout the day. Collaborative reflection is the way for teachers to stand back from their personal practice to consider how to co-ordinate their attack on teaching.

The same might apply to students: How much or how often are students involved in reflecting with help on their learning methods? How much 'sharing the theory' occurs with students? What analysis of transferability, adaptability, flexibility, theory into practice, theory from practice, making and testing connections and links occurs with students in our schools?

How come, despite the fact that these are the qualities which universities and employers and governments alike demand of school graduates, we in schools leave their development and students' power over them to chance? We let some kids work it out for themselves and let many fail to do so. The wider school system rarely suggests, let alone legislates or sets up the conditions for inter-disciplinary connections. And the school itself lets teachers make the connections if they wish, but rarely gets teachers together for the purpose, rarely demands it or timetables it, rarely even has such stuff on the agenda.

The subject and its content provide the organizing principle in the secondary school; the individual teacher's classroom, supported by specialist injections, in the primary school.

I have spent many years working with teachers at the margin of their pedagogy-in-practice. I refer both to the cutting edge of their teaching and to that sub-group of teachers at the pedagogical margin, those who are active explorers of their own teaching. I have rarely seen all the teachers working collaboratively together for the educational good of all the students in all the school's classrooms. I now believe that only in the *institutionalization of good pedagogical practice* will we appreciably improve learning outcomes for the whole of the school's student population.

My next question becomes, then: What conditions might be established which will allow this to happen and which will guarantee that the school must attend to such essentials? School policies, for all the teachers, need to be about pedagogy, about assessment policies and tasks, about a practical learning theory, about what thinking and doing and knowledge is valued across all classrooms.

Now it's time for me to declare my colors. What would I like to see as the school's pedagogical policy if I could conjure it up?

I want to argue that there really are only a couple of basic approaches to teaching from which to choose. Essentially, there is the *behaviourist approach* (call it the teacher 'chalk-and-talk' model, 'jug to mug', 'traditional', 'teacher-centred') and the *constructivist approach* (the 'workshop' model, interactive and dynamic, learner-centred, exploratory). The inconsistencies and variations between teachers stem largely from the choice between one approach or the other, or from *ad hoc* movement along the continuum between the two. More particularly, they come from each teacher's judgements and decisions about the 'what, how, why, when, for whom, in what order, and how well' factors of classroom programming and action. They come from each teacher's sense of 'tact and timing in planned interventions' into students' learning processes. They come from the varying sense of and sensitivity to pace and degree and timing and order in what students do in their classroom life. Inevitably they come from each teacher's implicit learning theory, but relatively rarely from the teachers' articulated and explicit learning theory, shared with learners.

I reject the behaviourist approach. I am a constructivist.

In these terms, how do Shelley's teachers emerge? James Harrison is pure behaviourist (but perhaps he at least comes clean about it) and Fred Makin is hopelessly behaviourist by default. Elaine Braden is behaviourist in effect, if not in implicit intention. Her instincts would probably respond well to some constructivist enlightenment, but her impact on students doesn't reflect this much. Sean Croker is confused, even though I doubt he knows it. He moves along the continuum between the two views of the learning and teaching world, essentially acting according to his sense of the possibilities and merits of individual students, engaging with the 'elite' students, effectively fostering passivity in the rest. He'll have some stances about teaching and learning, but he certainly hasn't got a thought-through teaching and learning theory! From the snippet I've provided, I'll bet that Shelley's Business Education teacher is rampantly behaviourist and unblinking about it. And Joanne Castle is constructivist, of course.

So what I see suggested in my teacher portraits, and is more widely observable in schools, is a hotchpotch of pedagogy and a melee of methods. While the methods are variable, they are drawn from implicit pedagogy that is 90 per cent the same across the school — behaviourist. But is is a hotchpotch for the learners. It ignores their needs and capabilities, and it contradicts the very purposes for their being in school. It is a hotchpotch because it isn't educationally logical and coherent. And, not least, there is always likely to be a Joanne Castle or two at large to confound the tenor of the school day. Such teachers can make life in the school quite uncomfortable for others, for themselves, and certainly for the students who must try to fathom what's going on as they move through their uneven school day.

It shouldn't and needn't be like this. If the school negotiated the articulation of its pedagogy, starting from informed learning theory, so that it is consistent for the school as an educational entity, then a practical teaching and learning theory for the school would emerge. The school would develop and act upon a negotiated set of teaching and learning principles. From this theory-into-principle teachers would derive a whole realm of methods to employ variously in their classroom practice — just as teachers have always done. But the difference now would be that disempowering contradictions between class and class, teacher and teacher, for the learners would be replaced by a kind of harmony of operational purpose.

Counterpoint would be part of the school's texture. All would not be mindless conformity. A healthy (and therefore, of course, constructivist) school would be full of contrapuntal themes and shifting methodological rhythms — but all arising from a purposeful coherence of understanding about what the music and orchestration of the school's educational life is all about.

Great variety would be evident. Stop such a school at any minute and across it I could visualize students in groups exploring; pairs doing experiments; whole classes in lecture mode with their teachers; teachers working one-to-one with students as the rest of the class is in activity; students presenting to their class; silent students with heads down; noisy classes and quiet classes; teachers asking questions and teachers answering questions; students doing likewise; and so it goes ad infinitum.

But the variety of method is not haphazard. Method would arise consistently out of a school's agreed policy on pedagogy-principles and practice. Method would not be merely a matter of whim, habit, background, preference, enthusiasm or weariness of the individual teacher. It would be to do with the *interrelationship* between the 'what, how, why, when, for whom, where from and where to, and how well' questions which determine teachers' programming as it translates into classroom learning practice. In short, pedagogy would be consistent in such a school and methods would derive from that pedagogy. Ideally, I'd like to be assured that:

- any activity or method employed in any classroom of the school could be reconciled with the school's negotiated pedagogy and teaching-learning principles;
- the informing philosophy is constructivist rather than behaviourist;
- therefore there is a strong emphasis on action and production;
- the students understand what they are doing in an active, constructivist way, know why they are doing it and where it is heading.

Then we'd have variety with vision! And in Shelley's school, we'd see a set of scenarios emerging which is rich in its range of teaching-learning resources, but consistent in its dedication to the development of her learning power, across and through her school life. Shelley could truly become a learner in the school, rather than the object of an ad hoc mix of teachers.

But I'm assuming that the school would decide on *my* preferred learning paradigm. It's more likely that, at first, Shelley's school would negotiate. I see this as preferable to having no agreed policy. At least the likes of Joanne Castle would know that she must adjust considerably or seek another, more empathetic school for her constructivist view of teaching and learning. Similarly, Shelley and her parents, informed of the school's intentions, would be at liberty to explore alternative schooling for her. Of course, my own belief is that the exercise of the school seeking to articulate its pedagogy would at least provide opportunity for teachers such as Joanne Castle to argue her view of the world, and perhaps persuade others to compose exciting education with her. Who knows, even the parents might get a say!

A word is appropriate here on the audit question which seems to bewitch, bother and bewilder most teachers, schools and systems. Given ownership of a policy on pedagogy the staff could declare its pedagogical intentions and its proposed practice and lay itself on the line to be monitored and audited on such a basis! Imagine the staff members declaring that they will accept responsibility, as a logical outcome of their school's pedagogical position, for monitoring and auditing and accounting for their own classroom practice across the school!! That could be a school with the sun on its brow and a most fortunate clientele of parents and students.

Difference With Reasons

The pattern of Shelley's journey through her school day is most evidently true in secondary schools, where the absence of coherent development in students' learning becomes apparent period by period. In the primary school the story unfolds year by year. Though here, too, teachers may habitually vary methods for different segments of the curriculum with the same class day after day: groups for some things, whole class or individual work for others; hypothesizing in some subjects, rote learning in others.

Methodological variety can be very healthy, if there is pedagogical reason to it, rather than unreflective custom (mathematics in the morning when they're fresh; social studies projects in the afternoon, when they're tired) and if there are considered inputs related to valued outcome. I want the reasons for difference between teaching approaches to be learning-related. I want the basis for teacher preference and teacher style to be drawn from what is best for students in their learning. I want differences to be complementary, not contradictory.

From my own schooling, as well as from my observations of teachers during my career, my own experience as a teacher, and my parental interest in my children's teaching, I know well the frustrations and confusions for the learner. Too often told to think with no opportunity to do it; to shut up when the need is to talk and work something out; to answer a dumb question, when the burning need is to ask an interesting one; to move on to the next mechanical task, when the value would be in working more fully through the one engaging at the moment.

In Summary

My points to emerge from this part of the argument are that:

- pedagogical contradiction, breeding methodological incoherence, teaches confusion and saps learning power, at best switching students on and off according to whether the approach happens to be apt and engaging or not;
- all methods are not all equally good; teaching method, consistent with a learning theory, should arise from consideration of where learners are in their learning, not from subject 'habits' or teachers' preferences;
- the impetus for the school's educational program ought to be the learner, in the school — not the teacher, in the classroom;
- a coherent educational institution is likely to be one which has argued and agreed on its pedagogical base: its teaching theory-in practice;
- unless this view of school cohesion is negotiated and owned amongst all its staff, it cannot work in practice — largely because like the captain of a ship, the teacher is all powerful in his or her classroom and because teacher attitude is a key determiner of the energy and conviction to be brought to bear on making any approach work well or not;
- the school should support the teachers in the application of valued approaches to teaching and learning in all its classrooms.

In arguing for a new vision of schooling I seem to have uncovered a litany of school inadequacies. There are some obvious reasons why schools are as they are: a course to get through and no time to stop; if you give the individual student attention, you lose the rest of the class; marks must be recorded at assessment time, whether the work is done or not, and so on. I don't believe we need to accept such reasons as satisfactory. I reckon that the outcomes won't be good enough if the learning processes aren't good enough, and it's the teacher who controls the learning process. For my kids, I want the parts, pattern and sum of their teaching to be learning-based, developmental, complementary and cumulative.

Depite the above critique, I don't believe that the whole story of our schooling is impoverished to the point of desperation. So much of what schools and teachers do is good. It's just that it can be so much better.

So far I have suggested how schools may become better by dint of their own collaboration and negotiation about learning theory. I now wish to examine how a centralized school system can help to bring this about.

Part B — The System

Most school systems produce some kinds of materials for teachers. They might take the form of teacher or student texts, syllabuses, subject guidelines, teachers manuals and policies, administrative instructions and resource and management paraphernalia, and often testing programs and examinations.

From all this central stuff, teachers take on board what they must, what interests them and what they think will help. There doesn't seem much evidence around to suggest that systems' policy statements and associated rhetoric have been able to change very much. Not much of it actually gets into the classroom and certainly very little of it changes the way teachers do things in their own domain. Except at the margin, I doubt that pedagogy has changed much in the last hundred years, even though the written down curriculum, resources, and system policies have changed substantially (see, for instance, Cuban 1984). Not coincidentally, I'm unaware of the quality of classroom outcomes changing much in the same period either. The kinds of outcomes in terms of the cognitive knowledge students acquire have altered, of course: new subject domains and disciplines have emerged; and all sorts of abilities have been fostered very much more over the century — in technical control over machinery, physical abilities and health care, public speaking, social awareness and so on. Children stay on longer at school with consequential rises in national literacy rates and academic qualifications.

But these are not the things I'm talking about here. I'm on about the *quality* of the outcome and the level of higher order skill developed in our students when we compare, say, the 1960s with the 1980s. Content and resource relevance are relatively easily introduced — computers instead of manual typewriters, the Middle East instead of Vietnam as world trouble spot, the latest economic theory — by comparison with pedagogical relevance. A nation more economically developed and socially just requires a people imbued with powerful higher order thinking and doing skills, a people positively challenged by and able to apply abstract knowledge and skills to new and difficult conceptual and practical tasks in ways complementary and cooperative with each other's contributions. It is in this kind of relevance that I see little sign of progress in many decades. Public schooling systems across the globe need urgently to address this question of quality of thinking as we approach the twenty-first century.

Western Australia: A Case

Context

In Western Australia a bold new approach to publicly funded education has been underway since 1988. In essence, the government-controlled, state-wide system has taken on the twofold process of:

- devolving educational responsibility to the school level, from a state-wide system that has traditionally been quite centralist in curriculum resource management, policy and administrative terms; and
- reorienting the whole system from an 'inputs' model to an 'outcomes' model with concomitant focuses on performance indicators linked directly to objectives and cost-efficiency.

The tradition has been a government system which controls all public schools in the state, employs and certifies teachers, provides virtually all school funds through itemized allocation or central accounting, issues syllabuses, mounts state-wide exams, offers professional development programs, judges and rewards teachers by their preparation rather than their results, and so on. Public accountability has really also only existed at the system level.

The system is still centralized to the extent that schools must operate within a centrally-determined framework, which includes the provision of syllabuses (government bureaucracy, the Ministry of Education). Whether the school must adhere to them is an interesting matter for present debate in Western Australia. After all, syllabuses clearly are inputs, not outcomes. The latter are what the new deal is all about, and it is the school's business to determine which are relevant and appropriate inputs to achieve the prescribed outcomes.

The framework, still under determination, is to include the declaration of system goals of education and the definition of required student outcomes (knowledge, skills, and atttitudes by subject area and level of schooling) and attainment levels ('benchmarks') to be achieved in the curriculum. By and large, the outcomes mandated are to be broad, at key points in schooling (perhaps eight from kindergarten to Year 12 or the final year of formal schooling) and are to focus on key learnings within subject areas.

Now schools are receiving an annual gross allocation of funds with responsibility for managing their expenditure across most of the items a school must deal with, from paying for electricity to finding and funding professional development for its teachers. They must set up 'school-based decision-making groups' with defined composition, representing the school and its community, guaranteeing that administrators, teachers, parents and students have input into school decision-making. They must develop a 'school development plan' which must meet the approval of the District Superintendent, a systemic inspector and accountability officer. In turn, the school development plan will be the basis for school accountability to the system and government.

The school development plan is interesting in its requirements and purposes. The central policy or system level requirement for it is laid down as this:

1 All schools must have a school development plan which states their intentions for ensuring effective outcomes within the resources available.

2 The school development plan must include:

- the purpose of the school;
- indicators of the school's performance;
- details of how the school will monitor its performance;
- local and Ministry priorities that need addressing;
- how these priorities will be addressed; and
- the allocation of school resources to ensure effective outcomes.

3 All schools must give parents opportunities to participate in the planning process in accordance with Education Act regulations. In this way, the school demonstrates its accountability to the local community.

4 All schools must present their school development plan to the district Superintendent before the plan becomes operative. Through this, the school development plan provides a basis for demonstrating the school's accountability to Government. (Western Australian Ministry of Education, 1990)

So in Western Australia the system has become explicit about the framework for the curriculum which in turn the school is required to enact. Sophisticated planning and developmental skills are called for and considerable involvement from all members of the school community is required. What we have, in sum, is a situation of explicit devolved responsibility, from the centre to the individual school, for the delivery of the curriculum; and this is accompanied by equally explicit accountability for the school's planning and performance. The new orientation is towards outcomes and accountability. While this may seem to readers still to be a heavy 'top-down' approach, it represents an explicit agenda which schools are now in a position to negotiate. While there are requirements, there are also new opportunities for school self-determination. A context for achieving what I have argued for in Part A has been established.

The school's challenge and opportunity lie in enactment. The point is that the system doesn't dictate *how* the school is to proceed with its curriculum enactment. Defining outcomes doesn't deliver them. The system says: 'Here is the framework; here is a defined set of outcome requirements and goals (but with plenty of latitude for school choice, relevance and diversity), and here is your quota of money and resources. You now have the responsibility for doing it and, within very reasonable limits, you are free to do it in your own ways'.

This is a high order challenge, and it is demanding a high order acceptance. Because of the imposition without negotiation of this challenge, the reaction in schools has so far been very uneasy on a continuum from rejection to grudging acceptance, together with demands for new conditions and salary scales for teachers now required to take on new tasks and duties — such as being required to participate in whole school planning! While industrial problems and an analysis of Western Australia's teething difficulties are not the issue in this chapter, the fact that very many teachers are simply not interested in the school beyond their own classroom and subject is a most disturbing indication of the future perspiration which will be needed to realize the Western Australian system's inspiration.

It's disturbing because the central issue I am examining is what the school might do when faced with this challenge and this opportunity; to be more than a loose collection of individual teachers and to reexamine instead its capacity to be a holistic unit.

What will schools make of this requirement for whole school planning? So far in Western Australia, I see little progress beyond the surface and organizational features of the curriculum — beyond timetabling and curriculum choices offered, beyond specialized curriculum focuses the school might decide to take on, such as aeronautics, or theatre arts, or languages; though I'm pleased to report that greater deliberate attention to social justice and equity issues is already emerging.

But so far the connections between school development planning and the crunch pedagogical issues aren't being made. This is still typical: a school acknowledges it has a serious student failure problem because it is located in a low socioeconomic area; it recognizes that literacy levels are below state norms; it halfheartedly prepares a school development plan — but it doesn't, in any substantial way, recognize the links between these 'separate' events. It almost certainly doesn't see that the school development plan might address the failure and literacy problems by a concerted pedagogical attack across the full curriculum and in all the classrooms.

School development planning also means that the school can no longer legitimately duck addressing the issue of the quality of teaching across the school, even though state schools in Western Australia still don't have any power over staff selection which remains centrally determined. A truth that most systems throughout the world are loath to admit is that all teachers are not equal and excellent. Some teachers are pretty ordinary; some, inevitably in a large school and large system, are less than satisfactory. Ditto for principals, who ultimately take responsibility for their schools' performance. The sheer numbers of teachers, principals and schools required to serve our student populations guarantees that hard truth.

However, when attention is called to the outcomes, via performance indicators of the entire complement of the school's teachers, then the school has to rethink how it can help its struggling few or many teachers to come up to scratch and deliver the goods. So in which aspects of teaching do we find the greatest difficulties emerging for the weak teacher? The answer is discipline and pedagogy. What's more, I'd argue that control problems are often directly linked to pedagogical problems. The gist of this chapter is that pedagogy is the major issue which schools must address.

These kinds of issues cannot be resolved by legislation. Their resolution in Western Australia can only be negotiated — if they are to work. The opportunity is there, but the recognition and the will typically are not — yet. I believe that, through negotiation at the whole school level and between schools and the system, both are possible and then real growth in the quality of student outcomes will not be far away.

It is all too easy to enter another round of token school policies and practices and another round of 'Yes, buts'. Unless the new deal makes a difference to the quality of student outcomes, it's really a waste of time and a mere sop to the political expedient of locating responsibility at the same place as accountability lies. Systemic requirements and frameworks can only be effective in achieving better outcomes for students if schools take up the challenge to negotiate the how of making it happen.

Jon Cook

The Power of Peer and Whole School Pressure

What the system can do, and indeed has done in Western Australia, is legislate for a context to be created which provides the opportunity for *whole school* treatment of key educational issues. Some might argue that to negotiate this would be a better way to go. The answer is posited that evolution will never bring about such sweeping changes; it requires a revolution, which equates in peace time to legislation: You make things happen by giving people no choice in the matter. This, of course, is what examinations have always done. It is an intriguing question as to whether schools will resist this new systemic 'interruption' or whether it will indeed be a catalyst for educational reform.

One key educational issue ought to be the school's pedagogical base for the kinds of reasons exposed in this paper. If the school can't duck operating holistically, as a kind of educational collective, then at least the chance is there that really worthwhile focuses will emerge, beyond the level of uniforms, behavior codes and spelling policies.

Besides requiring enlightened collective planning in schools, the system can uphold, espouse and enact principles which include valuing of the constructive capacities of learners' minds. In its examining and assessing requirements, the system can place emphasis on higher order thinking, on problem posing and problem investigation, and on reflective capacity, so breaking the reproductive cycle of testing which values recitation and catechistic application of formulae. Teachers and schools will rightly seek to ensure that students are successful in terms of the publicly valued 'standards'. Systems can be a dynamic force for reform by setting new kinds of standards, requiring new kinds of teaching and learning.

The system in Western Australia is creating an enforced opportunity for schools to address key issues at the school level. But while the system sets conditions, it can't negotiate much. Real negotiation about students' learning can occur at three levels: in the school, between teachers; in the classroom, between teacher and students; and between students as they learn.

Some useful negotiation can, however, occur between the school and the system over the content, quality and effectiveness of school plans. In the end, all will depend on whether schools and teachers intend to work in this way. To secure this intention the school must negotiate. The reason is simple enough: you can legislate for overt behavior, but you can't legislate people's thinking. You can only legislate what you can directly monitor and control and people's thinking is beyond that pale. Just as students in school need to see purpose and to develop ownership, so teachers need to take part in processes where they can begin to share control over what is done. It is my hope that by inviting schools to be more self-determining within explicit constraints, we may help them to reexamine old controlling habits and to establish new understandings about how children will learn in this place.

My belief is that the school as a unit can influence, subtly infiltrate, or cajole and even enforce good pedagogical behaviors in its teachers — a kind of reverse of schools' longstanding ability to stop certain behaviors from occurring. The school that says all classrooms will be silent is usually very capable of seeing that its teachers toe the line. Or if you nail the desks to the floor, it becomes awfully hard to mix and match them in different groupings according to learning need. What joy to turn this school power around to positive effect and make good things happen!

Conclusion

The system can provide a context and certain enlightened imperatives, as in Western Australia. The school can provide the collective power through negotiating that aspect of the curriculum called pedagogy: the one that in enactment determines the quality of students' outcomes.

In Western Australia the opportunity exists for schools to see themselves as a pedagogical power base, impacting directly on teachers' behaviour in their classrooms in terms of how they teach and how well their students learn. The opportunity is there for *the school to become the determiner and organizing principle for powerful pedagogy applied throughout the school.*

When we take the quality of learning as our goal, nationally and internationally, I suggest that currently the systems are failing, experimental groups of teachers are failing, inspired individual teachers are failing, if our goal is to extend needed reform across schools. The trouble is that teacher groups and individual teachers at the margin can only succeed at the margin. My evidence? After the enormous number of action research projects into aspects of pedagogy; after the thousands of classroom investigations by teachers into their own practice; after the many important 'movements' that have emerged and gained some currency amongst teachers (language across the curriculum, the role of language in learning, collective and collaborative learning, school-based curriculum development, action research pushes, and so on); after all this great work that has occurred in the last couple of decades, so little of it all has penetrated into whole school consciousness and action.

Governmental and political groups are failing to meet global learning challenges. Systems (bureaucracies) and political pushes (governments) can have great success in controlling, constraining, and delineating. What they haven't done, and I think can never do, is much to *liberate* teachers towards the exploration and achievement of more powerful and demonstrable learning processes and outcomes for students, governed by the need for a more powerful economic and socially just force in the nation.

Only the teachers themselves can achieve this learning-liberation. And they can only achieve it if they negotiate and come to own and believe it. And only the collective power of the whole school staff can achieve it for all the teachers with all the students in all the classrooms.

It's worth aiming for; and there's not much left to try.

Reference

WESTERN AUSTRALIAN MINISTRY OF EDUCATION (1990) *School Development, Planning, Policy, and Guidelines*, Perth, Western Australia.

Chapter 17

One, Two, Three, Four: How Do You Stop the Classroom War? Two, Four, Six, Eight: It's Easy, Just Negotiate

Pat Thomson

It's not hard to see negotiation as a simple formula. You just go in and follow a few straightforward steps and it all happens. Kids can tell you how to do it.

Maria

Maria is classified as one of our students at risk. I first came across her because she had been the name given by several parents. They said she was encouraging their kids to take drugs. Not only did she sniff butane they said, but she got their daughters to do it too. Maria was one of those young women whose feelings about herself and life were clearly written in her slouch, the tousled black hair obscuring her face, in her continual truancy, and in her refusal to look any teacher in the eye. In a tearful interview that lasted several hours, Maria demanded counselling: She had problems she wouldn't dare talk to us about she said. She thought that most of her problems at school were related to failure in Maths: This was a sore point and she preferred to talk about her several bouts of running away and living on the streets.

She eventually described instances of teachers asking her why she bothered staying at school, greeting her return to the class after several days' absence with an, 'Oh, you finally decided to grace us with your presence. . . .' By detailing her home situation, problems with particular teachers and her lack of achievement in Maths, Maria had almost planned out her own intervention programme. We decided to go with the signposts she had constructed for us. The counseling was organized, special Maths tutoring by a senior student was provided at the same time as her least favourite subject, some of her classes were changed so that she could start afresh with different teachers. Her attendance improved. She combed her hair out of her eyes.

A group of student teachers came to the school. Maria was one of the guides for the walk around the school. 'You've got a lot to say about what teachers should be like', I said. 'Why don't you let these prospective teachers hear them? Get them while they're young! Tell them what to do before they're let loose with kids!' After the tour was over, Maria wanted to stay and hear what else was being said. The student teachers were given a run through of the school philosophy — getting kids to stay at school and be successful at the 'hard stuff' was a key feature. Words like empowering and rigour were tossed around: all kids needed a fair go despite their backgrounds, we said. When we got to the bits about how you actually did it in the classroom, Maria wanted to speak. She Said:

> 'It's easy. You say what you reckon' we have to do, and you give us your ideas about how we can do it . We go and think about how we want to do it, and then we talk about it with youse and sort it out. We've gotta have some choice or we won't learn. If we negotiate, we'll do it (most of the time).

At 14, Maria knew the essential steps of negotiation. It's hardly a complicated dance. She already knew that it wasn't foolproof; it didn't automatically produce results. The kids might still resist, be turned off, be downright lazy, disorganized, or they might get distracted by outside events. Equally, the teacher may not always have done all the preparation necessary to make the performance a successful one. There is no guarantee that these steps work well all the time. Yet, Maria knew that if you felt you owned what you had to do and had been involved in its shaping, then you were more likely to be interested in it, would see the relevance of it, and in fact, would do it. . . . (probably).

* * *

Lee Shulman (1987) has suggested that the act of teaching is making connections between the lives, experiences and needs of particular students and with what the teacher carries around in her head — knowledge about specific subjects, knowledge about kids, schooling and education, skills and competencies drawn from particular disciplines and beliefs about learning and the world. Teachers use a variety of ways to make those links. They use analogies, metaphor; they structure experiences that they know the kids will like; they get the kids to explore their experiences and so on.

This connection making, teaching, is both theoretical and practical; it is learned on the job and is learned over time. There is no instant teacher — just add kids and it's done. There is only a continuing process, strongly associated with particular kids and classes, a higgledy, piggledy assortment of skills and understandings, a reserve tank of ideas and a trailer load of unresolved problems. In other words, we all learn how to teach. We do not come out of preservice training already highly competent. We only have the raw materials. We process them and refine them on the job, in our own classroom, with our own classes.

* * *

I started my teaching-learning with what we might now call 'at risk' kids. They were the ones who yelled out, walked out, acted out, broke out. They abused their bodies, the property of others and anyone handy. They hated themselves, their parents, schools and teachers. Most of them were street smart: many of them were clever but untaught in anything but crime school.

I started a school for these kids: you saw the alternative school all over the world in the 1960s and 1970s, so you know what they were like. They had high staff-student ratios, a pretty free-wheeling curriculum, a number of tatty arm-chairs. The kids all chainsmoked and called the teachers by their first names. The teachers were all vaguely different to their peers in 'real' schools and they were all highly idealistic.

Many of these schools did not last long. When the teachers got tired, the school closed. When the kids got out of hand, the school closed. When the kids didn't learn anything, the school closed. When the system was no longer willing to pay, the school closed. Those that survived earnt the support of education systems; they had a tough-minded kind of approach to teaching and learning that maintained both social order and produced real educational gains for the kids.

As I look back now (some 15 years later) on my six years running that school, I suspect that in fact I learnt more than the kids. I learnt the foundations of my teaching with those the conventional school had failed. They were not going to 'student' for any traditional 'teach'. They taught me, often by the trial and error method, how to teach so that they would 'student'.

The first thing that I learnt was that I couldn't yell at them. If there was work to be done, and they weren't doing it, then the quickest way to guarantee that it would never be done was to yell. Straight away I was into a mode of relating to them that forced me to learn a new authority, based on reason, based on what I knew and could do, and, yes, on sanctions. The power of the system was there whether I behaved like a harridan or not. The second lesson was that sometimes you had to use the system, even if you thought it was no good. When a large young man bears down on you brandishing a lump of two by four, it's no time to consider his traumatic childhood.

Having got rid of both the Rambo and the *laissez faire* romantic approach to kids, it was time to see about learning.

The school had begun with the premise that what the kids needed most was the 'stuff' to get a job. They needed to know how to read and write; they needed Maths; they needed to understand how the system worked so that they had some chance of making it work for them. They needed to know about food, health, sex, drugs, the law and money. They were the bottom of the barrel, the most messed around, and they deserved extra. They were angry, and most had every justification for their anger. There was just no point in suffering further for it, we thought. It didn't change things for you or any other battered kid, if you ended up in jail. Far better to sort yourself out and put that anger to some constructive use. Empowerment was the name of the game.

But how did you teach it? You could lecture and hector the kids, or you could provide them with large amounts of factual information to read and digest. That didn't work. That method was the same one that they had rejected in their other schools. If the teacher says it's something you must know, it's no good. Rebel!

The first clue came early in the piece. We already knew about behavioural contracting — a social work kind of process that got the kids involved in their punishments. You got the kids to own the fact that they had chosen to do something wrong and that there should be some kind of punishment as a consequence and then you drew up a contract about what they would do. If they'd stolen some other kid's property, they might have to earn some money to replace it, or do something for that person. If they had been late for an appointment and made everybody wait, they might have to give up some of their free time. We arrived at The Consequences through a period of negotiation with the kid. It was crucial that they had some ownership of the punishment, we believed, because then they also owned responsibility for the original bad behaviour, and didn't go around and blame it on everybody else or on circumstances.

It is always a shock to kids the first time they have to choose their own punishment. Some of them are terribly hard on themselves, and the negotiation is more about trying to get them to find something reasonable. 'No, putting yourself in detention for a month is not acceptable. All you've done is refused to follow directions. How about something less extreme? (By the way, is that what happens to you at home/at your old school?)'

Others are very resistant and know that this is the thin edge of the wedge, part of the plot to make them consciously take control of what happens to them. They often take a while. The conversation usually goes like this:

T: Why are you in trouble do you think?

S: Because I got in a fight.

T: And why is it against the school rules to fight?

S: I dunno.

T: What happens to you if you walk around fighting?

S: You get locked up.

T: And what do you think about that?

S: Not fair. My Dad says you ought to be able to hit someone if they're hassling you.

T: So I could just come up to you if you were hassling me and thump you and that'd be OK? You'd accept that would you? You wouldn't want to thump me back or get all your mates to find me later?

S: I'd get you back.

T: Would this have solved the original problem? Would you know what you'd done to me in the first place? I doubt it. You'd just keep going round doing the same stuff to everybody and wondering why you always got into fights.

This bit can go on longer — but you get the idea.

S: Huh.

T: So there's no difference between the rule here at school and the rule outside.

S: 'Spose so.

T: So what do you think should happen to people that go 'round breaking the rules?

S: They get punished.

T: Yes. And they find out what they did wrong so they can stop doing it. And what do you think is a good punishment for fighting?

S: Dunno.

T: What do you think should happen to you, because you were fighting and broke the rule?

S: Dunno.

T: I could give you some time to think about it. You could try to come up with a punishment that might help you not to solve your problems by thumping someone as your first option. Or I could give you some things to choose from. Or I could make your decision for you — but

that would be your choice to have me decide. What's it going to be
— you have some time, I give you options or you decide I can choose?

This is negotiation under pressure. Like a chess game, there has to be some
kind of move made. Whatever happens, kids have to know that they choose it,
deliberately, and that they are in control. This is not about equal power sharing.
This is about the first step with naughty kids — getting them to recognize that
they do make decisions about what they do, and that if they keep choosing to
break the rules, there will be consequences as a result of their actions.

This approach is often criticized as being a choice about the colour of the
rope that's meant to hang you. In my view this is a false analogy. In my process
you get to decide whether hanging is a good punishment, one that would help you
learn so you wouldn't do it again when you next had the opportunity.

This is hardly an infallible process. Sometimes, despite knowing the consequences, the kids may well still choose to break the rules (just like adults).
Sometimes, there might be very good reasons for deciding to break the rules. We
were careful to let the kids know that some of the teachers had been involved in
the anti-conscription (the Australian draft) campaigns of the 1960s and early
1970s, and that we knew that sometimes you did make deliberate decisions to
break rules and laws. But we pointed out we were conscious of what we were
doing, informed, with full knowledge of what would happen.

Shane

Shane was an arsonist. He'd successfully burnt down his former school and had
been so proud of what he'd done that he'd voluntarily owned up. A spell locked
up and then quite some time under supervision to follow: attendance at our
school was part of his sentence. He was a weedy little thirteen year old, with
sandy hair and a thin freckled face: a not very attractive kid until he smiled and
showed a fine array of crooked, nicotine stained teeth in the standard engaging
urchin grin.

Shane had been naughty. Well, that goes almost without saying — he was
always naughty. I can't remember what his particular sin was, but I remember the
train of events that followed.

> *T:* Shane, you've broken the rule, again. You've taken up too much of
> my time. The other kids need some help too. If you've got the
> energy to do this kind of stuff, you've got the energy to do some
> hard work. It's about time you put something back into this place
> and stopped draining it.
> *S:* What do I have to do?

He knew the ritual well.

> *T:* Something you think needs doing round here: as long as its hard
> work and not sitting on your bum I don't care what it is.
> *S:* I dunno.
> *T:* Well, how about the garden? You could do some weeding. Or there's

> always the common room — you could clean that up. Or how
> about . . .
> *S*: The garden.
> *T*: OK. Now what will you need to get together before you do the
> garden?

The trouble with these punishments was that they required so much getting together. Silence. Would I make a fight out of this bit or would I be helpful?

> *T*: You'll need the shovel and the fork and probably a wheelbarrow.
> *S*: How much do I have to do?
> *T*: Oh, at least a trailer full.
> *S*: Huh, we haven't got a trailer.
> *T*: That's not going to get you out of it. We'll hire one.

Stop. Check the negotiation. This feels more like me making the decision.

> *T*: Are you sure you want to do the garden? If it's too hard to go off
> and get a trailer, you can always choose something less difficult to
> organize.

. . . into my car and off to get a trailer. So far, this punishment was making me work. Shane hadn't lifted a finger yet. However, he hadn't lost interest either which was a major bonus. I knew that if I continued to show that I thought it was important that he face the consequences of being naughty and actually did something, we would have made a small gain with him. If I actually managed to get beyond the teacher/naughty kid dynamic, the you'll-do-this-because-you've-been-a-turkey routine that had obviously been Shane's major pattern with adults, I'd have made significant progress.

On the way back to the school, Shane looked at me and said, 'How much do you cost?' 'What do you mean?' I puzzled. This wasn't the regular form of yes-butting that I knew normally accompanied punishment. 'Well, what happens when they hire you? How much to hire a teacher?' 'Oh', I laughed, 'I wasn't hired, I was appointed'. What on earth was Shane on about? Stock response: when you don't know what they're driving at, give a slightly off centre answer. (At that time, I didn't realize that it was OK to tell kids how much you earned. They knew it was heaps compared to what they were likely to have, anyway. They usually just wanted to know how big the heap was.)

Shane got back to school and started to dig and weed. After an hour or so of tearing at the tough grass, he came inside. This was another danger time — he could so easily give up now, and I knew that I had to keep him on track and not buy into any little plot he might have for getting me to yell or say something that would cause him to stalk off in a huff.

> *S*: If you weren't hired, what happens when they want to get rid of
> you? They'll fire you, eh? Like my Dad. He got fired. One day they
> just didn't want him anymore so they told him to leave, just like
> that, after eight years, they just kicked him out, it's not fair, they shit
> me.

T: It's a bit different for teachers. If anything was to happen to me, it'd take a long time, and I'd end up being dismissed, not fired. But it'd take ages.

I didn't know where this was going, but it wasn't a disciplinary conversation.

S: My Dad was just like the trailer you know. They just hired him for a while and then left him when they didn't want him. That's what'll happen to youse?

I had no idea why Shane had suddenly come up with this. There was no logic attached to it that I could see. I certainly hadn't planned it. But somehow and for some reason he'd alighted on this particular topic. Of course, I'd read Freire, but hadn't had any idea about how you might actually get it to work. This was my first lesson in it.

Words were actually very important. Reflecting on your experience and making sense of it were important. The direct metaphor was important.

Shane and I sat down for a while and had a bit of a yarn about trade unions and alienation and the vagaries of mutli-national corporations and then both went outside and kept digging and weeding. While we worked, we kept talking — what had his father's options really been, what happened next.

Shane had plenty to tell me about what had happened to his family and neighbours. I had a bit to say about things I'd studied and read. We had a long conversation. Shane was happy to listen to what I had to say, because he'd located the topic. I was happy to talk in a different way with him about things that mattered to him and to me. I had to be careful about the way I said things. I couldn't use the words that I was familiar with. But Shane had shown me that it was possible to be accurate and not use the familiar academic discourse. I had to be careful to let him have his say. It would be too easy for me to leap in and dominate the conversation with all my book learning, my adult self-importance, my teacher behaviour. Our new relationship was fragile and unfamiliar to me. Was Shane really learning if I wasn't talking all the time? I found myself giving bits of information and asking questions that helped him keep his talk going. He talked more than I did. I listened. I found out a lot about him. He hadn't burnt down his old school in a fit of revolutionary pique when his father was sacked — the sacking was a few days before, and the arson some time ago. But he did tell me about what he liked doing with his Dad, and what had happened when his Mum left and how he had to look after his three younger brothers most of the time when Dad was off drowning his sorrows at the local.

This information came in very handy and helped me sort out some more things that would interest Shane at school. He started reading books about fishing, so he could surprise his Dad with the things he knew. He went to work at the local child care center so he could get some ideas and skills to help with the littlies. He started tinkering with the school lawn mower so that he could maintain the bit of garden he'd taken responsibility for.

I'd like to say that our relationship changed from that day on. Well it did and it didn't. One thing at a time. We established a different kind of dialogue, and both of us searched for ways to find it between the bouts of naughtiness and exasperation and rebellion.

I never did find out why he'd played with fire; I did notice, just a few weeks ago, an item in the newspaper that said his youngest brother had just been caught setting fire to the local primary school.

Shane became a mechanic.

A Brown Bag

The episode summed up a set of things for me. I have a little brown bag of principles that have been feeding all my practice since then.

1 Kids want to have real talks with teachers. They don't want to stay in the position where they either have to rebel against or accept the teachers' words. They want to establish good relationships.

2 Learning is not always planned. As a teacher you have to watch for the magic moments.

3 The kids give you clues about how to reach and teach them. You just have to listen.

4 The content, the 'stuff' that is talked about and learnt, has to be real to the kids. The process is only half the equation. What you teach is as important as how you teach.

5 There is some content that is really important — and kids know it. Who am I? How do I fit in the world? Why is the world like it is? What do I do if it's not fair? How do I make it work for me?

6 You have to have real conversations with kids where both parties have real things to say. Between you, you can start to deal with the questions. Conversations can't be a one-way street: They have to be reciprocal. (Habermas said it more elegantly.)

* * *

Somehow I learnt that the behaviour negotiating process was just as applicable to the formal curriculum. There wasn't any A-Ha! about it, it just seemed to happen . . .

You could ask them to nominate a punishment. You could just as easily say to a kid,

> What do you think you really have to learn? Here you are a school dropout, and now you're here. What one thing do you reckon' you could do to improve?

They always knew. Invariably, it was reading and writing. They never actually said,

> Well I have a poor self concept caused by the fact that when I compare myself to other kids my age, I discover that there are a few things I can't do. Because those things are the same things that are socially important and also are crucial to both school and work success, my life chances are diminished by them. In fact, my anti-social behavior is in some way linked to my failure to achieve in the basics of schooling.

It's just as well that they didn't say all this, because if they had we might have been inclined to give them assertiveness training, confidence building and advanced hug courses. Because they said, 'Readin' and writin', we just went straight on.

> Well here's your options. You can just get a couple of books and read them and then we'll have a yarn about them. Or you can read a page or so aloud to me, and we'll see if you're as bad as you think you are. Or you could write down something — like why you hated reading and writing in your old school — and we'll talk about it. Or we could give you a kind of test that might tell us some things that are useful and it might not. What do you reckon'?

Sometimes it took a while to get to the point where the kids would own the learning program, but you could eventually get there with even the toughest nut, because they owned the problem. If they were very behind, you often had to get them to read in a private situation, but they soon discovered that there wasn't much shame attached to learning and joined in the normal classes. That of course had to be negotiated too. It seemed to work wonders for their self concepts — nothing like finding out you're not stupid and that you really can read.

I stayed in the alternative school for six years and then moved into the mainstream. I was interested to see how much of what we did was transferable.

* * *

I discovered that going into mainstream schools changed the dynamic only slightly. The two schools I've been in since have been poor — working class I'd prefer to say — where the kids have differed only marginally from those in the alternative. They are still resistant to being told, and to being told off. They can give teachers a really hard time.

It's certainly harder to find the time and space to give each kid the individual attention that you need to establish the dialogue. It's not possible to drop everything and just do something like going off to get a trailer. Kids come in big blocks for limited periods of time, and there are lots of them. The adults they deal with aren't necessarily a coherent and philosophically compatible group, and there are many different standards and little rules for kids to maneuver around. But the principles still hold. I learnt to negotiate with groups.

> Well, this is English, and I'm told that we have to read a class novel, and I thought it would be good if we all picked it, rather than have me pick it. Whaddya reckon'. . . .? Well, in order to pick a book we'd better work out how we decide what makes a book interesting to read. What I want you all to do is to think about a book you really liked. What was it called? What was it about? Write down the name of it, if you can remember it. Now this is the hard bit. Do you remember what you did when you first picked up the book? What do you do when you are faced with making a choice about whether a book will be interesting? There will be a set of steps that you follow. You mightn't have thought about them before, but you certainly do them. Close your eyes and see if you

can picture yourself going into the library and choosing a book. What do you do?

I always read a bit of the first page, for example, to see whether I like the way the book is written; sometimes I just read a few lines and decide that it wouldn't be my cup of tea, and put it back. What do you do?. . . .

[List emerges. I write it up on the board.]

Now I just happen to have with me a few sets of books. How about we divide into groups and each have a set. Then each group will look at the books and talk about which ones they'd like to read. (Use the list we've got on the board about what to do when deciding on a book to read.) Then each group will make two recommendations to the whole class. . . . What the book is, why it'd be good to read, and how you decided.

[This would be spelt out on a sheet I'd give each group.]

OK? You remember your rules about groups? No putting other people down, everyone gets to talk. . . .

Now we're going to report back, and then we'll have a vote to decide on which book we'll all read.

Now this scenario can easily lead on to groups going away and reading the books before they make the whole group decision. They can each write a recommendation — book review — before the whole class discussion and vote. The groups can be constructed according to the first few stages of the 'Jigsaw' game (home groups and expert groups; a home group has a mixed set of books, the expert has the same book. Expert groups read a book and jointly decide on whether it is worth reading and why and then report back to their home group. Home groups then decide between all the books based on the recommendations of the expert groups). The major difference between this model and the cooperative learning model so often espoused (Slavin, 1985; Johnson, 1980) is that there is no 'right' body of knowledge to be tested at the end. There are no questions and no class competition to see if everybody has learnt the 'stuff'. Instead, there is a decision.

What has happened is that:

1 The kids have all let the teacher and each other know what kind of books they like reading. This will be useful to the teacher who learns something she can use later, and to kids, because it provides a 'test driven' class list that can be used for independent reading.
2 The kids have generated a shared set of strategies based in their experiences that can be used to select books.
3 The kids have worked in groups.
4 The kids have practised giving opinions and reasons to support those opinions.

And, depending how it is structured, they may also have read a book, written a review (using a similar list method as a starter). Most importantly, they will have made a real decision. They will have chosen their class novel.

For me, negotiation always combines with decision making at an individual or group level. The decision is always a real one. Kids do not engage in negotiation or collaborative activity just to regurgitate a set of material or to please the teacher. They engage in these processes in order to decide on what comes next. Whatever they decide they'll do. This is not an abdication by the teacher. In my book selection example, it's clear that I've already doctored the choices, so I can educationally justify whichever of the books they choose.

What it does mean is that I'm going to have a hectic few nights work, looking at their final choice and deciding on how it can be used to further the goals of the syllabus. I can't have a neat program worked out miles in advance. I can only plot out parts of it.

I might have already decided that the kids will have to demonstrate an appreciation of plot and character, but may go no further than that: I may then negotiate, partially or fully, the assignments on that basis.

Brown Bag 2

I add to my brown bag:

Negotiation leads to a real decision and action based on that decision.

* * *

Negotiation does not always lead to perfect solutions. A few years ago I was teaching a class of thirteen-year-olds. We had, using the kind of process established in the example above, worked out a six month program. It seemed fine to start with but then it started to fall apart. They wouldn't do the work required. They started to complain. 'This is boring'.

They started to argue.

'No, it's not, I like it'.
'Well that means you're boring then'.

I started to worry. What was happening? 'What's going on?' I asked them. 'You designed this program. How come you don't want to do it?' 'We do'. 'Dunno', came the simultaneous replies.

Social interaction was at an all time low. All my attempts to try to resolve the issue using a whole class negotiation just foundered. I said:

'I'm stuck. I don't know what's going on. How about I try to survey each one of you individually and see if I can make any sense out of it?

I constructed a lengthy survey that recanvassed all of their likes, dislikes, feelings about each other, the course, their particular learning needs. What I discovered was that a grand case of hormones had split the class asunder.

What I now had, six months later, was one group of girls who were far more mature than the rest of the class. They found all the work we'd originally set was far too babyish. I then had another group of girls who were feeling really out of it because half of their friends had suddenly ceased to be their friends and snubbed them constantly. They no longer had interests in common. They were prepared to stay with the original course provided they didn't have to work with the boys.

The boys were conscious that all the girls were somehow different. They wanted the original course to be more macho, more boylike.

I explained the results of the survey to the class. It made sense to them too and we negotiated that we would have a new program that consisted of a common core and three separate strands for the three groups. The common core content became a discussion about changing male and female roles, changing interests and whether macho novels and romance novels were a sensible way to go. The process became the content.

Brown Bag 3

The teacher can make the act of teaching part of the syllabus. The learner can discuss what works for her and him.

* * *

Sometimes there is a more complicated set of negotiations, particularly if there is a major piece of individual or group work as the summation of the course.

A couple of years ago I taught a final year Women's Studies course. It had two core units, a third unit that was to be chosen from a group of six, and a fourth unit that was an individually negotiated major project. The two core units were to provide the understandings, the basic theory and the competencies that the girls would need in order to accomplish their individual work.

An initial conversation with the class established a short list of skills they thought they might need: how to interview people, how to conduct a survey, how to take notes from a text, how to summarize the content of a film, how to run a group, how to write a letter, and so on. This list basically set part of the shape of the assignments that had to be done in the first half of the year. If the set content we were doing was on women and work for example, then an assignment might be to design a survey that examined an aspect — to be negotiated — of women and work, such as the number of local shop assistants who were part time or the incidence of sexual harassment in the fast food chain shops adjacent to the school.

What was negotiable was clear. What was non-negotiable was also clear. The girls in fact had set some of the non-negotiables when they established what they would need to do in order to complete the requirements of the course.

We knew that we had to cover a set of 'facts' and we had to learn a set of 'skills'. This was established at the beginning of the year and we all knew it. All that happened then was that I involved them in the process of working out how we would do that. We kept the list of 'skills' that they had compiled in the classroom, on the pin up board, and we dutifully ticked them off as we accomplished them. We kept a running record of our coverage of the course.

I hadn't forgotten to bring along my little brown bag of principles. Whenever I was negotiating with the girls they were there. The 'stuff' should be real, not artificial. The way the girls learnt how to run a group was to run a group not just learn the theory and be part of a group themselves. They actually ran discussion groups with junior high school girls looking at non-traditional careers such as engineering, plumbing and building. Part of their assessment was their own self-evaluation of how they'd done: the other part was feedback from their group.

The way they learnt to write a report was to investigate sex stereotyped behaviour in an infant school, using an observation technique chosen from a short list I provided. They compared their findings with the literature, getting information from text, and then wrote reports that were presented to the teachers from the infant school. These activities were relevant to the girls — they chose the ones that were important to them — and they had meaning — they drew on their experiences and knowledge. Better still, things often happened as a result of what they had done.

Their work in the infant school had examined the girls and boys behaviour in the yard. They found that the boys used the play equipment most of the time, whereas the girls mostly sat and talked. The teachers were concerned about this and followed up the girls' research with some interviews and further observation. As a result, a special program to encourage girls to be more active has been introduced.

Another of my students observed interactions in the classroom. She was supposed to be doing a standard interaction study to see whether the boys talked more than the girls. However, she become distracted while doing the tick the column exercise and started to listen to what they were talking about. She noticed that the girls often talked about their families, particularly their mothers. Their worlds were largely relational and domestic. The boys, on the other hand, seemed never to refer to their homes, but rather spoke entirely about their fantasy lives or teased each other. There was also a lot of shoving, pinching and poking amongst the boys. As a result of her report, the class teacher initiated new classroom strategies that began with the class being read the report. They then discussed the findings and worked out some strategies to reduce the low level physical violence in the room.

The girls' final major projects varied enormously. They had to come up with a topic that they wanted to know about and negotiate its content, method and the final form of its presentation. They had about seven weeks to get it together — as well as meet the requirements of their other four subjects. The project was a quarter of their final marks and the criteria on which it would be marked were spelt out in the syllabus. The girls knew what they had to do to pass, and what would make their work of credit standard. As part of the negotiation they had to indicate how they would meet the criteria.

One student worked with a small group of younger girls to present a self-scripted play about adolescent health issues to the school. Another conducted an evaluation of the course and reported on it to the local tertiary institution. Another investigated homebirths for her sister, another interviewed successful women in sport and made some recommendations for the school.

The topics they chose were drawn from their interests and the course, but many also contained a strong commitment to social action. In my experience, this often follows on from being able to make real decisions and from looking at the real world. You do see that all manner of things need a bit of attention and that research and information are an essential part of a problem solving exercise. This is not wildly radical. It is essentially what people do when they decide to try to get their local authority to fix up the road, or when they petition their local government representative for better or different services. It is what being a good citizen is about. It is taking some control over the things that affect you and that you can do something about.

The girls were able to demonstrate that they could exercise significant initiative and had good organizational skills. They were often able to present convincing written and verbal reports that did have an impact on the immediate environment.

They were encouraged to make their curriculum a part of the school and community improvement process. Student participation became more than being part of the Student Representative Council, or sitting on a school based committee. Student participation becomes at the same time part of the method of the classroom and part of the change process in the school.

* * *

A class discussion about the problems in the yard during a health lesson led a group of seven to twelve year olds in my school to approach the school governing body with a proposal for a new playground. After negotiation, they took on the responsibility of getting together some concept plans and costings. With a small amount of help from their teacher, they persuaded a local company to hire a bus, drive them around to all the local playgrounds that contained the company products so they could test them out, and provide them with lunch as well.

* * *

The Senior Students Representative Council received many complaints about racial harassment. One of the things they decided to do was to try to promote some visual images of the school community in harmony. After negotiation with the school governing body, the Art staff, and the school administration, they wrote a grant application to pay for an artist to come and work with students, painting several large murals. The application was successful. Individual students negotiated to become part of the mural project; involvement fulfilled part of their Art course requirements.

Negotiation about real things leads to empowerment.

* * *

Many final year subjects have the major individual project as an integral part of the syllabus. Consequently, many courses lower in the school also use the same method to ensure that the students have the experiences necessary to be successful in the important last year at school.

The major project is not too dissimilar to the 'final performance' suggested by the Coalition of Essential Schools (Sizer, 1984, Wiggins, 1988). It recognizes that by their last year of school, students should be undertaking large pieces of work that integrate what they have learnt, and demonstrate their capacities.

There is nothing in the writing of the 'essential school movement' that would state that the final performance has to be set by the teacher. However, the examples that are quoted, while they are far from the multiple choice tests they replace, are still usually prescribed by the teacher.

What makes the Australian model different is that the method, content and final product are all negotiable. They are not set by the teacher. What is set are the criteria — in terms of content, skills and understandings that have to be demonstrated. This shifts the curriculum from transmission, or reproduction of knowledge, to one of production and partnership.

It is the difference between the Foxfire approach (Wigginton, 1986) to teaching and learning and cooperative learning *à la* Johnson (1980), Slavin *et al.* (1985). In Eliot Wigginton's school, the kids had a say in the decisions about who would be interviewed and why, and they were involved in every aspect of the production of the Foxfire books, whereas in the Johnson classroom, the kids work together on what the teacher alone has decided (see, chapter 15).

I would have to ask if learning can really be said to be authentic, if the decisions about what are to be learnt and assessed are entirely predetermined and continue to be predetermined by the teacher or an examining authority?

This is not to suggest that kids do not need to learn particular bits of 'stuff' and that sometimes they will not recognize or know that they need it. They will not be experienced students, like my Women's Studies class, who can come up with a good list. In fact, there were lots of things that that class did have to just 'eat' in order to make sense of the topics. In the evaluation conducted by one student as her final project, the assignment that was the most 'popular' was a straight research task. The girls nominated in their original list that they needed to know how to get information from a variety of sources. I decided that they needed to know about women who had made major contributions to our state. The task was simply a list of names, and the question: 'Who were they and what did they do?' The students could choose to work in groups or as individuals. They could use interview, film and book as their information sources and could present their information in any form they liked. The next most 'popular' assignment was another research task: 'To investigate the history of the struggle for equal pay'.

Why did the girls find these two, seemingly dry and most 'bookish' tasks so stimulating? I can only conclude from their responses in the evaluation and from the discussion that occurred amongst them that it was because the 'stuff' was so new and so intrinsically interesting and significant. They discovered that women had been responsible for the establishment of a number of organizations and institutions, including the local child health services, that they encountered everyday, and they had never known. They'd discovered that the battle for equal pay was both historical and current, and that there were women, including their mothers, grandmothers and teachers, who had been directly affected by it. Both pieces of 'stuff' helped them make meanings out of their direct network of experiences. They began to see that there were reasons for things being like they were and these were the product of human action and decision. There was not necessarily a mysterious 'they' that decided everything but there were social forces that shaped what could be done. In other words, the 'stuff' was useful knowledge.

Sometimes neither the girls nor I recognized what they needed to know. One lesson early on in the course as we were struggling with the nature/nurture debate (a key concept that was prescribed in the syllabus), I wrote 'Biology is destiny' on the board. After it, I wrote, 'Freud'. 'What does the saying mean?' I started.

S: Miss, before we do that, what's that word after it? Fried, is it?
T: It's Freud. You all know who Freud was?

Wrong. Nobody knew who Freud was. So I decided to digress and talk about Freud for a while.

I made that decision knowing two things: That I would have to be the source of the information because there was no way we had time to try to read anything much about Freud; secondly, that meant that we would be in for a bout of chalk and talk — with me doing a lot of the talking. We ended up spending the best part of the week talking about Freud and his theories. It made sense of lots of things they recognized — why the psychiatrist used a couch, why lots of films and books were based on the idea of the unconscious, why lipstick commercials were like they were. . . . One of my treasured memories is of one of the students rushing out of the room at the end of the lesson, sprinting up the passage to where one of her friends was studying, hooting and hollering with laughter. . . . Hey, you'll never guess what you're supposed to be doing when you water the lawn with the garden hose. . . .

Working class kids do not have the same access to these cultural artifacts. They cannot attribute the layers of meaning to things they read and see because they just do not have the knowledge. Mike Rose (1989) writes about influential talk. He suggests that the academic discourses are full of influential talk that are both a foreign tongue and also a foreign set of concepts:

> The discourse of academics is marked by terms and expressions that represent an elaborate set of shared concepts and orientations: alienation, authoritarian personality, the social construction of the self, determinism, hegemony, equilibrium, intentionality, recursion, reinforcement, and so on. This language weaves through so many lectures and textbooks, is integral to so many learned discussions, that it's easy to forget what a foreign language it can be. Freshmen are often puzzled by the talk they hear in their classrooms, but what's important to note here is that their problem is not simply one of limited vocabulary. If we see the problem as knowing or not knowing a list of words, as some quick-fix remedies suggest, then we'll force glossaries on students and miss the complexity of the issue. Take for example, authoritarian personality. The average university freshman will know what personality means and can figure out authoritarian; the difficulty will come from a lack of familiarity with the conceptual resonances that authoritarian personality has acquired in the discussion of sociologists and psychologists and political scientists. Discussion. . . . You could almost define university education as an initiation into a variety of powerful ongoing discussions, an initiation that can only occur through the repeated use of a new language in the company of others. (p. 192)

Because poor kids don't know how to talk and write this new language, they often appear to have essay writing problems or note-taking problems. There is no doubt in my mind that one of the tasks of the teacher is to try to reveal and teach those hidden meanings — to help kids crack the codes of their world. That will mean taking advantage of the appropriate moments in the classroom, being prepared to be the source of the information, being prepared to 'teach' in the most traditional interpretation of the word. Some of this may not be negotiated with the students, but if there is a productive relationship between teacher and class, it will not matter if it is not. You don't have to negotiate everything.

Teaching the influential talk often means being prepared to leave the predetermined syllabus and being confident enough abut the relevance and the usefulness of the information to do so. It means knowing enough about the lives, experiences and knowledge base of the students to have some idea of what they need to know and how to connect the school and academic 'stuff' with them in ways that will make sense. When I talked about Freud with my class, I talked about the soapies that I already knew the girls watched, advertisements that appeared in teenage girls' magazines and the lyrics of songs on the current pop charts. I also introduced new material — the Oedipus legend — they'd never normally come in contact with it. That, in turn, led us into some discussion about incest which we picked up later in our topic on health.

I often get in trouble at home for watching particularly trite movies and soapies. I also religiously watch rock and roll programs, listen to the most popular radio station and buy *Dolly* magazine. However, while that is a good way to keep up with the general cultural milieu of the students, it is not sufficient to help me get to know particular kids.

At the alternative school, I could just sit down with kids and talk. In mainstream schools, I've had to develop a far greater range of tricks to enter the kids' world.

* * *

Teachers very often, particularly if they are English teachers, start the year off with activities that will both reveal the students' skills and also tell the teacher something about the students.

I often plan to start the year off by examining the concept of adolescence because it gets me into the who-am-I-and-what-is-going-on discussion. Last year, day one, I suggested to my class of seventeen year olds that in order for me to see what they could do and for me to understand them a bit, they should write about something they remembered from their childhood — nothing too dramatic, but something moderately important. I told them a little story about my father trying to teach me to swim by being lowered off the local jetty on a rope — a miserable failure because I just developed a fear of heights as well as water. I talked about how it was all because I needed glasses and nobody knew until years later. . . . I'd just experienced being lowered into a kind of bottomless blurry pit. I told them about how wonderful it was when I finally got my specs and saw everything in focus for the first time. . . .

At home a couple of nights later, I picked up the heap of papers and prepared for a little light read. I expected the odd broken arm, maybe a fight with a sibling, maybe a lost bike, maybe a first dog.

> . . . . The trouble with me is that I hate all men. This is because my
> father. . . .

And not one of these, but five! Five kids who were prepared to write to a perfect stranger that they had been abused children. . . . Another wrote about seeing her father die of a heart attack, somebody else saw their house burn down. . . . This is nothing too dramatic? This is only moderately important? This is what I'm going to build my course around? This is not what I asked for or expected.

This class had learnt that 'studenting' meant revealing all to your teacher. A spill-your-guts curriculum. I wondered what other teachers had done. Had they marked the work — this one an A grade piece of abuse, this other only a C? Had they tried to deal with the issues raised; if so, what training had they had? Had they dealt with these matters on a one-to-one basis or had they had a class discussion, a kind of forced classroom based encounter group? Had they encouraged the kids to keep on writing this kind of material — a let's really get it all out and wallow in it over and over again, if it gets said often enough it will all be better. . . .

There is no doubt that some of this writing was powerful. There is no doubt that their experiences were real. Had the kids learnt that their teachers were not able to deal with the topics and gave them high marks for realism, high marks for expression, high marks for content? I did in fact ask around and discovered that at least one student had been dining out on the heart attack piece for three years; it never failed to produce a good grade. Up till then. I didn't grade the work at all.

Just as well that I'd had all that time with the delinquents. Somehow it was a delicate balancing act of dealing with individuals in a counselling situation, getting them to read and get information that might help them make sense of what had happened, taking up the general issues with the class and getting them to move on. We read books and watched films and had people talk about the topics that had emerged. I also tried several other tacks to find out what they thought.

But the incident left me wondering. . . . Doesn't this make the teacher into some kind of middle class voyeur, peering at the lives of working class kids, never revealing themselves to anything like the same extent? Are all teachers equipped to deal with this? Are all of them trustworthy and will they keep confidentiality and not talk about what has been revealed to their colleagues in the staff room? What experience do we really want and need in order to be able to teach the kids? What is the real 'stuff' for the classroom and what isn't? I've had kids write stunning stories and poems about things they know about — aboriginal deaths in custody, the experience of the refugee, breaking and entering, running away. Often these are semifictionalized and dramatized; they are not simply a retelling of something that has happened. Some have obviously been through some process of reflection and refinement, some have been married to reading about the topic. Are these OK? Why are some OK and others not? My brown bag awaits a resolution.

A further problem: What if the kids' interests and values are unacceptable? What if the girls just keep writing Mills and Boon romances, if their personal writing reinforces a passive femininity (Gilbert, 1988, 1989; White, 1989)? What if the boys keep writing about killing people, about abusing women, about getting drunk and driving motor bikes down the local drag strip? Are all these OK? When do you exercise some control and say, 'Look, this is really not on'.

David

David was in my children's literature class. He was an irritating kid, but as bright as a button — you know the sort, they always ask the questions that require an hour's explanation, by which time the bell has gone and you forgot the homework.

When we went into the junior primary classroom to work with the little kids, he was very put out by the violence in the boys' stories. 'Why do they let them do that, Miss? It must help make them more aggro than they already are'. I was too smart to be caught out by this one (an unusual occurrence) and suggested that he ask the teacher concerned.

She said it's important that they write about what they want. She said if she stops them then the boys just won't write and they are already worse at writing than the girls. She said they wrote better if they wrote about things they were interested in and then she said it was about freedom of expression.

You mean that if she stopped them, it would be the teacher censoring what they wrote?

Yeah, but she makes decisions about what the kids should learn and that's not censorship. I mean the teacher always has some say in what's going on — whether they need to know adding up and what history they should know and stuff. Why should this be any different?

So what would you do, David?

I'd just tell 'em not to write that stuff, and then I'd find out some other things they were interested in. You can't tell me that all they think about is beating people up and killing them.

And what if they stopped writing?

Well, what's worse, not writing or writing dangerous horrible stuff?

David was pretty sure what he would do, but it's a question that troubles me: What is worse?

Negotiation is never just about getting the kids to do what interests them. Either in the realm of values, skills or content, there will be a teacher intervention. There will be a point where the teacher will have to decide what is acceptable and what isn't, what needs to be learnt. Sometimes, as in the case of the boys who want to write war fantasies, this can still lead to conflict and an imposition of school and teacher over the student. Empowering working class kids doesn't mean that they can do whatever they want or what they think they need.

Garth Boomer (chapter 20) suggests that the pragmatic radical sometimes gives way in the short term in order to achieve longer term goals. We teach kids how to pass tests that we thoroughly disapprove of because not to pass them would penalize them severely. They wouldn't get jobs or get into the university. We try to balance out the toxic with the good 'stuff' so that there isn't educational death during the year nor any permanent long term side effects. It sounds easy, but like the problem of the boys and their fighting stories, it isn't.

And a slick bit of negotiation or a good dose of empowering content won't provide the answer. Take the issue of pacing and labeling. Do you recognize this scenario?

- All kids learn at their own rate.
- Some kids are slower than others.

- Pulling kids out of class for special help means that they are not learning other things like how to be part of the class (social skills).
- Pulling the kids out of the class means that they are labeled as slow.
- If they are labelled as slow, the class teacher will teach them slowly and they will learn slowly (the Pygmalion effect).
- If they are compared to other kids, they will be labeled as failures.
- They will feel like failures and will learn more slowly.
- If they are not compared to other kids we will never know if they are catching up.
- If we do not recognize them as slow we will never be able to accelerate them.
- Trying to force kids to learn at a rate that is not theirs' will mean they will feel like failures and will fail.

The classroom teacher hears a variety of conflicting research and expert opinion on each of these assertions. While we may make headway on the curriculum and method, and while we will make differences for some kids, we will not fundamentally shift the inequities that reside in the education system until we make some sense of this piece of contested territory. Changing the content, making it inclusive of the kids' experiences, values and cultures is crucial. Giving them choices, revealing the decisions that can be made and where they will lead are crucial. Teaching students to negotiate is crucial. These are necessary but hardly sufficient.

There is still no magic formula that will make all kids successful at school work. The pragmatic/radical does not expect it.

Tony

I met one of the kids from the alternative school just the other day. He's a fairly successful rock and roll musician and only comes back home when the band is on tour. I had to argue my way into the venue to see him and there's no doubt I caused a bit of amusement when I suggested to the hefty bouncer guarding the performers' privacy that he should just tell Tony that one of his old teachers was here to see him. I gather that there was some considerable amazement at the enthusiastic response and the big hugs that went on when I got into the room.

Tony said everybody else in the band had hated school whereas he had liked it. I asked him what he thought he'd learnt. (Every now and then I suspect that I have never taught anybody anything.)

> Well, I read lots of good books. And you guys encouraged me to do music. I've forgotten all the Maths and stuff. We did lots of it, but you just forget it you know. I guess that I learnt social skills.

I groaned inwardly. What had happened to empowering?

> I always think of my old teachers as real friends. Most people only think of one or two of their teachers like that, but you were all my friends.

You really got to know me, you know, and I got to know you, and I never felt put down. You took me seriously.

Well, that was nice anyway.

You know that stuff we had to do all the time, you know, negotiate about stuff? Well, I do that all the time with these guys [the band]. They always get me to do all the stuff with the record company. I just go in and negotiate and we don't get screwed.

Bad luck about the choice of words. I always used to tell him that four letter words should be used positively not as terms of abuse. Guess I lost on that bit of turf but gained more important ground.

References

BRANDT, R. (1988) 'On assessment of teaching: A conversation with Lee Shulman', *Educational Leadership*, **46**, 3, November.

HORACE COALITION FOR ESSENTIAL SCHOOLS (1990) 'A final performance across the disciplines and the common principles for the coalition for essential schools', Providence, R.I.: Brown University, March.

GILBERT, P. (1990) 'Authorizing disadvantage: Authorship and creativity in the language classroom', in CHRISTIE, F. (Ed.) *Literacy for a Changing World*, Victoria: Australian Council for Educational Research.

GILBERT, P. (1988) 'Stoning the romance: Girls as resistant readers and writers', in CHRISTIE, F. (Ed.) *Writing in Schools*, Geelong, Victoria: Deakin University Press.

ROSE, M. (1989) *Lives on the Boundary*, NY: Penguin.

SHULMAN, L. (1987) 'Knowledge and teaching: Foundations of the new reform', *Harvard Educational Review*, **57**, 1, February.

SHULMAN, L. (1989) 'Teaching alone, learning together: Needed agendas for the new reform', in SERGIOVANNI, T.J. and MOORE, J.H. (Eds) *Schooling for Tomorrow: Directing Reforms to Issues that Count*, Boston: Allyn & Bacon.

SIZER, T.R. (1984) *Horace's Compromise: The Dilemma of the American High School*, Boston: Houghton Mifflin.

SLAVIN, R.E. (1985) *Cooperative Learning*, NY: Plenum.

SLAVIN, R.E., JOHNSON, R., JOHNSON, D. and VASQUEZ, B. (1985) *The Cooperative Learning Series*, Virginia: Association for Supervision and Curriculum Development.

WHITE, J. (1990) 'On literacy and gender' in CHRISTIE, F. (Ed.) *Literacy for a Changing World*, Victoria: Australian Council for Educational Research.

WIGGINTON, E. (1986) *Sometimes a Shining Moment: The Foxfire Experience*, NY: Anchor Books.

Chapter 18

Why We Learn is What and How We Learn: Curriculum as Possibility

Cynthia Onore and Bob Lubetsky

We've been finding it ironic, of late, that with all the talking and thinking and writing and observing we've done on curriculum negotiation, that we haven't spent enough time looking at the concept of curriculum. We have focused our attention on the thorny issues which coalesce around how to build a curriculum collaboratively with students. We have voiced slogans about how curriculum is the coming together of method and content, and that no curriculum is or can ever be neutral. We've worried about how the curriculum negotiation process can embrace all learners and how it can bring together the intentions, experiences, and ways of being of all learners, of teachers and students alike. All of these issues have been investigated thoroughly both in *Negotiating the Curriculum: A Teacher-Student Partnership* (Boomer, 1982) and in the current volume. We worry, however, that we may have forgotten to ask what curriculum might become.

We find ourselves wondering just what a new formulation of curriculum might be, given all we now know and believe, and about the consequences of treating what we teach, how we teach, and who we are as a continuous thread. Somehow, we've accepted that asking the four questions transforms the X in all that emerges as what we want and need to know about. We've focused on the curriculum composing process through the vehicle of negotiation without addressing the ways in which we might need to think about curriculum differently. And so, we wonder in what ways is curriculum transformed by the process through which we build it? Are there issues that we need to address about the nature of curriculum which are not revealed by negotiation as we've been defining it in this volume and in our work of the past ten years? Perhaps, we've begun to think, there are other issues and other questions that teachers need to examine in order to deepen and extend the ways we think about curriculum. By thinking of curriculum as knowledge, or content, or skills, we're in danger of limiting it. But what else needs to enter into our thinking about curriculum?

These questions arose for us quite recently when we glibly responded to a teacher's question about how the pluperfect tense in French could possibly be anything other than what it is whether you negotiate the curriculum or not. We answered that, Yes, the pluperfect would be changed. But what were we really saying? It was clear to us that this teacher might want to question herself about her purposes in choosing to study the pluperfect with her students. But our answer to her question depended upon another set of questions and speculations: Did we really mean that the pluperfect would be changed by how we came to know it? Did we mean that what we might ask about the pluperfect and what we might learn about it would form what we believe the pluperfect to be?

And the answer is, yes; we meant what we said. What we want to do in this chapter is to explore the issues that entered into our thinking and build on what we already know about curriculum and curriculum negotiation. It is our intention to draw an enriched picture of curriculum negotiation which will invite the wider social and political contexts into conceptions of curriculum and into places where teaching and learning are conducted.

Critical and Humanistic Pedagogy

Our thinking has been affected by the body of literature called critical pedagogy. We've learned about the location of schools within the larger society and the necessity to scrutinize and resist schooling as an institution of cultural reproduction. Critical pedagogy has sought to challenge the assumption that schools play a major role in developing a democratic and egalitarian society. From the now classic *Schooling in Capitalist America* (Bowles and Gintis, 1976) to the current writing of Giroux (1988), Aronowitz and Giroux (1991), and others (Apple, 1982, for example), critical pedagogy explicates the various ways in which schools reproduce and reinforce existing relationships of social inequality and thereby promote a society based on hierarchies of race, class, gender, and other forms of difference.

Oftentimes, however, these concerns have been addressed without much attention to the nature of interactions within the classroom. While being a 'transformative intellectual' (Giroux, 1988) helps us to see the importance of challenging the inequalities which exist in society, it doesn't tell us much about the kind of work teachers and students need to do in the classroom in order to see themselves differently and to act differently.

We've also been greatly influenced by humanistic educators and the progressive movement (Dewey, 1938/63; Kohl, 1967; Kozol, 1967; Holt, 1964). Advocates of this perspective focus on the classroom and wish to uncover the most humane structures that are child-centred and make central the thinking, experience, and questions of learners. From this point of view, the classroom can constitute a 'time out' for exploration and enactment of social relations which do not exist in the larger society, even though these educators surely wish they would. But we also find that humanistic/progressive educators who have looked closely at the nature of social relationships within the classroom have often failed to take into account the larger roles of schooling in society and how those roles enter into classroom relationships. Behaving critically and transformatively in the world does not automatically flow from a humanistic set of relationships in the classroom.

Unifying a humanistic view of the classroom with critical pedagogy is difficult, but essential, we think. Bringing these two elements together requires that we see school as a contested terrain with competing purposes. One purpose focuses on helping students to see themselves differently and to think critically and creatively, while the other presses on the student to 'fit in' to the job market and into the society in acceptable ways. There is a potential to resolve the tensions by acting together differently and by examining what, how, and why we are learning. A synthesis of the thrusts of each of these perspectives can help us begin to think about both curriculum and schooling. The outcome of this struggle can never be known in its particulars but the effort to change the connection between curriculum and society launches us in the direction of transforming both. We are seeing and seeking a unity between transforming the world and transforming the classroom. It is interesting that society brings together, in a most effective way, an authoritarian view of the classroom and an uncritical pedagogy. It makes transforming relationships among people and ideas in the classroom difficult, at best, and certainly renders a critique of the socio-political context impossible by being its mirror. And that's what we're struggling against.

To unite progressive education with critical pedagogy results in an enriched and problematized concept of curriculum. Curriculum can represent a coming together of understandings of the social and cultural relationships in the larger world, the reformulation of relationships within the classroom, and organized bodies of knowledge called subject matter. Additionally, however, curriculum defines a terrain in which a struggle for social justice can be engaged. Curriculum negotiation, by extension, is a process, a problem, and a project to link transformative social relations within the classroom to transformative social relations in the world at large, to yoke together the cultural origins of students' questions and understandings with the cultural origins of organized bodies of knowledge.

We would suggest that what we want to struggle for is what ought to form the curriculum — that is, how we ought to compose the experiences, knowings and behaviors of teachers and students, as well as how to incorporate organized bodies of knowledge. In the end, the classroom is and must be a place of struggle, uncertainty, and alchemy, with an ever-shifting mix of ingredients and an ever-shifting search for the union of form and content, organized bodies of knowledge and students' questions, understandings and experiences. In short, critical pedagogy and humanistic pedagogy represent ends of the same thread, the thread of school in its transformative possibilities both within and outside the classroom. Classroom curriculum then is the field of inquiry within which the struggles to transform the classroom and the world is waged.

Curriculum as Community

We've selected Garth Boomer's concept of curriculum composing (chapter 3, this volume)[1] as a jumping off point for illustrating one aspect of a humanistic pedagogy of which we've been critical. What we want to try and pin down is not the ways in which it invites students to share in the curriculum process, the ways in which teachers must acknowledge and include learners' intentions, or even the ways in which the authority and power relationships between teachers and students are altered by negotiating the curriculum. Instead, we will look at the ways in which Boomer's curriculum excludes the sociopolitical world from its attention and intentions, how the 'content' of the curriculum is more or less static and set prior to the coming together of a particular group of students and a particular teacher in a real place and time, and how it might encourage student passivity by separating, in its effect, how we think about the world from the way we choose to be in the world.

Boomer literally and figuratively centres learning on the classroom. Children are invited to participate in classroom activities and to define, in a limited way, what their participation should include. They are asked to bring with them and to share what they already know. Others are invited in as audiences for student work — librarians, community members, parents, and other experts. Finished products are to be shared with a wider audience, other classes, other schools, outside community members. While students are encouraged to reflect on their own values, they are also being asked to grow 'towards the stated and implicit values of the school' (p. 44).

What is troublesome in all of this is that there is a limited corresponding movement outwards — from the classroom into the world. We don't intend to limit our concept of curriculum to the literal movements of teachers and children out of the classroom, although there is much to be said for this way of thinking about curriculum activity (see, chapters 9 and 17 and our own example later in this chapter). But we do want to challenge the ways that the focus of attention is on this inward movement and explore what becomes possible if an outward impulse is integrated into the curriculum as well. We think that a key to ways in which schools can operate in order to prevent connecting individuals in a conscious (or unconscious) manner to the existing social order is, paradoxically, to unite the classroom with the community.

Maxine Green (1988) has suggested that we need to 'render problematic a reality which includes homelessness, hunger, pollution, crime, censorship, arms build-ups, and threats of war' (pp. 12–13). Rather than studying math, science, social studies, and language, we need to study who we are and the world we inhabit. This means that we cannot merely accept the content of the curriculum as a set of givens to be negotiated. We must problematize the curriculum. Problematizing the organized bodies of knowledge called subject matter means questioning ways in which subject matter is a reflection of the world seen through a particular cultural lens; connecting these bodies of knowledge to who the learners are and how we act in the world, through our studies, allows us to attend to the social order so that we can, in seeking to understand it also simultaneously change it (Schön, 1983).

One place to begin problematizing is to think that what occurs in the classroom is connected with thinking and being in the world. To treat content, pedagogy and environment as separate or separable, is to separate school from society. To make these connections requires more than bringing together academic and personal/experiential knowledge. It requires framing issues that arise from the intrusion of injustice and inequality into the classroom. If connections among the various aspects of the curriculum are to be redefined and thereby altered, so must relationships between the participants in this process of alteration, the teachers and the students. In order for relationships in the classroom not to mirror those of the larger society they cannot reproduce the contours of dominance and submission, hierarchy and power which exist outside the classroom. Community-building within the classroom, and community-building between schools and the social world outside the classroom, are, for us, the lynchpins of reformulating what we mean by curriculum.

We assume no clear cut questions or answers, or even a specific fund of knowledge on which to draw which can be anticipated in advance of the process of exploration and investigation or in advance of meeting and knowing the learners, but we are insisting on examining who we are in the world. Nonetheless, the essential questions, in contrast to what Boomer has suggested, cannot be set out in advance by teachers. We cannot separate who the learners are and the moment in history we inhabit from what their essentialities might be. And so, we must resist viewing the content of the curriculum as ready-made. We must negotiate not just how and what we will learn but why we will learn as well.

Thus community-building is a struggle about possibilities, those of coming to see ourselves differently, seeing others in new ways, and seeing ideas as opening up potential spaces for inquiry. Further, if what occurs in the classroom is connected to what occurs outside the classroom (that is, if what we think is connected to the ways we choose to be in the world), then community-building has implications for the way things can be outside the classroom.

Community is a complicated notion, in large part because we have so few experiences of it. There is a problem even if we have more experiences of it. This rests on the fact that we are divided in our loyalties between our individual needs and what we perceive as the needs of a group with which we have membership (Bellah *et al.*, 1985). One resolution to the conflict between individual and collective needs lies in being able to see correspondences between the satisfaction of our own needs and the missions and goals of the group. Certainly, communities built on caring, concern, and trust enable us to find correspondences and, so, for classrooms or any other group of individuals to build community requires both a shared sense of purpose as well as consistent expressions of caring, concern, and trust.

As a result, there is nothing automatic in creating a classroom community. But while acknowledging that community building takes time and is a struggle, we also want to suggest that we cannot wait until we have a sense of community in our classrooms in order to act as a community. In a recent article by Maxine Greene (1991), we find a way to frame the process of acting 'as if' and its benefits. Greene quotes Vaclav Havel writing from prison about what stands in the way of his becoming united with others in a common enterprise:

> If I consider the problems as that which the world is turning me into — that is, a tiny screw in a giant machine, deprived of humanity — then there is really nothing I can do. . . . If, however, I consider it as that which each of us . . . has the basic potential to become, which is to say an autonomous human being capable of acting responsibly to and for the world, then of course there is a great deal I can do. (p. 542)

By focusing on what we may become, not only on what each of us is at present, we make new roles, relationships, and actions possible. In this way, all teaching is an act of faith. We act now on the basis of a set of hoped-for future relationships, and trust that in acting 'as if', we can bring these hoped-for relationships into being.

Redefining relationships in the classroom, while important, is not an end in itself. What we can learn from building a community in the classroom is that there need not be a conflict between individual needs and the needs of the group. We may even see that sometimes there are purposes our work and learning can serve which are larger than ourselves. Recognizing those kinds of purposes helps to form a link to communities outside of the classroom. The potential to connect the classroom community to the world outside of school is enriched by a curriculum which brings the outside world in and moves the world of the classroom into contact with society.

None of this is possible if we fail to recognize that knowledge is a social construction, that it results from the conversations that occur. It is only reasonable to prevent these kinds of redefinitions if we objectify all relationships — those among ideas and those among people — and act as though any of them is independent of context.

The Teacher's Role in a Community

The role of the teacher is so important, although problematic, to be sure. The teacher must be able to see 'the ends in the beginnings' (Dewey, 1902/1971). She must recast students' understandings, cultures, and experiences, reenvisioning at the same time potentials for learning. In this way, she honours who her students are in the present while exploring who they may become. To do so requires casting classroom conversations so as to bring together the community and the classroom, and orchestrating a language of hope and possibility as learners and teachers struggle to speak across difference, as they struggle to create a sense of community. This is the teacher's special expertise, and in this way she is not the equal of the students. She may not be able to predict what students will name as their essentialities, their necessities, nor can she predict the outcomes of investigating these. But she knows how to engage herself and the learners in conversations that will bring these to light.

Finding a language to describe the dialectic between the teacher's theories and values and the students' needs and desires is difficult. Miles Horton has created a metaphorical description that comes as close to our sense of the teacher-student relationship as we've been able to find. Horton (1990) describes it this way:

> I like to think that I have two eyes that I don't have to use in the same way. When I do educational work with a group of people, I try to see with one eye where those people are as they perceive themselves to be. I do this by looking at body language, by imagination, by talking to them, by visiting them, by learning what they enjoy and what troubles them. I try to find out where they are, and if I can get hold of that with one eye, that's where I start. You have to start with where people are, because their growth is going to be from there, not from some abstraction or where you are or someone else is.
>
> Now my other eye is not such a problem, because I already have in mind a philosophy of where I'd like to see people moving. It's not a clear blueprint for the future but a movement toward goals they don't conceive of at the time.
>
> I don't separate these two ways of looking, I don't say I'm going to look at where people are today and where they can be tomorrow. I look at people with both eyes simultaneously all the time, and as they develop and grow I still look at them that way, because I've got to remind myself constantly that they're not all they can be. . . .
>
> If you listen to people and work from what they tell you, within a

few days their ideas get bigger and bigger. They go back in time, ahead in their imagination. You just continue to build on people's own experience; it is the basis for their learning. (pp. 131–132)

Like Dewey, Horton believes that teachers must be able to see two things simultaneously. They must have a clear sense of their own values, intentions, and goals and they must enter into the worlds which their students construct. The hope here is that in bringing each of these visions into focus at the same time, that a teaching/learning context and a curriculum will emerge which represents a cointentionality. It is not so much that teachers have a set of intentions which is opposed to or distinct from the students' intentions, but that a teacher is expert in seeing her intentions in her students' intentions. Curriculum, then, is an enactment of the issues and concerns that are generated by this super-imposed set of views.

In addition to thinking differently about intentions, as Horton (1990) has done, we also want to look at what and how teachers' knowings relate to those of students. Questioning the teacher's role and her expertise can help us avoid enacting and reproducing relationships based in dominance and submission. Many radical educators, most notably Freire (1970), have suggested that teachers must become learners with their students in order to transform learning. Some (McLaren, 1988) have suggested that teachers must be students of their students' understandings and that in so doing teachers may come to 'relearn' and reexperience what they already know. The teacher who, however, begins with the assumption that what she knows is what needs to be known, will have difficulty listening to and understanding the voices of students, particularly those students who have suffered oppression outside the classroom or those who express their understandings in ways which Ellsworth (1990) has termed 'non-rationalist'. By this, she means modes of argument and analysis which do not conform to the dominant forms of expression in the academy.

The teacher's expertise might be construed as 'knowing not to be an expert' (Horton and Freire, 1991, p. 131), and thus how to organize experiences so that students can retain control of the teaching-learning transactions and, further, that knowledge, which is different than anyone's individual contribution, can be constructed. The teacher does not re-experience what is already known, because both the teacher and the student are constructing a new understanding, not just re-experiencing one. The process of negotiating the curriculum is no longer so much a matter, then, of forging links between distinct and opposing intentions and understandings, but organizing experiences which allow intentions to be expressed, problematized, and developed.

Curriculum as Cultural Conversation

We are certainly not arguing here for eliminating any unique function for the teacher. Nor are we suggesting that the teacher lacks valuable expertise or intentions. Rather, we are attempting to redefine the teacher's role so that she might best support students in maintaining the locus of control over learning, their active construction of knowledge, their connections to their lived experience. We think that the effort to engage in these sorts of supports has the potential to make the critical link to the world outside of school by making school knowledge depend for its generation upon students' knowledge of and in the world, by helping students connect who they are outside of school to what they are in the process of coming to know inside of school. This kind of connection doesn't happen simply by virtue of redefining classroom relationships for, as we pointed out earlier, recognizing that social inequality and injustice expresses itself inside the classroom and struggling against it doesn't translate necessarily into challenging social inequality outside of the classroom. The effort to tie what occurs in the classroom to the quest for social justice is enhanced, we think, by continually examining and problematizing patterns of relationships in the classroom, by naming and rexamining who we are in the world. As we are now defining this pattern, it is the very stuff of the curriculum — the ongoing conversation between students and teachers.

To think of curriculum as conversation which composes a terrain of inquiry helps us define another role for the teacher. All members of the classroom community have attitudes, beliefs and dispositions which both reflect the culture from which each person comes and which enter into the conversation. If the teacher must resist the temptation to take control over learning, what, then does she do with the beliefs and attitudes she has? Horton (Horton and Freire, 1990) is helpful here. He says, 'If I really believe in what I want people to believe in, I don't tell them about it. I believe it. . . . Once they look at it, if they don't accept it, then I've gone as far as I can' (pp. 195–196). In other words, teachers need to demonstrate their beliefs through their actions. Beyond that, teachers must modify their vision of future possibility in light of the learner's current beliefs and attitudes. It's so hard when you believe so deeply in the importance of particular ideas or activities to let those go when students tell you that what they hold dear is incompatible. Nonetheless, it's important for us to strive to be sensitive to students' needs and to keep focused on finding compatibilities that can be built on rather than focusing only on resistances.

Above all, we do not wish to set the child, the curriculum, and the teacher's expertise in opposition to each other. There are tensions among the three, to be sure, but they are not opposed in the sense that any of them should have the power to nullify or override the others, nor that they must compete for ascendance. Instead, they must be seen as forces which have the potential to bring to light and to deepen understandings among divergent perspectives, to operate dialectically, to redefine one another as they are brought together. What Dewey (1902) has termed 'seeing the end in the beginning', (p. 12) and Horton (Horton and Freire, 1990) has termed having 'some vision of what ought to be or what they [learners] can become' (p. 98), Freire (Horton & Freire, 1990) asserts as 'knowing man's moment of information' (p. 98). This defines a further dimension to the teacher's expertise, knowing not just what is important, but when it is important.

From this perspective, until you know the learners, how can you know the essential questions? In this way, the teacher can never set in advance the essential questions which will animate the curricular conversation. She can only ask, what is there in this subject which contains essentialities and necessities, not only for the child as she now presents herself, but also for the child as she grows? This requires questioning the child, seeing and knowing the child in the present. The teacher must also ask, what is there in the child which is a living motivation? This living motivation inheres in present-day obstacles or problems which the child could address if the facts and the ways of knowing contained in the assumptions of the discipline were mastered. This requires an interrogation of the discipline as well. These questions and their emergent answers are the essential questions of the curriculum. They seek to uncover who the learners are and how they and the subject of study might grow to relate. Subject matter is thus a beginning, an end, and the means to the end, all at once. Learners are likewise beginnings, ends and means. The teacher must be an expert in seeing the ends in the beginnings.

In order to make links to the world, classrooms must be places in which we actively recognize that, as Marion Brady (1989) has argued, all knowledge is a culturally-imposed structure. What is known is determined as much by the questions we ask as by the questions we don't believe are worth asking. If, for example, the curriculum is eurocentric, questions about why this is the case and how the meanings generated by investigating this curriculum exclude other meanings are essential questions which would be ignored if we focus the curricular conversation solely on the curriculum as given. Therefore, cultural investigation is a critical component of any study because of what culture conceals as well as what it reveals. We want to suggest that learners investigate not only their own questions but that they also interrogate the cultural origins of their questions. In so doing, the cultural origins of the teacher's questions and the ways of knowing embodied in any organized subject matter are also objects of investigation. We believe that these inquiries are at the heart of multiculturalism. Raising these issues creates yet another role for the teacher. The greater the number of voices and perspectives, the richer the curriculum.

Curriculum as Radical Middle

We would like to call this concept of curriculum a 'radical middle', the space which unites the vernacular — the student and the world outside of school — to the arcane — the organized subject matters and ways of knowing characteristic of schooling. One of the problems of definition we have had throughout this chapter derives from the fact that we don't seem to have a language which adequately conveys the meanings we are trying to build. In this case, we will be borrowing our language from Twyla Tharp, the choreographer and dancer. She terms her choreographic style the 'radical middle' because in order to create a new dance form she has borrowed the metaphors, movements and imagery of common, everyday walking and gesturing across cultures. This is, for her, the vernacular. But her choreography is also firmly rooted in the classical style of western ballet, which she sees as arcane. When they intermingle, what results looks like neither one taken separately, although it is possible to analyze the origins of each movement and locate them somewhere on the continuum between the vernacular and the arcane. Nonetheless, she strives always to bring together each of these in order to construct a new movement. What we see is fresh, yet oddly familiar and strange simultaneously. From our perspective, the radical aspect of her work is its insistence that both past and present forms are of equal value. She rejects neither historical nor contemporary expressions of meaning.

When translated into educational terms, Tharp's radical middle seems to us to be very close to Dewey's (1938/63) vision of progressive schooling. Classroom study should be, according to Dewey, an amalgam of the past and present, inquiries which build upon the meanings of history and attend to the meanings of current reality. Only in this way can schooling be both preparation for and enactment of transformed social relationships. The vernacular, in the classroom, is all that learners and teachers bring with them from their cultures outside the classroom and from their lived experiences. The organized bodies of knowledge and ways of knowing of schools is the arcane. When successfully brought together what emerges is a transformed territory of meaning, containing elements of each but not simply a union of them. What results is a space which has changed each of them in the process of being constructed. Not only does the concept of the 'radical middle' help us think about curriculum in humanistic terms, it also helps us to see yet another connection between the classroom and the social and political settings outside the schoolroom.

A Case in Point

Students in one high school where we've worked for a number of years have been participants in this new vision of curriculum. As part of their requirement for graduation, they must participate in community service activities, a nonnegotiable constraint on their learning. What has happened in the classroom as a result of their engagement in working in a local nursing home is illustrative. In conversation with their faculty advisor, the students have shared their horror at the treatment that the residents of the nursing home are receiving from the staff there. As a result, the teacher has taken on the students as her apprentices in making these injustices public and in attempting to change the situation in the nursing home.

As a result, their in-school curriculum has helped them to take the actions in the world which their contact with the world has made an essentiality. The students have participated in discussions with the administration of the home, written press releases about their work, met with political leaders and presented their written reports to them, and have been studying how our society goes about responding to a crisis of the sort they have uncovered in this nursing home. Much of the work the students have done has drawn on organized bodies of knowledge from sociology and political science, to be sure. In addition, their understandings of the treatment of the nursing home residents rests on their understandings of their community. They know more and better about who the residents of the home are, what kinds of relationships these people have with their families, and how social reforms are enacted in their culture.

They understand power and authority differently from their teachers, or from their political representatives. And this knowledge has been brought to bear on the collective actions they have taken with their teachers. Each of the participants has been enriched, modified, and transformed by their collective actions in the world. And, the subjects of study have been brought to life in ways none of the participants might have imagined at the beginning. Even to write of what has occurred in the analytic way we have, distorts what actually happened. Because, above all, no matter how we look at the parts of this situation separately, they do not resemble the totality of what has happened. The totality is a radical middle, a curriculum of emancipation and transformation both within and outside of the classroom.

We certainly believe that teachers ought to know as much as they can about the cultures of their students. But we think that it is both too easy and too dangerous to make this statement and stop. Such a statement objectifies knowledge by making culture into a body of information. What the teachers in the example above have learned about the culture of their students is very much a product of the situation and events in which they have come to know their students' understandings. Even the students' expressions of their cultural patterns are changed by engaging in real actions in the world. They have seen parts of their community which would have been hidden to them had they not had to solve the particular problems that became essentialities for them. In other words, what the students and teachers know about their cultures is an aspect of the inquiries they launched, the reflections they engaged in, and the work they did both individually and collectively.

Coming Full Circle

We're trying to forge a different way of thinking about curriculum by suggesting that the learner and the curriculum be joined, that method and curriculum be seen as faces of the same coin, that past and present hold equal sway over our investigations, that community both inside and outside the classroom be objects of study and active constructions, that community represent both individual rights and collective responsibilities, that critical pedagogy and humanistic pedagogy come together to help us unite altered relationships within the classroom with the struggle outside the classroom for social change, and that the culture of the learners, the culture of the teacher and the culture of the school play equally essential roles in forming the curriculum. And further, none of these unions would be possible without a constructivist view of knowledge and all of them rest upon our belief that knowledge is always contingent and partial.

So we're back where we began: what and how we learn is fundamentally changed by why we learn. The question that our colleague posed to us about the pluperfect in French can now be more adequately addressed. Obviously, we are arguing against studying this or anything else as an isolated skill. About that assertion, we have no doubt. But what the study of the pluperfect might look like if it were part of a curricular investigation like the one we have tried to sketch here is much more difficult to define. We know an inquiry would rest upon the learner's own questions, the group's interrogation of the sources of those questions, the connections of those questions to actions in the world, a critique of its study in light of demands by the school or the state that it be studied, the teacher's vision of who the learners might become through their learning and relationships in the classroom not based on dominance and oppression.

How we define the shared enterprise in which this, or any other investigation proceeds, and whether the conversations provoked by an investigation are growth-producing comprise how we can assess the curriculum. These are also the elements of the situation which determine the potential for changes in the meanings of the subject and in how we see ourselves as learners and teachers. They redefine the subject-matter of study itself. It is that redefinition of the subjects of study and reconceptualizations of ourselves and each other which are our prospects for a transformative curriculum.

If curriculum can be truly liberatory, and we believe it can, then it can become so only by our ability to see the means of study and the ends of study as a unified whole. We must ask why we are studying what and how we are studying to ensure liberation. We have many questions about what this new curriculum might look like. We don't know very much about the ways in which the constraints and obstacles in schools and in ourselves might alter our view. What we think we have is a set of principles which will help us seek and find local solutions to the problems raised. More than anything, perhaps, our arguments are simply a call to action. We know what sorts of actions we'd like to launch but certainly do not know where they will lead.

It seems appropriate to end with Dewey because he seemed to be struggling with many of these same issues a long while ago. We know he had a vision of a democratic society, a world of justice and equality. He says, 'We are free not because of what we statically are, but insofar as we are becoming different from what we have been' (quoted in Greene, 1988, p. 3). We do know that thinking of curriculum negotiation in the problematic and dynamic ways we've defined here will surely make us different.

Note

1 Our goal here is to stake out a different ideological territory and this chapter provides us a needed contrast. We recognize, however, that Boomer presents another view in chapter 20 of this volume. Readers wanting to compare Boomer's current thinking to his earlier work are directed to that chapter.

References

APPLE, M. (1982) *Education and Power*. London: Routledge and Kegan Paul.

ARONOWITZ, S. and GIROUX, H.A. (1991) *Postmodern Education: Politics, Culture and Social Criticism*, Minneapolis: University of Minnesota Press.

BELLAH, R., MADSEN, R., SULLIVAN, W.M., SWIDLER, A. and TIPTON, S.M. (1985) *Habits of the Heart: Individualism and Commitment in American Life*. NY: Harper & Row.

BOOMER, G. (1982) *Negotiating the Curriculum: A Teacher-Student Partnership*, Sydney: Ashton-Scholastic.

BOWLES, S. and GINTIS, H. (1976) *Schooling in Capitalist America*, NY: Basic Books.

BRADY, M. (1989) *What's Worth Teaching*, Albany, SUNY Press.

DEWEY, J. (1902/1971) *The Child and the Curriculum and the School and Society*, Chicago: University of Chicago Press.

DEWEY, J. (1938) (Paper edition 1963). *Experience and Education*, NY: Collier Press.

ELLSWORTH, E. (1989) 'Why doesn't this feel empowering? Working through the repressive myths of critical pedagogy', *Harvard Education Review*, **59**, 3, August, pp. 297–324.

FREIRE, P. (1970) *Pedagogy of the Oppressed*, NY: Seabury Press.

GIROUX, H.A. (1988) *Teachers as intellectuals: Towards a Critical Pedagogy of Learning*, Granby, MA: Bergin & Garvey.

GOODLAD, J. (1984) *A Place Called School: Prospects for the Future*, NY: McGraw-Hill.

GREENE, M. (1989) *The Dialectic of Freedom*, NY: Teachers College Press.

GREENE, M. (1991) 'Retrieving the language of compassion: The education professor in search of community', *Teachers College Record*, **98**, 4, p. 542.

HOLT, J. (1964) *How Children Fail*, NY: Dell.

HORTON, M. (1990) *The Long Haul: An Autobiography of Myles Horton*, NY: Doubleday Press (with Herbert Kohl and Judith Kohl).

HORTON, M. and FREIRE, P. (1990) *We Make the Road by Walking*, Philadelphia: Temple University Press, pp. 98, 195–6.

KOHL, H. (1967) *36 Children*, NY: New American Library.

KOZOL, J. (1967) *Death at an Early Age*, Boston: Houghton Mifflin.

McLAREN, P. (1988) 'The liminal servant and the ritual roots of critical pedagogy', *Language Arts*, **65**, 2, pp. 164–179.

SCHÖN, D.A. (1983) *The Reflective Practitioner: How Professionals Think in Action*, NY: Basic Books.

SIZER, T.R. (1984) *Horace's Compromise: The Dilemma of the American High School*, Boston: Houghton Mifflin.

WIGGINTON, E. (1986) *Sometimes a Shining Moment: The Foxfire Experience; Twenty Years Teaching in a High School Classroom*, NY: Anchor Press/Double day.

Chapter 19

Negotiating the Curriculum: Archeologists in Search of Meaning

Nancy Lester and Garth Boomer

How do we talk about issues in education? What do our conversations sound like and what can we learn from these dialogues? If curriculum negotiation is not to become simplified and fitted-in to the reigning school culture, can talking to learn play a role in keeping curriculum negotiation dynamic and fluid?

Although some of these questions may have been at the back of our minds when we decided to audiotape our conversation on negotiating the curriculum, they seem now to have the power to shape this conversation in order to be able to provide it as a demonstration of professionals engaged in reflective practice conversation. Our original intention to audiotape was actually a compromise. We weren't sure whether we could co-write a chapter on negotiation, although we wished to so some kind of collaborative effort for the book. We thought that taping our talk would give us a draft text from which we could craft a more formal piece.

As it happened, the audiotape provided us with a new kind of text. We could have chosen to craft it further, but since both of us had done so with other chapters in this book we decided against that route. Moreover, we thought, generalized descriptions of negotiating the curriculum and necessarily eclectic accounts of classroom practice are likely to fail to represent the subtle, qualitative ebb and flow of the language of negotiated meaning. Stylized and formal theoretical discourse about negotiation, likewise, will inevitably sweep over the traces of the dialogues upon which or from which the discourse has been built.

We began to consider that our talking might, in itself, be valuable if left in its raw form. We know that we strike a delicate balance here. The possibility that our readers will take this conversation as a self-promoting format is a risk we have decided to take, because there is another way to read this conversation and it's the possibilities there that we are trying to move towards. We believe the text which we have made through informal talk illustrates and represents the kind of thinking and talking which is the stuff of negotiation and thinking about negotiation. A scaffolding of ideas is being shaped and reshaped. Out of labyrinthine entanglements, we seem to reach new levels of interim agreement in a quest that can have no ending; only the temptation of newly revealed horizons.

We take up the discussion at a point where we are considering Ellen Skelly and Stephanie Siegel's difficulties in 'coming clean' with students about their teaching agenda (Chapter 6). Ellen and Stephanie noted that students seemed not at all

266

interested in their attempts to lay bear what, as teachers, they had previously con-
cealed about their intentions.

Having considered and discarded the idea of interrupting this text with our
meta-text, we realized that the text should speak for itself. We invite our readers to
join at any point in the conversation where they are provoked to do so.

N: Of course, students seemed not to hear. In effect, they were experiencing a foreign language. To learn a foreign language you've got
to get right in there and start doing it to really be able to speak it
and to understand it. When you try to speak a language of 'constraints' or 'non-negotiables' you're speaking a foreign language to
students.

G: Yes, you can't simply transmit meaning. The students need to be
immersed in action which will give meaning to empty terms. I'm
reminded of an example given, I think, by Michael Polanyi (1966),
of interns in medicine observing for the first time a specialist at
work interpreting an X-ray which showed cancer. The interns saw
nothing of what the specialist saw. In due course, however, after
many such episodes they progressively came to see what the specialist could see all along. Similarly, the students will not hear what
you're saying for a while. It will not signify, but gradually, through
enactment, they'll begin to understand.

N: You know, it's taken me from 1984 to 1990 to feel I have a reasonable understanding of negotiating the curriculum. If it's taken me
that long, what can you expect of a class of kids which you might
have for only twelve weeks or fourteen weeks? Even now since
we've opened up this conversation and are beginning to build new
language around the ideas; even while we're doing it, we're changing how we see it.

G: It just struck me that one of the tenets of negotiating the curriculum
is to start with what the kids already know. So instead of launching
into a coming clean spiel, teachers would do better to say something
like this: 'Now, we're about to start a new unit of work. Tell me
what you think's going to happen. Let's see how good you are at
predicting'. Then they'll probably put up a whole range of
commonsense predictions based on teaching they've experienced in
the past. In this way, they'll begin to articulate their theories about
how schools and teachers work.

N: So then the teaching/learning model is or culture is . . .

G: Yeah, so you actually invite them to articulate the theories that they
have and don't know that they have about how schools work and
how this sequence will probably work.

N: But even asking students what they know about school is such a
foreign question. How can you be sure that they won't resist even
at that level. Some will, of course.

G: Yeah. They might be wary of saying some of the things they know.
They'll probably trot out what they think you want to hear.

N: Maybe.

G: But as they get more at ease with you, they may offer their secret

267

perceptions of how they deal with school and what they think school's
on about.

N: This suggests that 'becoming more at ease' prefigures 'coming clean'.
It seems trite, but developing a classroom culture which is based on
trust between and among students and teacher is the first step.

G: After they'd predicted, I might say: 'Well, I'm going to surprise you.
I'm not going to teach it that way'.

N: Well, would it be better before you even say that to ask: 'Why
should we do it that way?' 'What are the reasons you can come up
with for: Why is it the way it is? Why does it have to be that way?'
If you can get students to question why it's that way, then maybe
they can see that there are other ways and that the other ways are
not so terrible. They've probably had it ground into them that there
is only one way of doing it.

G: Wouldn't it be brilliant, if they could come through their own questioning of commonsense to something like negotiating the curriculum. Then you can say, 'Interesting, I've come to similar conclusions and I want to give it a go. Let's try it!'

N: You could build the structure with them.

G: Take them and yourself on a journey. Push the envelope with regard to their present understanding of schools and learning.

N: I think you're right. We ask teachers to question their assumptions,
beliefs, and theories about why it is the way it is. Why shouldn't
students be engaged in the same process?

G: What's going to derail this kind of approach?

N: Well, when I read your reply to Ellen and Stephanie (chapter 7), I
made a note that, paradoxically, we're asking both teachers and
students to buy into the culture and resist the culture. We are governed by a ruling discourse which we're asking people to accept and
resist at the same time. I think there's a legitimate reason to resist
an invitation to try negotiation. A student might legitimately say:
'Everybody else is learning the other way; at least the majority are.
Certainly the ones who are getting the jobs and getting into colleges
of their choice and getting the money don't do it this way. Why
should I do it this way?' Kids should ask it. And how do we answer
them? One answer that John Mayher suggested I give, but I'm not
sure how true it is, is that the best private schools, the elite schools
engage students in this kind of learning. (Ted Sizer (1984) also
makes this argument.)

G: Bob Connell, an Australian academic, wrote a book, *Making the
Difference* (1984), which suggested that working class schools should
observe the way ruling class schools latch onto power and appropriate their strategies. Let's appropriate their secrets for *our* purposes
in relation to *our* lives.

N: But my worry is that the ruling class schools are really doing advanced fill-in-the-blank. Maybe it's not the way they're taught that
gives them the edge. Perhaps the crucial difference is almost a sense
of smugness about the inevitability of achievement among elite
students. An almost God-granted expectation. In fact, elite students

buy right into the transmission/commonsense model because that fits them best to pass the SAT (Standardized Achievement Test) test and to get advanced placement. They'd resist alternative ways of teaching and learning.

G: I think the big secret of ruling class schools is that the moment kids step across their thresholds they're treated as very important persons who are going to make it. They are going to be successful readers of the culture and power figures within the culture.

N: Why aren't students in ruling class schools ever asked to critique their own role in society? They're lacking the kind of critique we're asking these kids in public schools to make. I'm really divided. I want to make public schools places where there's an intellectual environment, where people talk about ideas. But, on the other hand, I want ruling class schools to do what I'm also asking public schools to do, which is to question why it should be done this way and what the purpose of schooling is. That is never questioned.

G: It's immaculately given. Divinely there.

N: We want ruling class schools to question not only the school's governing frame, but the society's governing frame.

G: So how do you shake up ruling class schools?

N: You don't have them any more!

G: That's not a possibility at the moment. What I'd do is change the examining system. Teachers and schools are largely framed by what the society values. If you can change what society values, then ruling class schools will quickly accommodate. The truth is that if, let's say Pitjatjantjara (an Australian Aboriginal language) were made a requirement for university entrance, ruling class schools would soon be doing it better than the Pitjatjanjara people themselves.

N: But that's not the way to change them. You've got to ask different kinds of questions that require the kind of critical reflective thinking you and I value.

G: Sure. The most radical thing we can do in education is to change the kind of assignments that kids are being set.

N: Talking about private and public education has been an interesting diversion. In fact, it's not been a diversion at all. It's enabled us to set up a contrast between two seemingly different kinds of education and see not only the differences but some pretty basic similarities. We've even come up with an hypothesis that might help remedy the problems. But let's get back to this notion of 'foreign language'. I've been using Giroux's (1985) term 'transformative intellectual', and teachers I work with are really turned off by the notion. They say it's jargon. Why do they label it that way? I think it's a way of distancing themselves from engaging in learning. I'm now getting angry about this stance. I think we should adopt this language and then take it over.

G: Not adopt it, but engage with it.

N: Engage *in* it, because by engaging in it, we begin to own it. We define it ourselves. The other way we're constantly at battle with it. That's not helping us change ourselves or recognize who we might be.

G: We develop an insidious kind of deafness to language we stigmatize as jargon.

N: We don't take it on, because we decide it's somebody else's language and that language is being used to describe us in ways we'd never name ourselves. It's a foreign language being used to describe us. I need to work at it myself. So when you talk about 'coming clean', 'authenticity', 'negotiation', 'explicitness', what does it mean? Students are likely to reject such language.

G: You might as well talk to them about capitalists or differential expansion. We're back to a 'language in the content area' problem. The content here is negotiating the curriculum. Actually, the language is education. Education has not been on the school curriculum. It is a foreign subject with a foreign language. To use a theological metaphor, the high priests of education have the language.

N: It's natural for me to get angry when I'm hit with abstruse language. I have to come back. Don't pull away because if you pull away, you're letting them run over you. I want to say: 'No, I'm going to deal with these words. I'm going to deal with this concept; try to understand what that means; tell you if my meaning is in any sense related to your meaning; whether this has anything to do say about my role and practice'. That's a much more active stance. You're not lying down. You're not going into the ovens.

G: If you are oppressed or relatively powerless with regard to anything, how do you come back at what is powering at you?

N: How do you learn even how to do that? How do you learn that it's alright to do that? You've already said (chapter 7) to Stephanie and Ellen that the kids are taught very well not to take it on.

G: To collude; unwittingly collude in their oppression.

N: Yes and no. They've been taught how, so now it's wittingly.

G: I don't know whether this is a side track or not, but I think there's unwitting collusion too. When I taught, a bit like Mr Keating in *The Dead Poet's Society*, I experienced the power of charisma, which so takes over the minds of students that they'd go anywhere.

N: Hallelujah!

G: I'm very worried about charismatic teaching, which cunningly papers over its own designs. It so naturalizes, it so engages that it actually kills off resistance. Which sorts of teaching actually encourage resistance and an answering discourse? The charismatic is as much a menace as the mundane transmitter. One numbs people's resistance by being boring, the other obliterates resistance by being exciting.

N: I think the answer lies in constantly trying to uncover layers of meaning. On both the student's and teacher's part. What we're talking about is that we don't yet know what it means to negotiate; that it's a constant negotiation of the meaning of what negotiating means. I'd be happy if I could help students constantly, like an anthropologist, an archeologist, to keep digging. Archeologists seek the roots of cultures; when and where tools were invented, how they developed over time and according to need. When we hope to get students to investigate where their beliefs about teaching and learning derive from, we're asking them to dig into their personal and communal experiences for the roots of their school culture in order to help them discover why they do what they do. I suppose another good metaphor would be ethnographer. Accepting Clifford Geertz's (1988) theory that genuine, democratic, critical ethnography can only be produced if we recognize and make explicit the value and belief frames through which we 'see' the culture we're attempting to learn about, this metaphor for teaching and learning is also quite powerful.

G: If we could get the so-called oppressed to the point where they're starting to have the kind of insights and capacity to resist that you and I have the world will be transformed! But seriously, I'm not coy about wanting to get people thinking in a resistent way and then saying what they think. We're all prisoners of a kind of tact. Even when we resist we rarely go to the next step, to be tactless enough to say that we think otherwise.

N: So is negotiating the curriculum really educating for discontent?

G: Yeah. Educating for pleasurable discontent.

N: For interruption. But I worry. We produce a society of interrupters and then what happens to the community? You've said elsewhere that autonomy is not what we're after. No man is an island.

G: If we could get all segments of society to read the world against the grain what would happen?

N: I'm not sure. I don't want to think about that. I think at this moment in my time and where I am I want people to be questioners. I want people to challenge. I want people to peel away. Somebody else will then have to deal with what happens if people really begin to do that on a massive scale. It seems so important for me. What I say to my students all the time, and I said it particularly this summer is: 'What *are your assumptions* here? You just said something here in class. What are you assuming with that statement?' Because if you don't question where it is that you came from and what gave you the reason to say what you said, then there's no way of you knowing whether what you said has either meaning for others, or is, in the context in which we were discussing, meaningful. Because if your assumptions are from a private, elite school and you have no knowledge or understanding of a world other than that, how can you apply those values to a world that's not your own? So, I help students continually to try to question their assumptions about how they view the world. That's what seems to be negotiating the curriculum's end. To question in order to reveal. Gee, I don't care what happens after that. I'll be dead in twenty years.

G: We need to become gently alienated from ourselves.

N: That's exactly what I mean when I say 'uncover your assumptions'. Step out of where it is you are. That's what we mean when we say play the 'believing game' (Peter Elbow, 1973).

G: I'm worried about that. I want to play the disbelieving game. What's the difference between playing the believing game and the disbelieving game?

N: Well, if you play the disbelieving game, you can't immerse yourself. From the start, you're questioning and alienating yourself from it.

G: So you need to see the film, *and then* critique it.

N: You need to *be in* the film. I think the believing game is a legitimate thing to play as long as you can say, 'You can at the end of this reject everything you've done, but won't you be better off in your argument of rejection, having had the experience of it, then not having had the experience'. Talking about games, what about writing a dictionary? A fictionary?

G: A fictionary of negotiating the curriculum.

N: But even that, you see, is transmission. A dictionary is transmission. Students who are asked to look up vocabulary in the dictionary and to use words in a sentence often use words inappropriately because they've looked only at the first definition. So, we have to write the ultimate, deconstructive dictionary.

G: Exactly. A dictionary that deconstructs itself; that continually falls in on itself.

N: Then we'd have to make it a dialogue. But as you bring in additional vocabulary that also has to be deconstructed. That's the hard one. That involves reciprocity.

G: So, we're into a dialogue of negotiating what we mean.

N: So let me start. Of course, you realize that E.D. Hirsch has a dictionary of cultural literacy?

G: I think we should take that on and mock it.

N: Here is our . . .

G: . . . cultural literacy of negotiation.

N: Our answer to E.D. Hirsch. OK. Negotiating the curriculum. A dictionary's definition. Very short. We'll show how language can be really packed. '*Negotiating the curriculum*: educating for resistance'.

G: But that's pretty cryptic. What does, 'Teaching for resistance', mean? Teaching for 'standing in opposition'. Is negotiation actually teaching people to be in opposition?

N: Maybe it's that. Negotiating the curriculum is 'teaching for a position from which to oppose'.

G: I think that's negative.

N: OK, so give me a positive.

G: I'd want to go beyond opposition to the point where you actually break the barrier of opposition and start to attack, thereby provoking opposition. Because to be really powerful in opposition, you have to know what it's like when you're being opposed.

N: What are you saying?

G: If you're always in opposition, you are basically in a reactive mode. To be a really powerful opposer, you have to have been in a position where you are dealing with the opposed and seeing what happens when the opposed oppose you.

N: Now you're playing a dirty game. You're being a transformative intellectual.

G: Am I?

N: Yeah. Because you're trying to change things as well as think about

them. Maybe that's even a better definition of negotiating the curriculum: 'Understanding things to change them'.

G: You know, our dictionary is developing into a dialogue which touches
down every now and then on a definition that just won't do.

N: What we're trying to say in this chapter is that the value here is in
the dialogue. The more we share our understandings of it, the more
we learn. Not only about each other's understandings, but our own
understandings of it. Going back to the it.

G: We always come back to it.

N: But there is no *it*. There are *its*. Plural.

G: But if you continually keep trying to define further, like Hamlet,
you'll lose the name of action. You've eventually got to operate as
if there is an *it*, even if it's an interim measure. But you don't want
to stay with *it* too long. You might become a lotus eater, comfortable and complacent about it. You might get to the point where
there is no opposition.

N: And for you that's the *most* dangerous place to be. Let's say I've
told my undergraduate students: 'Negotiating the curriculum is
teaching for resistance'. They'll write that down in their notebooks
and expect to get a test which says, 'Define negotiating the curriculum'. They will write, 'teaching for resistance'. And what we're
saying is 'Don't believe that'.

G: No, what we're really saying is . . .

N: . . . believe that, but, at the same time, try to find out what that
means.

G: All right, let me try a correct answer: 'Negotiating the curriculum
is teaching so that students will believe you for a short time and
then disbelieve you for a short time'.

N: But now we're back to assessment. I accept what you just said
because we've built an understanding together. What if a student
did give me the answer 'teaching for, resistance?' What would I say
to that student?

G: I'd fail that answer. But if it said that and then said in brackets:
['The fact that I have given this answer shows that I've understood
the hegemonic forces of assessment which I am hereby resisting by
putting this in brackets'] . . .

N: . . . you'd give it an A++.

G: No, there must be a better answer.

N: 'Negotiating the curriculum is learning'. See, I'm trying to turn
resistance into learning.

G: Learning the game and why the game.

N: How to question it. Consider people who speak the Black English
Vernacular who have learned Standard English and, as a result,
become disenfranchised from their native communities. How to they
become not disenfranchised? How to have both worlds? Is there
parallel processing in life?

G: Are you going to put that forward as your next definition?

N: 'Negotiating the curriculum is parallel processing for life'.

G: I don't understand that.

N: It means resisting and conforming at the same time.

G: So what's your definition?

N: 'Learning how to be a parallel processor'.

G: I'd say, 'And at the same time distrusting parallels' Parallel processing means you can live compatibly with two worlds without ever bringing them into conflict.

N: You're saying the problem with being parallel is there's never touching, there's never connection. It's like what appears on the EEG heart monitor when a person dies. Two parallel lines. That means you're dead.

G: So that the new definition is, 'Understanding that parallelism is death?'

N: Well, at least that an understanding to live in two parallel cultures that don't touch or conflict is a kind of sterilization of both cultures, sending them both to perdition.

G: Maybe you and I are like parallel lines beginning to deviate and touch occasionally at moments of agreement. Perhaps negotiation is 'Reaching agreement!'

N: Well, I suppose that's what the real dictionary would say. Trite. I think that's what talking to learn means. Not to agreement so much as to understanding the other.

G: 'Negotiation means reaching interim agreements or provisional agreements'.

N: Provisional agreements, until there's something new to question in the provisional agreement. Sort of like this . . .

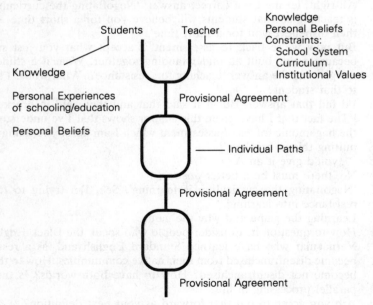

G: You and I have just reached a new provisional agreement about negotiation. It's much changed since we talked about it in 1984.

N: We're imagining schools that produce resisters, critiquers and questioners.

G: So what we ought to be doing instead of teaching for upward social mobility is teaching for social space, social capacity to effect one's circumstances. To defend oneself against the worst effects of society.

N: I think we have to say this is a process of education for changing the world. If we change schooling in this way, then we're going to change society.

G: Schools cannot compensate for society, but they can and do influence it.

N: I want students to go out there and say, 'Listen, there are inequities out here and I'm not going to stand for this. I know how to critique them. I know how to read them. I learned how to do it in school. I learned how to set a problem'.

G: Critical readings. Critical designing. Critical evaluation.

References

CONNELL, R.W. *et al.* (1984) *Making the Difference,* Sydney: Allen & Unwin.

ELBOW, P. (1973) *Writing Without Teachers,* London: Oxford University Press.

GEERTZ, C. (1988) *Words and Lives: The Anthropologist as Author,* Stanford, CA.: Stanford University Press.

GIROUX, H.A. (1985) 'Teachers as transformative intellectuals', *Social Education,* May, pp. 376–79.

POLANYI, M. (1966) *The Tacit Dimension,* NY: Doubleday.

SIZER, T.S. (1984) *Horace's Compromise: The Dilemma of the American High School,* Boston: Houghton Mifflin.

Chapter 20

Negotiating the Curriculum Reformulated

Garth Boomer

This book amplifies the voices of teachers whom I consider to be bold educational reformers working towards the realization of possibilities in the contested sites of schools and institutions. These teachers are, in my view, 'polyattentive', inquiring intellectuals, highly aware of constraints and *cul de sacs* while equally alert to opportunities to make gains in transforming classrooms, schools, and institutions. They are robust innovators who are both radical and practical, visionary and strategic.

In this summary chapter, I wish to explore teacher roles and dilemmas in the enactment of principles of negotiation. Specifically, I want to dispel any images of soft romanticism and *laissez-faire* utopianism which may have become falsely associated with the negotiating teacher. I want to celebrate the tenacity of teachers who not only survive, but daily make contributions to a new social order through the emancipation and encouragement of minds.

The Educational Radical

'Radical' is a word which has been hijacked into the world of politics, usually with negative connotations, to refer to the 'extreme left' — implying instability, emotiveness and revolutionary zeal. Taking the word back to its core, however, we can see that it more rightly refers to a person or an action which tries to go to the root of things, below surfaces and rhetoric, to examine complexities lying beneath the alleged *Truth*. My radical is a kind of sceptic or non-conformist in the sense of always searching for alternative interpretations. Accordingly, the 'radical' person even in my sense of the word is likely to be seen by the more accepting members of society as a burr under the saddle, a killjoy, an unwelcome critic, a meddler and often as a heretic. The radical will be a pain to the settled but in turn has to live with the pain of the social unease and ostracism which usually attends the intellectual fringe-dweller. Needless to say it is the intellectual radicals, the implacable, dissatisfied detectives who keep science progressing, who push out the philosophical horizons, who invent new interim solutions to persisting riddles. The radical is a questioner and questions are subversive but necessary if we are not to ossify and seize up. Socrates, in this sense, was the archetypal radical.

Democracy, theoretically, depends on an informed, questioning citizenry capable of choosing and discarding. Theoretically, then, a thriving democracy would comprise radical people. In practice, however, democracy is flawed.

It seems that most citizens seek, as their goal in life, contentment and harmony which often translates into an intellectual life which is largely unexamined and fixed. Indeed one could see democracies as a continuing struggle between settling and unsettling forces. It is safer, though more boring, to conform. It is safer to belong to a club, a sect, a team that offers a predigested, predisposed set of rules and beliefs. It is comforting to 'belong'. Because democracies give power and point to the will of the people, they will reflect the general disposition of the masses. If most people basically want to be told by someone sensible what to do, they will vote for people they think will increase their comfort and safety. They will not vote for 'radicals' as I have characterized them. By this analysis, democracies could be in danger of promoting a form of thoughtlessness and easy compliance.

This book is about educating for the antithesis of thoughtlessness. It is about constructive mindfulness, critique and evaluation. In short, it is about learning and learning never to become fixed. It is about the formation of a collaboratively radical democracy which values enquiry and negation as essential elements in the progress of civilization. It is about pleasurable discontent. Its vision is a cohesively unsettled democracy beyond smugness, self-satisfaction, slogans and righteousness.

My ideal radical enquires to bring greater empathy, subtlety and understanding to the society, not to tear it apart. The radical's project is greater collective wisdom. This is not, then, a book about the cult of the free-thinking individual. It is about the individual in society and society in the individual. It is about sophisticated co-existence which never quite reaches the finality of 'belonging'.

Tolerance and intolerance as absolutes are unacceptable. Gentle but conditional affection for others is to be balanced with a gentle alienation from oneself and the society. We are forever in danger of having our constructs harden into bigotry and of believing our own or someone else's latest summation. We need to seek always to be ideologically *provisional*.

This does not mean that we should think, like Hamlet, so precisely on the event that we lose the name of action. The logical extension of this stance is not some kind of post-modern society, so self-aware and subtle that it paralyses itself with provisionalism. We must in the end act as if our provisional readings are correct and our action should be in the direction of what we provisionally believe to be most just, constructive and ethically defensible. The radical is not without direction and passion. It is, in fact, through acting with passion that the radical tests hypotheses in order to reach a more subtle formulation. Siegel and Skelly in chapter 6 and Louth and Young in chapter 13 illustrate this mix of passionate action and dispassionate analysis which attends radical inquiry. Pat Thomson in chapter 17 shows how hard won principles inform her actions but never in such a way that they become unquestioned commandments.

The Epistemology and Politics of Negotiation

Negotiating the curriculum in schools, as set out in chapter 1, argues for classrooms in which teachers invite and allow students to help construct and enact the learning journey. A key point in the rationale is that engaged, intentional students, who also have the capacity to resist and question, will learn more and better than students who are programmed and instructed against their will or with their will having been 'motivated' by a persuasive teacher. Because chapter 1 is necessarily local and contained within the life of the classroom, it is in danger of leaving the impression that 'negotiating the curriculum' is merely a new teaching technique which will produce better learning. It has been a major project of this book to demonstrate that negotiating the curriculum is a way of being and acting which transcends technique and formula. At the level of mere sloganism it is a dangerous opiate. It is as an invitation to infinite reconstrual through action and reflection that we have presented it in this book illustrating what we mean through case studies of teachers at work.

In order to understand better the philosophical and political underpinnings of negotiation one needs to set the work more globally within the context of education systems and national/international economic and political regimes.

Certainly, this book attests to the power of negotiating the curriculum in improving student learning but it also builds up progressively a view of society and a political orientation within that society. 'Negotiating the Curriculum' can be taken up as a technique or a formula and used in schools by almost any teacher. It would not, however, be acknowledged as being within the spirit of this book unless it were accompanied by the frame of mind and view of teacher and student emancipation both explicit and implicit within the book. If the overriding concern of teachers is their control of the classroom organization and the curriculum as opposed to increasing student control and questioning, then we will have a form of pseudo-negotiation where the negotiation is simply a more subtle technique for charming students to take part willingly in the prefigured curriculum designed by the teacher. There is a world of difference between the teacher who consciously strives for the progressive 'radicalizing' of learners, in the sense described above, and the Dale Carnegie-type teacher who uses negotiation as a sweetener or a lure into the disguised but largely unchanged frames of the teacher's headset.

Such pretenders to negotiation are likely also to have an epistemology to match the crypto-dominant politics implicit in their teaching. Schools, like society, are riddled with a commonsense view of knowledge (Mayher, 1990) as 'stuff' which exists 'out there' and which can be taken and transmitted by a skillful teacher, through instruction, into the heads of learners — accompanied by various practice, drill and enforcement protocols. Nancy Lester, in chapter 15, sets out graphically how the transmission wolf can be dressed up in progressive clothing under the name of cooperative learning. In assessing the political and educational project of any classroom sequence, it is necessary to unearth the teacher's orientation towards knowledge and to develop a sense of what image of the human brain the teacher is working on. To do this an observer needs to peer beneath cosmetics and surface methodologies (group work, project work, interactive drama, etc.) to see what purposes the methods are serving. It is relatively easy to understand how a teacher with a 'transmission' view of knowledge, accompanied by a conception of the human brain as imitative and malleable through judicious external imprinting, is likely to have a politics characterized by conservatism, conformity and subjection of the masses by enlightened keepers of wisdom.

By contrast, the negotiating teacher as represented in this book, is a *constructivist* working on a view of the human brain as an interpreter of life's phenomena, inducing rules and building constructs (mini theories) of how the world wags. The constructivist understands that information, facts, data are received and interpreted according to the current constructs of the learner. They are thus shaped and built into new constructs, new 'knowings' (rather than 'knowledge'). With this view of learning, it is not a matter of whether or not to negotiate. There can never be exact congruence between what a teacher or a textbook means to mean and what a learner makes of that meaning. The dance between teacher and taught represents a continuing negotiation of meaning. Misunderstanding or rather partial understanding is inevitable but the quest to build progressively better mutual understandings is at the heart of teaching and learning. The teacher's key role is to ensure that learners do not learn to shut down their construing and reconstruing apparatus. The mathematics students in Susan Hyde's classroom, chapter 4, construct their own definitions before encountering textbook formulations. And so they come to the ruling discourse of mathematics critical, alert, and prepared to argue.

Politically, the constructivist is almost certain to settle on the 'liberal' side, with a strong sense of diverse cultures and world views and a strong sense of contested democracy. There will be degrees of difference from the more strongly individualistic constructivists to those who have more sharply honed understandings about how groups interact to negotiate the ruling discourse and delineations of truth.

This all amounts to the observation that this book, at a deep level, is about the uses and abuses of power in education. 'Transmissionists' are likely to contend that once people have mastered the knowledge 'basics' some will go on to power. Constructivists would say that some come to construe themselves as powerful and others learn to construe themselves as relatively powerless, the aim of radical educators being to try to redress this imbalance.

It is not drawing too long a bow, I think, to suggest that the classroom regimes which teachers establish (at whatever level of education) represent microcosms of the kind of community/society which they value. The analysis would have to be made at the deep level, not just on the basis of such things as desks in rows and formal features. One would want to know whether the teacher power is being used to emancipate or subject; whether individuals feel confident to question or feel cowed; whether rules are imposed or collectively built; whether ethnic minorities are included or marginalized and so on. The teacher's presentation of self (e.g. as fount of received wisdom as opposed to intrepid seeker) and orientation to others is possibly more profound in its teaching than the formal curriculum. The teachers represented in this book hold in common the vulnerability and the excitement of being palpable learners in their own classrooms, demonstrating that which they espouse. In order to promote student emancipation, of course, they need themselves to be emancipated or at least fighting for their own emancipation.

In this way, students will/can come to see their teachers enacting the same kinds of behaviors, beliefs, stances, and values which they are being asked to grapple with. In this way they may learn how to be and do what they see their teachers being and doing in their classrooms. There is no more powerful learning than that which comes as a result of seeing master craftpersons doing what they preach and attempt to teach. Students' disaffection and skepticism towards teachers, learning, knowledge, and schooling might have more to do with not seeing their own masters enacting what they, themselves, are supposed to be learning how to do than with anything else.

On Pragmatism

Life in education is a constant series of armistices between the ideal and habitual. Inertia in education has been well-documented (Cuban, 1984; Mayher, 1990). Educational institutions with few exceptions are permeated with structures and practices which relate to the factories which followed the industrial revolution and the development of the Taylorist/Fordist production line techniques of the early twentieth century. Mass education brought with it all the paraphernalia of mass control. School staffing is hierarchical/bureaucratic in design; classrooms, architecturally, have moved from rectangle (suited to one teacher and monitors in very large classes) to square (one teacher plus up to thirty or so) but are still premised on an out-front instructor/vigilante/ transmitter; the curriculum is divided into parts (subjects) and then further subdivided; lessons tend to have characteristic parts; assignment and homework protocols have changed little over the decades; system controls through testing regimes and teacher promotion criteria remain well entrenched; textbooks, by and large, are premised on behaviourist/transmission psychology; 'streaming' or 'tracking' of students persists overtly or covertly.

The history of 'radical' education reform could be seen as a history of failure to grip. It could be argued that the hypothetical 10 per cent who fought for Deweyan interactive classrooms in the early twentieth century have successors today in a 10 per cent who continue to strive to usher in a new regime of 'constructivism'. Yet, militaristic organization of schools still persists. The dominant paradigm of schooling has not changed in one hundred years.

Those with a radical orientation are ripe for the slaughter if they do not realize this. The prognosis for longevity of a naive radical in the mills of education is not good.

The radical teacher must be a hard-nosed pragmatist keeping alive principles and long-term goals, but having a canny sense of what is achievable, what is not worth the energy and what, however slight, might constitute strategic gain. The radical teacher must also seek out networks of support. Alone, even the pragmatic radical is at risk. Susan Hyde (chapter 5), a negotiator who has moved from being a teacher and faculty head to being principal of a complex secondary school, has encapsulated her current wisdom as an idealistic activist. She has, through years of struggle, setbacks and success, learned how to be effectively strategic, though never safe.

Pragmatism is not synonymous with capitulation or weakness. It is about knowing when to act and when not to act; knowing what is possible and what is doomed; weighing consequences and benefits; deciding what to say and what not to say; taking out insurance; having safety nets; not driving oneself insane with mocking images of unreachable utopias. To be pragmatic is to place the emphasis on effective action without denying the power of imagination and dreaming of better worlds; on the achieved and achievable rather than on the chronicles of failure. The quest for pragmatism is a kind of warfare on illusion. It is a search for sharper and more subtle situational literacy — the capacity to 'read' and assess what is going on with both groundedness and wisdom.

This book testifies to pragmatic teacher literacy. To know 'what is going on', or even to wonder what might be going on, means having an all-encompassing fish-eye-lens taking in the backgrounds, capabilities and aspirations of the learners and their parents, knowing the structures, habits and values of the school, reading the wider politics of the system and society (particularly its economics), and understanding the ebb and flow of interactions and struggles in the arenas of gender, race, ethnicity and class. It also means having a good sense of history, and an understanding of the antecedents of the status quo.

In order to position oneself as an actor in education, there is a need to have a feel for trends and power plays; for the flux and subtleties of new schemes, slogans and hypes. All this is needed to allow an assessment of where there is room to move, where there are possibilities and where there are dangers. 'Know then thyself' must be supplemented by 'know then thy world'. This is indeed a tall order and goes beyond the realms of pragmatism to demand theorized practice and practical theories.

On Constraints

Pragmatic radicals in the elementary classroom are less constrained than their high school counterparts. The capacity to work all day with the same group of students and the flexibility of programming that this allows is more conducive to negotiating the curriculum in its fullest sense than in the high school where lessons are framed, where students move frequently from teacher to teacher across 'boxed' subjects and where courses tend also to be divided into units or semesters of limited duration.

The less time a teacher has with students, the less rapport, mutual understanding and room for progressive negotiation there is likely to be. The student will therefore tend to be more programmed than programming, subject to the fixed requirements of a tightly prefigured course. In the elementary school, there is more scope for the building of a micro-community in which rules, protocols procedures and the curriculum can be mutually constituted and modified over time, although we can readily find alarming examples of elementary schools which seem intent on boxing and partitioning the curriculum.

Both the high school and the elementary school teacher, however, share systemic and school constraints. Even where schools are deemed 'private' or 'independent', closer examination will show that the school operates within a system of some kind (a church organization, or a community of like philosophy such as we find in Steiner Waldorf schools).

In public or state systems, depending on the bureaucratic regime, national economic constraints and political will, amongst other things, schools may be constrained by curriculum mandates (tight or relatively flexible), by fiats about texts, tests and accountability, by rules and criteria for teacher recruitment and promotion, by resource provision and by a range of other requirements such as rules on corporal punishment or student suspension. These, at least in overt enactment, become non-negotiables for the school and teachers within the school.

One usually finds within systems ongoing consultation, contestation and flux as participants within and outside the system debate and dance around issues. Teachers who rightly give priority to their students are often unaware of this. Interestingly, at least from my experience, systems over the past three decades have tended to be highly active in wanting to intervene and change schools (for better or worse). The evidence (Rand, 1974; Cuban, 1984) suggests, however, that while there is seemingly tight coupling and instrumental linking between educational bureaucracies and local schools, system-initiated innovations rarely lead to sustained take-up in schools. Systems can demand or require but implementation is perfunctory, if not subversive, and certainly as old demands are replaced by new, the earlier reform dies through lack of sustenance. By contrast, schools, which seem loose amalgams of individual teachers without strong overt institutional binding, actually manifest surprising curriculum and pedagogical homogeneity because they are, in fact, tight-knit cultural formations determined by custom and inertia.

It is a moot point, in any case, whether teachers in public school systems feel more constrained by system requirements than by the less obvious ethos, culture, and peer habits within the school community. My guess is that local constraints are likely to be the more palpable in most schools.

This is not to deny the power of systemic constraints. Systems, too, have their less obvious cultural traits which, along with deeply embedded structures, shape and hold the school culture. Ironically, even when people within systems move to change schools, say through new curriculum guidelines, they are often thwarted by semi-invisible implants within their own system. Indeed, it could be that system rhetoric is often a 'decoy discourse' which is rendered inoperable because it is denied by unspoken but cemented messages contained within assessment and promotion structures and rules.

For instance, the curriculum guidelines may call for greater interactivity, group work and problem solving in the classroom. At the same time, state tests in literacy and numeracy may reinforce recitation, drilling and exercise work. This coupled with meaningfully loud silences about promotion opportunities for those who run tight, quiet classrooms and deliver what is wanted (as represented by the tests), leads to a confirmation of the status quo in the face of contradictory overt exhortation from the system.

The pragmatic radical needs to know of such contradictions and fractures within systems for where there are contradictions there are opportunities to move. The curriculum guideline that seeks greater interactivity between students can become powerful cover for the radical teacher in the crossfire of conflicting ideologies and pedagogies within the school. The system has provided scriptures which can be cited against its deeper self. Its inherent schizophrenia becomes a virtue for the innovating teacher.

Similar fractures, contradictions and 'messes' (see, Schön,1983, for more on 'mess') occur in schools. There is always likely to be considerable mismatch between what is said and what is done; between the official line and the cultural understandings amongst the entrenched staff. ('This is how we do things around here'.)

A school may, for instance, have a highly detailed elementary social studies course which the staff may know (but do not say overtly) is essentially unteachable in its entirety. There may then occur a silent collusion, a kind of underground resistance amongst staff, which leads to outward indications that the course is being taught while in truth teachers are being highly selective and idiosyncratic in what they choose to do behind closed doors. Of course, the advent of a principal who mandates across-school tests in relation to the espoused social studies curriculum would add an interesting new dynamic to the culture of benign resistance.

There are always surges and counter-surges of power in schools, as there are in classrooms. Teachers differ amongst themselves. System injunctions come and go. Parent groups jostle and lobby, some formalizing their power through school boards and councils. The more subtly teachers can read these flows, counter-flows and cross-currents, the more strategically effective they are likely to be. Heightened capacity to read the system at all levels is a prerequisite for the successful pragmatic radical.

Developing the Wider View

Reading the system means going beyond education, especially to a reading of national and international politics and economics. Education has always been used to serve economic/political ends because it is an early powerful agent in will formation, attitudes and orientations. When the economy needs more technicians and less manual workers, the systems and schools will be pressured to include more technical studies courses and to keep students at school longer.

Interestingly, western capitalist society is currently demanding more flexible, self-reliant workers and is making these demands on a schooling system which has formerly served society well by ensuring that the bulk of graduates is compliant, conforming and imbued with an individualistic/ competitive, as opposed to a collaborative/teamwork ethic. Teachers, surprisingly, have a new, if questionable, ally in big business with respect to some of the collaborative work they wish to do in schools.

As a backdrop to political-economic maneuvering, there is the fascinating momentum of ideas and the panorama of history. My concerted, but necessarily superficial reading about what is happening in the arenas of academic disciplines, is that in the 1990s quite profound paradigm shifts are taking place. It seems that Cartesian dualities — the enlightenment linear rationality of cause and effect — indeed, the whole world of Newtonian physics upon which so many of our practices and metaphors of the world are built, are about to be overthrown by new theories which question continuity in evolution and history (Gould, 1989), take account of pattern within chaos (Gleick, 1987) and which blur mind/body distinctions (Bergland, 1985).

In the social sciences, the work of Foucault (1977) amongst others, has led to a better understanding of the highly subtle interaction of the micro ('a thought at its very inception is an act') with the hegemonic discourse. Traditional Marxism is being seen as too crude to encompass the subtle readings which are arising out of new feminist class and ethnicity (Lather, 1988 enquiries). It seems to me that we could be at one of those discontinuous points in evolution where there is about to be a major upheaval. Perhaps we are about to witness a post-modern revolution which will transform societies, cultures and, therefore, schools in quite unforeseen and unimagined ways.

All this has been to set negotiating the curriculum in a complex context so that it is clear that the writers in this book are not merely purveyors of a new teaching technique. This is a book about the teacher as 'transformative intellectual' (Giroux, 1988) initiating students into new ways of acting in a changing world; about the teacher as inveterate seeker after wisdom, modeling such an orientation to the world in the enactments of the classroom.

The Negotiation

Thus, the pragmatic radical enters the classroom with a rich apprehension of the context and constraints which impinge on the negotiations which are about to take place.

Presuming that the teacher has not met the class before, a whole new set of essential readings is about to begin. Each student comes with an agenda, a context and a set of constraints which will become part of the classroom equation whether they are acknowledged or not. The teacher, as archaeologist, has the task of unearthing and allowing the expression of the meanings and views which the students bring at least insofar as they relate to enacting the curriculum.

A major tenet of negotiating the curriculum is that students will learn most where they feel *they must* learn. Kelly (1955) says that we learn most in the areas of our greatest anxiety. If students are not 'anxious' (in the sense of curious, tense, uneasy, desirous) in areas where the teacher wants to or is constrained to teach, then the formal instructional programme is likely to be aborted or to take on all the attributes of ritualistically/catechistically going through the motions. Student *intention* is the key to learning success. The securing of student intention is at the heart of good teaching as it is portrayed in this book. It must be recognized that students who resist have intention. Resistance is not unintentional. It has meaning which needs to be voiced and heard and used in negotiating.

Such intention is not magically secured. It has to be negotiated painstakingly, probably very precariously and impurely at first, ideally building to the point where there is reserved or provisional trust between teacher and taught; where there is a sufficient critical mass of previous shared endeavour for students to feel that, with will and effort on all sides, good and useful things can and do happen in this classroom.

It would be a rare achievement, not to mention suspicious, if a teacher could walk into a new class and begin to negotiate the curriculum as set out in chapter 3 from the very beginning. Given schools as they are, the odds are that the students will not previously have experienced a teaching/learning context in which they have been invited to collaborate in the conduct of the classroom including the enactment of the curriculum. They may have experienced some teachers who are more or less humanistic and others who are highly militaristic and authoritarian. Certainly, if they are beyond, say, year 3 most will have learnt well and truly how to 'student' when teachers teach (Green, J., 1988). 'Studenting' means knowing how to produce the required artifacts and knowing, among other things, the often covert rules of question answering and turn taking. Both teacher and student engage in 'procedural displays' (Atkinson and Delamont, 1990) which become almost automated in the rituals of teaching and 'studenting'.

The negotiating, pragmatic radical will almost certainly be faced with the need to undo and rewrite the rules of procedural display. This cannot usually be done overnight. Students will tend to resist changes to the game. At its most intense, this will take the form of considering the teacher to be more than a little crazy. Siegel and Skelly in chapter 6 and Louth and Young in chapter 13 show how this kind of student resistance can impact upon the negotiating teacher. Students will apply quite intense pressure to 'normalize' the teacher. In this they may even recruit parents by carrying home tales of bizarre behaviour which in turn become missiles for assault on the school principal.

Of course, if the changes to procedural display are explicitly negotiated over time and if the new regime works in the students' terms, then students can become teachers' greatest advocates with parents, with other teachers and with the principal.

A teacher who has a view of learning and learners as set out in this chapter *cannot help* but negotiate the curriculum. The view of the student as 'born scientists' and the drive towards progressive emancipation is so strongly internalized that it becomes part of the pedagogical fabric. But the surface manifestations of the internalized world view may be highly variant according to contexts, constraints and local conditions. An observer of such a teacher at work will not see the immaculate enactment of the formulaic ideal as set out in chapters 2 and 3.

In one class, with a history of being disruptive and underachieving, the teacher may in early days adopt an explicit, highly structured non-negotiable regime with the intention, progressively, of inviting gradual student participation in assignment selection and in evaluation of the success of teaching/learning sequences. In another class taught by this same teacher in the previous year, understandings may be so advanced that the teacher and class together plot a full unit of work in which responsibility for teaching certain topics is taken up by selected groups. A common feature of both classrooms will be teacher *explicitness* about what is non-negotiable, about what is to be covered, how it is to be covered and most significantly how it is to be assessed (including upon what criteria). See Nancy Lester's detailed account of such explicitness at the university level in chapter 11. While the scope and degree of negotiation will vary strategically across classes, the teacher will always take pains to make the teaching and the curriculum *opaque*. I have described this elsewhere as a kind of Brechtian alienation effect (Green, 1988).

Most teaching is somewhat analogous to naturalistic theatre which is effective by so enthralling or capturing the audience that they suspend disbelief entering into the constructed world of the drama as if it were natural. Brechtian theatre operates on the principal of setting up *patently constructed* images of life as mirrors for critique and evaluation. A Brechtian-type classroom will similarly present the curriculum as a construct which can be critiqued and evaluated by the students. This may be an engrossing and disturbing classroom but it is not enthralling. The naturalistic classroom presents as TRUTH. The epic classroom, as I call it, presents as a laboratory for the scrutiny of alleged truth. Susan Hyde, chapter 5, illustrates how a teacher can formally and deliberately commission student critique of the enacted curriculum.

For the teacher who is at the preliminary stages of disassembling procedural display, on the way to a more fully negotiated curriculum, it is important even within a highly constrained, largely non-negotiable curriculum to build into the non-negotiable regime 'a pedagogy for the oppressed' (Freire, 1970). The way in which the new is presented, the opportunities to talk about the new and to bring student experience into conversation with the new and the opportunity to evaluate what has been learnt, must be built in. Pat Thomson, chapter 17, presents a range of portraits which demonstrate the complexities and nuances involved in the tentative search for linkages between the culture of students and the valued curriculum of the teacher.

In a way students cannot be expected to know the benefits of negotiation until they have pleasurable intimations of what it means and what it can do for them. That is, teachers must, at the same time as they are teaching the required curriculum, put negotiation of the curriculum, including school, on the curriculum. Students must be taught what negotiation of the curriculum is, what it can do, and *how to do it.* If students' question asking capacities in schools have atrophied, they must be revivified and legitimated. If students cannot work in groups, they must learn to do it. If students cannot evaluate their own work, this too must be learnt.

Herein, we see one of the reasons why advanced negotiation is so often abandoned by teachers. The drive to *get through* the curriculum, albeit in a desultory way, often leads to panic about time. The kind of meta-teaching and teaching of new capabilities which negotiation requires can be seen as an impractical superimposition on an already imposing curriculum.

If, of course, the aim is actual, demonstrated learning of the required curriculum as opposed to relatively hollow recitational presentation, then one *must*, in this book's terms, take the time to develop structures and behaviours which will allow students to talk, read, write, think and act themselves into understanding. It is a question of mirages of learning as opposed to real oases. If one takes the longer view, time taken to learn things properly and tenaciously *now*, is far more efficient than having repeatedly to revise and relearn that which has been repeatedly taken on piecemeal, superficially and precariously and therefore soon lost.

In fact, the negotiating teacher can demonstrate that, even within the time limits imposed and given the curriculum to be covered, *better results* can be achieved even by the traditional testing devices used by the school. While the negotiating teacher may take more time initially to secure intention and connection with the students' worlds, once secured, that intention leads to more intense, more energetic and more deep-seated learning than in the case of the reluctant student motivated and harried through an essentially decontextualized set of mind exercises.

Compare the knowledge of certain terrain in the case of a tourist who has been driven through in a tourist bus with traditional blurbs, as opposed to that of an adventurer (under guidance) who has, with map and compass, traveled the same territory and had the opportunity to talk it over with fellow travelers and an expert afterwards.

The Rigour of Negotiation

Because negotiation has sometimes been characterized by critics as a *laissez-faire*, indulgent student-centred regime which lacks rigour, it is necessary to make clear that this is not so.

In the first place, where a teacher has certain non-negotiables imposed (e.g.

a mandatory course in mathematics which will be externally examined), these non-negotiables must be declared and explained to the students. ('We have no choice about these matters but we do have some discretion in how to handle them'.) Over and above these, teachers, personally, will have some things which they will not easily yield up as negotiable. If the teacher knows that to learn students must have opportunity to activate the known, discuss the new and try things out in practice, then these opportunities must be built into whatever curriculum programme is negotiated. They will, however, be built in *and explained* as being seen to be necessary. They are not to go unquestioned. Student evaluation of the *efficacy* of certain methods must be included. The non-negotiables imposed by the teacher are not 'untouchables'. They can be challenged and questioned. The learning regime described by Lester (chapter 11) is highly structured, rigorous and demanding while at the same time allowing/requiring considerable student choice, decision making and self-determination.

Teachers, with their superior experiential wisdom and knowledge of the system, will have very strong views about what needs to be learnt if students are to 'make it' in society. They will not, and should not, yield easily, if at all, in insisting that these things are covered. Of course, having mandated certain things, the pressure is then on the teacher firstly to justify and secondly to teach in such a way that students actually and powerfully come to learn what is valued.

It is particularly important with students who are 'at risk', because of their class, ethnicity, race, gender, isolation or disability, that teachers *insist* on the learning of certain 'secrets' and passwords of the dominant culture, including, in particular, the acquisition of dominant cultural capital and privileged subjects such as mathematics. Pat Thomson includes such issues in chapter 17. The concept of 'strong' and 'weak' choice is important here. It became increasingly fashionable in the 1970s and 1980s to offer students, particularly secondary students, wider and wider curriculum choices. This was often justified by arguing that if students had such choice, then they would be more motivated to study what they chose. It was also justified in terms of individualizing the curriculum to suit student needs.

Now this wider range of subjects was still taught by the same range of teachers. There was not, therefore, concomitant choice of teachers by students. That is, there was not a greatly increased pedagogical choice. The new subjects would be taught in the same way as other subjects by the same group of teachers.

It is not hard to see, also, that widened curriculum choice of this kind leads to a tracking or streaming of subjects (in terms of content, challenge and privilege) and consequently to a streaming of students, with the so-called 'disadvantaged' being further disadvantaged by choosing or being counseled into 'less valuable' subjects and so gradually sliding off the edges of the school into the less powerful positions in society. This is weak choice.

A more rigorous social justice programme would decide on what is important and valuable for all and *mandate it* for all on the curriculum. The challenge to teachers then is to render this content teachable and achievable by all. The pedagogical pressure is then to find ways of engaging the minds and intentions of all, particularly the 'disadvantaged'. The only answer, as this book asserts, is, *within* the mandated non-negotiables, to enter into a form of negotiation where, provided the key goals are achieved, choice is offered in *how* this can be done. This is strong choice.

Pat Thomson, in chapter 17, shows how teachers who have a strong social justice drive need to balance *insistence* with a great degree of flexibility and ingenuity in the negotiation of 'ways in' to the valued territory. This may mean in the first instance strategic abandonment of the valued territory, in order to secure some prerequisite knowledge, confidence and attitudinal positivity.

In the negotiated curriculum of the pragmatic radical as outlined above, hard headed judgments are made about what can and cannot be done, always keeping in mind the desired state. If to fight parents on the matter of reporting student progress by normative grades from A to E would be to put the whole negotiation project at risk and to discredit the teacher, then a decision will be made, *at this time*, to go along with this form of reporting even though it is not in keeping with the principles of the teacher. This is not weak capitulation. However, while meeting parental requirements and conforming overtly to their expectations, teachers can find ways and means of discussing and negotiating grades with their students that are in keeping with teachers' principals. It is a strategic survival mechanism. One can go along with a decision while still critiquing it and waiting for the right time to have it changed.

The Negotiated Classroom

What, then, might distinguish a negotiated classroom? One should find, in the first place, a shared detailed understanding between teacher and students of what is going on, what needs to be done and how it will be done. Secondly, one would find student readiness to ask questions — procedural, substantive and speculative. There would also be group work and whole class reflection/evaluation episodes. A good deal of argument, negotiation and discussion would occur when it came time to evaluate assigned work. The 'feel' of the classroom would be one of engaged, intentional industry where tension to complete work is self or group-imposed rather than teacher imposed.

A litmus test of such a classroom would be that students continued to work purposefully when the teacher left the room. It would be a classroom in which the teacher could often be seen teaching (to whole class, group, or individual) but with the consent of the learners and often *as commissioned*. Furthermore, it would be a classroom that teachers could leave in order to work collaboratively with colleagues on school-based professional education endeavors. Often teachers feel guilty to leave their 'charges.' This is patronizing and contradicts their claims to be promoting student empowerment over their own learning. If school-based professional education is going to happen *now*, some provisional arrangements must be made *now*. This could be one beginning.

Conclusion

This book has explored what happens when highly principled, reflective pragmatic radicals set out to negotiate the curriculum. It is in the tradition of Dewey, Bruner and Freire in valourizing the minds, intentions and cultures of the learners but it places such ideals in the highly contested, messy and constrained contexts of institutions (elementary schools, high schools, universities and education systems) where vision and pragmatism contend.

Whereas ten years ago some of the ideas now further explored in this book were not well digested by those outside schools, it is becoming evident that in all industrialized countries further development, culturally and economically, will depend on the wise and judicious use of brain power. Business and industry now face the need for the same kind of transformations proposed for education in this book, although they may not share the same emancipatory, democratic project.

Negotiating the curriculum has become an economic and cultural imperative as, in a fractured and multifarious world, we seek to find the means of sustainable evolution. The curriculum negotiator, without guilt about what cannot be done at once, will seek to secure classrooms, schools and systems which free human beings to think; to learn and to work together in a common but not unexamined cause.

References

ATKINSON, P. and DELAMONT, S. (1990) 'Procedural display and the authenticity of classroom activity: A response to Bloome, Puro, and Theodorou', *Critical inquiry*, **20**, 1, pp. 63–69.

AVERCH, H.A., CARROL, S.J., DONALDSON, T.S., KIESLING, H.J. and PRINCUS, J. (1974) *How Effective is Schooling?* (A Rand Educational Policy Study), NJ: Educational Technology Publications.

BERGLAND, R. (1985) *The fabric of mind* Melbourne: Penguin.

CONNELL, R.W., ASHENDEN, D.J., KESSLER, S. and DOWSETT, G.W. (1982) *Making the Difference*, Sydney: George Allen & Unwin.

CUBAN, L. (1984) *How Teachers Taught: Constancy and Change in American Classrooms, 1890–1980*: NY: Longman.

FOUCAULT, M. (1977) 'Preface', *Language, Counter Memory, Practice: Selected Essays and Interviews by Michel Foucault*, NY: Cornell University Press.

FREIRE, P. (1970) *Pedagogy of the Oppressed*, NY: Seabury Press.

GIROUX, H.A. (1988) *Teachers as Intellectuals: Toward a Critical Pedagogy of Learning*, Granby, MA: Bergin & Garvey.

GLEICK, J. (1987) *Chaos: Making a New Science*, NY: Viking.

GOULD, S.J. (1989) *Wonderful Life: The Burgess Shale and the Nature of History*, NY: W.W. Norton & Company.

GREEN, B. (1988) *Metaphors and Meanings: Essays on English Teaching by Garth Boomer*, Australia: AATE (distributed by NCTE in the USA)

GREEN, J. and HARKER, J.O. (Eds) (1988) *Multiple Perspective Analysis of Classroom Discourse: Volume XXVII*, Norwood, NJ: Ablex Publishing Corporation, p. 24.

KELLY, G.A. (1955) *The Psychology of Personal Constructs*, NY: Norton.

LATHER, P. (1988) 'Feminist perspectives on empowering research methodologies', *Women's Studies International Forum*, **11**, 6, pp. 569–581.

MAYHER, J.S. (1990) *Uncommon sense: Theoretical Practice in Language Education*, Portsmouth, NH: Boynton/Cook-Heinemann).

SCHÖN, D.A. (1983) *The Reflective Practitioner: How Professionals Think in Action*, NY: Basic Books.

Selected Bibliography

BERGER, P. and LUCKMAN, T. (1971) *The Social Construction of Reality*, London: Penguin.

BRITTON, J.N. (1970) *Language and Learning*, Coral Gables, Fl.: University of Miami Press.

BRITTON, J.N., BARNES, D. and ROSEN, H. (Eds) (lst ed.), TORBE, M. (replaced Rosen in 2nd ed.) (1969/1986). *Language, the Learner, and the School*, Portsmouth, NH: Boynton/Cook Publishers, Inc.

BROWN, R.G. (1991) *Schools of Thought: How the Politics of Literacy Shape Thinking in the Classroom*, San Francisco: Jossey-Bass Publishers.

CUBAN, L. (1984) *How Teachers Taught: Constancy and Change in American Classrooms, 1890–1980*, NY: Longman.

FREIRE, P. (1970) *Pedagogy of the Oppressed*. NY: Seabury Press.

GIROUX, H.A. (1988) *Teachers as Intellectuals: Toward a Critical Pedagogy of Learning*. Granby, MA: Bergin & Garvey.

GREEN, W. (Ed.) (1988) *Metaphors and Meanings: Essays on English Teaching by Garth Boomer*. Victoria, Australia: Australian Association for the Teaching of English.

LESTER, N.B. and ONORE, C.S. (1990) *Learning Change: One School District Meets Language Across the Curriculum*, Portsmouth, NH: Boynton/Cook-Heinemann.

MAYHER, J.S. (1990) *Uncommon Sense: Theoretical Practice in Language Education*, Portsmouth, NH: Boynton/Cook-Heinemann.

POPKEWITZ, T.S. (Ed.) (1987) *Critical Studies in Teacher Education: Its Folklore, Theory and Practice*, NY: The Falmer Press.

REID, J.A., FORRESTAL, P. and COOK, J. (1990) *Small Group Learning in the Classroom*, Portsmouth, NH: Heinemann Educational Books; Toronto: Irwin Publishing.

ROSE, M. (1989) *Lives on the Boundary*. NY: Penguin.

SCHÖN, D.A. (1983) *The Reflective Practitioner: How Professionals Think in Action*. NY: Basic Books.

SIZER, T.S. (1984) *Horace's Compromise: The Dilemma of the American High School*, Boston: Houghton Mifflin.

Index